BURT FRANKLIN: RESEARCH & SOURCE WORKS SERIES
Philosophy and Religious History Monographs 138

THE CHURCH UNDER THE
COMMONWEALTH

A HISTORY

OF THE

ENGLISH CHURCH

DURING THE CIVIL WARS AND UNDER
THE COMMONWEALTH

1640-1660

BY

WILLIAM A. SHAW, Litt.D.

EDITOR OF THE "CALENDAR OF TREASURY PAPERS," AUTHOR OF THE
"HISTORY OF CURRENCY," ETC.

IN TWO VOLUMES

VOL. I.

BURT FRANKLIN REPRINTS

New York, N. Y.

Published by LENOX HILL Pub. & Dist. Co. (Burt Franklin)
235 East 44th St., New York, N.Y. 10017
Reprinted: 1974
Printed in the U.S.A.

Burt Franklin: Research and Source Works Series
Philosophy and Religious History Monographs 138

Reprinted from the original edition in the University of Illinois
    Library at Urbana.

Library of Congress Cataloging in Publication Data

Shaw, William Arthur, 1865-1943.
    A history of the English church during the civil wars and under
the Commonwealth, 1640-1660.

        Reprint of the 1900 ed. published by Longmans, Green, New York.
        1. Church of England—Government. 2. Church of England—History.
    I. Title.
    BX5073.S5 1974   283'.42   78-184708
    ISBN 0-8337-4389-9

To the Memory of my Father,

JAMES SHAW,

Died 20th June, 1899.

PREFACE.

THE scope of this work is intentionally restricted. It is not a history of religion in England during the years 1640-60. It is therefore not concerned either with the history of Dogma or with that of the Sects or of the three Denominations. The history of the Congregationalists as such, or of the Baptists as such, or of the Presbyterians as such, or of the Quakers as such, or of any of the Sects as such, must be sought in the separate histories of those bodies.

The bearing of the present work is quite different. The years 1640-60 witnessed the most complete and drastic revolution which the Church of England has ever undergone. Its whole structure was ruthlessly demolished—Episcopacy, the Spiritual Courts, Deans and Chapters, Convocation, the Book of Common Prayer, the Thirty-nine Articles, and the Psalter; the lands of the Bishops and of the Deans and Chapters were sold, and the Cathedrals were purified or defiled. On the clean-swept ground an entirely novel Church system was erected. In place of Episcopal Church Government a Presbyterian organisa-

tion was introduced, and a Presbyterian system
of ordination. For the Spiritual Courts were
substituted Presbyterian Assemblies (Parochial,
Classical and Provincial), acting with a very real
censorial jurisdiction, but in final subordination to
a parliamentary committee sitting at Westminster.
Instead of the Thirty-nine Articles the Confession
of Faith was introduced, and the Directory in place
of the Book of Common Prayer. New Catechisms
and a new metrical version were prepared, a parochial survey of the whole country was carried
out, and extensive reorganisations of parishes
effected. Finally, the equivalent of a modern ecclesiastical commission (or let us say of Queen Anne's
Bounty Scheme) was invented, a body of trustees
was endowed with considerable revenues for the
purpose of augmenting poor livings, and for years
the work of this ecclesiastical charity and reorganisation scheme was earnestly pursued.

There is hardly a parallel in history to such a
constitutional revolution as this, and it is upon the
constitutional revolution as such that I have kept
my attention steadily fixed.

So much for the scope of the work. As to its
contents, a part (a little more than half) of the
first chapter formed the introduction to the "Minutes
of the Manchester Classis," edited by me for the
Chetham Society in 1890.

The substance of a smaller part of the last
chapter formed the introduction to the first volume
of the proceedings of the "Plundered Ministers'

Committee," similarly edited for the Lancashire and Cheshire Record Society in 1893. This latter, however, I have entirely recast and rewritten.

Finally, portions of the whole book were read at Manchester College, Oxford, in February, 1899, in a series of lectures under the Hibbert Trust.

With regard to the appendices, I have not made the slightest attempt at forming a *corpus* of documents or *pièces justificatives*. Such an attempt would be perfectly impossible except to the Historical Manuscripts' Commission, or to the Master of the Rolls. I have confined myself to publishing definitely chosen parts of such materials as are never likely to be published in calendar form, or by the Historical Manuscripts' Commission.

To be explicit. It is presumed that if ever there is a Calendar of the work of the various committees which dealt with Church affairs during the years 1645-60, the material of that calendar will be drawn only from the authentic records of those committees. Of these records I give a detailed account in Appendix IV., vol. ii., pp. 457-76 *infra*. Now, outside this well-defined class of material, there is much besides.

In particular (firstly) there is all the wealth of personal reference contained in the *Commons' Journals* and *Lords' Journals*. For the period 1640-45, *i.e.*, anterior to the commencement of the definite records just referred to, there are preserved in the *Lords' Journals* (and nowhere else) hundreds of cases of clergymen tried, imprisoned,

sequestered or ejected ; or, on the other hand, promoted or nominated to benefices by the Parliament.
In an imperfect way Walker, with literally incredible toil, went through the journals whilst they
were still unpublished with the object of taking
out the first of these classes. Without distinction
I have taken them all out *ambulando.* As I have
read the journals systematically for the whole of
the period, it was an easy part of my task to
take out these cases. But it is safe to assert
that no person (say, editing a Plundered Ministers' Calendar) would ever draw up such a
list. It could only be done by careful verbatim
perusal of the *Commons'* and *Lords' Journals,* and
to perform that perusal simply for the sake of
recovering individual ministerial cases would be
distracting. This class of material will be found
in Appendix II.

Many of the original papers (petitions, etc.)
relating to the ministerial cases which are recorded
in the *Lords' Journals* are still preserved amongst
the MSS. of the House of Lords. See the Calendars of them in the Historical Manuscripts Reports,
especially Report VI. If it is asked why I have
abstracted the *Journals* and not included these
papers, the answer is that the Calendars referred
to are indexed, and therefore the material is
accessible ; whereas, in the case of the *Journals,*
the indices are so hopelessly inadequate under
the head of personal- and place-names that the
material is absolutely inaccessible.

Secondly. All the evidence relating to the success of the Presbyterian system during the years 1646-60 has become hopelessly scattered. The scribes of the various classical associations quietly walked off with the records when the Restoration came, and either destroyed them or handed them down to their descendants as private property. It is certain that such scattered material as this will never come within the purview of a Record Office Calendarer.

All this material, so far as I have discovered it, is contained in Appendix III.

Thirdly. It is extremely unlikely that any Calendar of (let us say) Plundered Ministers records would ever include the accounts of the sales of Deans and Chapters' lands, and of Bishops' lands, or, again, the accounts of First Fruits and Tenths which I have here printed. These accounts form a distinct class. They do not form part of the Records of any Commonwealth Committee, and would be almost necessarily neglected by a calendarer. These accounts will be found in Appendices VII., VIII. and IX.

The three classes of documents therefore which I have printed are such as the historical world cannot possibly ever hope to receive at the hands of an editor of the records of the Plundered Ministers' Committee. But if ever a Calendar of Plundered Ministers' Records should be given to the world, then the documents which I have selected for publication here would make, together with that calendar, a complete whole, or as complete a whole as it is now possible to reconstruct.

Besides this (to my mind important) point there is the further point of the interest of the documents themselves. In their entirety I believe they cover the whole country, and I hope it will be found that very few parishes indeed are unrepresented in one or the other of them.

What this means only the local antiquarian can adequately understand. Parochial histories invariably break down over the Commonwealth period. It is not, or not merely, prejudice. The period is not yet understood. The parish registers were neglected. The confused character, or legal status or position, and the conflicting numbers of the various parochial incumbents, the actual uncertainty as to who was the incumbent, the almost entire ceasing of the work of Episcopal ordination, and in consequence of the registering of admissions and the neglect on the other hand of ever keeping a register of such ordinations as were performed by the Presbyteries—all these causes have combined to make it as yet impossible to piece together the history of any parish for the years 1640-60.

I really cherish the hope that my book will inaugurate a new era in this matter, and that both in our county histories and in the increasing number of our parochial histories we shall see an end of that " 1640-60—*blank* " system. The period was by no means blank.

If any person is investigating the history of any

parish, and wishes to construct a list of the incumbents during the years 1640-60, let him proceed as follows : (1) Go to the Augmentation Books at Lambeth which are described in Appendix IV., pp. 467-76. There is at Lambeth a manuscript index of places, and he will have no difficulty in finding the particular parish in which he is interested.

The material he will get from this source will cover mostly the years 1652-58.

(2) For the earlier period 1645-52 he is reduced to a more scattered body of records, a difficult but still a workable body to handle. The three volumes at the British Museum, and the eight volumes at the Bodleian, have *indices locorum*. The material drawn from this source will cover the years 1645-50.

(3) For the period 1640-45 he will be reduced, I fear, to—my book and to the appendices there contained ; with the added advantage that those appendices contain incidental indications of value for practically the whole period.

This must be my justification for the length to which I have drawn out the appendices.

May I conclude this preface with a reference to a personal matter. Some nine or ten years since, when I was engaged in making collections for this work, I formed the purpose of visiting all the London parish churches with the object of examining (1) the vestry minute-book, (2) the registers, (3) if permitted, the parish chest itself in the hope of recovering any possible classis minute-book. The result was disastrous. In some few cases I met with distinguished courtesy, mostly with cold indifference, in more than one instance with most painful rudeness. The courtesy came from the incumbents, the rudeness from the parish clerks. I quickly found that my wish was hopeless of attainment, and I dropped it in despair.

Now let there be no misapprehension as to the value of the materials which I was obliged to forego the use of, and which is practically sealed to the historical student. Dr. Freshfield has worked at it in the cases of several parishes. In that of Bartholomew Exchange he has, regardless of expense, published the vestry minute-book verbatim up to 1676.

The pages of my book will show what valuable material he has put at the disposal of the historical student, and how heavily I have drawn upon his work. But what is one parish to the whole, and why should the historical student be reduced to the accidental generosity of any individual, however enthusiastic? My thanks to Dr. Freshfield are incapable of expression, but it has made my heart ache to think that there exists a world of first-hand historical material like that he has published and practically absolutely inaccessible.

It is a gross scandal that historical documents at all, not privately owned, not pertaining to the private ownership of any one, not relating to the private affairs of any one, should be locked up and rendered inaccessible as they practically are.

Parish registers and vestry minute-books do not belong to the incumbent. He is a mere bird of passage, a person who has the minding of them for some brief period. That is all, and a most unfit person he is. No other country in the world would supinely witness as we do, and have done, the waste, decay, destruction and falsification of parish registers. I remember, some years since, being shown by a minister the registers of his parish. The first volume had decayed, and the remains were kept in a tin box, each tattered leaf being carefully *rolled in tissue paper*. That meant that every time the leaf should happen to be inspected the brittle membrane would have to be unrolled. What prospect was there of those fragments surviving any handling at all? I advised the parson to put the fragments into the hands of a skilled London binder.

It is literally scandalising to think of parish registers being left in such keeping. All parish registers and all vestry minute-books earlier than the accession of Queen Victoria ought to be instantly removed to public and safe keeping—to some specially organised side of the British Museum —where they would not only be accessible to the historical student, and not only be bound and safeguarded against further decay, but also subject to the proper provisions of scholarly handling. If he does his duty, an incumbent should actually sit with a person who is examining his registers, and very irksome it is both for the incumbent and the

searcher. Whereas, at the Manuscript Room at the
British Museum there is every available precaution,
there is every perfection of convenience, there is
that ever present atmosphere or tradition of
scholarly handling and keeping, not to mention the
unspeakable convenience of having every register
within call without having to write or to travel all
over England for it.

There is neither sense nor reason in delaying
to do with the Church of England historical
registers what has long since been done with the
Dissenters' registers.

In conclusion I have to acknowledge—as every
student of the seventeenth century has—invaluable
help at many points received from Mr. Firth ;
and also assistance from Mr. Weich, librarian
of the Guildhall. Above all am I indebted to my
wife for help throughout, in the compilation of
the book, in the correction of proofs, in the identi-
fication of place names and in the total construction of the index.

CONTENTS.

VOL. I.

CHAPTER I.

CHAPTER II.

VOL. II.

CHAPTER III.

b

CHAPTER IV.

APPENDICES.

ANALYSIS OF CONTENTS.

VOL I.

CHAPTER I.

Ecclesiastical Debates and Legislation, 1640-43.

CHAPTER II.

The Assembly's Constructive Work, 1643-47.

§ I. The Thirty-nine Articles.

§ II. Church Government.

§ IV. *Jus Divinum* of Presbytery.

VOL. II.

CHAPTER III.

THE PRESBYTERIAN SYSTEM, 1646-60.

CHAPTER IV.

PATRONAGE AND FINANCIAL ADMINISTRATION.

CHAPTER I.

THE ECCLESIASTICAL DEBATES AND LEGISLATION OF THE LONG PARLIAMENT UP TO THE MEETING OF THE ASSEMBLY OF DIVINES.

1640-1643.

THE civil wars under Charles were the outcome of causes that had been at work for more than two generations. Since the consolidation of the nation under Elizabeth—since 1588—a twofold growth had been silently going on—of Constitutionalism in the civil life, of Puritanism in the religious life of the nation ; and the wars became a necessity when this twofold progress could no longer be contained and controlled by the old forms, by the old civil and religious institutions. And yet an attentive consideration of these civil wars will reveal their phenomenal nature. The years 1640-45 were the most revolutionary that this country has ever passed through. In the domain of the civil as well as of the religious agitation there is noticeable an extraordinary accentuation of feeling as the breach between King and Parliament widened, and it was this accentuation of feeling that led to the revolution itself. At the opening of the Long Parliament the expectation of change and the determination for it were general, but a much milder reform would have satisfied in December, 1640, than a year or two later. This is true of both the phases of the agitation—of the religious as well as the constitutional demands of the nation.

As compared with this rise of principle, the mere accident of the usurpation of the army, and of Cromwell, is insignificant. It is not to be wondered at that the army mastered the Parliament, nor that the victory of the army resulted in the monarchy of Cromwell. It is of much more importance that, when the accident of this usurpation had been swept away, the return was made to the constitutional standard, not of 1639, but of 1641. So much of the work of the revolution, at least, was to endure and to become the basis of the constitutional progress of the succeeding century.

Accentuation of feeling, 1640-43, and its effect on Puritanism. It is quite as true that these first years of the Long Parliament witnessed a similar accentuation of feeling and rise of demand in the second phase of the struggle—the religious agitation. The general idea of Church reform that obtained in November, 1640, had become insufficient and useless in June, 1641, and the scheme of June, 1641, was swept away by the events of 1642 and 1643. It is such a desertion of its original basis that makes one hesitate to speak of this as the Puritan Revolution, for the forms of Church discipline and government that were finally adopted were not contemplated by—did not grow out of—Puritanism proper. During the years 1640-48 English Puritanism itself underwent a revolution, and this fact must be recognised before the character of the period can be rightly understood. The steps in that revolution are marked by the debates on the Root-and-Branch Bill in 1641, and by the calling of the Assembly, and the adoption of the Solemn League and Covenant in 1643.

At the opening of the Long Parliament as much stress was laid upon religious as upon civil grievances, but the attitude of the Parliament was essentially lay—unclerical. In past years the clergy had largely intermeddled in secular affairs, and mostly in the interest of an unconstitutional executive. It was necessary, therefore, to secure the national existence against any such danger for the future—to restrict bishops and clergymen to their spiritual function. Again, Episcopacy had shown itself intolerant of the Puritanism of the parochial clergy. The Commons were resolved to assert and foster that Puritanism. These were the principles underlying the first legislation of the Long Parliament on matters of religion. But as the breach widened, so did the bounds of these principles. Episcopacy itself, the machinery of government of the State Church, was called into question, and it was resolved to replace it by some less centralised system, that would give a share of the government to the parochial clergy and put an end to the dependence of the bishops upon the Crown. It is probable that, without the necessity of calling in Scotch aid, and of adopting the Solemn League and Covenant, the Long Parliament would have resolved upon a system of Church government that might be called Presbyterian, though in a sense very different from that usually conveyed by the term

Revolution-ary adoption of Presby-terianism.

But events did not permit of such orderly evolution. The course of the war made it necessary to call in Scotch aid, and the condition of obtaining it was the adoption of the Covenant. The main facts of the result are well known. The Parliament was pledged to the adoption of Presbyterianism, and all through the years 1643-48 the work of its establishment was in progress in various stages. In many parts of the country the Presbyterian system was not set up; wherever established, there were restrictions on the power of the Presbyteries such as were unknown in Scotland; but with these limitations it still remains a fact that these years witnessed a real attempt at the enforcement upon the English nation of a Presbyterian system. Abstractly considered, the phenomenon is the most remarkable in English history. The main feature of a rigid Presbyterian system is the censorial power exercised by the Presbytery. The Scottish Kirk Session and the English Congregational Presbytery of the year 1647 took cognisance of the morals of the congregation, held investigations in regular form, and decreed punishment by suspension, being further empowered to call in the civil arm for the enforcement of this sentence. No system could be found more repugnant to the essence of English civil, constitutional, and national sentiment, and the attempt at the enforcement of such a system during the civil wars was nothing less than a blind conflict with that national sentiment. This, too, was at a time when there were in the minds of men vague and visionary notions of freedom nourished by the wars. Hence the phenomenal nature of this

English civil-war Presbyterianism, as judged from the point of view of the nation at large.

Nor is its strangeness less striking when viewed from the standpoint of clerical feeling merely. There have been only two occasions in the history of English dissent in which the Puritan clergy have favoured a pure Presbyterian system. The one was under Elizabeth, the other was the case in point during the civil wars. In both cases the movement stands apart from the general body of Puritan sentiment, from the general stream of Puritan protest. The broad principle underlying sixteenth and seventeenth century dissent was Puritanism merely, a spiritual perception expressing itself at different times in different forms—in the early days of the Reformation in scruples as to the vestments and the rubrics, that seemed to savour of Popery ; later, in the merely scholastic Sabbatarian controversy ; later still, in a rigid Calvinism as opposed to an apparently laxer doctrine of grace ; and again later, in the inculcation of greater morality of life, and greater regard for the means of grace and the Lord's day, as opposed to the immorality and the Sunday sports of the England of Charles. And this continued to be the main basis and character and current of English Puritanism even under the explosions of Elizabethan and civil-war Presbyterianism. The Presbyterianism of the days of Elizabeth was an academic movement principally, never in a national sense a clerical movement. It was apparently confined to three counties and London, and to a small portion of the ministers even of these counties. It never asserted itself in

English Puritanism never genuinely Presbyterian:

either under Elizabeth

actual organisation, and fell away before the close of Elizabeth's reign. There are no traces of any inheritance of the ideas or influence of this Elizabethan Presbyterianism by the English Puritans of the days of James I. and Charles I. The Presby- terianism of the Civil War was a more vital and concrete phenomenon, but none the less was it an abrupt and startling and illogical expansion from the basis of English Puritanism. And in sentiment the broad stream of Puritanism still flowed underneath. It is represented in the biography of the time in its entirety by one man—Richard Baxter. So vivid was his perception of the essential nature of Puritanism that he could not recognise the real existence of a Presbyterian system or party.

> Though Presbytery generally took in Scotland, yet it was but a stranger here, and it found some ministers that lived in conformity to the bishops' liturgies and ceremonies (however they might wish for reformation), and the most that quickly after were ordained were but young students in the universities at the time of the change of Church government, and had never well studied the points on either side; and though most of the ministers then in England saw nothing in the Presbyterian way of practice which they could not cheerfully concur in, yet it was but few that had resolved on their principles; and when I came to try it, I found that most that ever I could meet with were against the *jus divinum* of lay elders, and for the moderate primitive Episcopacy, and for a narrow congregational or parochial extent of ordinary churches, and for an accommodation of all parties in order to concord (*Autob.*, i., 146).

On the statement of fact Baxter's testimony will be found to break down in more than one instance. The significance of these words lies in their tone. They represent Baxter's attitude, and

the attitude of many others ; they are the expression of the constant element of Puritanism, as
opposed to the mere accident of the Presbyterianism of 1643-7.

In November, 1640, the general frame of mind
in the country, as in the Parliament, was negative,
not positive—destructive, not constructive.   There
were grievances existing in certain aspects of the
Church system, inseparably linked with that system,
and hateful by their offending.   There were men,
too, who had been instruments and promoters of
those grievances.   On these points there was no
hesitancy.   Men's minds were made up as to some
things which should no longer continue—as to
some high places of iniquity that should be cleansed.
But the notions of a new state of things were
vague.   In the opening harangues the subject of
religious grievances was only one with others—
civil, judicial, parliamentary—and a large part of
the consideration which the purely religious question received in those harangues was devoted to
the expression of fear as to a universally suspected
Popish plot.

With regard to the state of feeling in the
country at large, it is not difficult to generalise.
It is not to be denied that, as events proved later,
there already existed in the country a Root-and-
Branch party.   It appears from Baillie's letters that
the London petition had been started *immediately*
after the meeting of the Parliament, and that at
the same time, or very shortly after, petitions of a
like nature were got up in Kent, Essex, and ten
or eleven counties.   But in November, 1640, the

General atti-
tude in 1640
on the subject
of religious
grievances.

general feeling, as evinced in the petitions, was not such. For the clergy, the best statement of their position is given in the well-known Petition and Remonstrance. Two months before that petition was presented, there had been a very similar one preferred by two beneficed clergymen on behalf of many of the clergy of Lincoln. This petition complained of the increase of Popery, the renewing of idle and frivolous ceremonies, and the canons, and prayed that thereafter no canons should be made without consent in Parliament, that marriage might be lawful at all times, and that some severe law might be enacted against . . . the profanation of the Lord's day.[1]

Other petitions, as that from the churchwardens and sidesmen of London of the same date, complained of the articles of visitation and the oath of presentment exacted from churchwardens.

The petitions on grievances in 1640.

It is in such petitions, rather than in those advocating the abolition of Episcopacy, that can be discerned the true measure of reformation desired by the country at large ; and it is in this element, vaguely conservative and moderate, that we notice with the lapse of time and the progress of events, the change of attitude and accentuation of feeling which was so characteristic of the Parliament itself.

At the beginning of the session petitions poured in from the counties on the general subject of grievances. The names of fifteen counties which preferred petitions by the 9th November, are given in the journals and Rushworth. Some of them are preserved (those from Hertford, York, and

[1] D'Ewes' *Diary*, i., 8, 16th November ; Harl. MSS. 162, B. M.

Kent), and we may safely conjecture a similarity of
nature in all. The substance of the Dorset petition
was given by word of mouth by Lord Digby, in
one of those set speeches on grievances which will
be noticed immediately. "There was given to us
in the county court at the day of our election a
short memorial of the heads, that we might represent them to the Parliament: (1) ship money;
(2) pressing soldiers, and raising monies concerning
the same; (3) monopolies; (4) the new canons,
and the oath to be taken by lawyers and divines,
etc. ; (5) the oath required to be taken by church
officers to present according to articles new and
unusual."

The religious questions here raised are evidently
subordinate in position, and of small intrinsic importance as religious questions. Now, in this
matter of county petitions alone, notice the rise
of feeling. Sixteen months later the Lords, after Compared
having previously refused to sanction a similar with those
of 1642.
measure, passed the bill concerning ecclesiastical
persons (taking away the bishops' votes in Parliament and disabling all persons in holy orders from
exercising any temporal jurisdiction). On this
occasion a petition went from Kent to the Lords,
acknowledging with joy the good correspondence
between Lords and Commons in passing the bill
for the bishops' jurisdiction : "And we pray you
will go on with them to a thorough reformation,
especially of the Church *according to the Word of
God*".[1] During the agitation on this particular
bill, no less than twenty counties presented peti-

[1] L. J., iv., 571.

Chap. I.

1640.

The debate on grievances, November 7-10, 1640.

Grimston's speech.

tions praying for the passing of the measure, or returning thanks for it, in almost identical words.

The extent and the significance of such a rise in popular feeling can be traced and exemplified in the history of the struggle, and in the Parliamentary debates.

The Parliament met on the 3rd of November, 1640. The first set debate was on the subject of grievances, and was opened on the 7th by Harbottle Grimston, the very embodiment of a constitutional Conservative. With him the question of Parliamentary privilege preceded the question of religion, and, under the latter head, his attention was given almost entirely to the conduct of the late Synod, its canons, and the oath.[1]

They would have us at the very first blush swear to damnable heresy, that matters necessary to salvation are contained in the discipline of our Church, . . . and they would anticipate and forestall our judgment by making us swear beforehand that we would never consent to an alteration. Nay, they go further, for they would have us swear that the government of the Church by archbishops, bishops, etc., is *jure divino*. Their words are : " As by right it ought to stand," whereas we do not meet with the name of archbishop, bishop, dean, or archdeacon in all the New Testament. And whatsoever may be said of the function of bishop, it is one thing, but for their jurisdiction, it is merely *humana institutione*—they must thank the king for it.

After referring to the boldness of the Synod in granting a benevolence, he thus concluded :—

They which durst do this, will do more if the current of their raging tyranny be not stopped in time. Who are they

[1] The speech is given to Rushworth, iv., 34, but wrongly assigned to the 9th. D'Ewes' *Journal* corrects it.

that have countenanced and cherished Popery and Arminianism to that height it hath grown to in this kingdom? . . . Who are they that of late years have been advanced to any preferment in the Church, but such as have been notoriously suspicious in their discipline, and for the most part vicious in their lives? . . . Therefore, to put ourselves in a way for our redress and relief, I conceive it were fit that a committee might be named to take these petitions into their consideration . . . that the parties grieved may have just reparation, . . . and that out of them laws may be contrived and framed for the preventing of the like mischiefs for the future.

Grimston was followed by Rudyard,[1] who spoke of the Popish tendencies of the Court and prelates, and of the discountenance thrown upon the Puritan clergy; and by the fiery Sir Francis Seymour, who spoke little on the head of religion, and under that head only of the danger from Jesuits—the one aspect of the question which seems to us least real.

As might be expected, Pym's speech was the most representative. After speaking of the danger from the Papists, he alludes to the corrupt part of the clergy :—

Favourites such as for preferment prize not conscience, . . . and, worse than Papists, these are willing to run into Popery; and these, though severed, aim at one end, and to its achievement walk on four feet—at first softly, now by strides— and are near their ends if they be not prevented. The first foot is ecclesiastical courts—their action in discountenancing of preachers and virtuous men whom they persecute under the law of purity—their countenancing of preachers of a contrary disposition . . . and their frequent preachings and instructions to preach up the absolute monarchy of kings.

[1] Rudyard's speech in *State Papers, Domestic*, cccclxxi. No. 38 is a single oration, and so printed in Cooke's *Speeches in Parliament*, 1641, pp. 103-9. In Rushworth it occurs as several speeches (iii., pp. 1349, 1355, 1350, 1358, 1351, 1341, 1352).

It is needless to indicate further the nature of the debate. Pym had commenced his speech by moving for a reformation, finding out the authors of these grievances, and punishing them. Bagshaw concluded his similarly, thus :—

> In the interim, let them be made examples of punishment who have been the authors of all these miseries.

This merely general debate on grievances was continued on the 9th, on the occasion of the presentation of petitions from the counties. It was in this connection that Digby delivered to the House the message from Dorset already noticed. His condemnation of "such discontient divines," and of the conduct of the late Synod, was as vehement as any man's, and yet his subsequent change of attitude will be borne in mind. He was followed by Sir John Culpeper—destined likewise to a change of front. In the later debates of the following year, Episcopacy found no more vigorous defender than Culpeper ; but, in these early general debates, his condemnation of the canons and the ceremonies was clear and resolute.

The outcome of the discussion was the appointment on the 10th November of the committee of twenty-four for a declaration on the state of the kingdom, and a motion to refer the book of new canons to the examination of the Grand Committee for Religion.

These debates are very indicative of the attitude of the House. They show how small a place the questions which were later to agitate the Commons so violently—questions of Church government and organisation—had in the mind of the Long Parliament at its commencement, and how vivid, on the other hand, was its sense of the delinquency of particular members of the existing ecclesiastical system, and of the impolicy of the recently enacted canons.

It does not appear that the latter part of the motion was immediately acted upon. The debate on the canons did not commence until a fortnight after, and the vote on the subject was not taken until the middle of December; but it was with this subject of the canons that the real ecclesiastical debates of the Long Parliament actually commenced.

In the meantime the features of the situation were depicted in the petitions that poured in. The petition of the Lincoln clergy has already been noticed. The names of eight other petitions which were delivered in on these days (9th and 10th November) alone are preserved in the *Journals.*[1] They concern in their entirety the removing of the communion table, the railing of it in, the oath, and the articles put upon churchwardens and sidesmen, false doctrine, and irregularities of the clergy. Besides these matters there were submitted to the investigation of the Grand Committee for Religion all the cases of private injustice in the High Commission, or from the bishops' ordinaries. The num-

The clerical petitions.

---

[1] Sir Edward Dering's speech on the presentation of the petition of Thos. Wilson, rector of Otham in Kent, contained a most bitter attack upon Laud as "the centre whence our miseries grow" (*State Papers, Domestic,* cccclxxi., No. 49, 10th November; Rushworth, iv., 39). George Walker's petition as pastor of St. John Evangelist is given in *State Papers, Domestic,* cccclxxii., No. 37, 30th November.

ber of these (by 15th June, according to D'Ewes,[1] they had reached the extraordinary figure of 900) led ultimately to the appointment of sub-committees, " The Committee for Deprived Clergymen," and " The Committee for Scandalous Clergymen," afterwards notorious under the latter name.

On the occasion of the first report from the Grand Committee for Religion, bitter speeches were made by Sir Edward Dering and Sir John Wray. The former instituted an elaborate comparison between the High Commission and the Inquisition ; the latter called upon the House " to lay the axe to the root of the long and deep fangs of superstition and Popery " by moving " that the groves and high places of idolatry may be removed and pulled down ".[2]

But as yet the interest of the Commons was confined to the action of the late Convocation. It was determined first to pass a condemnation upon that body. After three adjournments of the debate, which was entirely legal, the House passed resolutions against the canons of 1640 in particular, and against the power of the clergy to make any canons without common consent in Parliament[3] (15th and 16th December).

Condemnation of the canons of 1640.

---

[1] D'Ewes' MS., vol. iii., p. 1021.

[2] 25th November, Wednesday (Rushworth, iv., 55 ; *Parl. Hist.*, ix., 147). In *State Papers, Domestic*, cccclxxii., Sir Edward Dering's speech is assigned to 21st November (Rushworth, iii., 1345 ; iv., 55). It concluded with a motion for a committee for discovery of the great numbers of oppressed ministers under the bishops' tyranny.

[3] C. J., ii., 51-2. ; L. J., iv., 273. ; Rushworth, iii., 1365 ; *State Papers, Domestic*, cccclxxxiii., Nos. 61, 67. The subsequent proceedings against the bishops in 1640-1 were based upon these resolutions. In March, 164¾, it was argued that the clergy had incurred a præmunire,

These debates were, however, as has been said, purely legal. As yet the subject of religious refor- mation had not been broached in the full House, and the first notice of the question is significant from its timidity. In the course of the previous week, 12th December, 1640, the Grand Committee for Religion had named a sub-committee to inquire into the state of religion in general. This committee reported to the Grand Committee, and on Monday, the 19th December, the Grand Committee reported to the House. According to their report [1] the sub-committee had pitched upon three points touching religion : (1) to inquire what is the cause of the decay of preaching ; (2) of the increase of Popery ; (3) of scandalous ministers. The House ordered that the sub-committee should be turned into a select committee—*i.e.*, directly from the House itself—and meet forthwith. It is indicative of the vague views and faltering attitude of the Parliament in its earliest months on the question of Church and religious reform, that on the 11th of December, the very day before the appoint-

Report on religion from the sub-committee for religion, 1640, 19th December.

and on 27th April an Act was introduced for punishing and fining the members of the late Synod (see the list of fines in Rushworth). This was replaced on the 3rd June by a bill for making void certain canons, and for the punishment of such prelates as were the makers of them. It was adopted by the Lords on the 12th of June, 1641, and it was on this bill that the form of impeachment was drawn up against fourteen bishops (C. J., ii., 165 ; *Verney Notes*, Camden Society, p. 83 ; D'Ewes' MS., ii., 657). Finally, the impeachment on such ground was not proceeded in, a fresh prosecution being instituted on the occasion of the withdrawal of the bishops from the Lords' House (30th December, 1641). The House returned to the subject of the canons and the punishment of convocation in 1642, but the outbreak of the war brought other issues to the front.

[1] D'Ewes' *Diary*, i., 87.

ment of the abovesaid sub-committee by the Grand Committee, the London petition[1] against Episcopacy had been presented. In its own words, the latter notorious petition prayed "that the government of archbishops, lord bishops, deans, archdeacons, etc., and their courts and administrations in them, with all its dependencies, roots and branches may be abolished, as dangerous to the Church and Commonwealth, and the cause of many foul pressures to the subject in liberties and estates, and the true government according to the Word of God established". To the petition was appended a list of twenty-eight grievances in the existing government, which may be noticed later.

The petition was signed by 15,000 hands, and not less than 1500 gentlemen of quality and worth attended in Westminster Hall on the day of its delivery.

Only a slight debate greeted the appearance of this petition, though its existence had been known some time. Sir Miles Fleetwood and Strode spoke generally and vaguely for a careful consideration of religion as the chiefest pillar of happiness. The Puritan D'Ewes was much more explicit. He did not deny there was much chaff in the petition, but he found some wheat in it also. D'Ewes' views on the Church and religion were, like those of many of his contemporaries, critical and not constructive. On almost every occasion on which we find him speaking on religion, he takes pains to draw a distinction between ancient and godly bishops, whom he reverenced, and the bishops of his own

[1] Rushworth, iv., 93-7.

"degenerate" days, who had their minds and
morals corrupted by the addition of their temporal
baronies.

Doubtless, *said D'Ewes,* the government of the Church of God by godly, zealous, and preaching bishops hath been most ancient, and I should reverence such a bishop in the next degree to a king. But I protest in the presence of God that if matters in religion had gone on twenty years longer as they have done of late years, there would not in the issue so much as the face of religion have continued amongst us, but all should have been overwhelmed with idolatry, superstition, ignorance, prophaneness, and heresy. As I allowed ancient and godly bishops, so I disliked their baronies and temporal honours and employments.

All the speakers who followed D'Ewes, with the exception of the Treasurer of the Household (the elder Vane), favoured the reception of the petition, and it was finally resolved that all the petitions[1] should be considered of on a certain day —the following Thursday. The roll of names attached to the petition was ordered to be sealed with the seal of the speaker and the two aldermen of London.

There was however a notable unwillingness on the part of the House in general to approach the consideration of this London petition, and of the general question of the government of the Church —of Episcopacy. The debate on it did not actually commence until the 8th of February, and yet the existence of the petition had been known, as has

---

[1] A counter petition in favour of the retention of Episcopal government had been presented on the same day, 11th December. The text of it is preserved in *State Papers, Domestic,* cccclxxxiii., No. 49.

been said, a month, and probably more, before it was presented. Writing on the 18th of November, Baillie states [1] that

> The town of London, a world of men, mind to present a petition, which I have seen, for the abolition of bishops and all their appurtenances. It is thought good to delay it till the Parliament have pulled down Canterbury and some prime bishops, which they mind to do as soon as the king has digested the bitterness of his lieutenants' censure. Huge things are here in working. The mighty hand of God be about this great work. We hope this shall be the joyful harvest of the tears which this many years have been sown in this kingdom. All here are weary of bishops.

In a later letter, on the 2nd of December, he informs the Presbytery of Irvine that

> The petition against Episcopacy, subscribed with some thousand hands, had been given in and pressed hard before now had not friends in both Houses, as more than two parts are, advised to spare the pressing of that conclusion till first they had put the whole bishops and their convocation in a præmunire for their last illegal canons, which now they are about, also till they have brought down some of the prime bishops for prime faults, which they have not will to essay till they have closed the Lord Deputy's process.

On the day after the presentation of the petition he writes as follows :—

> It was resolved that the petition against Episcopacy, root and branch, should be delayed till first we had gotten Canterbury down, and the Parliament had removed all the rest out of the House by a præmunire for their canons ; yet we are so delayed by Traquair's fencing for his own head ere we can come to the minor, where Canterbury stands to be concluded, as we hope, in a deep bocardo, that the people's patience could no longer keep in. So yesterday a world of honest citizens, in

---

[1] Baillie, *Letters*, i., 273.

their best apparel, in a very modest way went to the House of
Commons, sent in two aldermen with their petition—subscribed,
as we hear, by 15,000 hands—for removing Episcopacy, the
service-book, and other such scandals out of their Church. It
was well received. They were desired to go in peace and to
send three or four of their number on Thursday next to attend
some answer. Against that time, God willing, we will be in
hand with his little Grace, and sundry petitions of several
shires, to every one of which some thousand hands are set,
will be given in against Episcopacy.

As the petitions from the counties to which
Baillie here refers, were not presented to the House
until the 13th of January, it seems certain that
only the unwillingness of the House delayed them
so long; and even then the subject remained in
abeyance for a month further.

Unwilling-
ness of the
House of
Commons to
approach the
question of
Episcopacy.

Before the debates on these petitions in February, there were several occasions on which the
action of the Commons displays its disposition,
and verifies the above statement.

On Friday, the 8th of January, 164$\frac{0}{1}$, the *Subsidy
Bill* was under consideration. On that occasion
certain doctors of divinity were found to have been
inserted in the list of commissioners for the town
of Cambridge. A one-sided discussion arose as to
the exclusion of their names from the list. As far
as can be seen, all the speakers were in favour of
the motion. D'Ewes impatiently declared that in
his opinion the matter deserved no longer debate,
for it had been the old grievance of England that
clergymen intermeddled with secular affairs, "and
it was a great grievance now to be remedied, and
therefore we should much prejudice ourselves
now to admit it. So after one or two more had

spoken to it, all the clergymen were struck out." [1]

Four days later the Commons were called upon to consider the report concerning the standing or otherwise of certain committees. The question was proposed that the Grand Committee for Religion should continue to exist, and should take into consideration the action of the ecclesiastical courts, "and the government of the Church as it now stands," and present it to the House. There was, to all appearance, no division of opinion as to the first of these agenda, but the second was demurred to. It was proposed to substitute the phrase "irregularities of the government" for the word "government". In the end neither phrase was adopted, but another circumlocution invented, "the government of the Church as it is now *exercised*"; and this was not until after some debate, and with the admission of such palliatives as that with which D'Ewes concluded his speech in favour of the word government.[2] "Nor doubt I," said he, "however the question were put, whether of government or of the irregularities of the government, we should proceed with that discretion and moderation as to question nothing but what were fit to be questioned."

How long the Commons in their indecision would have postponed the consideration of the

[1] D'Ewes' *Diary*, i., 131; Harl. MSS., 162.

[2] The resolution in D'Ewes, i., 138, says simply, "the proceedings of the ecclesiastical courts and the government of the Church". Both the *Commons Journals*, ii., 66, and Nalson, i., 719, say, "the government of the Church as it is now exercised ".

subject of Episcopacy cannot be conjectured, but
in this matter it was not entirely master of itself.
On the 13th of January the resumption of the
subject was moved by Sir Edward Dering, the
occasion being the presentation of a petition with
which he was entrusted from his county, Kent.
The matter of it is identical, the wording almost
parallel, with that of the London petition.

By sad experience we do daily find the government in the
Church of England by archbishops, bishops, deans, and archdeacons, with their courts, jurisdictions, and administrations
by them and their inferior officers, to be very dangerous both
to the Church and Commonwealth, and to be the occasion of
manifold grievances to the subjects, their consciences, liberties,
and estates. The dangerous effects of this lordly power hath
appeared in their overruling with a hard hand all other
ministers, the suspension of many godly preachers, and restraining the lawful preaching of others, both for lectures and
for afternoon sermons on .the Sabbath day ; their encouragement of Papists' ceremonies and commendation of the Church
of Rome ; their enforcing antiquated ceremonies and the oath ;
their dispensation for plurality of benefice and abuse of the
ordinance of excommunication ; their claim of Divine right for
their office and jurisdiction, and assumption of temporal honours
and offices in the Commonwealth; and the iniquitous and
illegal proceedings of their courts.

It is therefore prayed (the petition concludes), that this
hierarchical power may be totally abrogated, if the wisdom of
this honourable House shall find that it cannot be maintained
by God's Word and to His glory.[1]

Among all our business (said Dering, in introducing the
petition), I observe one, a very main one, to sleep *sine die.* It
is a business of immense weight and worth, such as deserves
our best care. I mean the grand petition long since given
in by many thousand citizens against the domineering of the
clergy ; wherein, for my part, although I cannot approve of all

[1] Nalson, i., 74 ; Rushworth, iv., p. 135 ; Dering's *Speeches*, p. 16 ;
Proceedings in Kent, pp. 27-38.

that is presented to you, yet I clearly do profess that a great part thereof—nay, the greater part thereof—is so well grounded that my heart goes cheerfully along therewith. It seems that my county is of the same mind.

Two thousand five hundred names were appended to this petition. Another to a like effect was presented on behalf of the county of Essex by Sir William Masham,[1] and at the same time a petition of a slightly different nature was presented by Sir Philip Porter in the name of divers ministers of the county of Suffolk, desiring some relief from their burthens.

On the presentation of these petitions there was some difference of opinion as to the appointing of a day for the reading of them. Some were for fixing the day shortly, others for postponing it for some time. D'Ewes, sanguine and Puritanical, was for a speedy consideration of the question. He saw only the practice of adorations and heretic preachings, which still continued to deprave the Sabbath day.

It would be the greatest glory of his majesty's reign if we could change the greater part of the clergy from brazen, leaden —yea, and blockish—persons, to a golden and a primitive condition, that their authority might be warranted by their godly example . . . for it is evident that since the prelates have been debased and adulterated by the intermixture of their temporal baronies with their ecclesiastical function, all miseries and calamities at home and abroad have fundamentally risen from them.

In the end, Monday, 25th January, was appointed for the reading of the petitions and the discussion of matters in them.

[1] D'Ewes' *Diary*, i., 142.

Meanwhile the issues of the question were being decided outside the House.

Instigated by the rapid growth and activity of the Root-and-Branch party, the moderate Puritan clergy throughout the country determined to supply by one general petition a standard of the reform demanded by them in the name of the moderate majority alike of clergy and laity. Various petitions, signed in all by 700 to 800 clergymen, were drawn up and sent to London. There they were discussed at a meeting of representative clergy, and their substance drawn up into one general petition, the separate heads of grievance being appended in detail as a " remonstrance". All the signatures to the separate petitions were then attached to this so-called " Ministers' Petition and Remonstrance," and it was determined forthwith to present it to the House.[1]

---

[1] There has been a question as to the authenticity of the remonstrance attached to this petition from the ministers. The charge has been made by Royalist writers (first by Clarendon and after him by Echard) that a different paper was shown to the ministers subscribing, and that then their names were cut off and appended to the remonstrance. The truth of the affair can be easily discerned from D'Ewes' MS.

On the 1st February, Digby informed the House that some of the ministers who signed the petition disavowed the remonstrance. In reply, D'Ewes stated succinctly that the remonstrance had been framed out of several petitions or complaints sent out of several counties, " some being entrusted to draw the said remonstrance out of the said petitions ".

When, on the following day, these disavowing ministers appeared before the House, they were found to be no less personages than Dr. Burgess and Dr. Downing. It was then also found, as can be clearly seen from D'Ewes' narrative, that Digby had, from motives known to himself, instigated or magnified the reluctance of these two doctors to avow the petition, for by their own explicit confession, twice re-

No copy of this celebrated paper has survived, but its substance can be gathered from various sources, and from the debates upon it in the Commons.

The petition contained at least two main heads :—

1. Touching matter of doctrine corrupted.

2. Touching "corruption of matter of government in the Church ".

It would appear from a tract of Dering that the first head of doctrine touched upon the liturgy and the prayer book.[1] " The ministers do complain that the creed is often rehearsed, but they blotted out what they had put in ; that in one place it is over-short, and in one place dangerously obscure."

The Remonstrance consisted of " near fourscore heads," the following being hurried notes of some of them taken in committee :—

1. Church governors and officers are burdensome to all.

2. Bishops not of Divine institution, which they challenge.

3. Bishops assuming sole power of ordination and juris-diction.

4. Largeness of bishops' diocese. The inconvenience of it.

peated, they acknowledged that they avowed and allowed the petition and remonstrance, and only objected to the length of it, having been informed that the length of it would abate the edge of the House. On the other hand, it was shown by seven of the ministers in favour of the petition, who immediately previously had been called before the House (among them being Calamy and Marshall), that the names subscribed to the petition and remonstrance were taken out of the several petitions sent up. It further appears that the extracted petition and remonstrance had then been read, " in a large room, to upwards of fourscore ministers," Downing and Burgess themselves being of the number. On the whole, the procedure seems to me to be perfectly legitimate.

[1] Brit. Museum, E. 197, *A Collection of Speeches.*

5. Bishops delegating their powers to deputies, unmeet persons.

6. Bishops encumbered with temporal power and estate.

7. Bishops pretend to be the only supporters of the prerogatives of the king.

8. Bishops claim to be sole pastors in all parts of the diocese.

9. Confirmation by them only.

10. Sole probate of wills.

11. Bishops consecrate churches, etc., and make it necessary.

12. Bishops inhibit marriages at divers times of the year.

13. Bishops compose forms of public prayer containing matter of state.

14. Bishops imposing oath, as of canonical obedience *ex officio*, etc.

15. Bishops enforce subscription.

16. Commendams in bishops' hands.

17. The bishops' charge at consecration, but they observe it not.

18. Scandalous bishops, drinking healths, etc.

19. The burdens of bishops' officers and dependents and servants, being above 10,000.

Other points related to :—

Irregular presentations to livings.

Enforcing subscription to their opinions before granting institution.

Exaction of exorbitant fees for institution.

Induction often done " clancularlie and slightly ".

Notwithstanding institution and induction, ministers are forced to take licenses to preach from the bishops, their officials and commissaries.

They give licences to physicians, midwives and meat-dressers in Lent, which they have no relation unto as ministers.

They dispense with things unlawful, as pluralities and non-residence.

Other points apparently urged by the Remonstrance were the secular employment of bishops,

CHAP. I.

1640-1,
January.

their judicial power in Parliament, in the Star Chamber, in Commissions of the Peace, and at the Council table, and also the greatness of revenues of deans and chapters. The remaining heads probably comprised the various grievances as to ceremonies and the Prayer Book.[1]

The moderate *versus* the Root-and-Branch party.

Such was the statement of demand of the moderates, and as it stood, this Petition and Remonstrance was to form during the ensuing February and March the basis of the first real action of the House on matters of Church reformation. But it was not to pass unchallenged. It was presented to the Commons on Saturday, 23rd January, and on the following Monday petitions similar to that from Kent, calling for the abolition of Episcopacy, were presented from eleven counties—Hereford, Bedford, Sussex, Surrey, Cheshire, Warwick, Suffolk, Cambridge, Gloucester, Buckingham, and Norfolk.[2] Some of these were numerously signed —that from Suffolk with above 4400 names, that from Norfolk with 2000, etc.

On the Saturday previous (23rd January) it had been determined, after some debate, to read the Ministers' Petition on the Monday. But on that day came pouring in these very different petitions from the counties. The question then was, which of the two classes of petitions should be read, and if both were retained, whether the Ministers' Petition should not be retained first.

[1] See D'Ewes' MS., i., 184; *Commons Journals*, ii., 100 ; *Verney Notes*, p. 4 (Camden Society). In the third volume of D'Ewes there are two sheets which have apparently been misplaced (folios 117 and 129). They certainly refer to this matter.

[2] D'Ewes' *Diary*, i., 166.

In the end, it was decided to read the Ministers'
Petition on the 1st of February. On that day, after
wearing itself by an unsatisfactory discussion on
the exclusion from the debate of Dr. Edèn and Dr.
Parry, who had taken the new oath, the House
passed to the discussion of the second head of the
Ministers' Remonstrance touching the corruption of
matter of government in the Church, "in which so
many irregularities and wicked oppressions of the
bishops and their ministers, which were numbered
to be at least 10,000, were set forth, against godly
ministers and godly men specially, as it moved all
men's hearts that had any religion to a detestation
of them". The subject was not opened in debate,
Pym moving the appointing of another day for it.
It is significant of the later action of the House in
adopting the scheme of the Assembly of Divines,
that it should on this occasion postpone the consideration of the first head, touching matter of
doctrine, to that touching government, thereby
seeming to recognise their own unfitness for that
work. Clarendon's[1] most incorrect account of the
event is as follows :—

> The first malignity which was apparent there was not
> only in their Committee for Religion, which had been assumed
> ever since the latter time of King James, but no such thing
> had been before heard of in Parliaments, where, under pretence
> of receiving petitions against clergymen, they often debated
> points beyond the verge of their understanding, but by their
> cheerful reception of a declaration of many sheets of paper
> against the whole government of the Church, presented by ten
> or a dozen ministers at the bar, and pretending to be signed by
> 700 ministers of London and the counties adjacent (and of the

[1] I., 285.

London petition, but the House was then so far from being possessed with that spirit, that the utmost that could be obtained was that it should not be rejected, etc.), and for the ministers' declaration, one part of it only was insisted on by them and read to the House, which concerned the exercise of their jurisdiction and the excesses of the ecclesiastical courts ; the other parts are declined by many of them, and especially ordered "to be sealed up by the clerk, that it might be perused by no man" [these commas are Clarendon's, and have no authority], so that all that envy and animosity against the Church seemed to be resolved into a desire "that a bill might be framed to remove the bishops from their votes in the Lords and from any office in secular affairs".[1]

The House did not on this occasion at all debate the question contained in the second head of the petition. The only discussion which arose, was as to whether the Remonstrance, or so much of it as had been read, should be committed or not, and, if referred, then to what committee. Some would have had it committed to a new one to be named, others to the Grand Committee for Religion, and Mr. St. John, newly created the King's Solicitor, moved, to refer it to the Committee of Twenty-four. "All agreed that whatsoever committee should take it into consideration, should only prepare heads for the House to debate, and that they should also prepare like heads out of the other petitions, touching the grievances of the ecclesiastical government."[2] Thus it was moved that similarly heads might be collected for consideration out of the London petition, and presented along with the former. This motion was resisted, and

[1] It was nearly two months before such a resolution was worded, *vide infra*, p. 60.

[2] D'Ewes' *Diary*, i., 188.

among others by the ever ready defender of Episcopacy, Sir John Culpeper. He desired that the
London petition might not be referred at all, even
if the others were, since Episcopacy itself was
condemned therein, "and bishops," he declared in
his warmth, "are the main columns of the nation".
The sentence excited indignation, and would have
been followed by a hot discussion but for an
interruption of the sitting.[1]

The subject was not resumed until the 8th, but
on that and the following day a most memorable
discussion took place. There was not intentionally a set debate on Episcopal government; though,
owing to a misconception on the part of some of
the speakers, portions of the debate read as if
there was. The question was simply that which
had already engaged the attention of the House,
viz., the referring or otherwise of the Londoners'
petition to a committee, as well as the Ministers'
Petition and Remonstrance.[2]

The debate was opened by Sir Benj. Rudyard.
He inveighed against the want of simplicity in the
clergy, against their Roman ambition of a sumptu-
ous religion with additionals of temporal greatness,
and, repeating, perhaps, the very words of the
Ministers' Petition, declared how it behoved to
restrain them to the duties of their function, so as

---

[1] See in *State Papers, Domestic*, cccclxxvii. No. 2., a curious paper
of Grimston's argument in the House of Commons, 1st February,
concerning the *jus divinum* of bishops and Selden's answer thereto.

[2] "The only question," says D'Ewes (*Diary*, i., 206), "was whether
the London petition should be committed with the Petition and Remonstrance, but divers, mistaking the question, fell into a long and
large disputation."

they might never more hanker after heterogeneous extravagant employment, nor to be so absolute, so single and arbitrary in actions of moment as excommunication, absolution, ordination and the like, but to join some of the ministry with them, . . . that they might not have power hereafter to corrupt the Church and undo the kingdom. But although Rudyard thus strayed from the point of the debate, and although he thus expressed all that the thinking element alike of country and Parliament had conceived and determined on in the way of reform, he had no thoughts of the destruction of Episcopacy itself.

> When they are thus circumscribed, and the public secured from their corruption, I shall not grudge them a liberal, plentiful subsistence, else I am sure they can never be given to hospitality. Certainly, sir, this superintendency of eminent men, bishops over divers churches, is the most ancient, primitive, spreading, lasting government of the Church ; wherefore, whilst we are earnest to take away innovations, let us beware we bring not in the greatest innovation ever was in England. I do very well know what very many do very fervently desire, but let us well bethink ourselves whether a popular democratic government of the Church, though fit for other places, will be either suitable or acceptable to a regal monarchical government of the State. Wherefore, Mr. Speaker, my humble motion is that we may punish the present offenders and reduce and preserve the calling for better men hereafter.[1]

Rudyard was followed by the brilliant Digby, who at first kept more to the real point in debate.

> If I thought (said he) there were no further designs in the desires of some that the London petition should be committed than merely to make use of it as an index of grievances, then I should wink at the faults of it, and not much oppose it.[2]

[1] Rushworth, iv., 183.   [2] *Ibid.*, iv., 170-74.

He allowed that when the petition was first presented there would be more reason for the commitment of it—

As being then the most comprehensive catalogue we had of Church grievances, but now that the ministers by their remonstrance have given us so fair and full an index of them, without those mixtures of things contemptible, irrational and presumptuous wherewith this petition abounds, I do not know to what good end it can be committed. . . . What have we here? A multitude of allegations, a multitude of instances of abuses and depravations of Church government—and what informed from thence? Let the use be abolished for the abuse's sake.

Like every other speaker, Digby took occasion to record his indignation against the oppression that had marked the previously existing state of things. But in him it seems to be rhetorical.

Methinks the vengeance of the prelates hath been so laid as 'twere meant that no generation, no complexion, no degree of men, should escape it. Was there a man of nice and tender conscience, him have they afflicted with scandal *in adiaphoris*, etc.

But, rhetorical or not, he did not allow himself to be swayed by his own denunciation. He proceeded to expose, with most subtle ability, the difficulties of the situation.

To strike at the root, to attempt a total alteration, before ever I can give my vote to that, three things must be made manifest to me : (1) That the mischiefs which are felt under Episcopacy flow from the nature of the function, and not from the abuse of it, *i.e.*, that no rules, no boundaries, can be set to the bishops able to restrain them from such exorbitancies ; (2) such a frame of government must be laid before us as no time, no corruption, can make liable to proportionable grievances ; (3) it must be made appear that this Utopia is practicable.

In dwelling on the second of these demands, Digby uses a phrase that is very significant, as indicative of the almost universal impression of the time that the destruction of one system would be followed, as a matter of necessity and of course, by the erection of another.

> If we hearken to those who would quite extirpate Episcopacy, I am confident that instead of every bishop we should put down in a diocese, we should erect a pope in each parish, and . . . for my part I do not think that there is any such alliance as men talk of betwixt the mitre and the crown but from this reason, that upon the pulling down of bishops the governments of assemblies is like to succeed it; that to be effectual must draw to itself the supremacy of ecclesiastical jurisdiction."

Digby was not the only one who turned with discomfort from such an alternative. What he was prepared for he stated succinctly enough.

> Let us not destroy bishops, but make them such as they were in primitive times. Do their large territories offend? Let them be restricted. Do their courts and subordinates? Let them be brought to govern, as in the primitive times, by assemblies of their clergy. Doth their intermeddling in secular affairs? Exclude them from the capacity.

He concluded by moving for a standing committee of certain members of both Houses, with such a number of learned ministers as the House should nominate for assistants, to take into consideration all grievances and advise of the best way to settle peace and satisfaction of the government of the Church.

Falkland's speech.

He was followed in a similar strain by Falkland.

Like the other speakers, Falkland admitted to the full all the charges brought against the bishops

as promoters and authors of grievances, civil as
well as religious.

I doubt not bishops may be good men, and let us give good men good rules, we shall have good governors and good times. . . . I am content to take away all those things from them, which to any considerable degree of probability may again beget the like mischiefs if they be not taken away. If their temporal titles, powers and employments appear likely to distract them from the care of, or make them look down upon, their spiritual duty, and that the too great distance between them and the men they govern will hinder the free and fit recourse of their inferiors to them, and occasion insolence from them to their inferiors, let that be considered and cared for. . . . I am sure neither their lordships, their judging of tithes, wills and marriages, no, nor their voices in Parliament, are *jure divino*, and I am sure that these titles and this power are not necessary to their authority. If their revenue shall appear likely to produce the same effects, let us only take care to leave them such proportions as may serve in some good degree to the dignity of learning. If it be feared that they will again employ some of our laws with a severity against the intention of those laws against some of their weaker brethren, that we may be sure to take away that power, let us take away those laws, and let no ceremonies which any member counts unlawful, and no man counts necessary, against the rules and policy of St. Paul be imposed upon them.

With these things thus regulated, and their observation further guaranteed by triennial Parliaments, Falkland was persuaded there would be no reason to fear any future innovation from their tyranny, or any defect in the discharge of their duty, and therefore there would be no need on a few days' debate to change an order which had lasted 1600 years, and with it to change the whole face of the Church. For his purpose, therefore, the committing of so much of the Remonstrance as

Grimston's
speech.

had been read would be a sufficient basis on which to proceed.[1]

Falkland was followed by a man of a quite different cast of mind, and yet one who in this matter entirely coincided with him and all the previous speakers. Harbottle Grimston had the same terror of a hasty reformation, and his speech indicates clearly what he thought that reformation would be.

> I conceive it an easier matter for us *addere inventis*, to reform what is amiss in them and their government than *creare novum*, to set up a new form of government which we have had no experience of, nor do we know how it should suit either with the humours of the people or with the monarchical government; and it may be the new government which is so much desired, if it be brought in upon the grounds and foundations which some would have it, it will be out of our power ever to master it again, whereas the government already established, if the governors exceed their bounds, they may fall into a præmunire.

His scheme of reform is identical with that sketched by Falkland. Every branch of the bishops' temporal power he would gladly see abolished— their seats on the bench, at the Star Chamber, and at the Council board, even in Parliament, with the reservation of some to be always present as assistants to give their advice on spiritual matters when required; and the reformation of the High Commission, and the Official and Commissary Courts.

The debate had by this expanded from the somewhat narrow point really at issue to a general discussion of the question of Episcopacy, and it was

---

[1] This speech, as given in Rushworth, agrees in *substance* with the extract of it in D'Ewes' *Diary*, but not in the internal *order* of it.

on this wider ground that Nathaniel Fiennes rose
to meet the hitherto unanimous course of the discussion.   Fiennes was a Puritan, the second son
of Lord Saye, the most pronounced Puritan in the
Upper House.

He answered perfunctorily Digby's somewhat
frivolous objections to the petition itself, declared he saw no reason why the London petition
should not be committed, and then turned to the
more general question of the government of the
Church, as if to the more important and more
immediate subject of debate.   He touched first
upon the general defence of Episcopacy which had
been set up by Falkland and Digby.

As might be expected, he easily met the claim
of antiquity by a counter reference to the New
Testament proofs of the parity of a bishop and
preaching presbyter.   It was a stock argument.
But it is curious to notice how, when he answers
the argument drawn from the probability of danger
accruing to the State by the Church government
of assemblies, he tacitly admits the justice of the
inference that such and so narrow *might* the alternative come to be as a matter of history.   At the
same time he offers an alternative scheme of his
own, a scheme which was subsequently adopted in
the Root-and-Branch debates, and which indicates
clearly how even the Puritan mind of England
at this time turned from a Presbyterian scheme of
government with dread and aversion.

If it shall be cleared, as it is affirmed, that anything herein
doth strike at monarchy, I shall never give my assent thereto
as long as I live.   But, to clear that this is not so, I offer to

your consideration that by the law of the land not only all ecclesiastical jurisdiction, but also all superiority and pre-eminence over the ecclesiastical state is annexed to the Imperial crown of this realm, and may be granted by commission under the Great Seal to such persons as his majesty shall think meet. How if the king should grant it to a certain number of commissioners equal in authority, as he may do? This were an abolition of Episcopacy, and yet not diminution of monarchy.

He then proceeds to lay down at great length the evils that have resulted from the government and ceremonies of the Church. All the points he particularises were urged as freely by Culpeper as by Fiennes himself, but they differed in their conclusions.

To speak plain English, these bishops and deans and chapters do little good themselves, by preaching or otherwise, and if they were felled a great deal of good timber might be cut out of them for the use of the Church and of the kingdom at this time.

He therefore moved to consider, not a part only, but the whole matter, and to refer the London petition along with that part of the Petition and Remonstrance which had been read.

Sir John Wray,[1] Holles, Pym, Bagshaw, Cage, Robert and John Goodwyn, Strode, Hampden, Dering, Sir William Strickland, Cradock, Reynolds, Sir Jo. Clotworthy, Sir Ed. Hungerford, Sir Nevill Poole, Mr. Solicitor, Sir Walter Erle, Sir Hy. Mildmaye, Sir Jo. Evelyn, Mr. Peard, Sir Ed. Mumford

---

[1] D'Ewes, iii., 916. There are two accounts in D'Ewes' MS. of these debates; the one is in the first volume, the other is buried in the midst of the third volume folio 113b. The second is evidently notes taken on the spot, and the foundation of the more expanded but unfinished first account.

(Moundeford), Maynard, Crewe, Chadwell—all these, by far the majority of the talent of the House, followed Fiennes in his motion to have the London petition committed. In comparison with them, the opposing list is in matter of talent very insignificant —Mr. Comptroller Hyde, Waller, Selden, Vane (the elder Vane), Capell, Griffin, Holborne, Bridgman, Kinge, Mr. Kyrton, Sir Henry Rainsford and Palmer.

A different cast, however, was given to the debate when it was renewed on the following day (Tuesday, 9th February, 1640-41) by the proposition made on the 8th by Mr. Griffin that only some part of the London petition should be referred. This was the origin of the salvo which was made in the first resolution on the 9th, and it was supported by Mr. Treasurer of the Household (the elder Vane).

> We all (said Vane) tend to one end—that was, reformation—only we differ in the way. I desire, therefore, that those words in the petition which strike at the root and branch of it . . .

Here the report ends, but it is plain that Vane desired the exclusion of the words referred to, a proposal which was in substance identical with the subsequent reservation of the point of Episcopacy. It was evident that the weight of numbers and of opinion lay with the party desiring the committal of the London petition, and accordingly such a conclusion seemed the only way of escape for the favourers of Episcopacy. On the Tuesday, therefore, the speeches turned on this point, as to whether there should be any reservation or exception of any point in the referring of these petitions. Palmer and Whitelock desired to reserve the question of the total abolition. Holles contended against any such reservation. There are signs on this second day's debate of an increased violence and insolence on the part of the Root-and-Branch party. They called out to have the petitions of Gloucester and Hertford against Episcopacy read along with that from London, and, taking advantage of the disorder and misconceptions apparent in the debate, moved that the question to be put should be that of Episcopacy itself. Neither ruse succeeded, although the House was not thereby recalled to a more correct conception of the real matter in debate. It is evident that the turn which the discussion had taken was due to the precipitancy of the extreme members of both factions : the one through vindictive haste, the other through fear. Sir John Strangewayes declared that a parity in the Church would necessitate a parity in the Commonwealth. The argument provoked Cromwell into such a warmth of expression or attitude that there were cries from several to have him to the bar. Pym, Holles and D'Ewes all supported Cromwell on the mere point of order, and protested against the call, but they said nothing as to his views. The expression of opinion, however, from the acknowledged leaders of the constitutional party, whose views on Church matters were identical and went hand in hand with their views on the political exigencies, were not such. To all appearances, Hampden contented himself with announcing his wish to have the petition committed. The only expression of Pym's speech D'Ewes does not even notice. According to a tract written by Bagshaw at the Restoration, Pym expressed an opinion that it was not the intention of the House to abolish either Episcopacy or the Book of Common Prayer, but to reform both wherever offence was given to the people, and if that could be effected and consented to with the concurrence of the people and Lords, they should do an acceptable work to the people—such an one, indeed, as hath not been since the Reformation.[1]

All these men voted for the committal of the London petition, and, as will be seen, it was committed, but with a reservation of the point of Episcopacy.

That such was the just and general judgment of the House there can be no doubt; but even if it had not passed in this particular form—even if the point of Episcopacy had not been reserved for the separate and serious consideration of the House itself—it is plain in what sense the moderates wished the committal to be understood. If it was to consider of Episcopacy at all, it was not to consider of its abolition, but of its reformation, and, as a matter of fact, the committee did as much on this head when it did meet as it would have done if the resolution had passed without any salvo.

The proposal of this salvo was immediately and eagerly accepted by Falkland and Culpeper; the opposition from such speakers as D'Ewes and Bagshaw was more apparent than real. Bagshaw was for the retention of the petition and its committal.[2] But how?

---

[1] Bagshaw, *Just. Vindicat.*, Brit. Museum, E. 1019.
[2] Rushworth, iv., 186.

I do distinguish (said he) of a twofold Episcopacy. The first *in statu puro*, as it was in primitive times, the second *in statu corrupto*, as it is at this day, and is so intended and meant in the London petition. Now, I hold that Episcopacy in this latter sense is to be taken into consideration as a thing which trencheth not only upon the rights and liberties of the subject, but, as it now is, it trencheth upon the Crown of England in these four points, namely, (1) their claims of jurisdiction *jure divino;* (2) their maxim that Episcopacy is inseparable from the Crown of England; (3) the illegality of legislation without the bishops as a third estate; (4) their holding ecclesiastical courts in their own names. Upon these reasons, so nearly touching the right of the Crown in point of Episcopacy, I am for the retaining the petition, and for a thorough reformation of all abuses and grievances of Episcopacy mentioned in the Ministers' Remonstrance, which reformation may perhaps serve the turn without alteration of the government of England into a form of Presbytery, as it is in Scotland, France, Geneva and the Low Countries.

In the tract above cited, Bagshaw recapitulates his speech at a distance of nearly twenty years. In spite of a few verbal incongruities, the sense of his reiteration entirely confirms the view that Bagshaw, equally with the moderates—the bulk of the House —desired only a reformation of the " excresences " of Episcopacy, not of the function itself.

I openly declared my opinion concerning bishops for establishing them in their function according to law, and I have just occasion to profess to all, as in truth I do, that I was so far from the very thoughts of destroying bishops that, observing at the time of my reading, and divers years before, the great invasions that were made by them upon the common law of England, I knew no other way how to hold them up in their functions and just jurisdiction and in esteem and honour among the people as by reading in that law which gave them their just bounds and limits, and my sticking close to this opinion, and abhorrence of taking the Scotch Covenant, tending

to the utter abolition of Episcopacy, was the alone ground of
that load of affliction which lay long upon my body and
estate.

Identical was the position taken up by D'Ewes.[1]

I desired the question might be waived in respect of the
ambiguity of the matter, for if by Episcopacy is meant their
vain aerial titles of lordship, the spoils of the Crown with which
they are loaden, and their vast tyrannical power which they
exercise, so as the *totum compositum* of bishops as they now
stand and *tota sequela* be meant, I said I just gave my "Aye"
for the abolishing of them. But if by Episcopacy is meant
only their spiritual function as it stood in the primitive and
purest times, then I shall give my negative voice, for I should
highly prize a godly preaching bishop, and heartily wish we
might make ours such. I desired, therefore, we might first of
all, and unanimously, join to remove from Episcopacy those
adulterations and admixtures which we disliked, and then I did
not doubt that we should so far proceed with conjunction of
hearts and minds as there should not need to be any division
of opinion amongst us. I desired, therefore, we might for the
present lay aside the disputes of Episcopacy, or referring it, but
refer the London petition as it stood to a Select Committee.

By this time the mind of the House was
apparent, and its judgment a little clearer by the
perception of the incongruity of any debate of the
question of Episcopacy before the petitions themselves had been referred, much less debated.
Several speakers followed D'Ewes in his desire
to waive the question, and, seizing with unerring
instinct the general sense of the House, Lenthall
begged leave to read an order which he had drawn,
and which, with only the alteration of one or two
words, was the order subsequently adopted. The
final order ran in these words :— [2]

---

[1] D'Ewes, i., 210.   [2] C. J., ii., 81.

Ordered that the Committee of Twenty-four, with the addition of these six—Sir Thomas Roe, Mr. Holles, Mr. Palmer, Mr. Holborne, Mr. Fiennes, Sir H. Vane—do take into consideration that part of the Ministers' Remonstrance that has been read, and the petition of the inhabitants in and about the city of London, and other petitions of the like nature that have been read, to prepare heads out of them for the consideration of the House, the House reserving to itself the main point of Episcopacy for to take it into their consideration in due time.

As against this supremacy of the moderate section of the House, however, in the constitution of the committee the extremists certainly scored a victory. The Root-and-Branch men pressed for an addition to the committee of the younger Vane, Holles and Fiennes. Three others were named as a counterpoise—Roe, Holborne and Palmer—but the disparity of ability was so apparent that a division took place, when the nominations were confirmed by 180 to 145.

That this latter small gain was a victory for the extremists is evident from Baillie's account.

There was a great commotion in the Lower House when the petition of London came to be considered. My Lord Digby and Viscount Falkland, with a prepared company around them, laboured by formidable speeches and hot debates to have that petition cast out of the House without a hearing, as craving the rooting out of Episcopacy against so many established laws. The other party was not prepared, yet they contested on together from eight o'clock till six at night. All that night our party solicited as hard as they could, and the morrow some thousands of citizens, but in a very peaceable way, came down to Westminster Hall to countenance their petition. It was voiced whether the petition should be committed or not. By 36 to 7 voices, our party carried it that it should be referred to the Committee for Religion, to which some four or six more were added—young Sir Harry Vane, Mr. Fiennes, and some more of our firm friends.[1]

The committee thus appointed lost no time in meeting. In the *Verney Notes*, edited by Mr. Bruce for the Camden Society, there is a valuable account of a portion of its deliberations. Its first meeting was on the 10th of February; the report from it was made on the 9th of March. Within these limits—

The committee met thrice a week in the afternoon. Some sixteen of the remonstrant ministers attended them.[2] They (the committee) required satisfaction practically on that head which concerned government. . . . The ministers, by their speaker, Dr. Burgess, gave to the committee full contentment, and so much the greater by my Lord Digby and Mr. Selden's frequent opposition. The citizens also made good all the parts of their petition which the committee required to be proved.

Before this committee every other day some eight or ten of the remonstrants appear. Dr. Burgess is their mouthpiece. We did suspect him of being too much Episcopal. Yet he has carried himself so bravely that we do repent of our suspicions. The passages of the Remonstrance that yet has been called for, he has cleared to the full contentment of all the committee except Mr. Selden, the avowed proctor of the bishops. How the matter will go the Lord knows. All are for the erecting of a kind of presbyteries, and for bringing down the bishops in all things temporal and spiritual as low as may be. But their utter abolition, which is the only aim of the most godly, is the knot of the question.[3]

[1] On the 19th of February two other petitions against Episcopacy and the many abuses of their courts, from Cheshire and Devon, were presented to the House, and referred to the above committee, with the same restrictions as above. *Similarly* from Exon, 23rd February, Nottingham, Lancashire, Oxford, Buckingham.

[2] Baillie, *Letters*, i., 306.

[3] *Ibid.*, i., 302. Baillie's temperament influences all his statements of opinion, which are therefore of small value as compared with his statements of fact.

The first two meetings, of the 10th and 15th of February, were taken up by a consideration of the second and third heads of the Remonstrance.

2. The prelates' claim of Divine institution.

3. Their assuming sole power of jurisdiction and ordination.

It would seem as if, for the first three or four meetings, the committee was entirely in the hands of the ministers. Authorities were produced to prove that such a claim of Divine right had been made—Bishop Bilson, Andrewes, White, Davenant, Montagu, Dr. Pocklington, etc., and an equally long and significant list of references to Ignatius, Cyprian and the Councils, was brought forward to prove that in primitive times the bishops did not ordain or exercise jurisdiction alone, and to establish the identity of presbyters with bishops. On the former of these points some dispute took place between Selden and Burgess. Of the representations of the Episcopal party we have only one trace —their feeble objection that in "the work of ordination priests are taken in to ordain with bishops". Such an objection was easily answered, and the proceedings ended in a vote—

That the challenges of Episcopacy *jure divino*, as is complained of in the second article, in the sole power assumed by bishops in ordination and jurisdiction, by virtue of a distinct order, superior to a presbyter, is a material head, and fit to be presented to the House.

It is quite typical of the general situation that these points, especially the latter, should have been dwelt upon at such length. The point of the parity or disparity of bishops with presbyters was again

debated before the committee on the 17th, when
the disputants were evidently, as before, Selden
and Burgess. " Wherein," Selden asked, " in persons, places and causes, consists the difference
between a bishop and a presbyter?" Burgess's
reply lays down for us the tenets of that party
which was to acquire and retain through history the
name of Presbyterians.

1. Constantine I. His time we count the primitive time.

2. Consecrations and interdictions of Church licences,
sitting and ruling in civil assemblies and judicature, or acts
concerning matrimony or testament, were not used by bishops
or presbyters in ancient times.

In general, all jurisdictions were exercised in common, and
not by bishops alone.

For *Persons.*—They were all them that were within the
Church.

For *Causes.*—Offences in matters of faith or manners,
doctrine heretical or schismatical; all offences against God's
law so far as they were scandalous in any manner or degree,
brotherly admonitions, binding of delinquents, loosing of the
penitents.

For *Places.*—Ordinary or extraordinary. The ordinary
place was the Presbytery or Consistory.

The ministers then proceeded in the explanation
and defence of the remaining heads of their Remonstrance, and Nos. 4 to 7 of these articles were voted
by the committee to be material heads, and fit to
be considered of by the House.

It was plainly to be seen on which side the
weight of argument and sympathy lay, and the
exasperation of the prelatical party may easily be
imagined. One Richard Flood, a clergyman, who had
been present at the above meeting of the committee
on the 17th, came away in a rage, declaring he had

been among a company of rogues, who went about to pull down Episcopacy, and vowing to pistol Dr. Burgess with his own hand.[1]   Of the remaining heads of the Remonstrance, Nos. 9 to 19 were gone through in a similar manner on the 19th of February, from which date the *Verney Notes* cease on this point, the only other existing record of the debates of this committee being found in D'Ewes.[2]

It would seem that the subsequent debates in the committee up to the making of the report on the 9th of March abandoned the more general ground of the Ministers' Remonstrance, and in proportion became more aggressive and secular.   The matter for these debates, which were probably conducted by the committee without any further reference to the divines, was apparently furnished by the more extreme London and county petitions. For example, at the meeting on the 1st of March, the point in debate was the injustice and partiality displayed by the bishops in instituting to benefices.[3]

[1] D'Ewes, i., 236.

[2] It was probably in the light of this committee's debates that Nicholas (soon to be made Secretary) composed his remarkable paper preserved in *State Papers, Domestic*, cccclxxvii., No. 72.   He proposed, on behalf of the Court party, that the House of Lords should interest themselves in the question of Church government before the Commons had passed any resolution, it being doubtful how far they would go in their heat; this to be done by way of conference between the two Houses, and supplemented by the calling of a national Synod composed of a select number of divines of all the three nations, and, if possible, delegates from the Reformed Churches abroad, "in which may be resolved a uniform model of government to be presented to the Parliament of all the kingdoms for approbation".   It seems almost incredible that Nicholas could have put such propositions to paper, and I doubt exceedingly his authorship of the paper and the date of it.

[3] D'Ewes, *ubi supra.*

This will explain the apparent discrepancy between the votes already recorded and the final votes which were reported to the House on the 9th. The latter evince a more extreme and secular character. They show that the committee had referred itself to the divines only on those matters of antiquities and theology, of which, in the unanimous opinion of the age, the determination properly belonged to the clergy. But, in its judgment of the whole question, from the point of view of State policy and general justice, the opinion of the committee was the average opinion of the secular mind of the day, and the votes indicate clearly on what heads and aspects of the Church system the attention of the secular public and the House of Commons was fixed, and which parts of that system were to be the first to meet a challenge. The report was as follows :—

Die Martis, 9 Martii, 164$\frac{0}{1}$.

Mr. Crew reports from the committee for the Ministers' Remonstrance three heads for the debate and consideration of the House :—

1. Their secular employment, by which is intended their legislative and judicial power in Parliament, their judicial power in the Star Chamber and in commissions for the peace, and their employment as privy councillors and in temporal offices.

2. Sole power in ecclesiastical things, by which is intended ordination and censures.

3. The greatness of the revenues of deans and chapters, the little use of them, and the great inconveniences which come by them.[1]

The paper of reasons with which Crew supported

[1] C. J., ii., 100.

these motions is a strange document to be presented to a lay assembly :—

The reasons to prove the *first* are :—

1. That their office is to preach and teach, and not to meddle with secular affairs.

2. Because they are by this made judges of the property, etc., as judges in the Star Chamber, as justices of the peace, etc.

3. By this means they come wholly to neglect matters of the Church, contrary to Acts vi.

4. This is contrary to the command of the Apostle.

5. And of the Church of Chalcedon, and the constitutions of Ottobon.[1]

The arguments on the second head were :—

1 Tim. iv. and 2 Tim. i.—Timothy was ordained by the laying on of hands of the elders. So they are not to have sole ordination. Matt. viii.—Ordination belongs to the Church, and that cannot be one bishop alone. 1 Corinth. v.—The Corinthians are commanded to gather together to excommunicate the incestuous person. There are several examples vouched of bishops who ordained with their Presbytery.[2] So, likewise, many examples were brought against sole jurisdiction, and there were two canons in Sir Henry Spelman's councils that the bishop ought not to exercise sole jurisdiction.

To prove the third point or head he brought no reason, because the matter was plain evident.

Owing to other business brought down from the Lords, no set debate on the report took place on the 9th, but the temper of the House was seen significantly in an incident that occurred. Mr.

[1] D'Ewes, i., 298.

[2] See in *State Papers, Domestic*, cccclxxviii., No. 30, some propositions touching the Divine right of bishops and the distinction of his office from that of the presbyter. The main drift of this paper, which is dated 10th March, is that the King, Lords and Commons are competent judges as to the fitness of bishops as lords of lands, and so as a political order of men setting themselves upon their punctilios before their betters.

Pleydall (the constant debater for Episcopacy, and

amongst the first to join the Parliament at Oxford) rose to declare that in his opinion the committee had exceeded their powers, and intermeddled too far with Episcopacy.[1] Several answered him roundly in defence of the committee, and at a later stage Pleydall thought it discreet to explain himself, and made some slender satisfaction to the House by saying that he meant no hurt.

There can be little doubt that at this time it was in the mind of the generality of the House that the work of reformation could be accomplished by way of this committee. The House did not even let it be supposed that it had ceased with the presentation of its report, for on the same day an order was made that the committee should have power to send for witnesses the better to prepare the heads for the House.

The formal debate on this report was eagerly taken up on the following day, 10th March, 164$\frac{0}{1}$.

On that day the discussion was opened by Bridgman, son of the Bishop of Chester, with a motion to admit a certain divine (whom, upon pressure, he allowed to be Dr. Brownrig) to argue the question of the secular employment of the clergy before the House.[2] He was answered by Selden and others that, as the matter concerned only secular employment, there was no need of it, "for sole jurisdiction and ordination we might well have divines".

It is indicative of the waste of energy which

---

[1] D'Ewes, i., 299. [2] Ibid., iii., 937.

characterises this Parliament, due to its want of an organised and recognised leadership, that the House debated at length the *order* of the discussion, finally determining to adopt the following order in debating of the first head of the report, *viz.:* (1) Legislative and judicial power [of the bishops] in Parliament; (2) judicial power in Star Chamber and Commissions of Peace; (3) their employment as privy councillors at the Council table and in temporal offices.

Accordingly, the first day's debate was entirely taken up with the discussion of the first branch of the first head; and here, again, it ran upon the very narrowest lines. The question became entirely one as to the right by which bishops, historically and constitutionally, sit in Parliament; and this not only in the hands of antiquarians such as Selden and D'Ewes, and of lawyers such as Bagshaw, Whitelock and Glynn, but even of one purely and merely political, such as Pym himself. The only difference of opinion was as to whether bishops sit by tenure of barony or by right of diocese, having ecclesiastical jurisdiction, and as representing the clergy. The latter was the opinion of Selden and Bridgman, but with this exception there was neither opposition nor any deviation from the narrow argument. Even such a speaker as Culpeper, whom we should have expected to raise the debate into a higher plane of sentiment, contented himself with moving to have the question deferred. With equal docility, Pym followed [1] Glynn and others in

---

[1] With the single exception of a ludicrous comparison of the case of the bishops with that of Jonah: "Though Jonah came into the

their conclusion that the bishops could not be representative, and that they sat by one right in the Convocation and by another in the Parliament.

What is stranger still is the contrast between the wording of the resolution as it finally passed and the course of the debate itself. The final form of that resolution was as follows :—

> That the legislative and judicial powers of the bishops in the House of Peers in Parliament is a hindrance to the discharge of their spiritual function, prejudicial to the Commonwealth, and fit to be taken away by a bill, and that a bill be drawn for that purpose.

With the exception of a discussion as to the retention or rejection of the word " inconsistent " (predicated of the spiritual functions) found in an earlier form of the motion, and which was finally omitted, no discussion took place on the motives as laid down in the explanatory part of this resolution. The case is identical with that of the votes on the canons. The secular mind was resolved on the absurdity and iniquity of leaving such power and influence in the hands of Churchmen ; and the Commons therein wisely and faithfully represented the secular mind. The sense of the more fervently spiritual and sternly moral part of the nation was impressed with the beauty of the simplicity of true religious life, with the necessity of such simplicity for the heads of the religious organisation as much as for the lowest unit in it, and with the incompati-

---

ship by the Master's command, yet he, knowing he was not doing his Master's command, was to be thrown overboard, so these bishops, if they came in by Christ's commands, as I conceive they did not, and not performing their Lord's commands, are to be extinguished" (Moore's *Diary*, B.M. Harl. MS. 477, vol. ii., folio 313).

bility with this of high temporal status and potency. Of such phase of opinion a faithful reflex was found in the House of Commons, and stands expressed in their resolution of this day, notwithstanding that there is no apparent justification for it in the course of the debate.

According to Baillie, the votes passed unanimously, " not ten contradicting ".

The second head—the employment of the clergy in the Star Chamber and on Commissions of Peace —was reserved for debate on the following day,

Thursday, 11th March, when it was disposed of on equally technical grounds, and still more summarily. The statutes generally reputed as establishing the court were read, 3 Hen. VII., and 32 Hen. VIII., and in the latter it was noticed that " the clergy are inhibited to intermeddle in secular affairs, and so the matter was soon drawn to a question ".[1]

The resolution of the House was :—

> For bishops or any other clergyman whatsoever to be on the Commission of the Peace, or to have any judicial power in the Star Chamber or in any civil court, is a hindrance to their spiritual function, prejudicial to the Commonwealth, and fit to be taken away by a bill, and that a bill be drawn to that purpose.[2]

There is not even a trace that the point of the sitting of clergymen on Commissions of Peace, included in this resolution, was at all touched upon in the debate.

Owing to the preoccupation of the House with Strafford's trial, the third branch of the first head of the report was not deliberated upon until the

---

[1] D'Ewes, i., 307.   [2] C. J., ii., 102.

22nd March (Monday), when the House resolved that :—

For bishops or any other clergyman whatsoever to have employment as privy councillors at the Council table or in temporal offices is a hindrance to the discharge of their spiritual function, prejudicial to the Commonwealth, and fit to be taken away by a bill, and that a bill be drawn accordingly.

On the occasion of this debate, D'Ewes has preserved a lengthy pedantic speech of his own, which images most forcibly the hatred in the secular mind of the interference of the clergy in any department of temporal affairs. At no period in the history of this country has the deserving part of the clergy met with greater reverence and obedience within their own sphere than in the civil war period, and at no other period has the revolt—partly popular, still more legal—against clerical interference in matters outside the true domain of their activity, been more strongly and impatiently proclaimed. As might be expected, Hyde and the elder Vane contended that it was the inalienable right of the Crown to select its own advisers. As an antiquarian, D'Ewes could not but see the force and truth of the argument, but as a Puritan he had made up his mind against it, and D'Ewes was, on this matter, a Puritan first and an antiquarian after.

He roundly asserted that the counsels of the clergy had always proved dangerous and fatal. But the weight of his argument lay in the iterated and reiterated necessity of their attending solely to their spiritual function.

I deny not, as it hath been observed by Mr. Hyde, that they might be fit enough to advise at the Council table—yea, more fit it is to be feared than to preach—but this drew on a neglect of their other charge, which was more weighty.

Some discussion then ensued upon the second head of the report, concerning sole jurisdiction and ordination. But, conscious of its own want of special fitness for the debate, the House resolved to lay it aside for the present, and in the meanwhile to hear divines on the subject, and accordingly empowered the Committee for the Remonstrance "to hear such ministers as have desired to be heard on the sole power of bishops in ordination, and censure of such ministers, shall they desire it, and to hear such others as they shall think fit". Immediately thereupon it was ordered, on Hampden's motion, to go on with the third head of Mr. Crewe's report—*viz.*, deans and chapters—on the following day. The debate, however, was not taken until Friday, 26th March, when it was opened by D'Ewes.

D'Ewes was taking no mean part in the ecclesiastical debates of the Long Parliament, and his utterances, notwithstanding his pedantry, are typical of the two most important phases of thought in the Commons and in the nation at large ; its superstitious reverence for legality of form and its trenchant secularity ; in other words, the abrupt determination with which it resolved to assert for lay life—for national life—its proper independent sphere of action, and to banish clerical interference. Later in the year the Commons resolved to confiscate the revenues of the Church, those of the bishops to the Crown, those of the deans and chapters to good uses ;

and this after divines, both Episcopal and Puritan, had been heard before the Lower House, and after both parties (Dr. Burgess as well as Dr. Hacket) had pronounced it sacrilege to convert to secular purposes what had once been consecrated to God. The latter idea was common, and his attempt at overthrowing it is the merit of D'Ewes: "As the deans and chapters are now useless, we may well dispose of their revenues to better uses". He was not certain whether the pious donations of the eleventh century were sacrations to God or the devil, but he was quite certain that the patrimony of the Crown was as much sacration as the revenue of the Church.

We are not now singly upon a consideration of the estates of the Church, but of the estate of the Crown also, for the main question is not between the deans and a common person, but between them and the king. Here is *sacrum patrimonium* against *sacrum patrimonium*.[1]

He was followed in a lower strain of vituperation by Reynolds, Wheeler and Sir Edward Moundeford, speakers to whom Falkland could only reply with his habitual argument that the abuse of the institution or the evil lives of certain deans were not reasons for taking away deaneries. In his argument he was followed by Culpeper, who desired to see deaneries made useful rather than abolished, which latter, to his mind, threatened a decay of learning; and D'Ewes assures us "that of the many who spake after him, most spake to the effect that they might not be utterly abolished".[2]

The debate was adjourned. On the following

[1] D'Ewes, i., 359.   [2] *Ibid.*, iii., 948.

Monday Culpeper presented to the House a petition from divers deans who desired to be heard in
defence of deans and chapters. There was a decided
opposition to any reading of the petition at all, but
on the following day it was read and the request
granted. Owing to the pressing nature of Strafford's business, the divines were not heard for some
considerable time; and when, on 30th April, it
stood with the convenience of the House to hear
them, they did not appear. Thereupon a very ill-
tempered dispute arose, some proposing to go on
with the matter without any further reference to
them. These were, however, overruled, and Friday,
7th May, was appointed for the audience. As a
fact, it was not until the 12th of May that the
hearing actually occurred. On that day there
appeared on behalf of deans and chapters Dr.
Bargrave, Dr. Hacket, Dr. Ward, Dr. Brownrig.
On the part of the ministers who had signed the
Remonstrance appeared Dr. Burgess, Mr. Marshall,
Mr. White.

12th May, the
divines heard
in defence of
deans and
chapters.

The proceedings were opened by an extraordinary request from Dr. Bargrave, Dean of
Canterbury, who, after a few general observations
in defence of the institution of deans and chapters,
demanded that the consideration of the whole
question should be postponed, and in the meantime counsel assigned to them. The House declined to take any notice of the request, and then
the weight of the defence fell upon Dr. Hacket, at
that time minister of St. Andrew, Holborn. He
addressed himself to proving "the four points
undertaken to be proven by Dr. Bargrave, *viz.*,

Hacket's
arguments.

that deans and chapters conduce (1) to the glory of God; (2) the propagation of the Gospel; (3) the advancement of piety and learning; (4) the good of the Commonwealth ".

There is a remarkable timidity about this defence on the part of the usually trenchant Hacket. In support of the first "point" he instanced the daily prayers in cathedrals, and yet he was aware that objections were taken as to the manner. The abuse he confessed, and declared that all humbly desired the House to reform the same. In defence of the second "point," he came from prayer to preaching, and felt bound to confess that this had been too much neglected. "They desired that in each cathedral two sermons [should be preached] each Sunday, and that some lectures [might be prescribed] for the week-day which they would perform." The rest of the defence consisted of protestations as to the sacred nature of their property, the glorious estate of the English Church, and the threatening flood of ignorance which would rise on the abolition of deans and chapters.

Dr. Bargrave then delivered a Latin letter from Cambridge, and a petition from the officers of the Church at Canterbury, in favour of the continuance of deans and chapters, while Selden preferred a similar one from Oxford.

In the afternoon, after a few more remarks from Hacket, Burgess was heard in reply. His task was easy.

He agreed, as did the whole of his contemporaries, that the points laid down by Dr. Bargrave would, if fulfilled, be a sufficient justification of the institution. The real question was whether such ends were met by it, and, if not, by what could they be met; and it was easy for him, in support of the negative, to point to the [to the Puritan] objectionable formality of the prayers and music of the cathedrals, to the paucity of the preaching, and to the ease with which provision could be made for the continuance of the grammar schools, etc. But he was entirely at one with his antagonists in claiming for the patrimony of the Church a sacred character. "For sacrilege, he acknowledged that it ought not to be perverted, as the Casuists and the Puritans hold, to civil uses"; "and so," says D'Ewes, "the divines withdrew, and some spake to that which they had said on both sides, that they were to hold all the Church lands, and we were to have no more".[1]

Attitude of
Parliament to
the question
of appropria-
tion of dean
and chapters'
revenues.

We can form a tolerably good idea of the scheme that was in the minds of the portion of the clerical party represented by the remonstrant divines and Dr. Burgess from a tract extant among the king's pamphlets, "petition of divers of the clergy, . . . with five motions concerning deans and chapters".

The five motions are as follow :—

The deans and chapters may continue with these conditions :—

1. That they may be annexed to the parish churches in the great towns where the cathedrals stand.

---

[1] For the above account, see D'Ewes, ii., 556 ; Moore, iii., 518 ; Rushworth, iv., 269 ; Nalson, ii., 240. Bruce does not seem to have known of these jottings of Hacket's and Burgess's speeches in D'Ewes' and Moore's MSS. ; hence his introduction to the debates of this day in the *Verney Notes* (Camden Society), is vague and incorrect in detail.

2. That they may be elected in these places by the king, with the approbation and consent of the people.

3. That they may be enjoined to preach ordinarily twice every Lord's day at their parish.

4. That they may preach every Sunday once or twice in their courses at the cathedrals.

5. That they may be a *consilium* to the bishop in all matters of ordination and jurisdiction, so that nothing shall be done without them.[1]

On the other hand, there was a section of the Parliament which fearlessly advocated confiscation of the greater part of the property to purely secular uses.

On the very day preceding the above audience of the divines, the House had been in debate as to the manner of raising £400,000, urgently needed to meet the expenses of the two armies and the Scottish indemnity. On that occasion Peard brought forward a decisive paper scheme. It is worthy of notice :—

The deaneries do possess £28,400 (*old rent*). £8,400 to be allowed out of this £28,400 to rectories and churches now ill served. £20,000 is left of the old rent before named, worth £200,000 in true value. This, let to farm, will make £900,000 for twenty-one years and three lives, and this will be a superior way to raise money than any other, and will be a better security than any money granted can be.[2]

Characteristically enough the scheme received the support of Cromwell.

The House, however, was not prepared to go to such lengths at once. The debate on the deans and chapters was adjourned till Wednesday, 19th May, and on that day it did not take place, though an

---

[1] Brit. Museum, E. 170.   [2] D'Ewes, iii., 1007.

incident did which shows the apprehensions and distempers of the times. A fright was caused in the gallery by the fall of some plaster, and a rush ensued. Sir Thomas Mansell drew his sword " and came to the door of the House to inquire the cause, conceiving there had been some divisions in the House concerning deans and chapters, which matters had been ordered to have been debated this morning ".[1]

In the end, as it proved, the conclusion on this head of Crewe's report from the Committee for the Ministers' Remonstrance was not arrived at in the above connection. The orderly debates on that report were interrupted by the Root-and-Branch Bill, and when later the confiscations of the revenues of deans and chapters was voted, it was as a part of the Root-and-Branch Bill itself.

The first really effective legislation of the Long Parliament was, however, the result of the work of the above Committee for the Ministers' Remonstrance. In less than three weeks after the resolution on the first head, a bill to take away the bishops' votes in the Lords passed its first reading in the Commons as " An Act to restrain bishops and others in holy orders to intermeddle with secular affairs ".

The Bishops' Bill. 1640-1, 30th March.

Some eagerly pressed for its reading a second time the same day.[2]

From the beginning of the Parliament the national mind at large, and the majority of the Commons, had determined at least on such an item of reform. The production of the bill, therefore,

[1] D'Ewes.　　　[2] *Ibid.*, i., 377.

was immediately, but not merely, the result of the
resolution of the 10th of March.[1] In briefest
point, it was a bill to eject the bishops from the
House of Lords and the Star Chamber. It was
introduced and read a first time on the 30th
March, 1640-41.[2]

This "Bishops Bill" was read a second time on
the 1st of April, and reported on the 16th and
21st of April. On the following day a proviso was
added by the House, though opposed by D'Ewes
and others, exempting doctors of the two universities from the disability, and allowing them to act
as justices of the peace.[3]

The bill was read a third time on the 1st of The Bishops'
May, and immediately taken up to the Lords, and Bill in the Lords.
there read *primâ vice*. For almost a fortnight the
Lords did nothing with it, until the 13th, when,
on an impatient message from the Commons, they
condescended to read it a second time, and fixed
the debate on it for the 20th of May. The debate

[1] The concurrent legislation with regard to the status of the clergy
and their exclusion from Commissions of Peace will be noticed in
another connection, *infra*, p. 233.

[2] C.J., ii., 114.

[3] According to D'Ewes' *Diary*, folio 984, c. 182, and folio 477b,
85a, the debate on the proposition to exempt the two universities
took place on the 22nd April.

"A debate touching a proviso added to the bill for debarring
bishops and other persons in holy orders from secular employments,
by the Committee, for exempting the two universities. Mr. Whistler,
Mr. Maynard, Mr. Selden and others spoke that it might stand.
Others spoke to the contrary . . . I desired . . . that this proviso
might be left out, and that the divines in the two universities might
be left out with their brethren from being J. P."

In the *Commons Journals* (ii. 127), the resolution as in the text
was adopted on the 23rd.

continued for three days,[1] and on the 24th the House came to a composite resolution. It refused the bill as far as it related to the bishops' seats in Parliament, but adopted that portion of it which related to the Star Chamber :—

Resolved, That the archbishops and bishops shall have suffrage and voice in the House of Peers in Parliament.[2]

Resolved, That the archbishops and bishops shall not have suffrage and voice in the Star Chamber when they are called.

Three days later—on the 27th of May, the very day on which the Root-and-Branch Bill was first read in the Commons—the Lords, anxious to explain the nature of their act, appointed a committee to draw heads for a conference with the Commons. The paper of heads, as reported by the Earl of Bath, is exceedingly interesting :—

Whereas the House of Commons have said in their preamble of the bill that archbishops and bishops, and other persons in holy orders, ought not to intermeddle in secular affairs ; after long debate and consideration their lordships considered that by these words " ought not " they understood, not unlawfulness by any law, but conveniency or inconveniency; and among other reasons one principle did arise from the bill, for if this House conceived that if they thought it absolutely unlawful, they would not have put in these two provisos for the heads of colleges, and for such persons in holy orders to whom titles of nobility shall descend. For their right to vote in Parliament their lordships conceive that by the common and statute laws of this realm, and by ancient and continued practice, they have unquestionable right.

For inconveniency, their lordships yet understand not any such for certainty and weight that will induce them to

---

[1] Viscount Newark's speeches on the 21st and 24th of May are preserved in *State Papers, Domestic*, cccclxxx., No. 54, and in Cooke's *Speeches in Parliament*, 1641, pp. 305-13.

[2] L. J., iv., 256.

deprive them and their successors of that right; but if there be any to be given by the House of Commons, this House shall at a conference with them willingly hear and take them into consideration.·

For the bishops having no votes and suffrages in the Star Chamber, for their not being of His Majesty's Privy Council, for their not being justices of the peace, commissioners in secular offices, otherwise than in performing their duty as they are directed by law in some special cases, as plenary of benefice, loyalty of marriage, and some others; for their not having or enjoying any judicial place in any temporal court, this House hath fully assented.

Only it hath been offered to their lordships, on behalf of the bishops, that some consideration may be had of them in some particulars, as for the Dean of Westminster to have that corporation confirmed by Act of Parliament; for the Bishops of Durham, Ely, and the Archbishop of York for Hexhamshire, and for all in keeping court leet, and barons by their stewards, and all other courts that are executed by temporal officers, as formerly they have done, which their lordships conceive not contrary to the meaning of this bill.

The conference was held (27th May), and in answer the Commons determined to prepare reasons in defence of their vote. The reasons were reported to the House a week later (4th June).[1]

This paper is important as a statement of the opinion of the House (and the Commons even ordered it to be printed), and also for another reason, viz.: As originally reported by Pierpont, the paper contained eight heads or arguments, but, according to D'Ewes,[2] "The Lord Falkland, Mr. Nath. Fiennes, and one or two more gave some new reasons to be added to those former whilst we were voting the first six, and so it was ordered that they should retire into the committee chamber

Reasons of the Commons for the exclusion of Bishops from the Lords,etc.

---

[1] C. J., ii., 159, 167.   [2] D'Ewes, ii., 651.

and draw those reasons, which they did accordingly". It can easily be seen, from a comparison of the two forms of the paper, that Articles 7, 8, 9 of the final paper emanated from this strange combination, Falkland and Fiennes. The following is the final form of it (in the *Commons Journals* the final form of the paper is printed before the recommitment of it. The correction is due to D'Ewes, ii., 656) :—

Reasons of the House of Commons why bishops ought not to have votes in the House of Peers :—

1. Because it is a very great hindrance to the discharge of their ministerial function.

2. Because they do vow and undertake at their ordination, when they enter into holy orders, that they will give themselves wholly to that vocation.

3. Because councils and canons in several ages do forbid them to meddle with secular affairs.

4. Because the twenty-four bishops have a dependence on the two archbishops, and because of their canonical obedience to them.

5. Because they are but for life, and therefore are not fit to have legal power over the honours, inheritances, lives and liberties of others.

6. Because of bishops' dependency and expectancy of translation to places of greater profit.

7. That several bishops have of late much encroached upon the consciences and liberties of the subject, and they and their successors will be much encouraged still to encroach, and the subject will be much discouraged from complaining against such encroachment, if twenty-six of that order be to be judges upon those complaints. The same reason extends to their legislative power in any bill to pass for the regulation of their power upon any emergent inconveniences by it.

8. Because the whole number of them is interested to maintain the jurisdiction of bishops, which hath been found so dangerous to the three kingdoms that Scotland hath utterly abolished it, and multitudes in England and Ireland have petitioned against it.

9. Because the bishops, being Lords of Parliament, it setteth too great a distance between them and the rest of their brethren in the ministry, which occasioneth pride in them, discontent in others, and disquiet in the Church.

To their having votes a long time. *Answer :* If inconvenient, time and usage are not to be considered law makers. Some abbots voted as anciently as bishops, yet they were taken away.

That for the bishops' certificate for plenary of benefice and loyalty of marriage the bill extends not to them.

For the secular jurisdictions of the Dean of Westminster, the Bishops of Durham and Ely, and the Archbishop of York, which they are to execute in their own persons, the former reasons show the inconveniences therein. For their temporal courts and jurisdiction, which are executed by their temporal officers, the bill doth not concern them.

As it was still unconvinced by the arguments of the Commons, the House of Lords finally, on the 8th of June, 1641, rejected the bill on the third hearing.[1] Accordingly, here for the nonce is an end to it, and here too—but not for a moment merely—was an end to all dreams of a moderate Church reform.

Rejection of theCommons' Bishops' Bill by the Lords.

That such a result, however, was not intended by the Lords is plain. For some time they had been themselves intent on a scheme of Church reform, but from the more limited standpoint of objections to ceremonies and innovations. On the same day (1st March, 1640-41) on which they had issued their order[2] concerning the position of the Communion Table, the Lords appointed a most influential committee to consider of all innovations in the Church concerning religion. Five days later this committee was empowered to send

The Lords' project of ecclesiastical reform, 1st March.

The Lords Committee for Innovations.

[1] L. J., iv., 269. [2] See *infra*, p. 105.

for such learned men as they pleased to assist them.[1] The order was repeated on the 10th of March, and several names mentioned, "as the Lord Archbishop of Armagh, Dr. Prideaux, Dr. Ward, Dr. Twiste (Twisse), Dr. Hacket," who were to have intimation given to them by the Lord Bishop of Lincoln.[2]

On the occasion of the appointment of this committee, Mr. Gardiner has extracted from the Wodrow MSS. (Edinburgh) some slight account of the debate.[3]

> The Lord Saye spoke very freely against Episcopacy and the liturgy, constantly averring that he would never hear it. Bristol answered that there were some things indifferent pressed on men's consciences which must be taken away, but what was established by law no man might separate from it. Saye replied that they were now in *loco et tempore mutationis*, and therefore desired that a committee might be appointed for that effect.

Hacket has preserved some account of this committee.[4] Its constitution, apparently, subsequently changed; a portion of the original number was joined with the divines to form a sub-committee. Over both forms of it Williams presided. The list of those divines who did constantly attend is thus given by Hacket : Bishop of Lincoln, Primate of Armagh, Bishop of Durham, Bishop of Norwich, Dr. Ward, Dr. Prideaux, Dr. Sanderson, Dr. Featley, Dr. Brownrig, Dr. Holdsworth, Dr. Hacket, Dr. Twisse, Dr. Burgess, Mr. White, Mr. Marshall, Mr. Calamy, Mr. Hill.

---

[1] L. J., iv., 177.   [2] *Ibid.*, 180.
[3] Gardiner, ix., 298.   [4] *Scrinia Reserata*, part ii., p. 147.

Williams summoned the divines to the assistance of the Lords' Committee in the following important and ungrammatical letter :—

I am commanded by the Lords of the Committee for Innovations in matters of Religion that you know that their said lordships have assigned and appointed you to attend them as assistant in that committee, and to let you know in general that the Lords do intend to examine all innovations in doctrine or discipline introduced into the Church without law since the Reformation, and if their lordships shall find it behoveful for the good of the Church and State to examine after that the degrees and perfection of the Reformation itself, which I am directed to intimate to you, that you may prepare your thoughts, studies, and meditations accordingly, expecting their lordship's pleasure for the particular points as they shall arise, March 12, 164⁰/₁.

According to Hacket,

" The theological junto had six meetings in Westminster College, in all which time all passages of discourse were very friendly between part and part. The complainants noted the passages of some books that suited not, in their judgment, with the doctrine of our Church. They were condemned. Somewhat in ceremony and in outward form, as beside [sic, for residentiary] canon and supernumerary, they had their asking to bid it be restrained. Their exceptions against our liturgy were petty and stale—older than the old exchange—yet for their contentment the vote of the meeting did tend one way, to castigate some phrases, to publish the next printed books in all passages, from the beginning to the end, from the translation of King James's Bible, and to furnish the calendar altogether with passages of canonical scripture, expunging the apocryphal. The bishops had undertaken a draft for regulating the government ecclesiastical, but had not finished it. The sudden and quiet despatch of all that was done was attributed to the chairman's dexterity."

On the 5th of April, the Lords ordered the committee to meet on the following Thursday, thus indicating an intermission of its sitting. Dr.

Dell in a letter [1] of the 10th of April, 1641, un-
directed, but possibly intended for Nicholas, gives
the following fragmentary account of its deliberations at this time :—

> Our new committee for religion was appointed to have
> sate on Monday, in the afternoone last, but there being neither
> meeting nor adjournement it was left *sine die :* yet on Thursday
> in the afternoone, the Bishop of Lincolne, Durham, Winchester,
> Bristoll mett, where the assistants attended by some three
> score other divines of inferior ranke were present, and many
> temporall lords; and many points of doctrine and Church
> service being questioned among the rest one Lord sayd that it
> ought to be putt out of the creed that Christ descended into
> hell which he did not believe. Yesterday in the forenoone with-
> out any intimation or notice given to the other committees [*i.e.*,
> members of the committee] the same spirituall Lords and
> divines mett at the Bishop of Lincolne's lodging, where in
> lesse then two houres they condemned (as I am informed by
> the Bishop of Bristol, present) about fifty points in doctrine
> which they had mett with in severall Treatises and sermons of
> late printed amongst us; they had culled out a passage of my
> Lord of Cant[erbury] in his Starre Chamber speech, which
> they say is that *Hoc est Corpus meum* is more then *Hoc est
> verbum meum*, which the Bishop of Lincolne censured for that
> *verbum meum* did make *Corpus*, but would not further heere
> because his Grace was like to answer it shortly elsewhere.

There can be little doubt that a *résumé* of the
particular debate referred to above is contained in
"*a copy of the proceedings of some worthy and
learned divines appointed by the Lords to meet at
the Bishop of Lincolne's in Westminster*," which will
be found printed in the appendix (No. 1).

The paper consists of eighteen questions as to the
innovations in doctrine, appertaining to Popish
opinions, or the gross substance of Arminianism.

---

[1] *State Papers, Domestic,* cccclxxix., 24.

These are followed by references to three books deserving reproof, and by twenty-one questions on innovations in "discipline," which include the turning of the table altarwise, bowing, candlesticks, canopies, the rails, the reading of the second service, prohibiting ministers from expounding the catechism, suppressing lectures, and prohibiting conceived prayer before sermon. Then succeed three memoranda :—

1. That in all cathedral and collegiate churches two sermons be preached every Sunday by the dean and prebendaries . . . and one lecture at the least to be preached on working days every week all the year round.

2. That the music used in God's holy service in cathedral and collegiate churches be framed with less curiosity.

3. That the reading desk be placed in the church where divine service may best be heard of all the people.

The paper closes with thirty-five exceptions to imperfections in the Prayer Book. The exceptions are advanced rather as propositions than as resolutions. But it seems clear that they represent actual decisions of the Committee (Baxter, *e.g.*, in his autobiography speaks of them as "concessions"[1]), and that they were intended to be recommendations from the Committee to the Lords on the minor points of reform of doctrine and the Prayer Book.

Much greater interest attaches to the work of the committee on the subject of the reconstitution of the Episcopal function itself.

Various plans of reform were submitted, the chief one being Usher's "*reduction of Episcopacy*

---

[1] *Reliquiæ Baxterianæ*, part ii, p. 369.

CHAP. I.

1641.
Platforms of
reform of
ecclesiastical
government
submitted to
the Lords'
Committee
for Innova-
tions.

Archbishop
Usher's.

unto the form of synodical government".[1] This is the scheme that was oftenest quoted in connection with any idea of moderate reform or of comprehension, and was offered by the Puritan ministers at the Savoy Conference in 1661. It asserts that the preaching elders in common ruled the Church, that the president obtained his honour by good report, and that betwixt the bishop and the presbytery there was a harmonious consent in the ordering of Church government (speaking of the Church of Ephesus). It, therefore, makes the following proposals for the restoration of this ancient form of government by the united suffrages of the clergy, and for the accordance of the synodical conventions

[1] First published surreptitiously on the 25th November, 1656 (B.M., E. $\frac{894}{3}$) and authoritatively on the 17th December, 1656, by Nicholas Bernard (B.M., E. $\frac{897}{1}$). The imperfections which Bernard charges on the surreptitious edition are not formidable and leave the impression that the surreptitious edition was in accordance with the original MS. form, and that Bernard's was in accordance with Usher's last wishes. The MS. copy in the Lauderdale paper (B.M., addit. MS. 23113, f. 18) is in accordance with the surreptitious edition. This latter was reprinted at London, 25th June, 1660 (B.M., E. $\frac{1030}{3}$). The authorised version is preserved in Baxter's *Reliq. Bax.*, i., 238-40, and is reprinted in Elrington's Usher's *Works*, vol. xii. Usher acknowledged the authorship of his tract in conversation to Baxter, *Reliq. Bax.*, i., 206.

This tract is quite distinct from the utterly apocryphal tract, " *The Bishop of Armagh's direction concerning the Liturgy and Episcopal Government,*" London, 1642, B.M., 702, d. $\frac{8}{15}$. A MS. copy occurs in addit. MSS. 28273, fo. 31. This tract was reprinted in 1659 (E. $\frac{988}{15}$) and 1660 (E. $\frac{1030}{10}$), and is identical with (almost but not quite word for word with) Ephraim Udall's, " *Directions propounded and humbly presented to the High Court of Parliament concerning the book of Common Prayer and Episcopal Government,*" Oxford, 1642, B.M., 702, d. $\frac{8}{20}$. It was this tract of which Usher complained as an injurious and false aspersion and which was condemned (C.J., ii., 81, 9th Feb., 1640-1). It will be noticed that this date would put it before the time of Williams' Committee.

of the pastors of every parish within the presidency

of the bishops of every diocese and province: (1)
rector, churchwardens, and sidesmen to be turned
into a parochial presbytery; (2) rural deaneries to
be the basis of a monthly synod; (3) the diocese
to be the basis of a half-yearly synod; (4) the
provinces to be the basis of a triennial national
assembly.

Williams himself also offered a scheme for re-
conciliation on this head of Church government.

The principal points of his scheme were heads
three and four :—

3. That every bishop shall have twelve assistants, besides
the dean and chapter, four to be chosen by the King, four by
the Lords, and four by the Commons, for assistance in the
exercise of jurisdiction and ordination.

4. That in all vacancies those assistants, with the dean
and chapter, shall present to the King three of the ablest
divines in the diocese, who shall choose one to be bishop.

These two items enable us to identify with
almost absolute certainty the following paper [1] as
either by Bishop Williams himself for an agenda
paper for this Lords' Committee, or as representing
the outcome of the deliberations of that committee.

(1) All the B^{ps.} under 70 yeares old in theyr owne Dioces
being not sicke to preach every Lds day or pay 5 pound to the
poore.

(2) No Archb^{p.}, B^{ps.} or any other person being in orders &
having care of soules to be Judge of the Star Chamber or Privy
Counsellor or Justice of the Peace or a Commissioner from any

[1] *State Papers, Domestic,* Charles I., cccclxxxii., No. 1, without
heading or endorsement. Conjecturally, but incorrectly, assigned to
1st July, a date which the draft must have preceded by some time.
See L. J. under 1st July, 1641, and *infra* 73-5.

temporall Court under severall [sic ? for severe] penaltye & disabilites excepting the 2 universities, honourable persons by descent & Deane of Westminster in Westminster & Sᵗ Martins le Grand onely.

(3) 12 assistants to the Bᴾ· of every Dioces respectively to bee chosen out of every shire or county of England and Wales whereof 6 to assist the Bᴾ· & approve of every ordination of Ministers, one or two to assist in all ecclesiasticall judgement or sentence & to allow of appeales, 6 to be present in the heareing of appeales made to the Bᴾ· & the assistants to attend upon sumons under the penalty of 10ˡ.

(4) Election of Archbishops and Bᴾˢ· for the time to come to be performed by the Deane & the Chapter & all assistants in that Dioces, who are to recommende 3 persons in holy orders out of that or any other Dioces to the Kings Maᵗⁱᵉ who will be pleased to name one of them, that shall be consecrated and translated to the Bᵖʳⁱᶜᵏ within 20 days after the Congee deslier received, els the nomination is devolved to the King.

(5) No Deanes, Chapters or Residensiaries in Cathedrall or College Churches that have cure of soules to reside from theyr sayd cure above 60 dayes in the yeare : to preach 2 Sermons every Sunday & one Lecture in the weeke day in the place where theyr Cathedralls are situated upon a paine of a hundred pound to the King & losse of theyr profits for one yeare wᶜʰ is to goe to raise a stocke for the poore of that towne˙ & citty.

(6) The fourth part of the fines of all cases made by the Archbishops, Bᴾˢ·, Deanes, Deanes & Chapters, Dignitys, Prebendarys, as also of Mʳˢ·, fellowes, and schollars of colledges in both universities to be set aside to raise a stock to buy out all the impropriations of this kingdome: this money to bee delivered to collectors named by the Parliament who are to present clerks the first time to the sayd impropriations & afterwards for every [avoidance] the Archbishops, Bᴾˢ· & other Corporations from whence the money was raised [to present]: & of the remaining fine upon all impropriations the vicar or curate to be payd the tenth part.

(7) All Residentiarys that have a benefice with cure of soules to pay unto the Curate (who is to bee a preacher) for the time of his non-residence in proportion to the moity of the

entire value of such a benefice. And all double beneficed men
or pluralists to keepe a preacher that shall preach twice on the
Lords day upon the benefice from wch he shall be non-resident,
and to allow him an entire moity of the profits of the sayd
benefice for his labour and paines.

(8) The regulating of Courts Ecclesiasticall. No citation
to be issued forth before the Libell & the Articles be in. No
proceeding hereafter *ex officio mero* but the Judge & Register
shall pay the costs to the partie innocent. None to accuse
themselves in Criminall causes upon oathes imposed on them.
The defendant is to answer within 20 days after citation. Both
parties to examine theyr proofes within 4 months after. No
exception against the credit of witnesses but upon matter of
Record in a Court Civill or Ecclesiasticall. All causes to be
ended within the yeare. A competent number of Proctors &
Appariteurs to be assigned to every Consistory by the B^{p.} & 6
assistants. No suitor to goe to law upon trust in these Courts.
No Proctors to take fees for desiring continuance of days. No
more appeales but 2, one to the B^{p.} in person & his assistants
and the other to the Kings delegates the Arches & Audience in
matter of appeall set aside as unnecessary vexatious.

(9) The laws ecclesiasticall in use in this Kingdome to be
collected & abridged in the English tongue & by 16 learned
men to be named 6 by the King 5 by the House of Lords & 5
by the House of Commons; that Archb^{ps.}, B^{ps.}, Deanes, Archdeacons & Prebendarys may understand (wch now they doe not)
by w^{t} lawes they judge & the Kings people may likewise know
by w^{t} lawes they are to be judged.[1]

This committee proved entirely useless. Its
meetings were interrupted or intermitted, not, as
Hacket says, because its work was over in the first
six meetings, but by the pressure of business and
the course of events. For a time the House of

---

[1] For a more apocryphal but possibly contemporary scheme see
*Sixteen propositions in Parliament touching the manner and form
for church government by bishops and clergy of this kingdom.* B.M.
702 d. ⅜ London [June 8], 1642.

CHAP. I.

1641,
July 1.

The Lords'
Bill for regu-
lating
Bishops and
Episcopal
Courts.

Lords would appear to have been determined to wait for the results of its committee's proceedings ; and the bill " for the better regulating of arch- bishops, and for the better governing of courts ecclesiastical," the presentation of which to the Upper House will be referred to immediately, is to be regarded as the final form of the independent resolution of the Lords on the matter of Church reform.   But it cannot be gathered from the journals that this bill had been drawn up by Williams' committee, or that there had ever been a report made from that body.   The text of the bill has been recently printed by Mr. Gardiner.[1] It is interesting as showing the full length to which the Lords were ready to go in matter of reform of Church and Church government.

From another standpoint, however, the intro- duction of this bill into the Lords is to be regarded also as their answer to the violent debates which were in progress, in June, in the Commons on the Root-and-Branch Bill.   It was whilst the latter bill lay before the Commons' sub-committee that the Lords determined to take action.

The Upper House was not deficient in its regard for the importance of the subject of religion, and already voices had been heard deploring the differences between the two bodies in the matter. Nalson has preserved a paper which he describes as presented to the House of Commons,[2] and which is strongly indicative of the situation at the moment.   It is doubtless a paper intended to be presented to the Lords, or notes of a speech to

---

[1] *Const. Doc.*, pp., 94-106.   [2] Nalson, ii., 301.

be made by one of the Puritan Lords, Bedford or

Saye, or perhaps by Williams himself.

It is a doubtful case, in the heat of this dispute, how far the Commons may go in the declaration of their opinion, in which, if the Lords shall not concur, it may prove a great rock of offence between the two Houses. Therefore 'tis very requisite that the Lords of the Upper House do timely interest themselves in the discussion. To this purpose the Lords may be pleased to make a committee in their House for the reformation of Church affairs and government, and thereupon demand a conference with the committee of the House of Commons that the business may be handled by a consultation on both sides.

The fear expressed in such a paper must have been before the eyes of many in the Upper House, and it was doubtless partly the result of such a desire for compromise when the Lords took their last step in the matter of Church government. On Thursday, 1st July, therefore the bill was introduced into the Upper House—

For the regulating of archbishops, bishops, deans and chapters, canons, prebends, and the better ordering of their revenues, and for the better governing of the courts ecclesiastical and the ministers thereof, and the proceedings therein.

Evidently Nicholas looked to this bill of the Lords for the effecting of a working compromise. "We are still about the Church business," he writes on the 2nd of July, 1641, to Sir Thomas Roe, "which, if it were once accommodated, no doubt but all things else would be happily and quickly accommodated."[1]

[1] L. J., iv., 296, 298. *State Papers, Domestic*, cccclxxxii., No. 8. At one time the report was current in the country that the Lords had voted down the bishops in their House, and that the Church was to be governed by nine laymen in every diocese (*ibid.*, cccclxxxiii., No. 51).

The bill was read a second time on Saturday, 3rd July, 1641, and debated in a committee of the whole House on the 12th.   On the 23rd of October the Lords ordered it to be again read,[1] but no further trace of it appears.

The time for such a bill had, in fact, gone by. Had it been proposed in November, 1640, it would doubtless have been considered a complete satisfaction on all points complained of, and the scheme of Church government there indicated is that to which the majority of opinions gravitated, and which might have become more than an opinion but for the outbreak of the war.   But already by the middle of 1641 the growth of feeling had carried the question beyond the stage indicated by such a measure.[2]

The fate of the Commons' Bill against the

---

[1] L. J., iv., 308, 402.

[2] It is possible that the anonymous tractate entitled " Directions propounded and humbly presented to the High Court of Parliament concerning the Book of Common Prayer and Episcopal Government written by a reverend and learned divine now resident in this city," London, 1641 (a copy in *State Papers, Domestic*, cccclxxxvii., No. 3), belongs to the occasion of Bishop Williams' committee.   It argues in favour of both the Common Prayer Book and Episcopacy, but details certain emendations desirable in the first, and the following qualifications and conditions as equally desirable in the second, in order to reduce it to the constitution and practice of the primitive church :—

1. Bishops to preach ordinarily in their metropolitan church, or in parochial churches in their visitations.

2. To ordain only with the consent of three or four grave and learned presbyters.

3. To exercise suspension only with a necessary consent of some assistants, and that for such causes and crimes only as the ancient canons or the laws of the kingdom appointed.

4. Excommunication to be performed only by the bishop, with the consent of the pastor of the parish, and only for heinous and

bishops' votes in Parliament has already been noted. Chap. I.
On the 24th of May, 1641, the Lords rejected the 1641.
main head of it. Three days later, on Thursday, Introduction of the Root-
27th May, the Root-and-Branch Bill was intro- and-Branch Bill into the
duced into the Commons. The introduction of the Commons, 27th May.
measure is to be regarded as immediately due to
the rejection of the main head of the Bishops' Bill,
not as a threat or attempt at pressure on the Lords
to pass the Bishops' Bill, as a little attention to
dates will show.

> We are here in as great disorder as ever (writes Nicholas
> to Admiral Sir John Penington on the 10th of June). The bill
> which was passed by the Commons and sent up to the Lords
> to thrust bishops out of the Upper House, was last Monday
> cast out of their House, whereat the Commons are much
> troubled, and they have now a bill more sharp against bishops
> and the clergy, but it is conceived it will never pass to be made
> a law.[1]

Such a view of the transaction is entirely confirmed by a letter of Captain Robert Slingsby
to the same Admiral Penington and of the same
date [2] :—

> I suppose you have heard of the bill that passed the
> Commons House against the bishops in temporal employment
> and votes in Parliament, which was transferred to the Lords.

scandalous crimes; for lesser offences lesser punishments, and those
according to law.

5. Bishops not to demand benevolence for the clergy, nor exact
diet at their visitation, nor suffer their servants to exact undue fees
at ordinations and institutions.

6. That bishops and chancellors and officials may be subject to
the censures of provincial synods and convocations.

[1] *State Papers, Domestic,* cccclxxxi., No. 21.

[2] *Ibid.,* cccclxxxi., No. 22.

There their votes in Parliament only [were] voted to continue, but their other temporal employments taken away: Whereupon a bill was twice read in the Commons' House for abrogation of Episcopacy but not voted. In the meantime, at a conference betwixt the two Houses, the Commons propounded their reasons for passing the first bill entirely. Monday last Episcopacy was disputed on again in the Commons' House and hotly opposed and defended. The next day the Lords did throw the first bill quite out, and so left the bishops in the state they were before. This bred much murmuring in the city. The discourse of all men is they must now strike at Root-and-Branch, and not slip this occasion.

Dering's speech on its introduction.

The first reading of the Root-and-Branch Bill was moved by Sir Edward Dering, who, in a series of his own speeches, printed in the following year (1642), gives the following account of the transaction :—[1]

> The bill for the abolition of our present Episcopacy was pressed into my hand by Sir A. H. [Haselrig], being then brought unto him by Sir H. V. [the younger Vane], and O. C. [Cromwell]. He told me he was resolved that it should go in, but he was earnestly urgent that I should present it.[2] The bill did hardly stay in my hands so long as to make a hasty perusal of it. Whilst I was over-reading it, Sir Edward Ainscough [Ayscough] delivered in a petition out of Lincoln, which was seconded by Mr. Strode, in such a sort as that I had a fair invitement to issue forth the bill then in my hand, so I stood up.

The bill as presented by Dering was very short and intituled : *An Act for the utter abolishing and taking away of all archbishops, bishops, their chancellors, commissaries, deans, deans and chapters, archdeacons, prebendaries, chanters, and canons, and all other their under officers.*

[1] Brit. Mus., E. 197.   [2] C. J., iii., 57.

Dering's speech at the introduction of the
measure was hardly more than typical of the
general temper·of the House :—

> Mr. Speaker, the gentleman who spoke last, taking notice
> of the multitude of complaints and complainants against the
> present government of the Church, doth somewhat seem to
> wonder that we have no more pursuit ready against the persons
> offending. Sir, the time is présent and the work is ready. . . .
> I am now the instrument to present to you a very sharp bill,
> such as these times and their very sad necessities have brought
> forth. . . . I give it you as I take physic, not for delight, but
> for a cure—a cure now the last and only cure, if, as I hope,
> all other remedies have first been tried. . . . I never was for
> ruin so long as I could hope any hope of reforming. . . . My
> hopes that way are now almost withered.
>
> Sir, you see their demerits have exposed them *publici odii*
> *piaculares victimas.* I am sorry they are so ill; I am more
> sorry they will not be content to be bettered, *which I did hope*
> *would have been effected by our last bill.* When this bill is
> perfected I shall give a sad "aye" unto it, and at the delivery
> in thereof, I do now profess beforehand that if my former hopes
> of a full reformation may yet revive and prosper, I will again
> divide my sense upon this bill, and yield my shoulders to
> underprop the ancient, lawful, and just Episcopacy yet, so as
> that I will never be wanting with my utmost pains and prayers
> to root out all the undue adjuncts to it and superstructions
> on it.

The success which attended the measure must
have surprised its most sanguine supporters. It
seems plain, from some expressions in D'Ewes'
speech, that the bill was not at first regarded
very seriously, and it is also plain, from the
numbers on the division, that its numbers included
more than the mere Rooters ; that it included those
Puritans who wished for a reformed primitive
Episcopacy. "The utter abolishing of the bishops

and all titular ecclesiastics, with their dependants hath been agreed upon in the House of Commons, and met with less noes in the debate than the business of the Earl of Strafford had." [1]

D'Ewes'
speech.

I moved (said D'Ewes) [2] that I desired the bill might be read the second time, because I saw no inconveniency, *for it might rest as well after the second reading as after the first.* One thing was objected by the gentleman on the other side (Sir J. Culpeper), that he did not think the government of Episcopacy yet so past hope of reformation as we should yet need to enter upon this last and final remedy. I answer that the holding of their temporal employments be such as Diana to them as they will not part from, that there was little hope of other amendment, and for his desiring us to stay to see what the Lords would yet do with our bill lately sent up to them to debar bishops from all secular employments, and to take some time to debate the matter of Episcopacy and deans and chapters before we read the bill the second time, all this might be as well done after the second reading thereof, for it might be referred to a committee of the whole House, and a fit time appointed when all these particulars might be fully debated.

The bill was read a second time on the same day, the second reading being by 139-108.

Commitment
of the bill.

After the second reading a debate arose on the question of commitment. Hyde stood up to defend his beloved Church, and that government " under which it had continued many hundred years in great happiness ". Pleydall asserted that the bill aimed at the subversion of truth and peace; and wished it committed to the fire. In answering an objection made on this occasion by one of their speakers (doubtless Pleydall), and which had cer-

[1] Sidney Bere to Sir John Penington, 17th June, 1641 ; *State Papers, Domestic,* cccclxxxi., No. 42.

[2] D'Ewes, ii., 625.

tainly been made on other occasions often enough, D'Ewes used words which show us what has been already gathered from the debates in February, and is confirmed by the history of the Root-and-Branch Bill itself, that the House had not conceived any practicable scheme of Church government that might replace Episcopacy. The House shunned the question, and it was this disposition that led it to the adoption of the idea of a synod of divines. " Nor shall we need," said D'Ewes, " to study long for a new Church government, having so evident a platform in so many reformed churches."

Holles, Pym and Cage spoke directly against the government of the Church by bishops, and it was not until after a long and frequently renewed debate that it was ordered to be referred to a committee of the whole House. Even then a fresh and hot dispute arose as to when the debate should take place—the defenders of Episcopacy desiring it to be postponed till after the disbanding of the two armies. The ruse was too apparent, and signally futile; the debate was ordered for the following Thursday, 3rd June. It was not, however, held on the 3rd. It was moved for on the 7th, but did not actually commence till Friday, 11th June, 1641. At this point D'Ewes' *Diary* gives us an insight into the secret management of this memorable Parliament :—[1]

Sir Robert Harley, as I gathered, Mr. Pym, Mr. Hampden, and others, with Stephen Marshall, parson of Finchingfield, in Essex, and some others had met yesternight and appointed that this bill should he proceeded withal this morning, and the

[1] D'Ewes, ii., 692.

said Sir Robert Stanley moved it first in this House.   For Mr. Hampden, out of his serpentine subtlety, did still put others to move those business that he contrived.

D'Ewes again refers to this in another, the most picturesque, passage of his whole *Diary* :—[1]

Conceiving that the great business of the *Bishops' Bill* would not have been brought into the House till Monday next ensuing, 14th June, I went out of the House in the forenoon, after I had sitten there awhile, to walk in Westminster Hall behind the shops, near the Court of Common Pleas, when Mr. Stephen Marshall, minister of Finchingfield, came to me and asked me how chance I was not in the House, and desired me to make haste thither, because they were in agitation about this great business for abolishing bishops.   I told him I thought it was not possible, because I was but a little before come out of the House.   He answered me that it was undoubtedly so, and that some of the House had determined to call for it to-day.   I then asked him why I had no notice of this as well as others.   He told me they were sure of me.   I said aye, if you expect only my aye or no ; but if you expect of me that I should speak in the cause, you should in civility have given me notice.   As I hasted to my chamber near the hall to peruse anew those fragmentary notes which follow . . . but before I could peruse them half over, Mr. John Moore, a member of the House, came to my lodging to call me away, because the Bishops' [the Root-and-Branch] Bill was in agitation, which shows the hollow-heartedness of Mr. Pym, Mr. Hampden, and those other seeming wise men, who, though they relied upon me to speak, yet they concealed their intendment from me, that I might do below myself in speaking.

When D'Ewes entered the House, Pleydall was speaking against the bill and reading Latin quotations from the fathers.   In spite of his "unprepared state," D'Ewes spoke in reply at great length. His speech consists of his usual long-winded account

[1] D'Ewes, iii., 1014.

of the unpatriotic action of bishops in early English
history, and would not be worthy of remark were
it not for the temper he displays towards the close.
There was no flinching in D'Ewes' advocacy of a
new order of things :—

All grievances in inconveniences which may at first happen
in a new government will be remedied by frequent Parliaments,
and for the distractions which may happen in the meantime,
before a new Church discipline be settled, it may fully be provided for by a bill or act of twenty lines, in which I would
have a clause inserted for the severe punishing of tradesmen
and other ignorant persons who shall presume to preach.[1]

Fiennes and Clotworthy spoke generally to the
bill ; then it was taken piecemeal, and the preamble
was read and debated. The preamble was finally
voted in the following form :—

The preamble
voted.

Whereas the government of the Church of England by
archbishops, bishops, their chancellors and commissaries,
deans, archdeacons and other ecclesiastical officers, hath been
found by long experience to be a great impediment to the perfect reformation and growth of religion, and very prejudicial to
the civil state and government of this kingdom.[2]

As was inevitable from the situation, such a
preamble could not be rejected. It could not
indeed be opposed. Even Culpeper confessed that
of late years many calamities had happened by
them in the Church, but he weakly desired that
the words " long experience " and " government "
might be changed to " late experience " and
" governors," as he was not aware that it had

[1] D'Ewes, iii., 1015. In Nalson, ii., 298, there is a speech of
Rudyard's which belongs to this date. Nalson wrongly assigns it to
the 21st.
[2] 11th June, 1641, C. J., ii., 174.

been characteristic of Episcopacy in former times. From the nature of the case, such was the only argument open to defenders of Episcopacy. Although Culpeper received a crushing reply at the hands of St. John, the argument was iterated and reiterated.

John Crewe, of Northampton, a man of a very exact, strict life (and the fact moved D'Ewes to astonishment), desired rather a bill to restrain the bishops' power. Sir John Coke declared that by the same argument monarchy might be taken away. The debate was long and evidently fierce, for Hyde received, as chairman of the committee, a sharp rebuke from Fiennes for allowing Coke's words to pass; but late at night (and the debate began at seven in the morning) the preamble was passed, reported to the House and adopted.

The debate continued— on Episcopacy, 12th June.

On the following day, 12th June, 1641, the point for debate was the abolition of the offices of archbishops, bishops, etc. It is indicative of the small difference in matter of political tenets, and of the huge difference in sentiment, that the debate proceeded as hotly as before, and yet revealed very little fresh matter.

As on the previous day, Culpeper was driven by his own knowledge of matter-of-fact, by his own previous utterances, to acknowledge some measure of justice in the preamble. His only resource was to question the necessity of taking the most fatal and final course. "Agreeing first to the preamble, he said though they were in their persons an impediment, yet this should not make us to take them away; and, secondly, that before we abolish

the government, we should offer a new."[1] Falkland's objection was, on a plane of sentiment, low
and unworthy of him. Pleydall could only sigh
for the condition of religion, and weakly declare
that if religion would return to its primitive purity
we should return to it.

But circumstances gradually were making the
maintenance of such an attitude impossible. *Pari
passu* with the change that was taking place in the
moderates, who were for reform, the course of
events was adding to the acerbity and to the
clearness of view and constructive ability of their
opponents, and was simultaneously driving Falkland and the Episcopal party from a position in
which their opinions clashed with their sentiment
into one of mere antagonism to a party now at last
bent on a specific reform.

The rejection of the Bishops' Votes' Bill by the
Lords had been a matter of satisfaction to the
Root-and-Branch party. Sharper measures, they
thought, were now at hand, and D'Ewes, though D'Ewes'
far from a professed Rooter, did but reflect this speech.
feeling in his speech :—

I acknowledge it a great providence that the Lords refused
to pass our other bill. Truly, I think God gave no blessing to
it, because we did our work by halves; but now, when we
shall do our work thoroughly, we shall have no cause to
despair of a good result.

To Culpeper's demand for a platform, D'Ewes
could give no reply :—

It hath been objected that before we alter the old government of the Church we should establish a new one. For that

[1] D'Ewes, ii., 694.

it may be answered that before a new house be builded where an old one stood, the old one must first be removed,[1]

Husband's *Passages and Speeches of this Parliament* contains a speech of Sir Henry Vane. As printed it is assigned to the 11th, but doubtless it belongs to this debate of the 12th, and was uttered by the younger Vane.[2]

Vane's speech.

It is of interest as exhibiting the opinions of the man who was apparently the originator of the bill, and who certainly was the promoter of the scheme which was afterwards introduced into it :—

> For my part (said he) I am of the opinion of those who conceive that the strength of reason already set down in the preamble to this bill by yesterday's vote is a necessary decision of this question. For one of the main ends for which Church government is set up is to advance and further the perfect reformation and growth of religion which we have already voted this government doth contradict. . . . In the second place, we have voted it prejudicial to the civil state. . . . But to this it hath been said that the government now in question may be so reformed and amended that it needs not be pulled down quite, because it is conceived it hath no original sin or evil in it, or, if it had, it is said regeneration will take it away; unto which I answer, I do consent that we should do with this government as we are done by in regeneration, in which old things are to pass away and all things are to become new, and this we must do if we desire a perfect reformation, and growth of our religion, or good to our civil state, for the whole fabric of the building is so rotten and corrupt from the very foundation of it to the top, that if we pull it not down now it will fall about the ears of all those that endeavour it within a very few years.

He then passes in review the evils of the existing system, its affinity in character and deriva-

---

[1] D'Ewes, ii., 694.

[2] Dr. Nalson prints it, and ascribes it to the elder Vane.

tion with popery, its pride, encouragement of superstition and persecution of godly ministers, and its threatening attitude to the civil state, and concludes in a manner worthy of Cromwell himself :—

Lastly, and that which I assure you goes nearest to my heart, is the check which we seem to give to Divine Providence if we do not at this time pull down this government. For hath not this Parliament been called, continued, preserved and secured by the immediate finger of God, as it were, for this work ? Had we not else been swallowed up in many inevitable dangers by the practices and designs of these men and their party ? Hath not God left them to themselves as well in these things [army plots, etc.] as in the evil administration of their government, that he might lay them open unto us, and lead us, as it were by the hand, from the finding them to be the causes of our evil, to discern that their rooting up must be our only cure ?

On Hyde's report from the committee, the House resolved that the taking away of the several offices of archbishops, bishops, chancellors and commissaries out of the Church and kingdom should be one clause of the bill.

Although the debate had lasted seven hours, and it was nearly four o'clock when Hyde made the report, some in their eagerness to go on with the work called out to proceed with the bill after the vote had passed.[1] The debate was, however, adjourned until the following Tuesday, 15th June, 1641, when the House took up the consideration of deans and chapters, "and the rest of the rabble depending on them ".

D'Ewes seemed to think the treatment of this

[1] D'Ewes, iii., 1025 ; C. J., ii., 174.

subject to be his peculiar and sole heritage. As on a former occasion, he was among the first to speak; and, however, the House disrelished his long-winded discourses (though there is no inkling of such a fact in his egotistical *Diary*), it was glad to listen to his fearless opposition to the clerical claim of inviolability for the revenues of deans and chapters. In his opinion these were but the revenues left formerly for superstitious purposes to abbeys, etc. " Both the doctors," said he, referring to the previous occasion on which Hacket and Burgess had been heard at the bar, " did agree in the end that neither king nor public should partake of the Church revenue, but that it was sacrilege to take it away. To this I hope to give a clear and full answer."

The House had evidently made up its mind against deans and chapters; it recorded its decision on this day. Yet it required some satisfaction on the point of legal right and justification, and therefore listened gratefully to such speakers as D'Ewes and Thomas, the latter of whom entered into a long disquisition on the nature of the functions of deans in the time of Augustine, and thence traced their history to his own time.[1]

But it is evident that if no satisfaction of the kind had been given, the vote would have been the same. D'Ewes was followed by Glynn. Falkland, as might be expected, spoke in favour of the institution. Fiennes, Sir Thomas Widdrington and Peard as obstinately maintained the opposite. But

[1] Thomas's speech is given in Rushworth, iv., 285, and Nalson, ii., 283. The latter wrongly dates it 11th June.

the most surprising feature in the debate is Culpeper's speech as recorded in D'Ewes. It plainly indicates how little heart the Episcopal party had in their cause, and how purely their position was a matter of sentiment :—

> For deans and chapters, he thought them so to depend on the bishops, as the bishops being taken away the others must necessarily be abolished ; . . . but he desired that provision might be made for the maintenance of those during their lives that we should put out, and for the disposition of those revenues for the time to come that learning and piety might be thereby advanced.

In the afternoon the opposition to this head of the bill assumed a different aspect, though one equally futile, at the hands of Selden. In his opinion deans and chapters, not being a part of the government of the bishops, could not be included in the bill, therefore, their abolition was a *non sequitur*.[1]

The point was a puerile one for such a man to urge, and was easily answered by St. John and Pury.

The speech of the latter is very noticeable. Pury was an alderman of Gloucester, and, to meet Culpeper's scruples on the score of the ejected members, he laid down a scheme for the employment of the revenues of the dean and chapter of Gloucester.[2] It is noticeable as showing that, though his vote on this occasion was evidently engaged for the bill, he is not to be reckoned among the veritable Rooters — after sketching a provision for the existing members of the system thus :—

CHAP. I.

June 15, 1641.

Pury's speech.

[1] D'Ewes, ii., 706.   [2] *Ibid.*, ii., 707.

CHAP. I.

June,
1641.

If the dean and those prebends, being but seven in all to be now taken away, will be preaching ministers, there is a sufficient maintenance for so many of them as have not too much besides, and yet to reserve as large a salary as now is allowed for so many singing men then in holy orders as cannot preach, etc., etc. . . . Out of the manors and lands, the said cathedral living to be made a parochial church, £200 or more may be allowed for a learned preaching minister there, and £100 per annum each for two such others to assist him ; and then the rest of the said manors and lands may be employed to other godly, pious and charitable uses as the wisdom of the King and Parliament shall think fit.[1]

On Hyde's report the House *resolved* on the question :—

That all deans, deans and chapters, archdeacons, prebendaries. chanters, canons and petty canons, and their officers, shall be utterly abolished and taken away out of the Church ; and, secondly, *resolved* that all the lands taken by this bill from deans and chapters shall be employed to the advancement of learning and piety, provision being had and made that his Majesty be no loser in his rents, first-fruits and other duties, and a competent maintenance shall be made to the several persons concerned, if such persons appear not peccant and delinquent to this House.[2]

Owing to the pressure of business the bill was not proceeded with again till Monday, 21st June.

The debate
continued—
on Ecclesias-
tical Courts
and Regimen,
21st June.

The clause of the bill discussed on this latter day was that which provided for the abolition of the ecclesiastical courts, and the enacting of a præmunire against such as should hereafter fall into error.

The discussion was certainly the most momentous

---

[1] For the speeches of Pury see Nalson, ii., 289, and Portland MSS. (Nalson, xiii., 45).

[2] C. J., ii., 176, 15th June, 1641.

of all the ecclesiastical debates of the early years of CHAP. I.
the Long Parliament, and strikingly exhibits the June 21, 1641.
salient characteristics of the House. Even Hyde,
the most blindly thorough-going of the᾽ Episcopal
party, had a grudge against this element of the
ecclesiastical system. " Mr. Hyde himself said that
if they meddled with probate of wills or matrimony
they should incur a præmunire." There cannot be
detected in D'Ewes' account of this day's debate
any trace of dissent or division of opinion as to the
liability to a præmunire. Some members of the
House supposed that this clause of the bill would
affect the bishops' votes in Parliament, but, upon
explanation given that the clause only concerned
proceedings in ecclesiastical courts by and under
the power of archbishops, bishops, deans, etc.,
exercised by their commissaries and officials, and
did not at all touch upon any act performed by the
bishops in their own persons, or to their votes in
Parliament, no other dispute was made save as
to the date from which the præmunire should be
incurred.[1] The date fixed was the 1st of August.

It is very evident, from the nature of a verbal
addition made after the fixing of the date, that the
course of the debate was being very carefully and
skilfully managed. A qualifying clause was inserted
in these words (whoso shall exercise jurisdiction)
" otherwise or in any other manner than shall be
provided and allowed in the present act ". This
clause, together with the last clause of the bill in
its original form (viz., *and be it further enacted by
authority aforesaid that all ecclesiastical jurisdiction*

[1] D'Ewes, ii., 723.

Vane's
scheme of
organisation
of Ecclesias-
tical Juris-
diction.

Dering's
scheme of
same.

fit to be exercised within this Church and kingdom of England shall be committed to such a number of persons and in such a manner as by this present act (shall be) appointed), was meant to prepare the way for Vane's scheme, which was handed in almost immediately thereupon. For no sooner had Dering got up to urge the House, having regard to the chances of the bill in the Lords, to make some provision for the juridical government of the Church, and had offered to show the way by proposing certain provisions, than he was rudely and sharply interrupted, and before he could find opportunity to conclude his speech, the younger Vane had handed in a clause which in reality contained a new scheme for the Church jurisdictional government. The clause provided for the appointment of a body of commissioners, lay and clerical, to exercise ecclesiastical jurisdiction in every shire for a time. As soon as Dering had recovered from his surprise, he hastened to conclude his speech and to offer his alternative scheme.[1]

Dering's scheme is worthy of attention. It contains three points : (1) the circuit for future Church government, or the diocese should be the shire ; (2) in each of these, twelve or more chosen, able, grave divines to be appointed by Parliament to be of the nature of an old primitive constant presbytery ; (3) over each of these a president, " let him be a bishop, or an overseer, or a president, or a moderator, or a superintendent, or a ruling elder, call him what you will ".

[1] Nalson, ii., 300.

Here was the reduction and restoration of the
pure primitive Episcopal presidency.
Many in the House seem to have adopted
Dering's scheme, though there was a difference of
opinion whether the president of the presbytery
should be constant or only temporary and elective,
and so at the will of the presbytery.[1]   This is the
first division of opinion discoverable in the action
of the now triumphant majority of the Commons,
and the day did not close with a final vote, as had
the debate on the 12th and 15th; instead thereof
a sub-committee was named, and the three clauses
of the bill already passed, with the addition brought
in by Vane, were referred to its consideration.

On Thursday, 8th July, Prideaux reported from
the sub-committee to the Grand Committee certain
amendments and considerations on the Root-and-
Branch Bill.

The nature of the action of the sub-committee
is apparent from the notes of the report (for such
I take them to be) preserved in the *Verney
Notes* (p. 104, Camden Society).   They evidently
are in the form of recommendations, thus :—

[*Bishops and Deans and Chapters' Lands*].—The dean and
chapter's lands put to feoffees to satisfy the King's dues, and
  The feoffees to pay it to the persons now in possession. . . .
  Commissions to certify what lands the bishops, deans and
chapters now have, and what is paid out of those lands, and
also to certify what Church livings are under £100 per annum,
and also about chapels of ease.
  Jurisdiction.—Two commissions for Canterbury and York
for Archiepiscopal government, and nine or five commissioners
in every county to exercise Episcopal government.   All writs

---

[1] D'Ewes, ii., 723.

to be directed to the commissioners; all ecclesiastical courts devolved to them, and to meet monthly.

Ordination.— These commissioners give warrant to five commissioners to ordain any man into holy orders. (The) commissioners shall call three divines to punish heresy, schism, etc., according to ecclesiastical laws. For non-payment of fees he shall be as an excommunicate person, only he may come to church.

Relatively to the importance of it, this report (if such it is) met with little discussion.

On Friday, 9th July, it was adopted *in toto*, as to the matter of the first point, in the following resolutions, after a futile reiteration from Culpeper of the objections, on the ground of conscience, to the giving of the bishops' lands to the king [1] :—

1. That all lands, possessions and rights of all deans and deans and chapters shall by this bill be committed to the hands of feoffees to be nominated in this bill.

2. That all the lands and possessions of all the archbishoprics and bishoprics of England and Wales, except the impropriations and advowsons, shall by this act be given to the King.

3. That all impropriations and advowsons belonging to the archbishoprics and bishoprics of England and Wales shall be committed into the hands of feoffees in the same manner as the lands of deans and chapters are appointed to be.[2]

On the following day, 10th July (Saturday), the House supplemented these resolutions by another, making provision for the employment of the revenues :—

A competent maintenance shall be allowed out of the lands and possessions of the cathedral churches for the support of a fit number of preaching ministers for the service of every such church, and a proportionable allowance for the reparation of the said churches.[3]

[1] D'Ewes, ii., 772.   [2] C. J., ii., 204.   [3] *Ibid.*, ii., 205.

Passing next, on Monday, 12th July,[1] to the
second head of the report—jurisdiction—

The House resolved that such ecclesiastical power as shall be exercised for the government of the Church shall be transferred by this act into the hands of commissioners to be named in this act; secondly, that the commissioners, or the major part of them, named in this act shall have authority to appoint deputies and other officers to exercise the jurisdiction given to them by this act.

It has been generally noticed that in the former of these two resolutions there was an alteration in the policy of the House. In the proviso of Vane, which first moved this matter on the 20th of June, the scheme had proposed commissioners drawn equally from the clergy and the laity. By the vote of the 12th of July, all the commissioners were to be laymen. It is easy to understand how the general sense of the House went this way :—

Divers (says D'Ewes) spake touching the committing of all ecclesiastical jurisdiction to lay commissioners. Mr. Selden spake exceeding well to it, and showed that the said jurisdiction might be exercised by laymen.[2]

The constitution of the proposed commission was further discussed on the 15th and subsequent days.

It would seem, from D'Ewes,[3] that the House following out Prideaux's suggestions as reported

---

[1] I here follow D'Ewes, ii., 777, rather than the *Commons Journal*, ii., 205, the latter of which dates the first part of the resolution the 10th.

[2] D'Ewes, ii., 177.

[3] As the House was in committee, or through inadvertency, the resolutions of these days are not entered in the *Commons Journal*. They are preserved for us in D'Ewes, ii., 786.

from the sub-committee, determined on the establishment of two committees—the one as succeeding to the Archiepiscopal jurisdiction, the other to the Episcopal. The whole scheme was,. therefore, roughly as follows : The whole jurisdiction was to be in the hands of the chief commissioners (subsequently fixed at nine in number). These had power to delegate their functions, and by themselves and their delegates, ecclesiastical justice was to be administered in the several counties by county commissions (as inheriting Episcopal jurisdiction), and generally over the two provinces by two provincial commissions (as inheriting Archiepiscopal jurisdiction).

It was decided on the 17th that appeal should lie to the latter from the former.[1]

Such I take to be the meaning of the resolutions passed on the 15th and subsequent days of July.

Those of the 15th were in these words :—

(1) The commissioners appointed by this act for the several provinces of Canterbury and York, shall respectively exercise archiepiscopal jurisdiction within the said several provinces ; (2) All the ecclesiastical jurisdiction committed by this act to the commissioners, except the archiepiscopal, shall be exercised by these commissioners in every county of England except York and Lincoln, where they are to be appointed in the parts and ridings thereof.

A similar order was made for Wales.

Provisions for
ordination.

When the House came next in order to consider of the constitution of a body for the purposes of ordination, much more division of opinion was displayed than on the matter of jurisdiction. A

[1] D'Ewes, ii., 790.

motion was made to constitute five ministers in every county for the purposes of ordination, and this was the form in which the final motion passed. But it was strongly objected to by some lovers of the primitive presbytery. To their minds the right of ordination was inherent in every presbyter, and it seemed as illogical to constitute five men for the purpose as to allow the bishops to do it alone.

And it is probable that much division of opinion would have been displayed upon this head if it had not been pointed out, what was perhaps present as a menace to the minds of most, that a large body of the clergy at that moment was Episcopal in tendencies and scandalous in life, and therefore unfit for the work of ordination.

As finally resolved, the nomination of these five commissioners in each county was vested in the body of nine chief commissioners.

From the point of view of this narrative, these heads of jurisdiction and ordination are by far the most important elements in the Root-and-Branch scheme, showing as they do how the Parliament came to evolve a scheme of Church government, and what that scheme was, and how different from the Presbyterian system which was adopted four years later as a consequence of the alliance with Scotland.

The idea that the body of *clergymen and other ecclesiastical* persons forming " the Church " needed a distinct organisation and government of their own, was to the English mind of the seventeenth century as commonplace and self-evident as that parliamentary and legal systems were needed for

CHAP. I.

July, 1641.

Critical estimation of the Root-and-Branch proposals.

the laity. Hitherto this ecclesiastical body had been governed in the diocese by the bishop and his court in all matters relating to ordination, institution, trial for offence and suspension. The Parliament had now declared against such Episcopal system, and it was necessary to replace it by some other. Apart from the abortive schemes for a "modified" Episcopacy, there were apparently only two plans feasible : (1) a system of government by clerical assemblies, a Presbyterian system more or less after the Scottish model—all matters of ordination, trial and censure being determined by vote in the local assembly or classis, and appeals lying to the higher ranges of the organisation, the provincial and national assemblies ; (2) the alternative would be some such scheme as is contained in the resolutions of the Commons just described, by which the jurisdiction of the bishops' court was vested in the hands of a body of lay commissioners, who were to go on circuit in the spiritual courts, while the matter of ordination was referred in a similar way to a lay commission, all in actual dependence upon Parliament.

Had the course of events been different—had the English Parliament been left free to settle this question as its own instinct dictated—there can be no doubt that it is the latter scheme and not the former that would have been adopted. Such is the natural conclusion to be drawn from the above account of the ecclesiastical debates of the Long Parliament. It was only gradually that the House came to resolve on the abolition of Episcopacy, and that it faced the question of the discovery of a Church

system to replace it ; but throughout this course of
mental evolution the Parliament was thoroughly
true to the national instinct, and would have remained so had it not been that the course of the
war made it necessary to accept Scotch aid at the
price of the adoption of the Scottish Church system.

To return to the Root-and-Branch debates.

The remaining point for discussion was concerning the disposition and use of the revenues of
deans and chapters. This was agitated on the
27th of July, but for obvious reasons the matter
had to be left in abeyance. In answer to Culpeper,
D'Ewes urged that the House had, as a matter of
fact, yet " first to know what are the revenues of
the cathedrals, and what poor livings there are that
ought to have a maintenance ". This would, in the
ordinary course of things, be the work of a commission during the recess, upon the result of whose
investigations the House might, at the next meeting,
make a full disposition of the revenues. Accordingly the clause was left generally and vaguely
worded, ordering merely the employment of the
surplus for the advancement of the true religion,
piety and learning.[1]

Further than this the debates on the Root-and-
Branch Bill did not go. The bill rested in committee. The fright occasioned by Charles's journey
to Scotland drove the matter into the background.
One solitary attempt was made to revive the bill.
As late as the 13th of August, 1641, the Commons
determined to proceed with the discussion on
the following Monday. But the order was not

[1] D'Ewes, ii., 798.

followed out, and no other attempt was made.[1] After the parliamentary recess the Commons never went back to the project. Although, however, like many another of the early attempts at legislation on this subject, the bill was fruitless, it is not, therefore, to be disregarded. It stands as an illustration of the advance of opinion that had been made since November, 1640, under the force of circumstances which compelled the House to examine its own mind to know what it desired. And, at the

A standard of Anglican Puritanism essentially non-Presbyterian.

same time, it supplies us with a complete programme of purely Anglican Puritanism—lay and clerical alike. It shows what would probably have been the action taken, the Church system and government adopted, now that the House had been roused to settle the matter definitively if events had not necessitated the adoption of the Solemn League and Covenant.

The noticeable feature in these debates, and in the scheme elaborated in them, is the absence of any Presbyterian element. It is at first sight, perhaps, hard to realise the meaning and the truth of this. Almost every speaker of importance had expressed a veneration for the character of a primitive bishop, had claimed for every minister his share in the work of Church government by the restoration of the ancient primitive presbytery

[1] *State Papers, Domestic,* cccclxxxv., 26th October, 1641. Thomas Smith to Sir John Penington: "Our Parliament is once more met in full, and are very busy perfecting the businesses formerly begun, *viz.,* the devoting of bishops in the Upper House, and the pulling down of Episcopacy root and branch . . ." This, however, is only the assertion of a letter-writer and a pure misconception. The reference is only to the later Bishops Bill of October, 1641.

But there is the greatest possible difference between this and an advocacy of the Presbyterian
system, as it was understood in the seventeenth
century. *Then*, Presbyterianism was a clerical
system, encroaching largely upon the civil and
national life. It judged the actions and morals
of individuals; it haughtily arrogated to itself a
share in the national government. There was
nothing further from the mind of the English
Parliament and nation than to favour such a
scheme. What they desired was some practicable
plan for the ruling and ordering of an unwieldy
institution in order to make it more patriotic and
evangelical, and the scheme evolved during these
debates on the Root-and-Branch Bill was peculiarly
secular, indeed, astonishingly so when we bear in
mind the respect the age had for the clerical
function.

But a Presbyterian system as such had not
entered the mind of the Parliament.

Later in the year (20th November, 1641), in
the debates on the clauses of the Grand Remonstrance which concerned religion, Dering had
occasion to speak of Presbyterianism. His words
are as follows :—

Mr. Speaker, there is a certain newborn, unseen, ignorant,
dangerous, desperate way of Independency. Are we for this
independent way? Nay, sir. Are we for the elder brother of
it, the Presbyterial form? *I have not yet heard any one
gentleman within these walls stand up and assert his thoughts
for either of those ways.*[1]

Baillie, in his remarkably interesting letters,

[1] British Museum, E., 197, p. 100.

often expresses his belief that the triumph of presbytery was at hand, etc. There is not the slightest doubt that in his ignorance of the English constitution and character, and in his own too sanguine eagerness, he made a great mistake.

It must be borne in mind for the clearer comprehension of Baillie's view, which was not his alone, that on this point clerical opinion would naturally proceed more quickly than lay or secular opinion. The very idea of presbytery was one that appealed strongly to the professional instinct of the clergy, and it is remarkable with what swift unanimity the bulk of the clergy embraced it within a period of hardly more than two years from the date of these debates. Indeed for them—the clergy—the process of conversion began long before the Solemn League and Covenant. In October, 1641, for instance, one correspondent is found informing Viscount Conway, "our chiefest farmers have their loins girt with a divinity surcingle and begin to bristle up for a lay eldership".[1] But between this advanced clerical standpoint and the general standpoint of the laity and the Parliament there was a great gulf—a gulf that was actually never crossed.

Before passing to the train of events which led to the adoption of the Solemn League and Covenant, it is necessary to complete in one view the remaining portions of such legislation on religious matters as the Long Parliament passed whilst still its judgment was untrammelled by that Solemn League and Covenant.

[1] State Papers, Domestic, cccclxxxv., 22nd October, 1641.

1. *Innovations, Idolatry, Superstition.*

From the first moment of the meeting of the Parliament, it had its attention fixed on the innovations in Church service which had been introduced under the Laudian regime. On the 25th of November, 1640,[1] White reported from the Grand Committee for Religion the case of Dr. Layfield :—

CHAP. I.

1640.

Legislative action of the Long Parliament against Innovations and Idolatry.

He hath set the communion table altarwise, caused rails and ten several images upon those rails to be set at the altar. He bowed three times, (1) at his going to the rails ; (2) within the rails ; (3) at the table, and so on the return. But since the images were taken down upon a complaint made by the parish he hath bowed but twice, and that is within the rails which is an argument he bowed before to the images. I.H.S. he hath caused to be set in gold letters upon the table and forty places besides : said to the people " Heretofore we see Christ by faith but now with our fleshly eyes we see him in the Sacrament ". When these images were taken down he charged them with sacrilege. He refused to give the Sacrament to his people unless they came to the altar, though [they] having offered reverently kneeling to receive the same in the body of the Church. He caused one Boulton to be excommunicated for not coming up to the rails to receive, and refused to read his absolution. He said he would not for a £100 come from the rails to give the Sacrament, nay he would rather lose his living. . . . He tells them they must confess their sins, and he hath power to absolve them. . . .

The Committee was of opinion that even though he was a member of Convocation he should be sent for as a delinquent, and so the House ordered.

Similar charges of setting up idolatry and exercising acts of it in his own person were brought against Matthew Wren, Bishop of Ely.[2] In this case of Wren a special committee was appointed,

---

[1] C. J., ii., 35.   [2] *Ibid.*, ii., 54, 19th December, 1640.

which reported on the 5th of July, 1641,[1] but the ordinary course taken with regard to the almost innumerable charges of a similar nature seems to have been to refer the petitions or cases to the Committee for Scandalous Ministers.

The sense of the House, like that of the nation itself, was very precise and strong on this head of grievance of Popish innovations. When some few days after the opening of the Parliament the Commons decided to take the Sacrament, they deputed two members to request Bishop Williams, Dean of Westminster, to consecrate the elements on a communion table standing in the middle of the church, according to the rubric, and to have the table removed from the altar.[2]

The position of the Communion Table.

The House decided to proceed summarily in the matter by way of sending commissions into all the counties for the defacing, demolishing, and quite taking away of all images, altars or tables turned altarwise, crucifixes, superstitious pictures, ornaments and relics of idolatry out of all churches and chapels.[3]

Accordingly, on 5th February, 1640-41, a bill was introduced for abolishing superstition and idolatry, and for the better advancing of the true worship and service of God.[4]

[1] C. J., ii., 199, 19th December, 1640.

[2] Ibid., ii., 32, 20th November, 1640.

[3] Ibid., ii., 72, 23rd January, 1640-41.

[4] Ibid., ii., 79. Read a second time and committed 13th February, 1640-41 (ibid., ii., 84). On the 1st of June, 1641, the committee for this bill was ordered to stand and be continued as to the bill only (ibid., ii., 162, 183, 199). On the 15th of July, 1641, the committee was again ordered to stand (ibid., 212). Bill ordered to be reported 8th August, 1641 (ibid., 246). After this nothing further is heard of it.

Independently of the Commons, the House of
Lords took similar action in the matter. On the
16th of January, 1640-41,[1] they ordered that divine
service should be performed as appointed by the
Acts of Parliament of the Realm, and all disturbers
of the same severely punished, "and that the
parsons, vicars and curates in the several parishes
shall forbear to introduce any rites or ceremonies
that may give offence otherwise than those which
are established by the laws of the land".

On the occasion of their trial of Dr. Pocklington,
they ordered all the images and superstitions set
up by him as incumbent to be demolished, and
strictly commanded the bishop of the diocese to
see this done.

Some few weeks later, on the 1st of March,
1640-41, the Peers similarly ordered that every
bishop in his diocese should see that the communion table in every church "should stand in the
ancient place where it ought to do by the law, and
as it hath done for the greater part of these three
score years last past". At the same time the
Upper House appointed a committee of its own to
consider all innovations in the Church concerning
religion.[2]

As in the case of all the other ecclesiastical
legislation of the Long Parliament, the Commons
Bill for the abolition of superstition had a very interrupted career. On the 8th of August, six months

[1] L. J., iv., 134. This order was repeated almost verbally on the
22nd of April, 1641 (ibid., iv., 215).
[2] Ibid., iv., 174, 1st March, 1640-41. For the history of the
committee see supra, pp. 65-74.

CHAP. I.

1641.

The rails before the Communion Table.

after it had been committed, it was ordered to be reported.[1] On the occasion of this order the House further made a declaration to the effect that the churchwardens of every parish should have power and liberty within their own parish churches to take down the rails from about the communion tables, and to set up the said tables " in the same order as by the laws and rubric they be set. The House doth likewise declare that they hold it fit that no man shall presume to oppose the Discipline or Government of the Church established by law."

The concluding terms of this order were occasioned by the frequent anti-ceremonial disturbances and riots in churches which had occurred during the early months of the Parliament's existence.[2] That the order was momentarily ineffectual is proved by the recurrence of the subject two months later. On the 30th of August the Commons resolved that the—

Churchwardens of every parish church or chapel do forthwith remove the communion table to the east end of the church, chapel or chantry, where they stand altarwise, and place them in some convenient place of the church or chancel, and take away the rails and level the chancel, as heretofore they were before the late innovations.[3]

[1] C. J., ii., 246. *Ut supra*, p. 104 note.

[2] See L. J., iv., 100, 113, 30th November, 1640 ; L. J., iv., 215, 22nd April, 1641. In June, 1641, a mob of persons, during the time of the administration of the communion in St. Saviour's and St. Olave's, Southwark, rushed upon the communion rails and broke them down (L. J., iv., 270-71, 277, 318). Similar outbreaks of mob violence against the communion rails occurred at St. Thomas Apostle, London (C. J., ii., 194 ; L. J., iv., 295, 30th June, 1641), and in numerous other places

[3] C. J., ii., 278.

A committee was specially appointed to see the order carried out as far as related to the Universities and the Inns of Court, and to draw up the terms of a formal order.

This order was reported on the following day, 1st September.[1] After reiterating the regulation concerning the position of the communion table, it prescribed the abolition of scandalous pictures of the Trinity, etc., and of images from the Church, of tapers, candlesticks and basins from the communion table, and of bowing at the name of Jesus or towards the East. The order concluded with provisions for a return as to its due execution throughout the country. After some debate, which was renewed on the 6th of September, an addition was proposed to it for preventing all contempt and abuse of the Book of Common Prayer. This addition was, however, shelved, and on the 9th of September the Commons finally adopted the order with the object of presenting it to the Lords at a conference.[2]

The Lords debated this order on the 8th of September,[3] and agreed to the abolition of communion rails and images, but not to the enforced abolition of bowing at the name of Jesus. Without going further with the debate, on the following day they revived their own order of 16th January, 1640-41, for the performance of divine service as appointed by law, and invited the Commons to assent thereto. The latter hot-temperedly declined, and drew up a declaration of the point at issue between the two

[1] C. J., ii., 279.   [2] *Ibid.*, ii., 280, 287, S.P.D., cccclxxxiv., No. 16.
[3] L. J., iv., 391-92.

CHAP. I.
1641-2.

The Commons' Bill against innovations Feb.-Dec., 1642.

Houses,[1] stigmatising the order of the House of Lords as ill-timed and lacking in due authority.

During the recess which ensued immediately (10th September to 20th October, 1641), the care of this matter was left to a standing committee of the Commons, which took care for the dispersal of the (Commons') declaration through the counties.[2] No effect followed from such a step, however, and the matter of innovations generally rested in this undetermined state until the following February, when the Commons resolved that a bill should be brought in based in substance upon its orders already passed for taking away innovations.[3]

Accordingly, on the 16th of that month, there was read for the first time[4] an act for suppressing

[1] L. J., iv., 395; C. J., ii., 286, 9th September, 1641.

[2] C. J., ii., 289, Pym's Report, 20th October, 1641.

[3] *Ibid.*, ii., 427, 12th February, 1641-42.

[4] *Ibid.*, ii., 436, 16th February, 1641-42. Read a second time and committed 17th February, 1641-42 (C. J., ii., 437, 465). Reported 12th March and re-committed (*ibid.*, 476). Again reported 21st March and ordered to be engrossed with the amendment " that the time expressed in the bill for the levelling of the chancels shall extend to twenty years last past " (*ibid.*, 489). Read a third time, and passed in the Commons, 23rd March, 1641-42 (C. J., ii., 493). Read a first time in the Lords, 25th March, 1642 (L. J., iv., 669) ; a second time, and committed 29th March (*ibid.*, 679). It was named in the "*nineteen propositions*" in June, 1642 (C. J., ii., 598, 639 ; L. J., iv., 96, 160). It was again debated in the Lords on the 14th of July, 1642 (L. J., iv., 210, 212), and referred to a committee to consider of a proviso for the appointment by both Houses of commissioners in each county for the taking down the glass windows in the churches. On the 16th of July, with this amendment, it was read a third time and passed by the Lords, and sent down to the Commons (*ibid.*, v., 214 ; C. J., ii., 675, 677, cp. C. J., ii., 691, L. J., v., 248). Finally, on the 1st of November, 1642, the Lords accepted the Commons' amendments (L. J., v., 425), and the bill was ordered to pass, but as the time limited in the bill had lapsed, a short bill had to be prepared to prevent any inconveniences thereby

divers innovations in the churches and chapels of England and Wales.

The subsequent history of this ordinance is given in the preceding footnote. After it's elaboration the Commons, without expecting the king's assent to it, proceeded to act upon it. On the 24th of April, 1643, they appointed a small committee of nine to receive information from time to time of any monuments of superstition and idolatry in the Abbey Church at Westminster, or in the windows thereof, or in any other church or chapel in or about London, with power to demolish the same.[1] A few days later the powers of this committee were extended so as to include all superstitious monuments in any public or open place, or in or about any church or chapel.[2] Late in the following month the committee was ordered to take into its possession the copes in the "cathedrals of Westminster, St. Paul's, and Lambeth," and to see them burned or converted to the relief of the poor in Ireland.[3]

With the object of replacing the defunct "bill for the suppression of . . . innovations," a new ordinance for pulling down superstitious pictures,

The ordinance against superstitious innovations, 28th August, 1643.

(C. J., ii., 831, 2nd November, 1642). Seven days later order was taken for the removal of the crucifix, etc., and the proper placing of the communion table in Lambeth Chapel and Denmark House (ibid., ii., 843). In December the bill for taking away superstitious innovations was included for royal assent in the propositions for accommodation with the king then framing, (20th December, 1642 L. J., v., 504, 581-83 ; C. J., ii., 903). With a view to this the time limited in the bill was extended by amendments (C. J., ii., 904, 27th December, 1642).

[1] C. J., iii., 57, 60.   [2] Ibid., iii., 63, 28th April, 1643.

[3] C. J., iii., 110, 31st May, 1643, cp ibid., 347, 368, 422, 503, for like special orders.

crucifixes and altars, etc., was introduced into the Commons on the 19th of June, 1643.[1] It passed the Lower House on the 5th of July,[2] was agreed to by the Lords on the 26th of August, and finally passed on the 28th August, 1643.[3] All altars and tables of stone were ordered to be demolished before the 1st of November, 1643, the communion tables removed from the east end to the body of the church, the rails round it taken away and the chancels levelled, tapers and candlesticks removed from the communion tables, and crucifixes, crosses, images and pictures from the churches. The ordinance concluded with directions for the conduct of churchwardens, etc., in the carrying out thereof and for the preservation of monuments of kings or nobles, etc. In substance this ordinance was further repeated by an additional ordinance of 9th May, 1644, which also added that no copes, surplices, superstitious vestments, roods and roodlofts or holy water fonts, should be any more used in any church or chapel.[4]

2. *Pluralities.*

The legislation against Pluralities, 1641-3.

A less striking evil than that of superstitious and Popish ceremonies was that of PLURALITIES, with its necessary attendant non-residence. With the object of regulating this abuse a bill "con-

[1] C. J., iii., 134.

[2] *Ibid.*, iii., 155; L. J., vi., 133.

[3] L. J., vi., 198, 200; C. J., iii., 220; Rushworth, v., 358-9; Husband's (Folio), 307; Scobell, i., 53.

[4] Rushworth, v., 751; Husband's, Fo., 487; Scobell, i., 69. For the legislative history of this additional ordinance see C. J., iii., 470, 486; L. J., vi., 545-6; cp. also C. J., iii., 485, iv., 246. The subsequent attempts at legislation on the subject in 1645 and 1647 were undertaken with a view to the treaties with the king and were abortive. See L. J., vii., 54; C. J., iv., 349, 412, v., 351; L. J., ix., 513.

cerning pluralities" was introduced into the Commons on the 25th of February, 1640-41.[1]

[1] C. J., ii., 92. Read again for the second time, and committed as "an Act against pluralities of spiritual promotions," on the 10th of March, 1640-41 (C. J., ii., 100). On the same day another Act was introduced "for reformation of pluralities and non-residence," and read the first time (*ibid.*). This latter bill was read a second time on the 16th of March, and committed to the same committee as the first bill (*ibid.*, ii., 105, 129). From this point the two bills were apparently combined. The bill 'against the enjoying of pluralities of benefice and non-residency' was read a third time, and passed on the 19th of June, 1641. On the same date it was read a first time in the Lords (C. J., ii., 181; L. J., iv., 280). It was again read and debated in the Lords on the 19th of July (L. J., iv., 321, 332, 400) and on the 25th of October, 1641, and referred to a committee to consider of the king's chaplains the privilege of noblemen, and of heads of colleges, and also of a proviso for a pluralist to supply his extra livings with a curate on a moiety allowance (L. J., iv., 404). The Lords would appear to have contemplated reserving some of these extra livings for the supply of clergymen who had been persecuted under the Laudian regime (*ibid.*, iv., 410, 457). On the 11th of February, 1641-42, the Upper House agreed to its amendments on the bill, and requested a conference with the Commons upon it (*ibid.*, iv., 577). On the following 17th the Commons agreed to some of these amendments (C. J., ii., 438, 476). A conference between the two Houses was held on these amendments on the 23rd of March, 1641-42 (L. J., iv., 661, 664; C. J., ii., 493). On the 3rd of May, 1642, the Lords consented to waive the amendments which the Commons could not accept, with the exception of a proviso concerning the two Universities (L. J., v., 40). After a conference the Commons accepted this proviso, the date by which pluralists were to resign extra livings being amended from 1st June to 1st August, 1642 (C. J., ii., 555). Like all its fellows this bill was included in the "*nineteen propositions*" for the king's assent in June, 1642 (C. J., ii., 598; L. J., v., 151, 160, 211), and again in the propositions for accommodation with the king framed in December, 1642 (L. J., v., 504; C. J., ii., 903-4), for which purpose the date limited in the bill was again altered to 1st April, 1643. For this purpose the bill was again passed through the Commons, being read a third time on the 7th of January, 1642-43, as "an Act against the enjoying of pluralities of benefices by spiritual persons and non-residence," with the addition of a proviso concerning parishes where divers presentations or collations or portions of tithes have been used (C. J., ii., 917). In this form it was read a first time in the Lords on the 11th of January (L. J.,

The legislative history and fate of this bill was parallel with that of its fellows in all points—in its frequent interruptions and in its final rejection by the king, after a period of nearly two years.

3. *Scandalous Ministers.*

The almost identical history of the legislation on the subject of the treatment of Scandalous Ministers will be detailed in another connection (see vol. ii., chapter iv.).

4. *The Sabbath.*

Besides these three main heads of superstitious innovations in the churches, of pluralities, and of scandals in the lives of the clergy, the reforming zeal of the Long Parliament attempted futilely to embrace the lay evils of drunkenness, swearing and usury.[1]

v., 545), and a second time and committed on the 14th of January (*ibid.*, v., 553), and finally passed on the 16th of January (*ibid.*, v., 558). It was accordingly included in the fourth proposition presented to the King at Oxford (L. J., v., 581-83, 28th January, 1642-43).

[1] On the 1st of March, 1640-41, a bill was read for the first time for the suppressing of alehouses and tippling houses, and for the avoiding of drunkenness. References to the subject of this bill are not infrequent in the journals of the Commons. On the 17th of December, 1641, a small committee was appointed to prepare a declaration for quickening the justices of peace throughout the kingdom to put the laws in execution against swearers, drunkards and Sabbath breakers (C. J., ii., 348). This declaration was reported in the form of an ordinance seven days later, 24th December, 1641 (C. J., ii., 356). The House, however, preferred to proceed by way of bill, and ordered one to be brought in against Sabbath breakers, common swearers and drunkards, and to prevent the increase and suppress the great number of alehouses and tippling houses. The measure, however, went no further. The bill against usury was read a first time on the 2nd of March, 1640-41 (C. J., ii., 95), and again on the 15th of March (*ibid.*, ii., 104), and a second time on the 19th of March (*ibid.*, ii., 108). The measure almost immediately dropped out of sight, and no further reference to it can be traced, as was also the case with the bill against the importation

With regard to the observation of the Sabbath, CHAP. I.
1641. however, its Puritan spirit was more resolute. On the 10th of April the Commons ordered the Lord Mayor in London, and the justices of peace throughout the counties, to see to the execution of the statutes for the due observing of the Sabbath.[1] This step was followed by the introduction of a bill to restrain bargemen, lightermen and others from labouring on the Lord's Day.[2] As usual this latter measure was lost in the mass of undigested, multifarious, and in great part unfinished legislation which strewed and marked the Parliament's path. In the following December it harked back to its original idea of enforcing the existing statutes against Sabbath breakers, swearers, etc., and the form of an ordinance for that purpose was presented to the House.[3] Again changing their mind the Commons determined to proceed by way of a bill, and ordered the introduction of one "against Sabbath breakers, common swearers and drunkards, and to prevent the increase and suppress the great number of alehouses and tippling houses".

In its turn this proposition was lost sight of, and more than a year later the Commons decided

of foreign cards, read for the first time on the 4th of January, 1640-41 (*ibid.*, ii., 96).

[1] *Ibid.*, ii., 118.

[2] C. J., ii., 155, 24th May, 1641. Read a second time on the 3rd of June, 1641 (C. J., ii., 165). Reported from committee on the 14th of July, 1641 (C. J., ii., 211). Read for the first time in the Lords on the 24th of December, 1641 (L. J., iv., 488), and again on the 12th of January, 1641-42 (*ibid.*, iv., 508). A second time on the 15th of January (*ibid.*, iv., 514).

[3] C. J., ii., 356, 24th December, 1641.

VOL. I. 8

CHAP. I. to renew and revive its former order for the better observation of the Lord's Day, entrusting the execution of it to the Deputy Lieutenants of the Counties.[1]

It was not until the 6th of April, 1644, and after repeated appeals from the clergy, that the ordinance for the better observation of the Lord's Day finally issued.[2]

Closely related to this Sabbatarian legislation were the more abortive measures for the free passage of the Gospel, the bill for which was introduced into the Commons[3] on the 30th of March, 1641.

Reserving for future treatment such of the measures of the Long Parliament as touched upon the question of Church patronage and finance (see chapter iv.), and upon ecclesiastical jurisdiction see chapter ii.), two important series of measures or proposals complete this summary review of the religious legislation of the Long Parliament prior to the calling of the Westminster Assembly, *viz.* : (1) as to the Liturgy, the conduct and administration of the Sacrament and Divine service; (2) as to the Episcopal system.

The legislation concerning the Liturgy, 1641-2.

5. *The Liturgy.*

As to the former of those two both Houses had most clearly indicated their intention with regard to the restoration of the pre-Laudian manner of attending the administration of the

---

[1] C. J., iii., 80, 11th May, 1643.

[2] See it in Rushworth, v., 749.

[3] C. J., ii., 114. Read a second time on the 12th of April, 1641, and committed (*ibid.*, ii., 119, 130, 186, 209).

Sacrament, and the performance of Divine service in strict accordance with the law (see *supra*, p. 105).
It was quite in keeping with this conservative attitude that it prohibited the Bishop of Lincoln from publishing a prayer to be read at the time of public thanksgiving.[1] In the debates on the Grand Remonstrance the House on the whole preserved the same attitude though evidently with greater division and heat. During the progress of those debates, the proposal had been made to insert in the Remonstrance a clause concerning the Book of Common Prayer. This clause was offered on the 15th of November, 1641, and referred back to the committee. On the following day it was again read and gave rise to a fierce dispute. D'Ewes' account of the occurrence is as follows :—[2]

We then proceeded with the discussion of that clause again which concerned the Common Prayer Book, and the errors and superstitions of it, and at last it was resolved upon the question that the clause and all that which is therein contained concerning the Common Prayer Book should be laid out. But it was severally moved that a clause of addition might be drawn whereby we might justify the use of the Common Prayer Book till the law had otherwise provided. Mr. Pym moved that we might read the examinations which should have been read in the morning. I stood up next and moved in effect following, that two things had been now proposed—the one that a new clause should be drawn by which we might show our intentions to maintain the use of the Common Prayer Book till some alteration were made by law, the other that we might proceed to read those examinations which should have been read in the morning. For the first I can no way assent to it, for though

[1] C. J., ii., 280, 6th September, 1641.

[2] D'Ewes' *Diary*, Harl. MS., 163, Fol. 154a, Tuesday, 16th November, 1641. For petitions in favour of the Liturgy, September-November, 1641, see *Proceedings in Kent*, pp. 60 *seq.*

I gave my aye to the laying aside of that clause, but now in debate among us, which concerned the Common Prayer Book, yet it was not of any dislike I had of the clause itself for my heart went with it, but only because I thought it fit to be waived at this time that so we might discontent nobody, and for that which was said by the gentleman on the other side (*viz.*, Mr. Hyde), that many sober good men were afraid the Common Prayer Book should be taken away, I did believe some sober men might be of that opinion yet I durst boldly say that there were divers of the looser part of the clergy who were the defiers of that book, that if they were sober to read it on the Sunday they were scarce so all the six days before, and therefore at this time to add any other clause touching this particular were most unreasonable. I shall therefore second the motion of the gentleman at the bar which was in my thoughts before he made it (*viz.*, Mr. Pym), that seeing we have so much spare time to dispute the addition of unnecessary clauses we may proceed with the reading of those examinations which require haste.

But the House generally inclining to finish the said Remonstrance or declaration at this time, the clerk's assistant read the next clause concerning our intentions to dispose of the lands of the bishops and deans whereon divers spake, myself also briefly, and in conclusion the Episcopal party were so strong in the House as we were fain to lay aside this clause also.

In this passage D'Ewes enables us at once to understand the resolution which appears in the Journals of the Commons,[1] and the strength of the Conservative and Episcopal party in the House.

[1] C. J., ii., 317, 16th November, 1641.

Moved, that the clause that has been now read concerning the Liturgy shall be recommitted to the same committee that a clause may be brought in that may not cast any aspersions or scandal upon the Book of Common Prayer established by law, and to bring in a clause that may declare that this House does approve of a set form of prayer.

Resolved, upon the question that the clause or anything therein contained that concerns the Common Prayer Book shall be totally left out of this declaration.

In the course of the succeeding months, how- CHAP. I.
ever, the drift of events carried the Parliament far 1642.
from such a standpoint, and it made no concealment
of its intention to attempt a reform of the Liturgy
after advice had with the intended assembly of
divines. In this form it was stated in the "*nineteen
propositions*" in June, 1642.[1] Pending such action,
however, the situation, as regarded the Prayer-
Book and the performance of Divine service, was
decidedly uncertain, and great laxity and difference
of practice prevailed. The disorder was further
increased when the Parliament found itself driven
to utilise the cathedrals as magazines for ammuni-
tion, to melt down the bells for cannon, and to do
away with, or if possible to sell, the organs for
cash. In accordance with these new conditions
a joint order[2] of the two Houses prescribed as
follows—

> In these times of public danger and calamity . . . such
> part of the Common Prayer and service as is performed by
> singing men, choristers and organs in the cathedral church
> be wholly forborne and omitted, and the same to be done in a
> reverent, humble and decent manner without singing or using
> the organs.

6. *Episcopacy.*

That the Root-and-Branch Bill should have been The legisla-
dropped altogether after the recess is explicable tion concern-
ing Bishops,
only on the ground that the Parliament perceived etc., Oct.,
1641, to Feb.,
the necessity of the advice of an assembly of 1642.
divines for so momentous a measure, and possibly
also that it anticipated, however conjecturally, the

[1] C. J., ii., 598.
[2] L. J., v., 487, 12th December, 1642; C. J., ii., 881.

coming events which were to make even a modified Episcopacy an impossible alternative.

But on one point the Commons were insistent. They were determined to get rid of the bishops from the Upper House. On the 21st of October, 1641— the second day of the reassembling after the recess —a bill was introduced for disenabling all persons in holy orders to exercise any regal jurisdiction or authority. The bill passed the Commons in two days,[1] but rested practically unnoticed in the Lords

[1] Read a first and second time, 21st October, 1641, and committed to a committee of the whole House (C. J., ii., 291). Reported and engrossed on the 22nd, and read a third time and passed on the 23rd (ibid., 292-93), with the excision of the following clause : " Or any other temporal court whatsoever by virtue or colour of any law, statute, commission, charter, or otherways ". Read a first time in the Lords, 23rd October (L. J., iv., 402. See in the State Papers, Domestic, cccclxxxv., No. 29, 26th October, 1641, an account of a conference between the two Houses hereupon). Read a second time on the 4th of February, 1641-42 (ibid., 562), and committed to a committee of the whole House. Reported with slight amendments 5th February, and read a third time and passed, under the protest of the Bishops of Winchester, Rochester and Worcester (ibid., 564). The Commons accepted the amendments the same day (C. J., ii., 414), and sent back the bill to the Lords to be sent on to the king for his royal assent. On the 14th of February, 1641-42, the king passed the bill by a commission (L. J., iv., 580). He accompanied this favour with the following message : " His majesty observes great and different troubles to arise in the hearts of his people concerning the government and Liturgy of the Church. His majesty is willing to declare that he will refer the whole consideration to the wisdom of Parliament—which he desires them to enter into speedily that the present distraction about the same may be composed—but desires not to be pressed to any single act on his part till the whole be so digested and settled by both Houses that his majesty may clearly see what is fit to be left, as well as what is fit to be taken away "—words which it is absolutely impossible to reconcile with the non-possumus attitude assumed by Charles in the later treaties of Uxbridge, Newcastle and Newport. The Act, therefore, appears quite properly among the statutes of the Realm (v., 138), as 16 Car. i., c. 27 : " An Act for disenabling all persons in

until the egregious folly of the petition of the twelve CHAP. I. bishops on the 30th of December, 1641, alienated 1641-2. the sympathies of the Lords from them. The high indignation of the Lords was the Commons' opportunity, most men expressing a great deal of alacrity of spirit for this indiscreet and unadvised action of the bishops.[1] On the following day, therefore, the Lower House sent a message to remind the Peers of the bill against bishops' votes, and after some weeks' delay the bill passed the Upper House and received the royal assent by commission.

Further than this the Parliament did not go in the direction of either destructive or constructive independent legislation in Church matters. When next it took up the question of either bishops or Episcopacy, the war had broken out, and the Parliament had courted the aid of the Scotch. On the 26th of August, 1642, the Lords communicated to the Commons the declaration of the General Assembly of the Church of Scotland of the 3rd of August, 1642.[2]

The legislation concerning Episcopacy, Sept., 1642,-Jan., 1643.

> What hope (said this declaration) can the kingdom and kirke of Scotland have of a firm and durable peace till prelacy, which hath been the main cause of their miseries and trouble, first and last be plucked up root and branch as a plant which God hath not planted.

This declaration was debated in the Commons on the 1st of September, 1642. Without contradic-

holy orders to exercise any temporal jurisdiction or authority ". From the 15th of February, 1641-42, no person in holy orders could sit in Parliament, or in the Privy Council, or could be on any commission of peace, or exercise any temporal authority.

[1] D'Ewes' *Diary*, iii., 295a.

[2] C. J., ii., 738; L. J., v., 321.

tion it was resolved upon the question, that "the government of the Church of England by archbishops, bishops, their chancellors and commissaries, deans, deans and chapters, archdeacons and other ecclesiastical officers hath been found by long experience to be a great impediment to the perfect reformation and growth of religion, and very prejudicial to the state and government of this kingdom, and this House doth resolve that the same shall be taken away". As the main article of the intended reply to the General Assembly's declaration, this resolution was sent up to the Lords for their assent, and by them amended on the 9th of September.[1]

It was not, however, until the 22nd of November that the Commons nominated a committee to prepare a bill for the abolition of bishops, etc., out of the Church of England in accordance with its resolution.[2] Pending the completion of the bill, the Parliament determined at first to demand of the king, as one of the propositions for accommodating differences, that he should confirm the declaration passed in both Houses for taking away bishops, etc.[3]

Almost immediately, however, the decision was taken to hurry through the bill with the object of printing it in regular form for royal assent. On the 30th of December, therefore, the bill "for the utter taking away of all archbishops, bishops, their chancellors and commissaries, deans, sub-deans, deans and chapters, archdeacons, canons and prebendaries, and all chaunters, chancellors, treasurers,

[1] L. J., v., 345.   [2] C. J., ii., 858.
[3] L. J., v., 504, 20th December, 1642.

sub-treasurers, succentors and sacrists, and all vicars choral and choristers, old vicars and new vicars of any cathedral or collegiate church, and of all other their under-officers out of the Church of England," was introduced into the Commons, read a first and second time and committed.[1] As reported from committee, the bill contained a provision of feoffees for the lands of the bishops, etc., and the House thereupon proceeded to limit the number of them to seven, and to nominate them. In this form the bill finally passed Parliament on the 26th of January, 1642-43, and was included in the fourth proposition sent to the king at Oxford (L. J., v., 581-83). It did not, of course, receive Charles's sanction. The Act represents the last effort on the part of the Parliament at either destructive or constructive legislation on the question of Episcopacy, prior to the calling of the Assembly.[2]

CHAP. I.

1642-3.

[1] C. J., ii., 906.   Debated in committee, 14th January (ibid., 914), 17th January (ibid., 931), 19th January (ibid., 935). Reported from committee on the 21st of January, 1642-43, adopted, read a third time and ordered to be sent up (ibid., 937-38). Read a first time in the Lords, 23rd January (L. J., v., 569), and a second time and committed on the following day (ibid., 570). It was reported on the 26th of January without amendment, read a third time, passed and ordered to be sent in title to the king as a proposition (ibid., 572).

[2] The subsequent proceedings with regard to the bill for the abolition of Episcopacy are of interest only from the point of view of the negotiations with the king. With a view to the Treaty of Uxbridge, the Act was altered so as to include a destruction of the hierarchy in Ireland along with that in England and Wales, an amendment which was occasioned by the Treaty of Edinburgh, 29th November, 1643, with the Scotch, and by the terms of the Solemn League and Covenant. For the process of the alteration of the bill in the Houses, see C. J., iv., 43-4, 6th and 10th February, 1644-45. For the progress of the treaty itself, see the papers entered sporadically in the *Lords Journals*

The Assembly of Divines.

The idea of appealing to an Assembly of Divines for expert assistance in Church affairs had in one form or other been present to the mind of the Long Parliament for some time before the outbreak of the war. In the debates on the Ministers' Remonstrance, in the early part of 1641, the House had heard divines before its committee. The Lords had proceeded similarly in the case of their own projected reform of innovations in the Church (see *supra*, pp. 65-74). These were, however, merely occasional references to individual divines. But the idea of a systematic reference, on matters concerning the settlement of religion, to an assembly called *ad hoc* had been broached by more than one speaker in the debates on the Root-and-Branch Bill, and was explicitly avowed in the Grand Remonstrance in November, 1641.[1]

It was not until the following February, however, that the House proceeded to put its avowed determination into force. On the 12th of that month it ordered the knights and burgesses to bring in the names of such ministers as they severally and respectively thought fit to be employed for the settling of the affairs of the Church.[2]

(vii., 167 *seq*.), and Dugdale's Treaty of Uxbridge. For the propositions as presented at Oxford in November, 1644, see L. J., vi., 531 ; vii., 54 ; and for those at Uxbridge in January, 1645, and at Newcastle in July, 1646, see as above and Rushworth, vi., 309. For the subsequent treaty of December, 1647, in the Isle of Wight, in which the above proposition occurs as propositions 9 and 10 appended to the four bills, see L. J., ix., 408, 483, 499 ; C. J., v., 351 ; *Parliamentary History*, xvi., 405, 483.

[1] Rushworth, iv., 438, section 185 of the Remonstrance.

[2] C. J., ii., 427.

For a few more weeks the design slept. But on the 26th of March the Commons urgently appointed the Grand Committee to consider "what is fit to be done for the present in the matter of religion, and what will be further necessary to be done for the future." [1] At the same time they despatched an importunate message to the Lords to expedite the "declaration of the causes and remedies of our evils, especially because there is something contained in it that concerns the matter of religion which this House desires should be settled and established ".[2]

On this matter the Grand Committee did not sit until 4th April, when a committee was appointed to frame a declaration expressing the intention of the House to vindicate the doctrine of the Church from aspersions and concerning government, discipline and liturgy in the Church, and consultation to be had with divines thereupon.

D'Ewes' account of the debate preceding this resolution is as follows :—

Mr. Rous moved that some divines might be appointed to prepare the way to settle the Church in doctrine and discipline. On this it was generally moved that we should have a committee to prepare such a declaration as might include this. Sir Hugh Cholmley moved that we might first vote for it here, and only leave it to the committee to put it into words, which made me move in effect following. . . .[3]

[1] C. J., ii., 498, 26th March, 1642.
[2] "I came in between nine and ten.   Sir Benj. Rudyard was then ordering to appoint a day to consider of the matter of religion, to settle the distraction of the Church for the present and to provide for the future.   Divers spake to it, and at last it was settled for Thursday next" (D'Ewes' *Diary*, iii., 443, 26th March, 1642).
[3] D'Ewes' *Diary*, iii., 455.

Three days later this declaration was reported and accepted by the House :—[1]

> The Lords and Commons do declare that they do intend a due and necessary reformation of the government and liturgy of the Church and to take away nothing in the one or the other but what shall be evil and justly offensive, or at least unnecessary and burdensome, and for the better effecting thereof speedily to have consultation with godly and learned divines.

To this declaration the Lords assented on the 9th of April, ordering it to be published by the sheriffs in the counties and market towns.[2]

Consistently with this measure the Commons three days later reiterated its order for the nomination of divines by the knights and burgesses, two divines for each English county, one for each Welsh county, two for each university, and four for London.[3] From the 20th of April, 1642, onwards the Lower House was intermittently engaged in considering and voting the names of these divines.[4]

The bill for calling the Assembly of Divines.

The list of nominations being finished, a bill was at once introduced for the calling of the Assembly.[5] The extraordinarily chequered legislative career of this measure is given below.

---

[1] C. J., ii., 515, 7th April, 1642.

[2] L. J., iv., 707.   [3] C. J., ii., 524.

[4] " We went to the order of the day to name the several ministers that should be elected to be at the Synod, and so the names of the divines of Bedford, Buckingham and Berkshire were delivered in by the knights and burgesses of the said counties. When we came to the divines to be named for Cornwall, the several members, burgesses of that county, brought in several names, which after a long debate were at last agreed upon " (D'Ewes' *Diary*, iii., 475, 20th April, 1642). The entries of the separate votes run through pages of the *Commons Journals* from ii., 535-564.

[5] 9th May, 1642, read a first and second time, and committed to the whole House (C. J., ii., 564). Reported on the 13th of May and

The Solemn League and Covenant.

The Solemn League and Covenant was the determining factor in the final revolution of opinion which was ultimately forced upon the Long Parlia-

recommitted (*ibid.*, 571). Reported again on the 17th of May and ordered to be engrossed (*ibid.*, 575). Read a third time, 19th May, and passed with the proviso [the divines to debate, etc.] " as in their judgments and consciences they shall be persuaded to be most agreeable to the Word of God " (*ibid.*, 579). Read a first time in the Lords, 20th May (L. J., v., 76) ; a second time, 21st May, and committed to the whole House (*ibid.*, 78). On the 26th the Lords added sundry names of divines, and fixed the date of meeting for the 1st of July, 1642 (*ibid.*, 84 ; C. J., ii., 287), and hereupon a conference was moved between the two Houses. The Commons considered the Lords' amendments on the 31st May (C. J., ii., 595). The differences between the two Houses were considered at a conference, which was reported on the 1st of June (C. J., ii., 598), and on the 3rd of June the bill passed its third reading in the Lords (L. J., v., 101). In reply to the request of the Commons, the Lords sent away the bill for the king's assent (C. J., ii., 605, 4th June). Three weeks later they urged the Secretary to urge the king for his assent (*ibid.*, v., 154, 21st June). The royal assent not being obtained, the bill lapsed by the expiry of the time limited in it for the meeting of the Assembly. Accordingly a committee was appointed by the Commons to prepare a new bill (C. J., ii., 672, 14th July, 1642). This bill for giving further time for the meeting of the Assembly was read a first time and second time, and committed on the following day (C. J., ii., 673). The date of the meeting was hereby extended to 10th August, 1642. The bill was reported and engrossed on 16th July (*ibid.*, ii., 675). It, however, proceeded no further. On the 15th of September, 1642, a third bill was ordered to be prepared (C. J., ii., 767, 781). This bill was read a first time on the 6th of October, 1642, as " an Act for giving further time for the Assembly of Divines " (C. J., ii., 796). Read a second time, and committed on the same day. On the following day the committee reported its advice for the preparation of a new bill altogether. This was accordingly ordered (C. J., ii., 798, 7th October, 1642). Three days later the fourth bill was read a first time as " an Act for the calling and assembling together of an assembly of godly and learned divines to be consulted with by the Parliament for the settling the Church government and vindicating the doctrine of the Church of England from all calumnies and aspersions, etc." (C. J., ii., 802). It was read a second time the same day, and committed to the whole ment. From the first the influence of Scotland had tended in this direction. At the opening of Parliament, England and Scotland were nominally at war. Negotiations for peace had been begun at Ripon, which were shifted to York, and finally, in

House. From the 11th of October, the House sat in committee on the bill, and on the 13th it was reported with some alterations of names of divines (C. J., ii., 806). On the 15th of October it was read a third time and passed. On the same day it was read a first time in the Lords (C. J., ii., 809; L. J., v., 400). A second time, 18th October (L. J., v., 405). Considered in committee, 19th October, when alterations of ministers were proposed (*ibid.*, 407), reported, read a third time and passed. The same day the Commons agreed with the Lords' amendments (C. J., ii., 814), and the Lords thereupon ordered the Clerk of the Crown to prepare a commission for the passing of the bill, "and that it be speedily sent away to the king to be signed" (L. J., v., 407). The bill was accordingly named for the king's assent in the "*propositions for accommodation*" (L. J., v., 504; C. J., ii., 903, 20th December, 1642). With the object of bringing this bill, which was now lapsed, within a new time limit for the purpose of this negotiation with the king, a fifth bill was introduced into the Commons on the 27th of December, 1642 (C. J., ii., 904). Read a second time, and ordered to be engrossed on the same day. Read a third time on the 6th of January, 1642-43, and passed with certain alterations of names (*ibid.*, 916). Read a first time in the Lords on the 10th of January (L. J., v., 542), and a second time and committed on the 14th of January (*ibid.*, 554). Reported, read a third time, and passed on the 19th of January (*ibid.*, 564), with amendments, to which the Commons agreed on the 28th of January (C. J., ii., 947). The bill was immediately sent off to Oxford (*ibid.*, 948; L. J., v., 581-83). Of course the bill did not receive the king's assent. On the 3rd of May, 1643, therefore, a [sixth] measure was ordered to be prepared (C. J., iii., 68). This was read as an ordinance on the 13th of May (*ibid.*, 83) and committed. Reported with amendments and engrossed on the 20th of May (*ibid.*, 93). Carried up to the Lords on the 24th of May (*ibid.*, 99; L. J., vi., 60). Referred to a committee of the Lords on the 5th of June, 1643 (L. J., vi., 81). Reported on the 6th of June with amendments, among them the very material one of the addition of ten Peers and a proportionable number [*i.e.*, twenty] of the Commons to be made to the Assembly (*ibid.*, 84), and with the express exception of any right of jurisdiction to the Assembly (*ibid.*, 84). To these amendments the Commons substantially agreed on the 7th of June (C. J., iii., 119). A conference

November, 1640, to London. Whilst in London the Chap. I.
Scotch Commissioners did not confine themselves 1640.
to the mere work of negotiation. They intrigued
actively to fan the feeling against Episcopacy. The
Scotch Commissioners were accompanied by four Attitude of
ministers—Alexander Henderson, Robert Blair, the Scotch towards the
"to satisfy the minds of many in England who English re-ligious dis-
love the way of New England better than that of pute in Nov., 1640.
Presbyteries used in our Church [of Scotland]";
Robert Baillie, "for the convincing of that prevalent
faction against which I have written [Canter-
burians]"; and Gillespie, "for the crying down of
the English ceremonies for which he has written;
and all four to preach by turns to our commissioners
in their houses ".[1]

They arrived in London on the 15th of November,
1640, and if Baillie's words are an index of the
thoughts of the commissioners generally, they must

was held hereupon on the 10th of June, the Commons having insisted on
the retention of the reference to the Church of Scotland as intending
an uniformity with it. On this point the Lords gave way in the conference, and on the 12th of June, 1643, it finally passed the Lords (C.
J., iii., 126 ; L. J., vi., 89, 90). This form of the ordinance is printed in
the *Lords Journals*, vi., 92. But on the 16th of June an order was
issued for the calling of it in (C. J., iii., 131). The clerical omission of
"together with some members of both Houses" was corrected on the
17th of June (C. J., iii., 132), and so this extraordinary piece of legislation
was finished. The rules for the guidance of the Assembly were prepared by the Lords on the 29th of June, 1643, adopted by them, and
sent down to the Commons (L. J., vi., 114 ; C. J., iii., 149). After consultation in committee with some of the divines thereupon these rules
were accepted by the Commons on the 6th July (see the two forms of
the rules in L. J., vi., 114 ; C. J., iii., 156) with the exception of
clause 5, to which omission the Lords assented (L. J., vi., 123). The
form of oath to be taken by the members of the Assembly was voted
by the Commons on the same day (C. J., iii., 157).

[1] Baillie, *Letters*, i., 269.

have imagined that there was a Presbyterian faction ready to welcome them. The erroneousness of such an assumption has been already pointed out, but it would seem that the commissioners for some time proceeded with the negotiations under that impression.

> Think not (says Baillie) we live any of us here to be idle. Mr. Henderson has ready now a short treatise, much called for, of our Church discipline. Mr. Gillespie has the grounds of Presbyterial government well asserted. Mr. Blair a pertinent answer of Hall's Remonstrance.

On the occasion of Charles's declaration at Whitehall of the 23rd of January, 1640-1, that he would consent to no change in the estate of bishops, the Scots put into print " Mr. Alexander Henderson's very good reasons for their removall out of the Church".

The method of the treaty was to take one demand at a time, the Scots refusing to reveal the whole of their demands beforehand. In consequence, the eighth demand, which contained as its third head the demand of the Scots on the point of Church government, was not reached till the middle of February, 1640-1. In the uncertainty of the times preceding the condemnation of Strafford, both parties were reluctant to approach the question of uniformity of Church government, and it was only on the 10th March that the Scotch decrees concerning unity of religion were presented. But the unwelcome point was suddenly brought to the front by an act of imprudence—the publication by Henderson of

> That little quick paper proclaiming the constancy of our zeal against Episcopacy. . . . Divers of our true friends did think

us too rash, and though they loved not the bishops, yet for the honour of their nation they would keep them up rather than that we strangers should pull them down.

The result is told by Baillie thus :—

We give in a mollifying explanation of our meaning. Here we were put in a new pickle : the English peers were minded to have cause printed our explanation. This, doubtless, this rash and ignorant people would have taken for a recantation of what we had printed before. But, in the end of that explanation, we had professed that we had yet more to say to the Parliament according to our instructions against Episcopacy, so before we had said all out, the king thought meet neither to publish his proclamation nor our explanation. Evil will had we to say out all our mind about Episcopacy till the English were ready to join with us in that greatest of questions, but there was no remedy.[1]

On the 15th March the English Commissioners replied by desiring the Scots not to move the Parliament in that matter, and, after many passionate words from the Earl of Bristol, the Scots consented to lay it aside till after the conclusion of Strafford's trial. The complete demands under this head, therefore, were formally received by the Lords Commissioners on the 10th of April, and on the 14th were discussed by the Upper House. The first demand concerned uniformity of religion and conformity of Church government as a special means of preserving peace between the two kingdoms. But it was accompanied by an assurance from the Earl of Bristol that the same morning

The demand for uniformity of Church government.

[1] Baillie's *Letters*, i., 306-7. For this transaction see S. P. D., cccclxxviii., No. 70 ; L. J., iv., 159, 216, Hist. MSS. Rep., x., vi., 139 ; Portland MSS., i., 8-9 ; Tomasson tracts, E., 157.

Some of the principal lords of the Scots Commissioners told the Lords Commissioners that they could do no less but deliver in those papers, as they were commanded to do by those that employed them in this service, but yet told the Lords Commissioners that what answer it shall please both Houses of Parliament to return in their own time, they will abide and acquiesce with that.[1]

The various papers which had passed between the Commissioners were read at the same time.

These data were communicated to the Commons at a conference on the following day, and were debated in the Lords on the 20th of April,[2] but the subject was not noticed in the Commons till the 15th and 17th of May. On that occasion Hyde moved simply to adhere to the answers of the commissioners, but D'Ewes, afraid of offending "so friendly and so potent a nation," moved "rather the question of the affection of the Scots, yea though we never intended to pursue any part of what they desire".[3] The resolution finally adopted was as follows :—

This House doth approve of the affection of their brethren of Scotland in their desire of a conformity of Church government between the two nations, and doth give them thanks for it. And, as they have already taken into consideration the reformation of Church government, so they will proceed therein in due time as shall best conduce to the glory of God and peace of the Church.

From this answer both Houses refused to swerve, and with a verbal alteration it stood in that form in the final words of the treaty, as ratified by bill in August, 1641.

[1] L. J., iv., 216.   [2] *Ibid.*, v., 224.
[3] D'Ewes' *Diary*, ii., 191.

Two points appear plain from the account of Chap. I. this debate of the 15th of May, as preserved in D'Ewes' MS : (1) That the answer of the Commons was framed on a previously prepared, though more curt and ungracious answer of the Commissioners ; (2) that the House did not at all touch upon the substance of the Scots' request. The only division of opinion was upon the question of the use of the words, "and do give them thanks". The question of the uniformity of Church government—the substantive proposition of the Scotch paper—was not alluded to apparently by a single speaker.[1] Such was the fate of the first negotiation between Scotland and England on this subject of the introduction of a Presbyterian system into England.

When the subject was again taken up, it was on the initiative not of the Scots but of the English. That initiative was taken, however, only under the pressure of sheer necessity, and the course of the negotiations shows with what reluctance the final step of calling in Scotch aid was adopted. From the moment the outbreak of war became a certainty, it became an object of great consideration for either side to secure the neutrality or the goodwill of the Scotch nation. A diplomatic rivalry ensued on this merely negative policy, and it is plain that until the return of their commissioners from the

---

[1] *Cf.* Clarendon, iii., 294. There had been a general inclination to return a rough answer and reproof for their intermeddling in anything that related to the laws of England. But by the extraordinary industry and subtlety of those who saw that business was not yet ripe, and who alleged that it was only wished not proposed, and, therefore, that a sharp reply was not merited, the above gentle answer was returned.

Chap. I. futile negotiations at Oxford, in the spring of
1642. 1643, a party among the Scots themselves thought
neutrality the only likely attitude. They stood,
and it pleased them to think that they should so
stand, as mediator between two belligerent powers,
with a truly national loyalty to the person of their
prince, but with a full knowledge that their interests
lay with the English Parliament, and it required
the actual teaching of events to convince them of
the impracticableness of such a policy.

During this interim period of diplomacy, the
subject of Church government was at first avoided
by the English Parliament, and then handled with
The negotia- almost all their accustomed caution. On the occa-
tions between
the Parlia- sion of the meeting of the General Assembly of
ment and the the Scottish Church, which had been called for
Scotch, July,
1642. 26th July, 1642, the Commons drew up a declaration "how affairs stand here," wherein they assured
the Assembly that if war could be avoided

> We do not doubt that we shall settle matters . . . in
> Church and State to the . . . glory of God by the advancement
> of the true religion, and such a reformation of the Church as
> shall be agreeable to God's word.[1]

A previous declaration, in April, sent to the
Great Council, had been still more unsatisfactory
and vague. The reply of the General Assembly to
the former of these was of a nature to convince the
Parliament that Scotch aid, if ever required, would
only be obtained on one condition—an uniformity
of Church government. They complained of the
slowness of the reformation of religion in England,

[1] L. J., v., 228.

surmising that God had some quarrel with England
for this, and with a reference to the demand of
their Commissioners in the treaty of London,
1641, proceeded to lay down their main require-
ment :—

(4) The Assembly doth renew the proposition made by the
aforesaid commissioners for beginning the work of reformation
at the uniformity of kirk government. For what hope can
there be of unity in religion, of one confession of faith, one
form of worship, and one catechism, till there be one form of
ecclesiastical government. Yea, what hope can the kingdom
and kirk of Scotland have of a firm and durable peace till
prelacy . . . be plucked up root and branch.

(5) The prelatical hierarchy being put out of the way, the
work will be easy without forcing any conscience to settle
in England the government of the reformed kirks by assemblies;
for although the reformed kirks do hold their kirk officers and
kirk government by assemblies higher and lower in their strong
and beautiful subordination to be *jure divino* and perpetual,
yet prelacy . . . is almost universally acknowledged to be an
human ordinance.

This declaration of the General Assembly was
unanimously approved by the Secret Council on the
18th of August, 1642, and forwarded to the English
Parliament. It was communicated to the Commons
on the 26th, but not debated there till the 1st of
September. It will be seen from D'Ewes' notes of
this debate, and from the reply subsequently drawn
up, that the effect of the Scotch declaration was
instantaneous, but only in one direction. There
no longer remained any idea of a preservation of
Episcopacy in any form—modified, purified or
otherwise; but none the less the Parliament
avoided the giving of any pledge on the subject
of a Presbyterian system of government, referring

itself rather to the deliberations of an Assembly of Divines. On both points there seems to have been practical unanimity in these debates.

The debate of 1st Sept., 1642.   After the reading of the declaration of the Assembly,

> There followed (says D'Ewes) many speeches thereupon, I cannot say any debate, for all men argued for the abolishing of bishops after Mr. Rous had first made the motion, and scarce a man spake for them. About two of the clock Mr. Solicitor and others desired that we might put off the debate till Saturday morning next ensuing, because, it being a matter of great weight, we might argue it upon the greater premeditation. And I thought the House so strongly inclined this way as I went out of the House about the time, but, after my departure, the House sat till about three of the clock, and then voted the abolishing of them.[1]

The resolution, as it appears in the *Journals* of the House, ran as follows :—

> The declaration from the General Assembly of Scotland was, according to the order of this House, now again read.
>
> And the House fell into the debate thereof.
>
> *Resolved* upon the question *nemine contradicente* that the government of the Church of England by archbishops, bishops, their chancellors and commissaries, deans, deans and chapters, archdeacons, and other ecclesiastical officers, hath been found by long experience to be a great impediment to the perfect reformation and growth of religion, and very prejudicial to the State and Government of this kingdom, and this House doth resolve that the same shall be taken away.
>
> *Resolved* upon the question that this vote shall be one head of the Declaration to be prepared for answer to the Declaration from the General Assembly of the Church of Scotland.

Further, a committee was appointed to prepare this declaration: "They are likewise to declare the

---

[1] D'Ewes' MSS., B 312, 1st September.

mischiefs that have come to their Church and State
by Episcopacy ".[1]

Five days later (6th September) the reply of the
Commons to the Scotch declaration was presented
from committee and forwarded to the Lords, who
consented to it with a few verbal alterations.   This
reply deserves attention [2] :—

We acknowledge it an act of love that our brethren in The Parlia-
Scotland have bestowed their serious thoughts for unity of ment's declaration in
religion, that in all His Majesty's dominions there might be reply to the
one confession of faith, one directory of worship, one publick Scotch, Sept.,
1642.
catechism, and one form of Church government.   And although
it will hardly be punctually obtained and exactly, unless some
way might be found for mutual communication and conjunction
of counsel and debate in framing that one form, yet both
intending the same end, proceeding by the same rule of God's
word, and guided by the same spirit, we hope, by God's assistance, to be directed so, that we may cast out whatsoever is
offensive to God or justly displeasing to any neighbour church,
and so far agree with our brethren of Scotland, and other reformed churches in all substantial parts of doctrine, worship
and discipline, that both we and they may enjoy those advantages and conveniences which are mentioned by them in this
their answer, to the more strict union of both kingdoms, more
safe and easy government of His Majesty, and both to himself
and people more free communion in all holy exercises and
duties of worship, more constant security of religion against . . .
the Papists, and deceitful errors of other sectaries, and more
profitable use of the ministry, for the compassing and attaining
whereof we intend to use the labour and advice of an assembly
of godly, learned divines, for the convening of whom a bill hath
already passed both Houses.

The main cause which hitherto hath deprived us of these
and other great advantages, which we might have by a more
close union with the Church of Scotland and other reformed
churches, is the government by bishops . . . and . . . we do

---

[1] C. J., ii., 748, 1st September, 1642.   [2] Ibid., ii., 754.

declare that the government by archbishops, bishops, their chancellors and commissaries, deans and chapters, etc., is evil and justly offensive and burdensome to the kingdom, a great impediment to reformation and growth of religion, very prejudicial to the state and government of the kingdom, and that we are resolved that the same shall be taken away. And, according to our former declaration of the 7th of February, our purpose is to consult with godly and learned divines that we may not only remove this, but settle such a government as may be most agreeable to God's holy word, most apt to procure and preserve the peace of the Church at home, and happy union with the Church of Scotland and other reformed churches abroad, and to establish the same by a law which we intend to frame for that purpose, to be presented to His Majesty for his royal assent.

Its import.   Such a declaration is indicative at once of the past and of the impending action of the English Parliament on the subject of Church reform. The General Assembly of 1641 had appointed Henderson to draw up a confession of faith, a catechism, a directory for all parts of the public worship, and a platform of Church government, " wherein possibly England and we might agree ".[1] The succeeding Assembly of 1642 had been greeted by a letter from a number of English ministers at London showing their desire of a Presbyterian government. But such was not the attitude of the House of Commons. A few months later the Parliament was driven to throw itself unconditionally into the arms of the Scotch, but its whole precedent and subsequent action shows its determination to control the reconstruction of the national Church in its own sense—in a lay sense, in an English sense— by the help of an Assembly of Divines, and with

[1] Baillie, i., 364.

a desire of approximation to the best reformed CHAP. I.
1642.
churches, but none the less with a repugnance to
the pure Scotch Presbyterian system.[1]

At the conclusion of the General Assembly
(13th August, 1642), a standing commission had
been named to watch over the negotiations with
England. It was to this body that the Parliament's
declarations of September were sent. In their joy
at the nature of those declarations, they at once
proceeded to nominate a body of commissioners to
be in readiness to carry out actual negotiations;
but for this final step there was wanting the same
alacrity on the part of the Parliament.

At that time the king, being desperate of our assistance,
and the Parliament apprehending no need of it, we were no
more solicited by either, so for a long time lay very calm and
secure. But after Kentown and Brainford, or thereabouts,
when Newcastle had gathered his northern army, the Parliament thought meet to crave help from us, there was great word
of commissioners coming from them to our council, and it was
a wonder, if they desired any help, that they denied to use
better means for its obtaining. But such was their (as I take
it) oversight, that they used no other means but a declaration
of their desires to have our help according to the late treaty.[2]

The hesitation which Baillie notices in these Course of the
Parliament's
negotiations
words was not due to oversight, but to indecision
on the part of the Parliament. On the 2nd of with the
Scotch, Nov.,
November, 1642, the Commons passed a declara- 1642-August,
1643.
tion inviting Scotch aid. This declaration the
Lords put on one side, and although on the falling

[1] Clarendon (iii., 298) maintains that the Scotch imagined that
England would never accept their ultimatum of "uniformity". The
statement deserves no credit, but it is indicative of the *impression* of
one party.

[2] Baillie, *Letters*, ii., 58.

through of the negotiations between the king and the Parliament the Lords adopted it, a month passed before the messengers to carry the invitation were named. As it was, the expectation of an agreement with the king was strong enough to defer the adoption of this final step. The negotiations with Charles, which had been broken off in November, were renewed at Oxford in February, 1642-43. The "Treaty of Oxford" lasted from the 4th of March to the 15th of April. It was for the purpose of these negotiations that the Houses hurried through their bills for the Assembly and for the abolition of Episcopacy. Clarendon represents the adoption of the latter measure as a mere ruse, the House not intending to insist on it, "very probably their departing from their proposition of the Church might be the most powerful argument to the king to gratify them with the militia" (iii., 378). Such a view is a mere perversion of fact. The determination to abolish Episcopacy, and to reconstruct the national Church by the help of an Assembly of Divines, had come to the Parliament through the debates of 1641 and 1642, through the intensification of its own feeling and the rise of popular opinion. From that position it was impossible for the Parliament to recede, even if it had wished, and even though it knew that to insist on it would be fatal to the success of the negotiations. The Scottish Commissioners who had been destined for London had been detained in Oxford by Charles, and to the Parliament's request to allow them to proceed to London, according to their instructions, Charles replied on the 18th of April, 1643 by a

practical refusal.[1] On the 1st of May, the Commons CHAP. I.
accordingly took the final step, and requested the 1643.
Lords to join with them in sending members from
both Houses as commissioners into Scotland. It
was not until the 27th, and upon reiterated messages
from the Commons, that the Lords acceded to the
proposition, and named as their commissioner Lord
Gray of Warke. The Commons at once nominated
on their behalf Sir William Armyn and Henry
Darby. Three weeks later, the Commons added
to their number Sir Henry Vane (the younger) and
Hatcher ; but it was not until the 11th of July
that the Lords took the corresponding step of
nominating the Earl of Rutland. Meanwhile the
Scottish Estates had met on the 22nd of June, 1643,
and were waiting in great perplexity the arrival of
the promised commissioners.

> Yet there was no word of them. All did much admire
> that not so much as one excuse was made of this so great
> neglect. Some did conjecture one cause, some another. Some
> did think them so overwhelmed with plots and dangers that
> they were amazed. . . . Yet the most thought the greatest
> cause of their irresolution to flow from their division. The
> House of Lords was said to be opposite to the Commons'
> conclusion of craving our help.[2]

There is much truth in the latter surmise, but The Parlia-
it was not as a mere faction or party that the Lords ment's inde-
cision and
hesitated to invite into England a Scottish army final surren-
der to the
and a Scottish Covenant. But, whatever lingering Scotch.
hope either House may have had that the final step
might yet be avoided, was swept away by the events
of June and July, 1643 ; and the reflexion proves

[1] L. J., vi., 10.   [2] Baillie, ii., 79.

how purely a thing of necessity the Solemn League and Covenant was. Those two months mark the lowest point in the ebb of the Parliament's fortune. During the preceding three months Waller's plot, the treachery of the Hothams, the successive defeats of the Fairfaxes in Yorkshire and Waller in Devonshire, and the surrender of Bristol, had constituted an almost unbroken series of royalist successes. And there is a remarkable parallelism between these events and the action of the two Houses in the matter of the Scotch negotiations.

For instance.

Pym made his report concerning Waller's plot on the 6th of June. On the same day the Lords agreed to the ordinance empowering the Assembly of Divines to meet. Three days later the Commons ordered instructions to be brought in for their commissioners intended for Scotland. On the 27th of June was received Charles's proclamation declaring the Parliament no longer a free Parliament. On the same day the Lords agreed to the despatch of Corbett as a preliminary commissioner to Scotland. On the 30th of June, the Fairfaxes were beaten by Newcastle at Adwalton; the news of this was followed by the renewed treachery of Hotham at Lincoln (2nd July). Three days later the Commons resolved that the Scotch nation should be forthwith desired to send in aid and assistance. On the same day the Lords resolved

That this House will send two lords as commissioners into Scotland by this day sevennight, or sooner if they can be ready, and do concur with the Commons that one of their instructions shall be to desire the aid and assistance of the Scotch nation.

This parallelism could be further illustrated,
but it is needless. The facts which prove it are
well known. And, intrinsically, the interest of the Nature of the
question lies not in these minor fluctuations of Parliament's
capitulation
resolution on the eve of other great negotiations. to the Scotch.
The way for the Covenant had been paved, not in
1642, but in 1641, when the only chance for a
compromise on the Church question had been lost,
and when the Commons determined on a more
radical scheme, and with the aid of its own
Assembly. Such was the attitude of Parliament
at the opening of the war. Had the success of the
Parliament been immediate and decisive, as was at
one time expected, the Church question would have
been treated in a purely national sense, probably
on the lines sketched out in the debates on the
Root-and-Branch Bill. There may have been—
there doubtless would have been—some concession
to clerical feeling, but there would not have been,
as there subsequently was, a formation of presbyteries, parochial and classical, possessing censorial
powers, and proceeding by legal methods. There
would have been none of the Scotch element of
jurisdiction in the English Church of the years
1643-51. As it was, no sooner had it become
apparent that the war could not be finished at a
stroke, than the necessity of securing Scotland for
the Parliamentary cause was at once seen. The
only possible condition was the adoption of the
Covenant—of a uniformity of Church government
—so much was known from the first ; the question
then became one of time, or of the immediate
fortune of the war. Fortune declared against the

Parliament, and the Covenant was accepted. It may be that a slight portion of the Commons had no dislike for a pure Presbyterian system—it is certain that a Presbyterian party had sprung up amongst the clergy—it may also be that the course of the ecclesiastical debates of the year 1641 had educated the majority of the Commons, or had habituated them to the conceptions and terminology of a primitive Presbyterian system in the abstract, but none the less the final adoption of the Covenant was, under the circumstances, of the nature of a capitulation.

The adoption of the Solemn League and Covenant, August-September, 1643.

The instructions to the commissioners were reported by Pym from committee on the 12th of July, 1643, and agreed to and sent up to the Lords on the following day. The Lords agreed to them on the 15th. To these was subsequently added the declaration to the Assembly of Divines in Scotland, which was accepted by the Upper House on the 19th, under which date all the papers are entered in the *Journals*. There is no further trace in the negotiations of the hesitancy which had marked the proceedings of the last three months. The commissioners landed at Leith on the 4th of August; by the 18th the draft of the Covenant had been completed and despatched to the English Parliament. It reached London on the 26th, was at once referred to the Assembly, and adopted in principle in the Commons on the 5th of September. The arrival of commissioners from Scotland facilitated the speedy settlement of disputed points, and on the 18th the Lords adopted the Covenant. It was then solemnly sworn to by both Houses at St. Margaret's on the 22nd.

The conclusion was foregone, but there are two points that should, perhaps, be taken into consideration in the final estimation of the transaction. The first has been explained with great succinctness by Mr. Gardiner.[1] In the first draft of the Covenant, as agreed upon at Edinburgh, Vane had proposed an amendment by adding after the words, "the Church of Scotland in doctrine, worship, discipline and government," the words "according to the word of God". When the Covenant was referred to the Assembly of Divines at Westminster, this amendment was retained, along with another of the Assembly's own, defining the prelacy, which it was desired to abolish, as that which consisted in archbishops, bishops, etc. The scope of both amendments is plain. The former would pledge the Covenanted Parliament to the Scottish system only in so far as it was found agreeable to the word of God; the latter gave it freedom in the construction it put upon the word prelacy—in the view it took of the then existing Church system. Practically both amendments were retained in the final form of the Covenant.

Secondly, before its final adoption both Houses insisted on being satisfied by the Assembly at Westminster that the Covenant could be taken in point of conscience, and they joined in requiring the Assembly to set forth a declaration stating the reasons and grounds of the opinion which they had thereupon expressed of that lawfulness in point of conscience.

The latter exception is, however, under the

CHAP. I.

1643.

[1] Civil War, ii., 268.

circumstances comparatively meaningless. It did not detract from the simple fact that the English Parliament, under the pressure of necessity, had forfeited its future freedom of action in the matter of Church reform—that it had pledged itself to a particular policy.

CHAPTER II.

THE CONSTRUCTIVE WORK OF THE WESTMINSTER ASSEMBLY.

1643-1647.

§ *I.—The Thirty-nine Articles.* § *II.—Church Government.* § *III.— Presbyterian Jurisdiction or Discipline.* § *IV.—Jus Divinum of Presbytery.* § *V.—Ordination.* § *VI.—The Directory for Worship.* § *VII.—The Confession of Faith.* § *VIII.—The Greater and the Lesser Catechism.* § *IX.—The New Metrical Version of the Psalms.*

§ I.—*The Thirty-nine Articles.*

THE Westminster Assembly met on the 1st of July, 1643. After hearing a sermon from its appointed Prolocutor, Dr. Twiss, in the Abbey Church, it adjourned to Henry VII.'s chapel [1] to call the roll of its members. According to the ordinance of 12th June, 1643, the Assembly consisted of 10 English lords and 20 English commoners, sitting as lay assessors; 121 English divines; 3 scribes or clerks; and 8 Scottish commissioners, 5 of them clerical and 3 lay. The personale of the list, and the subsequent alterations in it owing to death, etc., can be seen in Hetherington, 103-6. On the first day the roll call revealed an attendance of sixty-nine, and Baillie says that the ordinary attendance of the English divines was about three score. [2]

On the same day, 1st July, the House of Commons read over the draft rules to be observed

The Assembly's revision of the Thirty-nine Articles.

---

[1] On 23rd September, 1643, an ordinance was passed to enable the Assembly to meet in the Jerusalem Chamber in the abbey, because of the cold of Henry VII.'s chapel (L. J., vi., 230).

[2] *Letters*, ii., 108-9.

by the Assembly in its debates,[1] and recommitted them to its own committee for conference thereupon with some of the divines. Four days later, Wednesday, 5th July, these rules were passed by the Commons along with two other resolutions. The first of these latter called upon the Scotch to send in aid for the preservation of the religion and liberties of the English kingdom. The second ran as follows :—

> Resolved upon the question that it shall be propounded to the Assembly of Divines to-morrow at their meeting to take into consideration the 10 first Articles of the 9 and 30 Articles of the Church of England to free and vindicate the doctrine of them from all aspersion and false interpretations.

The vote was carried up to the Lords the same day by Mr. Rouse, and agreed to by them.[2]

The rules for the debates and the above resolution were brought into the Assembly on Thursday, 6th July, and on the following Saturday it proceeded to resolve itself into three separate committees to consider respectively of Articles 1-4, 5-7, and 8-10. From Monday, 10th July, these committees accordingly sat in their several places. After two days' work in them the Assembly met on Wednesday, 12th July, and decided upon debate that in proceeding upon the Articles places of Scripture should be alleged for the clearing of them. Thereafter the Assembly, with the not infrequent interruption of other more secular work, settled down to its committee work on the Articles, passing the 4th Article on the 1st of

---

[1] C. J., iii., 150.
[2] *Ibid.*, 155-56 ; L. J., vi., 121.

August, and debating the three creeds on the 18th
of August.[1]
On the 22nd of August, 1643, the two Houses ordered "that it be propounded to the Assembly of Divines to consider of the doctrine of the 9 next Articles of the Thirty-nine Articles of the Church to clear and vindicate the same from all aspersions and false interpretations".[2] This work was interrupted during the whole of September by the consideration of the Solemn League and Covenant, and when the form of that agreement had been settled and sworn, both in England and Scotland, it was found that it necessitated a more immediate consideration of the question of Church government, with a view to the assimilation of the English Church system to the Presbyterianism of Scotland. "On Thursday, the 12th of October, 1643," says Lightfoot in his *Journal*, "we being at that instant very busy upon the 16th Article of the Thirty-nine Articles of the Church of England, and upon that clause of it which mentioneth *departing from grace*, there came an order to us from both Houses of Parliament enjoining our speedy taking in hand the Discipline and Liturgy of the Church."[3] This effectually interrupted the work of the Assembly on the Thirty-nine Articles.

The work interrupted and left incomplete.

In the course of its subsequent labours of 1643-46, on the various parts of the Presbyterian system which it developed, the Assembly worked whatever of the Thirty-nine Articles of the Church of

---

[1] Lightfoot, xiii., 8, 10.
[2] C. J., iii., 214 ; L. J., vi., 194.
[3] Lightfoot, xiii., 17.

CHAP. II.

England it thought worthy of preservation into the Confession of Faith, and in view of that disposal and arrangement of the matter proposed tacitly to drop the Articles altogether. But on the 7th of December, 1646, the Commons sent to require of it all that had been accomplished on the Thirty-nine Articles, with the text of Scripture attached as proofs.[1] Accordingly, on the 5th and 6th of January following, the Assembly re-read its former proceedings on the Articles, and ordered them to be transcribed and sent up.[2] It was not, however, until the 13th of April that Gower reported the Assembly's preface to the Articles.[3] The Scriptural proofs were ordered to be inserted two days later, and on the 29th of April, after an energetic demand from the House for the forwarding of these Articles, they were presented to the Commons by Dr. Smyth.[4]

There is nothing discoverable in the *Journals* of either House with regard to any proceedings of the Parliament upon them.[5]

The Articles revised and passed by the Assembly include 1-15, and are so printed in *The Proceedings of the Assembly of Divines upon the Thirty-nine Articles of the Church of England.*[6] This tract contains the

---

[1] C. J., v., 2; Mitchell, *Minutes of the Westminster Assembly*, 309.

[2] Mitchell, 318.   [3] *Ibid.*, 348-49, 352-53.

[4] C. J., v., 151, 156.

[5] The numerous references to the " articles of Christian religion " relate, of course, to the Assembly's Confession of Faith (see *infra*, 361, 365). The twenty articles of religion elaborated by the later Assembly of Divines of 1654 were a draft Confession of Faith or definition of fundamentals not an attempted revision of the Articles of the Church of England (see *infra*, 366, ii., 82-4).

[6] B. M., E. $\frac{4}{1}\frac{1}{0}$ without title page or date.

whole of the Articles 1-15 inclusive, together with the Assembly's preface. In the form in which they were inserted by the Parliament in the 14th proposition sent to the king in the Isle of Wight, to Carisbrooke Castle, December, 1647 (see *infra*, ii., pp. 59-69), the 8th Article and the preface were omitted. In this form they were reprinted in 1654,[1] and in Neal, Puritans, vol. v., appendix liii., and elsewhere.

§ II.—*Presbytery or Church Government.*

The draft form of the Solemn League and Covenant was received in London from the commissioners of the English Parliament in Edinburgh, on the 26th of August, 1643. It was immediately referred by the Parliament to the Assembly, and from that date onwards to the solemn taking of it by the two Houses on Monday, 25th September, it was the constant subject of debate between Assembly, Parliament and the Scottish Estates and the General Assembly of the Scottish Church. Regarding its adoption in England as a certainty, the General Assembly followed up the adoption of the draft of the Covenant by the appointment of commissioners to treat in England at first hand with the Parliament and the Westminster Divines, on all matters concerned with the evolution of that uniformity of Church system which was the main item in the Covenant.

The "Commissioners of the General Assembly of

The work of the Assembly on the subject of Presbytery or Church government.

---

[1] B. M., $\frac{814}{8}$. Articles of religion, or the 14 Pillars of the Church of England, presented to our late King Charles at the Isle of Wight, and now humbly tendered to the mature consideration of the supreme authority of this nation. 4to, London [8th October], 1654. The usually missing 8th Article and the Assembly's preface are reprinted by Dr. Mitchell (*Minutes of the Westminster Assembly*, p. 541).

Chap. II.
1643.

The Commissioners of the General Assembly of Scotland.

the Church of Scotland appointed to treat with the English Parliament or Assembly for the union of England and Scotland in one form of kirk government, one confession of faith, one catechism and one directory for worship," was a body composed of five ministers [1] and three elders.[2]

They were elected at a session of the General Assembly at Edinburgh, 19th August, 1643. On the following 9th September, the two Houses in London appointed a joint committee [3] to receive the propositions brought by the said commissioners from Scotland. The latter presented their credentials and papers to the Parliament's committee, and by them they were laid before the House of Lords on Monday, 11th September, 1643. As the commissioners had brought also a declaration to the Westminster Assembly, the latter body was empowered by a joint vote of the two Houses to appoint a committee of its own members to receive propositions from the Scotch Commissioners.[4] The Assembly therefore elected its committee (of twelve members) on the same day, 11th September.[5]

The Parliamentary Reception Committee.

This double committee of Lords and Commons, and the separate concurrent committee of the Westminster Assembly, are to be regarded as things of the moment, an organisation solely intended for the

---

[1] Alexander Henderson, Robert Douglas, Samuel Rutherford, Robert Baillie, George Gillespie.

[2] John, Earl of Cassilis, John, Lord Maitland, Sir Archibald Johnston of Warriston.

[3] The Commons' members, Mr. Solicitor, Mr. Pym, Sir Gil. Gerard, Sir J. Clotworthy (C. J., iii., 235). The Lords' members, Lord Viscount Saye and Sele, Lord Howard of Echt (L. J., vi., 211).

[4] C. J., iii., 237 ; L. J., vi., 211-12.   [5] Lightfoot, xiii., 13.

consideration of the Covenant, and for the formality
of the reception of the Scotch Commissioners
and their papers. According to Baillie, the commissioners when they came up to London were
desired to sit as members of the Assembly. This,
however, they declined to do, "since they came up
as commissioners for our National Church, they
required to be dealt with in that capacity ".[1] Whilst
willing as private men to sit in the Assembly, and
upon occasion to give their advice in points debated,
they insisted on being dealt with formally on the
matter of the treaty for church uniformity, and
demanded that a committee should be appointed
from the Parliament and the Assembly of Divines
to treat with them thereupon. " All these," says
Baillie, "after some harsh enough debates, was
granted to once a week, and whyles after there
is a committee of some Lords and Commons and
divines which meets with us anent our commission."
This latter standing committee to which Baillie The Parlia-
refers was appointed by order of the Parliament of Treaty Com-
17th October, 1643, as follows :— mittee.

Ordered that the committee [2] formerly appointed to treat
with the Scots Commissioners shall be the committee appointed
to join with a committee of the Assembly to meet and treat
with the divines from Scotland concerning a form of Church
government, directory of worship, confession of faith and form
of catechism.[3]

To this order the Lords assented three days
later.[4] On Monday, 23rd October, the Assembly

[1] *Letters*, ii., 110.
[2] *Ut supra*, p. 150, under date 9th September, 1643.
[3] C. J., iii., 278.   [4] 20th October, 1643, L. J., vi., 265.

received this order from the Parliament, and after some agitation "partly about the work to be done and what is like to be," the divines re-appointed as their committee the twelve divines who had been previously appointed to receive the papers from the Scots and to treat upon the Covenant.[1]

The Treaty Committee, therefore, was the same in personale as its predecessor; but, instead of being appointed for the treaty as to the Covenant, it was now constituted a standing committee for the treaty as to church uniformity.

Influence exercised by the Treaty Committee upon the work of the Assembly.

Baillie distinctly claims that this standing treaty committee of Lords, Commons, divines and Scotchmen stood behind the Assembly and prompted it for the time being in its debates on the important subject of Church government and officers. "To this committee," he says, "a paper was given in by our brethren [some of the Scotch divines] before we [Baillie and Rutherford] came, as ane introduction to further treatie. . . . According to it the Assemblie did debaite and agree anent the deutie of pastors."[2]

It is, of course, natural that few direct traces of such predominant influence, as Baillie here ascribes to this treaty committee, should be discoverable in the *Journals* of Parliament or in the Records of the Assembly. It would not be likely to be confessed. But the course of the narrative of the Westminster Assembly's work prove that Baillie has hardly overstated the case. At the time of the definite establishment of this treaty committee, 17th to 20th October, the Assembly

---

[1] Lightfoot, xiii., 27.   [2] Baillie, ii., 110

had been already for some days engaged on the Chap. II. debate of the crucial matters of Church government 1643. and discipline. The sudden interruption of the academic discussion of the Thirty-nine Articles on which the Assembly had been engaged, and the introduction of the more highly controversial topic of Church government and discipline, was doubtless due to the arrival of the Scotch Commissioners from the General Assembly. It was the immediate and logical consequence of the adoption of the Covenant. So much instantly must be ascribed to Scottish influence. How much more will remain to be traced.

From the 28th of August, 1643, onwards to 15th September, the Assembly had been almost entirely engaged upon the consideration of the Covenant on reference from the House of Commons. On the latter date, 15th September, 1643, the very day on which the first members of the Scotch Commissioners were received in the Assembly of Divines, the House of Commons ordered "that Mr. White do bring in an order for the Assembly to consider of matters of the discipline of the Church government".[1] On the following Monday (18th September) this order was rendered more express and drawn up as an ordinance, as follows :—

Upon serious consideration of the present state and conjuncture of the affairs of this kingdom, the Lords and Commons assembled in this present Parliament do order that the Assembly of Divines and others do forthwith confer and treat among themselves of such a discipline and government as may be most agreeable to God's holy word, and most apt to procure and

The question of Church government referred to the Assembly, 12th Oct., 1643.

[1] C. J., iii., 242.

preserve the peace of the Church at home, and nearer agreement with the Church of Scotland and other reformed churches abroad; to be settled in this Church in stead and place of the present Church government by archbishops, bishops, their chancellors, commissaries, deans, deans and chapters, arch-deacons, and other ecclesiastical officers depending upon the hierarchy which is resolved to be taken away; and touching and concerning the directory of worship or liturgy hereafter to be in the Church; and to deliver their opinions and advices of and touching the same to both or either House of Parliament with all the convenient speed they can.[1]

On Wednesday, 20th September, Sir Robert Pye was ordered to carry up this ordinance to the Lords for their concurrence therein. The Lords respited it " for a while ".[2]

On the following Saturday the Assembly, by the mouth of Dr. Temple, acknowledged the receipt of these instructions, " which we find to be a business of a large nature and will require time to give present satisfaction; yet, as time will give leave, they will fall on that work also ".[3]

On the 17th November, 1643, Baillie writes [from London] :—

At last the Assemblie of Divines have permission to fall on the question of Church government. What here they will do we cannot say. Mr. Hendersone's hopes are not great of their conformitie to us *before our armie be in England*.[4]

Acting upon this ordinance of 12th October, the Assembly began the consideration of the great

[1] C. J., iii., 246.   [2] *Ibid.*, 249 ; L. J., vi., 223.
[3] *Ibid.*, 252, 23rd September, 1643. It is to be noted, however, that it was not until the following 12th October that the Lords formally agreed to this ordinance for the Assembly to treat of a discipline and Church government (L. J., vi., 254).
[4] Baillie, *Letters*, ii., 104.

question of Church government. On Monday, 16th Chap. II.
October, it held a solemn fast as a preparative, 1643.
and on the following day proceeded to debate upon The Assembly's
the order of reference.[1] The divines voted to deal Committees
first with the question of government. Thereupon at work on it.
debate arose as to whether to proceed instantly
with the discussion of church officers or to settle
the precedent question, *viz.*, " whether there were
a rule for government to be had in the Scripture ".
The Independents put forth their strength in defence of the latter, but were outvoted—a foretaste
of the differences of opinion that were soon to
reveal themselves. The Assembly was then divided
into three committees as before, each having the
same question referred to them. Speaking apparently of no particular committee, but of all three,
Lightfoot says : " After dinner we met in the
committee, and the business we did was to collect
all the texts where mention of any church officers
is, and we set down very many upon which to
consider at our next meeting, and appointed then
to treat upon apostles, prophets, evangelists, and
the seventy disciples ".[2]

On Thursday, 19th October, the second and
third committees reported hereupon. The latter
committee found out of Scripture the following
officers : apostles, evangelists, prophets, pastors,
teachers, bishops or overseers, presbyters or elders,
deacons, widows. On this particular report the
Assembly debated in full session on Monday, 23rd
October, the disputed point being whether the list
of officers quoted was complete or not. The matter

---

[1] Lightfoot, xiii., 20. [2] *Ibid.*, p. 21.

was concluded in the morning debàte, and in the
afternoon the Assembly resolved itself into its
usual committees to agitate the question whether
a pastor and teacher were the same officer in
substance, "and after very long we concluded
affirmatively ".[1]   It was not until the 27th of
October that the first committee reported on the
question of officers in the Church. It found the
following church officers in Scripture, *viz.*, apostles,
prophets, evangelists, pastors and teachers, bishops,
elders, deacons, widows.

The office of
pastor in the
Church.
The divines debated in full session on this report
on Thursday the 2nd of November, and following
days. The debate commenced with the office of
pastor. It is at this point that Baillie's evidence
ut supra, p. 152, concerning the course of the
debates becomes pertinent. The Assembly first
voted the continuity and necessity of the office of
pastor,[2] and then proceeding to define his office,
stuck upon the question of the public reading of
the Word. Such public reading of the Word in
the public congregations was voted an ordinance
of God, but on the subsequent question whether
this public reading was the pastor's office, the
Assembly suddenly faltered. "When the thing was
coming to the very question, it was much desired
to delay the vote for fear of some inconvenience
that might follow. And hereupon it was put to
the question whether this should be put to the
question, and it was voted negatively, and so we laid
it by for the present and adjourned till Monday."[3]

---

[1] Lightfoot, xiii., 27.   [2] *Ibid.*, 36.
[3] *Ibid.*, 39-40, Friday, 3rd November.

It is of course permissible to see in these words some confirmation of Baillie's testimony. But it is to be noted (1) that the first recorded interference of the Scotch Commissioners in the debate did not take place until nearly a fortnight later, *see infra*, and (2) that there appears in effect to have been no break in the material continuity of the debate, for on the following Monday, 6th November, the Assembly voted the public reading of the Scripture to belong to the pastor's office,[1] subsequently adding thereto the further duties of catechising, sacramental administration, blessing, prayer,[2] rule of the flock, and care of the poor.

The inconvenience of the method adopted by the Assembly in its committee arrangements is curiously illustrated by the fact that after having thus traversed part of the ground it was drawn back again over it by the belated report of the second committee. On Wednesday, 8th November, that committee reported as follows :—

> The Church officers under the New Testament before the ascension of Christ were John Baptist, the twelve Apostles and seventy Disciples. After his ascension, apostles, prophets, evangelists, pastors, teachers, elders, deacons, widows.[3]

On this report the Assembly proceeded to resolve that pastors and teachers were one and the same for the substance of the office.

Almost immediately thereupon the chairman of the first committee reported five propositions advanced concerning the office of doctors and teachers, and the difference between it and that of the pastor.[4]

The office of doctor and teacher in the Church.

---

[1] Lightfoot, xiii., 40. [2] *Ibid.*, 40, 44-47.
[3] *Ibid.*, 43. [4] *Ibid.*, 44.

The report was laid by to be debated another day, but before the committee could set specifically upon it the Scotch Commissioners intervened with an *ex parte* declaration. They imparted their desires to the triple committee of Lords, Commons and Divines with whom they were in treaty, and from that body they were reported to the Assembly of Divines by Mr. Marshall on Tuesday, 14th November. In effect the Scotch Commissioners wished to lay down four permanent officers in the Church-pastors, teachers, ruling elders and deacons, the former three having the government in the Church. To this expression of opinion they added an enumeration of the four sorts of assemblies in their own Church, *viz.*, Church sessions or particular elderships, classes of presbyters, provincial synods, national assemblies.

The Scotch Commissioners intervene.

The report being read, which was very long, Dr. Burgess moved that Mr. Marshall would relate whether the committee had examined by Scripture that part of it which concerns Church officers.

To which Mr. Marshall answered that the committee had not debated them all but referred it to the Assembly.[1]

In the light of this communication the Assembly proceeded to the aforementioned report of the preceding 8th November, from the committee on the office of doctor and teacher—their identity or difference. The debate on this point endured for a week, from the 14th to the 21st November, and was carried on with extraordinary pertinacity and warmth. Baillie's account of the dispute is as follows :—

The Independent men, whereof there are some ten or

[1] Lightfoot, xiii., 51.

eleven in the Synod, manie of them very able men, as Thomas
Goodwin, Nye, Burroughs, Bridge, Carter, Caryll, Philips,
Sterry, were for the divine institution of a Doctor in every
congregation as well as a Pastor. To these the others were
extreamlie opposite and somewhat bitterlie, pressing much the
simple identitie of Pastors and Doctors. Mr. Hendersone
travelled betwixt them, and drew on a committee for accomodation in the whilk we agreed unanimouslie upon some six propositions wherein the absolute necessitie of a Doctor in everie
congregation, and his divine institution in formall termes was
eschewed. Yet where two ministers can be had in one congregation, the one is allowed according to his gift to applie
himself most to teaching and the other to exhortation according
to Scripture.[1]

According to Lightfoot's *Journal*, the first interference of the Scotch in the debate occurred on
the second day (Wednesday, 15th November) :—

Then returned we to the business again [*viz.*, of the
identity of Doctor and Pastor], and treating very largely of
this business, Dr. Burgess desired that one of the Scots
divines would speak on this business, which Mr. Henderson
did, advising that as the churches reformed have their eyes
upon us so should we have our eyes upon them and on this
point particularly.

It was after this urged that this [should be framed as the]
proposition. " The pastor and the doctor are equally ministers
of the Gospel," which when it was urged Mr. Henderson again
desired that we would be wary lest we give offence and prejudice
to other churches. He also after some further debates about
this spoke again, that we would not in metaphysical and
abstract notions consider of these things, but go to work to
determine what offices we think fit to be in the Church, without more ado.[2]

Notwithstanding this plain and coercive advice
the debate continued with undiminished tenacity

[1] *Letters*, ii., 110.   [2] Lightfoot, xiii., 53.

CHAP. II.

1643.

Ineffectual
attempt at
accommoda-
tion with the
Independents
on the ques-
tion of the
office of the
doctor.—
November,
1643.

and length until the following Friday, 17th November, when upon the motion of Mr. Henderson
the business was referred to a committee of six.
This committee reported on the following Monday
a series of five propositions of the nature summar-
ised by Baillie as above, but without apparently
conducing to any accommodation. " Mr. Henderson and Mr. Palmer offered several tempers for
accommodation, and so did others, and so we spent
the session without conclusion of anything, but
only determined this by vote, 'that we should
to-morrow first consider wherein we agree in this
question about pastors and teachers,' and for that
purpose was a committee chosen, and so we
adjourned." [1]

The following day, Tuesday, 21st November,
was spent in the consideration of six colourless
propositions from this latter accommodation committee, the use of a teacher or doctor for exposition
and doctrine being admitted, but practically nothing
more. [2] It is quite clear from the words in which
Lightfoot refers to the proceedings of the next day
that this conclusion was not an accommodation,
but an interim statement of a few commonplaces of
agreement, the main contention of the Independent,
viz., the necessity and divine institution of the
doctor being postponed until the Directory of Worship should come on for consideration. [3]

Much more crucial was the immediately succeeding subject concerning ruling elders, and the

---

[1] Lightfoot, xiii., 58.   [2] *Ibid.*, 58.

[3] *Ibid.*, 60. This point, a not unimportant one, could not be
gathered from Baillie's testimony at all.

division of opinion upon it was as clear and, if
anything, sharper.

The question was raised, on Wednesday, the 22nd of November, 1643, on the basis of a proposition reported by the second committee on the preceding 8th November, in the following terms :—

Besides those Presbyters which rule well and labour in the word and doctrine, there be other Presbyters who especially apply themselves to ruling, though they labour not in the word and doctrine.[1]

Quite early in the debate Henderson, as representing the Scotch members of the Treaty Committee, spake concerning this thorny business of ruling elders, " that however it be somewhat strange in England, yet that it hath been in the reformed churches even before Geneva, and that it hath been very prosperous to the Church of Scotland ".[2] At a later point in the debate Henderson again intervened, taking the prudential ground and proving the necessity of ruling elders to see to the manners of the people. The debate ran, however, mainly upon the lines of Scripture authority and interpretation. The Independents, supported by Smith, Gataker, Temple, Vines and others, argued strongly against the divine institution of the ruling elder. The main body of the Synod reasoned for it, and with this latter Baillie joyfully identifies himself and his brethren of the Scotch Commission.

" When all were tired it came to the question. There was no doubt but we would have carried it by far most voices ; yet because the opposite were men verie considerable, above all gracious and learned little Palmer, we agreed upon a com-

[1] Lightfoot, xiii., 43, 60.   [2] *Ibid.*, 60.

mittee to satisfie if it were possible the dissenters. For this end we meet to-day, and I hope ere all be done we shall agree. All of them were ever willing to admitt elders in a prudentiall way; but this to us seemed a most dangerous and unhappie way, and therefore was peremptorily rejected. We trust to carry at last, with the contentment of sundry once opposite, and silence of all, their divine and Scriptural institution. This is a point of high consequence, and upon no other we expect so great difficultie, except alone on Independencie; wherewith we purpose not to medle in haste till it please God to advance our armie, which we expect will much assist our arguments." [1]

One accommodation committee, but not that to which Baillie refers in these words of hardly concealed cynicism, was appointed on Friday, 1st December, after five days' debate. A week later, after days of equally futile dispute, on the 7th of December, a second committee for accommodation (the one mentioned by Baillie as above) was appointed to draw up heads of agreement, and then to draw up the ruling elder's office. [2]

The three propositions reported from this committee were adopted on the following day, Friday, 8th December.

Of these propositions the last asserted that some others beside the ministers of the Word, or Church governors, should join with the ministers in the government of the Church. [3]

Following this inconclusive beginning, the Assembly proceeded to debate the antiquities of the Jewish civil and ecclesiastical courts, and the position of the civil elder in respect to them. Day after day the discussion held, notwithstanding Sir Benj. Rudyard's plainspoken advice "to lay this

[1] *Letters*, ii., 111.   [2] Lightfoot, xiii., 75.   [3] *Ibid.*, 76.

subject by, for that it would prove but a weak Chap. II. ground to build our eldership upon the Jewish ".[1] 1643.

On the following day Lord Saye, reiterating The subject postponed. Rudyard's opinion, moved to waive the scrutiny as to the Jewish elders, and on an exhortation from Lightfoot to hasten the material things tending to settlement, leaving these speculations alone till leisure, the Assembly agreed to lay by the present subject for the present, and to proceed to the consideration of the office of the deacon.[2] Baillie in his *Letters*[3] asserts that in addition to voting the existence of Church governors, as joining with the ministers in the government, the Assembly actually came to a vote "that in the Jewish Church the elders of the people did join in ecclesiastick government with the Priests and Levites". This assertion is, however, not borne out by Lightfoot's *Journal* (*ubi supra*).

The office of deacon presented no points of The office of deacons in the Church. controversy like that of the doctor or the ruling elders, and the committee report "that it was the office of a deacon to take special care to distribute to the necessaries of the poor," was quickly adopted, Friday, 15th December,[4] though the discussion as to the exact nature and limitation of his office held till past Christmas.[5]

After two days further debate on the office of The office of widows in the Church. widows,[6] the Assembly had brought to a close what was practically the first portion or earliest stage of

---

[1] Lightfoot, xiii., 81.
[2] *Ibid.*, 83, Thursday, 14th December.
[3] *Letters*, ii., 117.   [4] Lightfoot, xiii., 84.
[5] *Ibid.*, 93, 28th December.   [6] *Ibid.*, 94-98, 29th Dec.-1st Jan.

its constructive work. Baillie asserts in effect that the Assembly hereupon was for a moment at a stand, "because the Committee [the Treaty Committee of Scots, Lords, Commoners and Divines] had prepared no other matter to compt of for the Assemblie to treat on. Sundrie things were in hand, but nothing in readyness to come in publick".[1]

Speaking later in the same letter,[2] and referring apparently to the debate of Friday, 29th December,[3] Baillie throws further light on this outside management of the Assembly's debates :—

> We were called out before twelve to dine with old Sir Henry Vane. Doctor Twisse was absent that day. Dr. Burgesse fell to be in the chaire. The question came : What should follow the Widows ? There were left some branches of the Apostles' and Evangelists' duties yet undiscussed. We thought these questions needless, and wished they had been passed ; but sundrie by all means would have them in, of designe to have the dependence of particular congregations from the apostles in matters of ordination and jurisdiction determined. The Independents foreseeing the prejudice such a determination might bring to their cause by all means strove to decline that dispute ; as indeed it's marked by all that to the uttermost of their power hitherto they have studied procrastination of all things, finding that by tyme they gained. We indeed did not much care for [*i.e.*, object to] delayes till the breath of our armie might blow upon us some more favour and strength.

---

[1] *Letters*, ii., 120. [2] *Ibid.*, 122.

[3] Lightfoot, xiii., 96. The debate on the Anabaptist letter from Amsterdam took place on Thursday, 28th December, and the debate to which Baillie refers on the day following, Friday, 29th December— a day also on which Burgess occupied the chair in place of Dr. Twisse (Lightfoot, xiii., 93, 96 ; Baillie, 121-22). The resolution as to the office of widows was voted on the 29th (the subsequent debate on 1st January being devoted to the Scripture proofs). Lightfoot was called to the city before this vote was taken, hence his *Journal* contains no reference to this important passage of arms which Baillie recounts.

However, that day, we being gone, the one partie pressing the debaite of the Apostles' power over congregations, the other sharplie declining, there fell in betwixt Goodwin and Burgess hotter words than were expected from Goodwin. Mr. Marshall composed all so well as he could. Men's humores, opinions, ingagements are so farr different that I am afraid for the issue. We doubt not to carrie all in the Assemblie and Parliament clearlie according to our mind ; but if we carie not the Independents with us, there will be ground laid for a verie troublesome schisme. Always it's our care to use our utmost endeavour to prevent that dangerous evil.[1]

Baillie's hopes and plannings were destined to speedy disappointment. The split with the Independents came swiftly enough. With such material of difference and strife it could not be averted though it actually declared itself in an unforeseen connection.

After its work on Church officers was concluded The Assembly as above related, the Assembly turned for a moment digresses to the subject of aimlessly back to add some particulars to its ordination. previous determinations as to the character and power of Apostles and Evangelists. And then, in spite of the wish of the Scotch to have on the question of the Presbyterian Church organisation, threw itself upon the consideration of ordination. The ensuing debate, which will be referred to more fully below,[2] held from the 2nd of January to the 2nd of February, 1643-44, and it was out of this question of ordination that grew the undesigned but inevitable split with the Independents concerning presbytery.

During the course of this debate on ordination, on the 19th of January, a formal report had been

---

[1] Baillie. ii., 122.   [2] *See infra.*, pp. 318-20.

made in the usual purposeless manner from the first committee concerning presbytery. The report was tentative merely and confined to proposing (1) that the Scripture holdeth out a presbytery in the Church ; (2) that a presbytery consists of ministers of the Word and such other public officers as the Assembly had already voted to have a share in the government of the Church.[1]

What notice was taken of such report does not appear, but at the following meeting[2] the chairman of what seems to have been the same committee[3] tendered a further report, the tenor of which was that there may be many congregations under one presbytery as in the Church at Jerusalem. The Independents were exceedingly opposed to the presentation of this proposition, and it cost an hour's sharp debate or more before the report was on the question admitted.[4]

Equally with its predecessor, however, this proposition lay for the time being unheeded, as did also the elaborate paper presented on 25th January by the Scotch Commissioners to the Treaty Committee, and from the latter to the Assembly concerning the Presbyterian Church system in Scotland

---

[1] Lightfoot, xiii., 115.

[2] Monday, 22nd January, 1643-44, *ibid.*, 116.

[3] The chairman of the committee that was chosen to consider of the presbytery (*ibid.*). This appears to have been simply the first of the three committees of the Assembly, the other two committees having similarly the work of jurisdiction and ordination respectively referred to them.

[4] On the 24th of January, the Commons ordered Mr. Rouse to hasten their resolutions concerning their settlement of the government of the Church (C. J., iii., 376). On the 16th of February following, an even more urgent vote was taken by the Lords (L. J., vi., 429-33).

and the fourfold system of assemblies—parochial, Сʜᴀᴘ. II.
classical, provincial and national.[1] The proposal 1644.
to refer this paper to the committee to which the
question of presbytery had been referred, was for
the moment lost on the opposition of the Independents.

The origin of these latter proceedings is thus
explained by Baillie :—[2]

> Being wearied with the length of their proceedings and
> foreseeing ane appearance of a breach with the Independents
> we used all the means we could while the weather was faire to
> put them to the spurrs. After privie conference with the
> special men [the leading Presbyterians of the Assembly], we
> moved in publick to have ane answer to our paper anent the
> officers of the Church and Assemblies thereof that we might
> give an account to our Church of our diligence. We were
> referred as we had contrived it to the Grand Committee to
> give in to it what further papers we thought meet which the
> Assemblie should take to their consideration. They [the
> Assemblie] were very earnest to have us present at their
> [three] committees, where all their propositions which the
> Assemblie debaited were framed. This we shifted as too burden-
> some and unfitting our place, but we thought it better to give
> in our papers to the Great Committee appointed to treat with
> us. So we are preparing for them the grounds of our
> Assemblies and Presbyteries. Also we wrote a common letter
> [dated 2nd January, 1643-44,] to the Commission of our Church
> desiring a letter from them to us for putting us to more speed
> in such termes as we might show it to the Assemblie.

When, however, towards the end of January The digres-
the Assembly found itself face to face with a dead- sion leads to
an incidental
lock, and that it could not decide the question of and prema-
ture re-
ordination by the London ministers until it had sumption of
the debate of
decided the precedent question of presbytery itself, Presbytery.

---

[1] Lightfoot, xiii., pp. 119-20. [2] *Letters*, ii., 131.

that question forced itself to the front, and had inevitably to be taken in hand once for all. As a result a mere side-issue had the effect of precipitating that collision between Presbyterian and Independent which the Scotch Commissioners had spent all their force in trying to avert.

On the 2nd of February the Assembly, by the urgency of Lord Saye, laid aside for the moment the question of the London ministers ordaining, and, in face of the opposition of the Independents, fell upon the above reported proposition that divers or many churches may be under one presbytery.[1] The scriptural examples in support of the proposition were brought in by the same committee on the 14th of February.[2]

The regular debate hereupon, which developed into the first great trial of strength between Independent and Presbyterian, began on Monday, 5th February, 1643-4, and for more than a month, until 14th March, the Assembly devoted itself to this theoretical, premature, merely declaratory debate of presbytery. The dispute ranged, not only over the question of representation of the separate churches in one presbytery, and the position of each of these in relation to that presbytery, but also as to the seat of jurisdictional power—the power of censure and excommunication, *viz.*, whether it lay with the particular congregation or the presbytery. After a fortnight's debate the negative opinions of the Independents were voted out, and the affirmative proposition ordered to be considered.[3]

Premature debate of Presbytery, Feb.-March, 1643-4.

---

[1] Lightfoot, 131; Gillespie, 9.   [2] *Ibid.*, 150.
[3] *Ibid.*, 170; Gillespie, 10-27.

On the 22nd Feb. it was voted that the number of believers mentioned in Acts i. 15 and other places belonged to the Church in Jerusalem as members of that Church,[1] and on the following day that the number of those believers in the Church in Jerusalem was more than could ordinarily meet in one place in one time in the exercise of worship and government.[2] To these votes were similarly added, on the 26th of February, that the many apostles and other preachers in the Church in Jerusalem import that there were many congregations :[3] on the 5th of March, that the elders of that Church are mentioned :[4] on the 7th, that the apostles did the ordinary acts of presbyters as presbyters in the Church of Jerusalem, and that this shall be brought to prove the Presbyterial government at Jerusalem :[5] on Wednesday, 13th March, that the instance of the Church of Jerusalem shall be brought to prove that many several congregations may be under one Presbyterial government.[6]

This point in the long drawn argument, however, was not reached without a certain amount of engineering. In his letter of 18th February, 1643-44, Baillie had asserted the wish of the Scotch Commissioners " againe to assay the Independents in a privie conference, if we can draw them to a reasonable accomodation, for that toleration they aim at we cannot consent ".[7] In a subsequent letter of 2nd April, 1644, and speaking of the debates prior to 22nd February, while still the Indepen-

---

[1] Lightfoot, 174.   [2] *Ibid.*, 181, 23rd February; Gillespie, 29.
[3] *Ibid.*, 182 ; *Ibid.*, 30-31.   [4] *Ibid.*, 195 ; *Ibid.*, 33-4.
[5] *Ibid.*, 203 ; *Ibid.*, 34-6.   [6] *Ibid.*, 214 ; *Ibid.*, 39-42.
[7] *Letters*, ii., 140.

Early
attempt at
accommoda-
tion with the
Independents
on the
subject of
Presbytery,
Feb., 1643-4.

dents held the field with their negative arguments against presbytery, Baillie gives some curious details of this attempt of the Scotchmen. He assigns no date to the meetings which he describes, but they must have taken place before the 22nd of February.

For to remeid these evills and satisfie the minds of all we thought meet to assay how far we could draw them in a private friendlie way of accomodation, but Satan, the father of discord, had well near crushed that motion in the very beginning. After our [the Scotch Commissioners] first meeting with some three [Presbyterians] of the Assemblie, Marshall, Palmer, Vines, and three of them [the Independents], Goodwin, Burroughs, Bridge, with my Lord Wharton, Sir Harie Vane, and the Solicitor in our house and very fair appearances of pretie agreement, Mr. Nye was like to spoil all our play. When it came to his turne in the Assemblie, he had from the 18th of Matthew drawn in a crooked informall way which he could never gett in a sillogesme the inconsistence of a Presbyterie with a civil state. In this he was cried down as impertinent. The day following when he saw the Assemblie full of the prime nobles and chief members of both Houses he did fall on that argument againe [then follows Baillie's description of Nye's discomfiture, of which Lightfoot gives an account under date 21st February, 1643-44, xiii., 169]. We had many consultations what to doe; at last we resolved to pursue it no further, onlie we would not meet with him except he acknowledged his fault. The Independents were resolved not to meet without him, and he resolute to recall nothing of the substance of that he had said. At last we were entreated by our friends to shuffle it over the best way might be and to goe on in our businesse. God that brings good out of evill made that miscarriage of Nye a means to doe him some good, for ever since we find him in all things the most accomodating man in the company.[1]

[1] *Letters*, ii., 145-46. On the 17th of February the Scotch Commissioners had drawn up a paper in which *inter al* referring to the order of the Commons to the Assembly to quicken their proceedings

Whether or not this incident interrupted the underhand workings of the Scotch Commissioners is not clear, but the subsequent attempts at accommodation between the Presbyterians and Independents appear to have been pursued if not to have originated in the Assembly itself. On the afternoon of Friday, 8th March, a committee was appointed for the purpose of accommodation, consisting of four Presbyterians[1] and four Independents.[2] Baillie adds to Lightfoot's account the assertion that this committee was to meet with a committee of four of the Scotch Commissioners "to see how far we could agree". He adds a pious ejaculation that his brother Scotch Commissioners were glad that what they were doing [contriving] in private should be thus authorised.[3]

The committee met several times, and agreed upon several propositions in which a presbytery was in substance granted by the Independents on prudential grounds of Church polity.[4] The further

Снар. II.

1644.

The Assembly takes up the project of an accommodation with the Independents, March, 1643-4.

(*supra*, p. 166, note 4), they desired the adoption of means thereto. The Lords and Commons made a merely conciliatory reply (L. J., vi., 460-61).

[1] Seaman, Vines, Palmer, Marshall.

[2] Goodwin, Bridge, Burroughs, Nye (Lightfoot, xiii., 206-7).

[3] *Letters*, ii., 147.

[4] Lightfoot, xiii., 214-15, 229 ; Baillie, ii., 147. The draft of the terms of an accommodation on the moot point of the relations between a classical presbytery, a congregational presbytery and a congregation was produced by Marshall at the first meeting of the new accommodation committee " as the results of our and their conference about accomodation before," 8th March, 1644. This interesting draft is preserved in Gillespie, 37. For alternative propositions offered to the committee on the following day by Mr. Vines, see *ibid.*, 38-9. Vines' propositions represented the minimum of Presbyterian concessions. The Independents' propositions which were handed in on the 13th, are preserved, *ibid.*, 40-1. Out of the three competing series five pro-

proceedings under this head were then again temporarily interrupted by the resumption of the question of ordination (see *infra*, p. 323).

By the 3rd of April, however, the Assembly had completed the doctrinal part of ordination, and had drawn its conclusions into the form of twelve propositions.[1] On numbers five and ten of these propositions there arose a fresh debate as to the word presbytery, and the nature of congregation, whether fixed or not. This led to a review of the votes already taken concerning presbytery, and on the afternoon of the 10th of April they were accordingly presented by the committee which had been appointed for the methodising of them, as follows :—

1. The Scripture doth hold out a Presbytery in a church (1 Tim. iv. 4 ; Acts xv. 2, 4, 6).

2. A Presbytery consisteth of ministers of the Word and such other public officers as are agreeable to and warranted by the Word of God to be church governors to join with the ministers in the government of the Church (Rom. xii. 7, 8 ; 1 Cor. xii. 26).

3. The Scripture holds forth that many congregations may be under one Presbyterial government. Proved by instance of the Church of Jerusalem [by arguments detailed].[2]

Upon the question, however, that those votes should then be transmitted to the Parliament a long agitation ensued, the Independents strongly opposing it. With a view to accommodation, therefore, the committee for methodising the above votes reported on the following day,

positions were agreed upon between the 13th and 19th of March, and provisionally reported to the Assembly on the latter day (*ibid*).

[1] Lightfoot, 237-38.   [2] *Ibid.*, 243.

Thursday, 11th April, proposing in a singularly inconclusive manner to insert the first two votes concerning presbytery into some proper place among the twelve propositions concerning ordination, and for the present to omit the third proposition concerning a presbytery over many congregations.[1] The report was disliked, and practically fell to the ground, and for two more days the Assembly discussed the fixity of congregations, resolving at last, on Monday, 15th April, "that fixedness or not fixedness of the congregations is indifferent as in point of government".[2] Well might Baillie write : "I cannot tell you what to say of the Assemblie. We are almost desperate to see anything concluded for a long time ; their way is woefully tedious. Nothing in any Assemblie that ever was in the world, except Trent, like to them in prolixities."[3]

On the following Wednesday, 17th April, Dr. Burgess reported a draft of the Assembly's votes concerning ordination and presbytery, drawn as ready to be presented to the two Houses.[4] After a hot debate they were ordered to be drawn up ready till the Parliament should call for them or the Assembly think fit to send them. When, however, on the 19th April, the Directory of Ordination was finally adopted by the Assembly it was decided to send up to the Parliament that Directory, together with the twelve propositions concerning the doctrinal part of ordination, and to

[1] Lightfoot, 244. [2] *Ibid.*, 247 ; Gillespie, 49-51.
[3] *Letters*, ii., 165, 12th April, 1644.
[4] Lightfoot, 249 ; Gillespie, 51-2.

CHAP. II.
1644.

Postpone-
ment of the
report to the
Parliament
on Presby-
tery.

lay aside for the present the draft votes concerning presbytery "as not yet to be sent into the two Houses".

We have given in to the Parliament our conclusions about ordination, whereupon we have spent, I think, about fortie long sessions. To prevent a present rupture with the Independents we were content not to give in our propositions of Presbyteries and congregations that we might not necessitate them to give in their remonstrance against our conclusions, which they are peremptor to doe when we come on that matter. We judged it also convenient to delay till we had gone through the whole matters of the Presbyteries and Synods to send them up rather in their full strength than by pieces; also [in this way] we suffered ourselves to be persuaded to eschew that rupture at this tyme when it were so dangerous for their bruckle state.[1]

The resolution, however, with regard to the non-forwarding of the votes to the parliament did not hinder the prosecution of the abstract debate of Presbytery which recommenced on 25th April, and from that date to the 10th of May, ranged over the vital questions of the power of congregations, the number of ruling elders in a congregation, and of the seat of the power of ordination whether in the congregation or in the Preaching Presbyter.[2] The decisive vote taken on the latter date, 10th May, that "no single congregation which may conveniently join together in an association may assume unto itself all and sole power of ordination," was carried by 27 to 19, and is to be regarded as one of the severest blows the Independents had yet received. Lightfoot notes in his diary that the business "had been managed with the most heat

[1] Baillie, *Letters*, ii., 169-70.
[2] Gillespie, 55-64; Lightfoot, 261-2.

and confusion of any thing that had happened

among us ".

Four days later the Committee for the Summary of Church Government made a report which diverted the Assembly to the question of Discipline or Jurisdiction,[1] a question which will be treated separately below. This diversion and the subsequent intrusion of the Directory for Worship had the effect of postponing for some months the consideration of the question of Presbytery.

In the middle of August, 1644, however, Warriston came up to London from Scotland bearing letters from the General Assembly there to the Assembly of Divines, designed to quicken the latter body. The letters were read in the Assembly on the 14th of that month[2] when Warriston particularly declared the passionate desires of the Scotch Parliament and Assembly and nation for the completion of the Church uniformity in accordance with the Solemn League and Covenant.[3] Immediately thereupon, 15th August, the Scotch Commissioners called a meeting of the Treaty Committee, and delivered into it a paper penned by Henderson concerning the evil of the delay in settling religion, and the earnest desire of the Scotchmen that some ways might be found out for expedition. Copies of the paper were taken to be presented to the Lords, Commons and Assembly respectively.[4]

This paper was read to the Lords on the 16th August, and is entered *in extenso* in the *Journals.*[5] In the Commons more note was taken of it. It

Intervention of the Scotch.

---

[1] Lightfoot, 262; Gillespie, 64.   [2] Lightfoot., 303.
[3] Baillie, ii., 220.   [4] *Ibid.*   [5] L. J., vi., 674.

was resolved that the Treaty Committee should inform the Scotch Commissioners of the progress made by the House in the matter of the ordinance for ordination, and further, that the said Committee should consider with the Scotch Commissioners how the whole Directory might be expedited.[1]

The reference here is probably to the Directory for Worship, and the compliance of the House was doubtless due to the timely need of propitiating the Scotch. "Also," says Baillie,[2] "we have the Grand Committee to meet on Monday [19th August], to find out ways of expeditione : and we have gotten it to be the work of the Assemblie itselfe to doe no other thing till they have found out wayes of accelerating ; so by God's help we expect a farr quicker progress than hitherto".

The recommendations on this head from the Grand or Treaty Committee were reported to the Assembly by Mr. Palmer on the following day, Tuesday, 20th August.[3]   The report was as follows :—

1. That the Assembly appoint a committee to draw up the Directory : which is already done.

2. A committee to join with the Commissioners of Scotland to draw up a Confession of Faith.

3. The Committee for the summary [of Presbytery or Church government], hasten their report about Church government.

4. The Assembly to return to the government.

5. Then to handle excommunication.

On items 3 and 4 no resolution was taken on the day of the presentation of this report, but some time before the 28th of August, the Assembly had

---

[1] C. J., iii., 593-94, 17th August.

[2] Baillie, ii., 221.   [3] Lightfoot, 305.

appointed to return to the question of government, CHAP. II.
and to hold to it till the conclusion of the erection   1644.
of sessions, presbyteries and synods.[1]

Accordingly, on the 4th of September, the
Assembly approached the debate on government,
and after some dispute, and acting apparently in
compliance with the wishes of the Scotchmen and
against the recommendation of the Treaty Committee drew up the preparatory question for discussion in the following form :—

Systematic debate of Presbytery begun Sept., 1644.

" It is lawful and agreeable to the word of God
that the Church be governed by several sorts of
Assemblies." [2] This proposition was under debate
on 6th September, and agreed to.[3] As the Assembly
had already discussed congregational and classical
Assemblies, it was thereupon agreed to debate first
of Synods.[4] This was accordingly done on the 13th
of September, on the proposition that " Synods are
one of these sorts of Assemblies whereby the
Church may be governed," but on the 16th of
September, the question was restated in the
following form : " The Scripture holds forth
another sort of Assemblies for the government of
the kirk beside classical and congregational, which
we call Synodical ".[5] The debate on this held
through the 16th and 17th and was voted on the
latter day,[6] when the succeeding proposition also
relating to the constitution of Synods, was propounded thus : " Synodical Assemblies are made

[1] Baillie, ii., 224.
[2] Gillespie, *Notes of the Debates and Proceedings of the Assembly of Divines*, p. 65 ; Lightfoot, **308.**
[3] *Ibid.*, 66-67 ; *Ibid.*, **309.**   [4] *Ibid., ibid.*
[5] Gillespie, **71-72.**   [6] *Ibid.*, **73** ; Lightfoot, **311-12.**

up of pastors and teachers and other Church governors". This last item of the enumeration represented the wishes of the Independents as against the Scotch and English Presbyterians. It was hotly debated during the 19th and 20th of September, and was only adopted on the latter day when qualified by the words, "when it shall be deemed expedient".[1] On the 23rd, therefore, the proposition was adopted in the following form: " Pastors and teachers and other Church governors as also other idoneous persons, where it shall be deemed convenient, are members of those Assemblies which we call Synodical, where they have a lawful call thereto ".[2]

The succeeding proposition was thereupon also ordered, " Synodical Assemblies may be of several sorts, as provincial, national and œcumenical ".[3] This was voted without much debate, but on the consequent question of the subordination of these Assemblies, of appeal, and of the seat of government in the Church, whether in the congregation or in the superior Assemblies, the old division of opinion again emerged. The debate on it raged hotly through four sessions, from 26th September to 1st October.[4] On the latter day the proposition was voted in these words: "It is lawful and agreeable to the word of God that there be a subordination of congregational, classical, provincial and national Assemblies for the government of the Church ".[5]

---

[1] Gillespie, 75-77 ; Lightfoot, 312-13.
[2] Gillespie, 78.   [3] *Ibid.*   [4] *Ibid.*, 78-84.
[5] The Scriptural proofs of the proposition were adopted on the following day (*ibid.*, 85-86; Lightfoot, 313-14).

The smooth and comparatively rapid progress made on these debatable topics can only be attributed to the drooping spirits of the Parliament in consequence of Essex's disaster in the West, though Baillie hints in one of his letters at something more.[1]

Two days before the vote of 25th October concerning suspension[2] was taken, the Lords, acting with a view to the propositions for peace which were then preparing, had deputed the Lord Admiral and the Earl of Pembroke to acquaint the Assembly that "in regard of the many divisions and distractions abroad, this House desires they would hasten the settling of the government of the Church".[3] The Lord Admiral reported on the following day, 24th October, that he had acquainted the Assembly of Divines with their Lordships' desires, "and they received the message with much joy, and will speedily set upon it".[4] On the same day the Commons sent to the Assembly, by Mr. Tate and Mr. Salway, for a report and despatch of the Directory and of anything else ready concerning Church affairs.[5] In consequence of this latter message,[6] which arrived on the 25th of October, the Assembly appointed a committee to methodise the votes already taken on the matter of Church government, ordering it to report on Thursday, 7th November.[7]

Scotch influence quickens the debate.

[1] 16th September, 1644. "We begin with Synods, and hope to make quicker despatch than before by God's help. We have sundry means of haste in agitation with our private friends" (*Letters*, 228).

[2] See *infra*, p. 249, under Discipline.   [3] L. J., vi., 31.

[4] *Ibid.*, 32.   [5] C. J., iii., 675; Whittaker's *Diary*, 327.

[6] The message of the Lords is strangely enough not mentioned in either Gillespie or Lightfoot's *Journals*.

[7] Lightfoot, 321; Gillespie, 96.

In the interim, the two Houses acting jointly, and under the excitation of a letter sent from Newcastle from the committee of the Estates of Scotland, which was forwarded to them on the 1st of November from the Committee for both Kingdoms, again sent on the 4th of November to the Assembly to request a return of how far they had proceeded concerning the government of the Church, "and speedily to send in what they have already prepared touching that matter, and to acquaint them that the Houses have received desires in letters from the committee of the Estates of Scotland to press an expedition in settling the affairs of the Church".[1] The repeated behests and appeals produced their effect in quickening the divines.

On the 8th of November Dr. Burgess read to the Assembly a draft of what they had finished in the preceding April concerning presbytery, with a view to its being sent to the Houses. The scribes compared the transcript with the original records, and the title "concerning some part of Church government" was adopted after some controversy.[2]

The part reported by Burgess pertained only to the presbytery, and was composed of such propositions as the Assembly had finished and had left lying by for report from the 10th to 18th of April, 1644.[3] After much tugging with the Inde-

---

[1] C. J., iii., 684-85; L. J., vii., 43, 45, 4th November, 1644. Baillie's exultation at the change of tone in the Parliament is discernible between the lines of his letter of 1st November to Spang (ii., 240).

[2] Lightfoot, 324.

[3] *Ibid.*, 243, 250; see *supra*, p. 172, and compare with the text of the humble advice itself (L. J., vii., 61).

pendents, who entered their dissent to the third
proposition,[1] *The humble advice of the Assembly*
of Divines . . . concerning some part of Church First Report
government was presented to the Commons on the on Presbytery
same day by Dr. Burgess.[2] It was ordered to be Assembly to
taken into consideration on the following Tuesday. the Parliament, 8th
On the 11th of November it was read in the Lords,[3] Nov., 1644.
and on the following day the House of Commons
took the propositions into consideration. At the
commencement of the debate Mr. Holland presented to the House the petition of the Dissenting
Brethren against the propositions concerning presbytery, desiring liberty to bring in their reasons of
dissent.[4] As the outcome of their debate, the
House requested the Assembly to state " what
those officers are that are intended in the second
proposition of their advice," and to present the
remainder of its votes concerning presbytery.

In reply to the latter request the Assembly
appointed a committee to draw up its votes on
presbytery, and two days later presented to the
Houses, on the 15th of November, its "humble
declaration" concerning those officers as above.[5]

On the 17th and 18th of November the House
proceeded in the consideration of one of the
propositions from the Assembly, *viz.*, that the
Scriptures hold forth a presbytery in the Church.[6]

[1] Lightfoot, 324.
[2] Friday, 8th November, 1644, C. J., iii., 691 ; L. J., vii., 51
Whittaker's *Diary*, 343.
[3] L. J., vii., 61.   [4] C. J., iii., 693 ; Lightfoot, 327.
[5] Lightfoot, 330 ; C. J., iii., 697 ; L. J., vii., 64, where the humble
declaration is entered in full.
[6] Whittaker's *Diary*, 348.

The debate was deferred, and until January the House was unable to return to the subject owing to the intrusion of the work of completing the Directory for Worship. (*See infra,* pp. 349-52).

On the 2nd of December the Lord Chancellor of Scotland made a speech in the Assembly touching the approaching meeting of the General Assembly of Scotland in the coming January, desiring with a view to it that the English Assembly would complete its work on Church government. The Assembly thereupon ordered the draft of its votes on Church government to be brought in on the following Thursday.[1] On the day prescribed the report of this draft of Church government was made,[2] and after being debated on 5th and 6th December, was voted on the 9th to be sent into the two Houses, some slight discussion being added on the following day on one of the sub-titles of the draft.[3] Accordingly, on the 11th December, the Assembly presented their draft to both the Houses as *The humble advice of the Assembly of Divines now sitting at Westminster concerning Church government.* In delivering it Dr. Burgess explained to the House of Lords that the Assembly having formerly brought up some papers [the first *humble advice* of 8th November], being three propositions concerning Church government, "they have now brought it up again in the same place [in the completed draft], where it is to be to co-here with other particulars".[4]

Second and full Report on Church government from the Assembly to the Parliament, 11th Dec., 1644.

---

[1] Lightfoot, 338 ; Mitchell, 12-13.
[2] Thursday, 5th December, Lightfoot, 339 ; Mitchell, 15.
[3] Mitchell, 17 ; Lightfoot, 339-41 ; Gillespie, 97.
[4] L. J., vii., 94 ; C. J., iii., 721.

The House of Commons ordered this second "*advice*" to be taken into consideration peremptorily on the succeeding Thursday, 19th December. Meanwhile, with a view to a full and deliberate debate, it requested the divines to send up all the remaining points of Church government. In reply to the request, Marshall informed the House,[1] on the 23rd of December, that all the material parts of Church government had been already reported to Parliament, and that there remained only the point of excommunication. In Baillie's sanguine expectation the end of this troublesome question was at last in sight.

We have (he says, writing on the 26th December), putt together all our votes of government, and sends them up to-morrow. The Independents have entered their dissents only to three propositions. "That in Ephesus was a classical Presbyterie; that there is a subordination of Assemblies; that a single congregation has not all and sole power of ordination." Their reasons against these three propositions we expect tomorrow. Against the end of next week we hope our committees will have answers ready to all they will say; and after all is sent up to the House by God's help we expect shortlie ane erection of Presbyteries and Synods here, for there appears a good forwardness to expede all things of that kind in both Houses since the taking of Newcastle.

Later, in the same letter, speaking of the literary labours of his fellow Scotch Commissioners, he again expresses this hopeful view :—

We have transmitted our answers to the Independents' reasons against our Presbyterie. They are well taken and now upon the press. We hope in the beginning of the next week to send up also our answer to their reasons against our Synods.

[1] C. J., ii., 730, 733, 20th and 23rd December, 1644.

CHAP. II.
1644-5.

We make no question but shortlie thereafter the Houses will pass an ordinance for the Government; what is behind, a good part will be ended and follow us to our General Assemblie; and all the rest, by all appearance, will be closed a month or two thereafter, for all men now inclines to a conclusion. God in his good Providence has made many things, especiallie the counsels of our enemies and retarders, to co-operate for His ends.[1]

The question of Presbytery debated in Parliament, January, 1645.

In view of this meeting of the General Assembly and Parliament, the Scotch Commissioners had, on the 1st of January, 1644-45, delivered in a paper to the Treaty Committee concerning giving an account to the Scottish Parliament and General Assembly of the proceedings of the English Parliament in the matter of Church government.[2] And with the fear of such an ordeal before their eyes, the Commons decided to take in hand immediately the question of Church government. On the 6th the House resolved that a presbytery consisting of ministers of the word and other public officers may be in a church. On the question being put whether the word congregational should be added to that resolution, it was resolved in the negative.[3]

[1] *Letters*, ii., 247-49.

[2] Mitchell, 24; C. J., iv., 7; L. J., vii., 122.

[3] C. J., iv., 11, 6th January, 1644-45. "It was resolved that of the three propositions concerning Church government sent from the Assembly we should join the first two together and make one of them, which was that a presbytery consisting of preaching ministers and other officers might be in a church; and that the two Scotch Commissioners who were this day to go to Scotland should inform the General Assembly there that we had passed that vote in the House; and for the third, that it was now in agitation" (Whittaker's *Diary*, 368). The entry in the *Journals* of the House of Commons is as follows: "The House of Commons, having received from the Hon. and Rev.

Still animated by this interested deference to the Scotch, the House resolved on the 14th of January, "that many particular congregations may be under one Presbyterial government," [1] and that this vote should be part of the ordinance [for Church government]. [2] On the following day a series of votes was adopted declaring pastors, doctors and teachers, elders and deacons to be officers of the Church, [3] and similarly eight days later (23rd January, 1644-45), to the following effect :—

Chap. II.
1644-5.

That there shall be fixed congregations.

That the ordinary way of dividing Christians into congregations is by the respective bounds of their dwellings.

That the minister and other Church officers in each

the Commissioners of the Church of Scotland a paper dated 1st January, 1644-45, wherein they desire to know what is done and what is in doing concerning uniformity of religion, returneth this answer :—

" That Episcopacy and the jurisdiction of it is by bill (which hath passed both Houses, and been presented to the king for his royal assent) taken away and abolished. The Book of Common Prayer and festival days, commonly called Holydays are by ordinance of Parliament taken away, and a Directory for Public Worship established by the same ordinance.

" Some propositions concerning Church government being presented to the House of Commons from the Assembly of Divines this one of great concernment that the Scripture doth hold forth 'that many particular congregations may be under one Presbyterial government,' is appointed to be debated in the said House upon the 6th day of this instant, January 1644-45 ".

" And the House of Commons hath by order sent to the Assembly of Divines recommending to their care the fitting of psalms to be sung in the congregations."

[1] " We passed proposition 3, about which there had been some dispute among the divines, with this alteration, leaving out the words 'that the Scripture doth hold forth,' and resolving it thus 'that many several congregations may be under one Presbyterial Government'" (Whittaker's *Diary*, 371).

[2] C. J., iv., 20. [3] *Ibid.*, 21.

particular congregation shall join in the government of the Church in such manner as shall be established by Parliament.

That these officers shall meet together at convenient and set times for the well ordering of the affairs of that congregation.

That many particular congregations shall be under one Presbyterial government.

That the Church shall be governed by congregational, classical and synodical Assemblies in such manner as shall be established by Parliament.

That synodical Assemblies shall consist both of provincial and national Assemblies.[1]

The completed votes of the Parliament on Presbytery prepared for the Treaty of Uxbridge.
On Monday, the 27th of January, 1644-45, Mr. Rouse carried up to the Lords the four substantial portions of these votes on Church government, *viz.*, concerning—

1. The officers in each particular congregation.

2. The government by particular congregations under one presbytery.

3. By congregational, classical and synodical Assemblies.

4. Synodical Assemblies to be provincial and national.

The Lords agreed to the votes on the same day,[2] and they were completed on the following day by the adoption by the Lords of the proposition concerning the geographical delimitation of congregations.[3] The speed with which such progress had been accomplished can only be explained by the necessity of presenting the votes concerning Church government to the king as a whole before the expiry of the twenty days limited for the Treaty of Uxbridge. It was with a view to the same object that the House desired the Assembly to hasten the finishing of Church government, and to

[1] C. J., iv., 28.   [2] L. J., vii., 158.

[3] C. J., iv., 33 ; L. J., vii., 159.

send in to the Parliament the remaining portions,[1]
the commissioners at Uxbridge having written
urgently for them. Under the influence of the same
stimulus too the Assembly passed and presented,
on the 4th of February, its advice concerning
excommunication and its advice for a directory
concerning admonition, excommunication, and
absolution (see *infra*, p. 257).[2]

It is not part of our purpose to tell the tale of
the abortive negotiations at Uxbridge on the subject of religion. The alterations which, in view
of these negotiations, the Parliament made in its
bill for the abolition of Episcopacy, and in these
propositions concerning Church government,[3] were
merely such as were necessitated by the Treaty of
Edinburgh, 19th November, 1643, between the
Parliament and the Scotch for uniformity of
Church government, a treaty which rendered the
inclusion of Ireland in the new Church system a
necessity.

The Treaty of Uxbridge fell to the ground, and
with it the bill which the Parliament had prepared
for the abolition of Episcopacy and the establishment of presbytery and the Directory. Thence-
forth the Parliament were left to establish its
Church system by its own act and authority.

From the middle of May, 1645, through most
of June, and into July, the Commons debated in
committee the business of the Church, *i.e.*, as to
the Directory and the putting into effect the votes
on government already agreed to by the erection

---

[1] 3rd February, C. J., iv., 40; L. J., vii., 169.
[2] C. J., iv., 41.   [3] *Ibid.*, 43, 44; L. J., vii., 179.

CHAP. II.

1645.

The work of the sub-committee of the House of Commons in preparing for the erection of Presbyteries.

of Presbyteries.[1]   For this purpose the committee of the House had appointed a sub-committee of its own members to draft proposals in conjunction with the divines and the Scotch.   The sub-committee appealed to the city ministers for their advice on the proposed Presbyterial organisation of London, and to the Assembly of Divines for some scheme applicable to the rest of the country. The city divines appear to have their draft of the classes of the London Province ready cut and dried.   But the problem of arranging such classes for the rest of the country was more difficult.

On the 26th of May a message was sent from the sub-committee to the Assembly requesting its advice concerning the constituting of congregational, classical, provincial and national elderships, with the object of drafting a scheme for dividing up the country into these various systems.[2]   An influential committee of the divines of the Assembly was appointed to prepare this matter with the assistance of the Scotch Commissioners.   It reported on the 29th of May,[3] proposing to establish provincial Synods coterminous with the various counties, together with sundry rules concerning the nomination of officers.   On the following day, 30th May, the first portion of this advice was taken up to the sub-committee of the House.[4] After perusal of the paper the sub-committee desired some addition concerning possible differences between the minister and people in the elections.[5]   The Assembly accordingly reconsi-

---

[1] C. J., iv., 180.   [2] Mitchell, 97.
[3] *Ibid.*, 98.   [4] *Ibid.*, 99.   [5] *Ibid.*, 2nd June.

dered their advice, and again presented it to the
sub-committee of the House on the 4th of June,
whereupon that body requested the Assembly to
draw a catalogue of sins which should justify
exclusion from the Sacrament. After being debated through four sessions, the requested catalogue was, on the 13th of June, ordered to be
carried up to the sub-committee.[1]

It is internally evident that Baillie's letter (ii.,
271-72) relates to this particular period, and that
it should be dated 3rd June, not 4th May. The
letter as usual throws much light on the interior
workings of the sub-committee of the Commons.

We have this fourteen dayes been upon our advyce to a sub-
committee of the House of Commons anent the execution of
our votes of government : for it is the work of that sub-committee to draw two ordinances, the one for the practice of the
directorie. . . . The other ordinance is for the erection of
Ecclesiastick Courts over the whole kingdom. For their help
herein they called the ministers of London to advyse them
for their city, and they sent to the Assemblie for their advyce
anent the rest of the kingdome. The city ministers have sent
them their unanimous advyce (for of 121 city ministers there
are not three Independents) for planting just after our Scotch
fashion an eldership in every congregation, of fourteen Presbyteries within the laws of communication, every one consisting
of ministers betwixt twelve and sixteen and as many ruling
elders ; and of a provinciall synod for London and ten miles
round about. The Assemblie have presented their advyce this
day. We went throw this forenoon session[2] unanimouslie
what concerns Provinciall and Nationall Assemblies, as yesterday what concerned Presbyteries and the days before Congrega-

[1] Mitchell, 103.

[2] 4th May was Sunday. There was no session of the Assembly
as usual from Friday, 2nd, till Monday, 5th May. The date of this
letter ought without question to be corrected as above.

tionall Elderships. They have concluded Provinciall Synods twice a year, Presbyteries once a moneth and Nationall Assemblies once a year, and after, every one of these as it shall be needfull. Herein the [geographical] greatness of this nation forces them to differ from us with our good lyking. Their Provinciall Assemblies cannot consist of all the ministers, but of so many delegat from every Presbyterie; for in sundrie of their provinces will be above 600 Churches which would make at least 1200 members in a Provinciall Synod: also their Nationall Assemblie is constitute of three ministers and two ruleing elders deputed not from every Presbyterie, but as it is in France and Holland from every Provinciall Synod, whereof there will be at least sixty. We shortlie expect an ordinance according to our advice and the execution presentlie upon the back of it.[1]

In another undated letter (which must be at least after 2nd June),[2] Baillie[3] again refers to the proceedings of the Assembly in reference to the Parliamentary sub-committee.

The condition of our Church affaires here is good. We are at a point with the government; and beginning to take the Confession of Faith and Catechise to our consideration. These eight dayes we have been on our advyce for the manner of choysing of elders in every congregation and division of the country into Presbyteries and Provinciall Synods. We hope now shortlie by God's help to see a Synod and fourteen Presbyteries in London and a session in every Church, just after the [Scotch] fashion.

On the 7th of July the debates of the sub-committee of the Commons were interrupted by the presentation of the completed draft of Church government from the Assembly. It is necessary for a moment to explain the genesis of this draft,

The completed draft of Presbyterian Church government presented from the Assembly to the Parliament 7th July, 1645, under the title *The humble advice concerning Church government.*

---

[1] Baillie, ii., 271-72, 4th May, 1645.
[2] See Mitchell, 99.   [3] Baillie, ii., 275.

which was something more than a duplication of CHAP. II.
the Assembly's advice to the sub-committee of the 1645.
House of Commons.

On the 1st of April, 1645,[1] propositions for the
supplement or completion of the votes concerning
Church government were reported to the Assembly
from two sources : (1) the committee for the supplement of government ; (2) the Assembly's committee. The Assembly proceeded to the debate of
the four propositions emanating from the former,
and by resolution passed the first of these, *viz.*,
that the congregation should be heard on its exceptions to a minister ordained to them. From the
10th to the 17th of April propositions two and
three were debated.[2] It was out of the latter
proposition concerning a member's renouncing his
membership that the debate upon the gathering
of churches arose, 18th April.[3] For a time this
put on one side the consideration of the perfection
or completion of the Assembly's work on Church
government, on which Dr. Staunton had made a
further report on the same day, 18th April.[4]

From the 23rd of April the Assembly, however,
returned to the consideration of Dr. Staunton's
propositions for the completion of the government.
The fourth proposition, concerning the power of
the civil magistrates in the suppressing of heresies,
was debated from the 1st to the 6th of May,[5] and
on the latter day was altered to the following
form : " The civil magistrate hath authority, and
it is his duty to provide that the Word of God be

[1] Mitchell, 75.   [2] *Ibid.*, 79.
[3] *Ibid.*, 82.   [4] *Ibid.*, 83.   [5] *Ibid.*, 87.

truly and duly preached, the sacraments rightly administered, Church government and discipline established and duly executed according to the Word of God ".[1]

On the same day the Assembly appointed a committee to methodise all its votes concerning Church government which had not yet been sent up to Parliament, and to consider what was wanting to the said votes,[2] thus anticipating by only a day an order of the Commons requesting them to hasten the despatch of the matters which concern the government of the Church.[3] On the 7th of May this committee reported various items concerning moderators of the assemblies, the election, etc., of ruling elders, and the summons issuing from these latter.[4] The discussions of these items occupied the Assembly through four sessions to the 15th of May. On the latter day[5] it was proposed to send up all the votes now drawn into the form of a "Draft of Government". Before this could be agreed to, however, differences arose as to the classical presbytery, which prolonged the debate to the 26th of May, when a message from the sub-committee of the Commons then sitting upon the question of the practical erection of Church government intervened (see *supra*, p. 188), and kept the Assembly, as already described, engaged till the second week in June.

Writing on the 17th of June, Baillie refers to this delay a little petulently.

---

[1] Mitchell, 89.   [2] *Ibid.*, 89.
[3] C. J., iv., 133, 7th May, 1645.
[4] Mitchell, 89.   [5] *Ibid.*, 95.

Since my last, 3rd June, there is by God's mercy a great CHAP. II. change of affaires here. Our progress in the Assemblie is but 1645. small. We fell in a labyrinth of a catalogue of sins for which people must be kept from the Sacrament and ministers be deposed. When we had spent many dayes upon this we found it was necessare to have ane [preface] and a general cause [? clause], whereby the Presbyteries and Synods behooved to be intrusted with many more cases than possibly could be enumerat, that yet it will be some dayes before the body of our Government goe up to the Houses.[1]

On the 16th of June, however, the draft of government was at last complete, with the exception of the preface, and was read and adopted by the Assembly,[2] and ordered to be sent up. Certain changes in the draft were reported and considered on the 20th of June,[3] and ordered to be carried up on a paper by themselves. Still later, on the 26th of June, the Assembly proceeded in the debate of the report of the committee for methodising of Church government.[4]

Little more progresse is made (writes Baillie, on the 1st of July), in Church affaires. The Assemblie has been forced to adjourne on fyve diverse occasions of fastings and thanksgiving lately every one whereof took from us almost two dayes. When we did sitt we had no reall controversie ; only petty debates for alteration of words and transposition of propositions in the whole Body of Government took up our time. Our luck will be very evill if once this week by God's help we doe not at last put out of our hands to the Houses all that we have to say of Government, the whole platforme there[of] really according to the practice of our Church.[5]

On the 30th of June the Assembly was engaged

[1] *Letters*, ii., 286.   [2] Mitchell, 104.
[3] *Ibid.*, 106.   [4] *Ibid.*, 107.
[5] *Letters*, ii., 291, 1st July, 1645.

in the consideration of the names of the ministers to be elected for the proposed classical system in London.[1] On the 3rd of July the draft was at length completed, and at last, after a further alteration on the following day, Friday, 4th July, was again voted to be sent up to the House on the following day.[2]

On Monday, 7th July, accordingly Mr. Marshall presented to the two Houses as *The humble advice of the Assembly of Divines concerning Church government,* together with the [Scriptural] proofs of several additional votes concerning Church government.[3] This paper is to be looked upon as incorporating the previous humble advice of December, 1644.

The debates in the Commons on the erection of the Presbyterian system.
Being now in possession both of the completed draft of government from the Assembly, and of the proceedings of its own sub-committee, the Commons at last, on the 11th July in Grand Committee, " proceeded in the debate of the directions of the congregational, classical, provincial and national Assemblies, according to a report made to us from a sub-committee ; London, Westminster, and the parishes adjacent being divided into twelve classes, which are to form one province ".[4]

Twelve days later Whittaker reported from the Grand Committee of the House the matter of Church government, and upon his report three resolutions were passed touching the manner of and qualification for election of elders for a

---

[1] *Letters*, ii., 108.   [2] *Ibid.,* 109.

[3] C. J., iv., 199 ; L. J., vii., 483.

[4] Whittaker's *Diary*, 439.

parochial and congregational eldership.[1] On the
same day the Lords sat down to the consideration of the Assembly's completed draft [*the humble advice*] concerning Church government, read it a second time, and referred it to a committee.[2] Proceeding with Whittaker's report, the Commons, on the 25th of July, 1645, completed their votes concerning the election of elders, and sent them up as an ordinance for the election of elders for the concurrence of the Lords.[3] They then appointed a committee to consider of persons fit to be a committee " to give directions for the choice of elders of congregational and classical presbyteries in the province of London, and to present the names to the House ". The said Commons Committee was further to prepare a letter to be sent from the Speaker to the respective Parliamentary Committees of the counties, requesting them to consider of and nominate certain persons, ministers and others, to be appointed by authority of Parliament, " who shall consider how the several counties respectively may be most conveniently divided into distinct classical presbyteries, and what ministers and others [*i.e.*, lay elders] are fit to be of each classis, and that they accordingly make such division and nomination of persons for each classical presbytery, which divisions and persons so named for every division shall be certified to the Parliament ".[4]

---

[1] C. J., iv., 215, 23rd July, 1645 ; Whittaker's *Diary*, 443. For Whittaker's position on this committee and for a characterisation of his MS. diary *see infra*, pp. 257-8.

[2] L. J., vii., 504. [3] C. J., iv., 218. [4] *Ibid.*

The House further empowered its committee to call in the assistance of divines of the Assembly or others for their assistance in the matter.

The ordinance concerning the electing of elders was read in the Lords on the 26th of July, 1645, and committed to a committee of the whole House.[1] On the 29th they made certain amendments. Six of the seven amendments the Commons promptly accepted, but the seventh, which exempted from the ordinance chapels belonging to Peers of the realm, they as promptly rejected.[2] Eventually, on the 19th of August, 1645, a compromise was agreed to on the point, and the ordinance accordingly passed both Houses on that day as *Directions for the Election of Elders.*[3]

The first Parliamentary ordinance for the erection of the Presbyterian government : the directions for the election of elders, 19th August, 1645.

After prescribing four rules concerning the manner of the election and the qualification of elders, the ordinance provides for the hearing and trial of all exceptions brought against any elder from the congregations by a body to be nominated by Parliament, with power to approve or remove him accordingly. It then provides that all parishes and places whatsoever, except Peers' chapels, shall be brought under the government of congregational, classical, provincial and national assemblies, and proceeds to depict the limits of the various classes which together should form the province of London. The Chapel of the Rolls, the two Serjeants' Inns, and the four Inns of Court, were constituted each a congregational presbytery and united into one classical presbytery. The parish churches of London, 137

---

[1] L. J., vii., 510.   [2] *Ibid.*, 515; C. J., iv., 224.
[3] L. J., vii., 543-44; C. J., iv., 242.

in number, were arranged in twelve other classes, and the whole thirteen classes constituted the province of London.

For the country at large the instructions already quoted for the choice of county committees to consider of the mapping out of the classical districts were repeated verbatim. For the universities the chancellors, vice-chancellors and heads were to consider and certify to Parliament concerning their arranging under classical presbyteries, "and the said several classes respectively being approved by Parliament, within their several precincts shall have power to constitute congregationall elderships where a competent number of persons so qualified for elders as aforesaid shall be found; and where no persons shall be found fit to be elders as aforesaid, then that congregation shall be immediately under the classical presbytery until the congregation shall be enabled with members fit to be elders". The congregational eldership was to meet once a week, the classis once a month, the provincial assembly twice a year (the first meeting to be determined by the aforesaid persons or committees appointed for the settling the various classical, etc., bounds). The national assembly to meet and sit as summoned by Parliament, and not otherwise, being constituted of two ministers and four elders from each provincial assembly (the provincial assemblies being similarly constituted of at least two ministers and four elders from each classis).

On the 17th of September, Mr. Whittaker reported from the Grand Committee on Religion, which had that day been engaged in the consider-

CHAP. II.

1645.

Measures proposed by Parliament for the execution of the ordinance, Sept.-Oct., 1645.

ation of the names of the tryers of elders [1] a letter to be sent to the standing Parliamentary Committees in the respective counties concerning the establishment of presbyteries in the counties. It was adopted, and ordered to be signed by the Speaker, and sent into the counties, together with printed copies of the ordinance and votes concerning the election of ruling elders. [2]

Six days later the Commons, vigorously following up their own ordinance, resolved on report from the Grand Committee for Religion, that a choice of elders within the province of London should be forthwith made. [3] In order to do this the Grand Committee proceeded energetically to consider the names of the tryers or judges of the elders to be elected in the province of London.

The names were reported on the 26th of September, were approved by the Commons on the same day, and by the Lords on the 29th. [4]

Finally on the 8th of October, 1645, the Commons likewise adopted from the Grand Committee for Religion the names of the tryers of elders for the two classes of the two Serjeants' Inns. [5]

In these ordinances the Parliament had at last outlined the new Church system for the nation. But the essence of Presbyterianism is discipline, the exercise of Church censure, and until the breath of that spirit had been breathed into the structure of the material fabric thus erected by the Long

---

[1] Whittaker's *Diary*, 464.   [2] C. J., iv., 276.
[3] *Ibid.*, 282, 23rd September, 1645.
[4] *Ibid.*, 288, L. J., vii., 607.   [5] C. J., iv., 300; L. J., vii., 637.

Parliament, it was impossible to put the scheme into execution. The professional clerical spirit, now thoroughly roused and self-conscious, would not contemplate the execution of the scheme until the point of jurisdiction had been assured to them, and although in the end that clerical spirit was doomed to a bitter disappointment, the play of such motive was strong enough to postpone the actual erection of the congregational and classical elderships from this date, October 1645, until July, 1646. The question of jurisdiction will be treated in the succeeding paragraph. Here it is only necessary to summarise the events of the intervening months up to the latter date, in so far as they bore upon the question of the erection of the Presbyterian system. When the Scotch Commissioners perceived what a difficulty would be made over the question of jurisdiction, they advised the divines to set up their presbyteries and synods for the present, with as much jurisdictional power as they could get, and after the system had been got to work, then to strive to obtain from the Parliament their full due power.[1] The Assembly, however, was of another mind, and in the end framed its peremptory petition, 7th August, 1645.[2]

It is strange that even in the midst of this crucial contest with the House, the Scotch Commissioners should have been expecting a speedy issue and an immediate erection of the presbyteries.

We expect this week (writes Baillie in August, 1645), that all over London elders and deacons shall be chosen for every congregation, and then in a week or two that the thirteen

Chap. II.

1645-6.

The erection of the Presbyterian system delayed by the action of the clergy.

---

[1] Baillie's _Letters_, ii., 307.   [2] _See infra_, p. 268.

Presbyteries and the Provinscall Synod within the lynes [of communication] shall be sett up, and so without delay in the other shyres, for orders are drawne allready for this effect.[1]

Two months later he is still, though less, hopeful :—

> Great wrestling have we for the erecting of our Presbyterie. It must be a Divine thing to which so much resistance is made by men of all sorts,[2] yet by God's help we will very speedelie see it sett up in spight of the devill. . . . Our greatest trouble for the time is from the Erastians in the House of Commons. They are at last content to erect Presbyteries and Synods in all the land and have given out their orders for that end; yet they give to the ecclesiastick courts so little power that the Assemblie finding their petitions not granted are in great doubt whether to sett up anything till by some powerfull petition of many thousand hands they obteine some more of their just desyres.

In a similar deluded spirit the House, on the 27th of October, 1645, ordered the Lord Mayor to inform the House what he had done on the order formerly sent to him from the Parliament concerning the election of elders.[3]

The dilatory action of the clergy supported by the city.

As it proved, the refusal by the Parliament of an unlimited jurisdiction to the eldership was for months an effectual and the only impediment in the way of the erection of presbyteries and synods. The ministers refused to accept of presbyteries with such limited jurisdiction,[4] and the lay spirit in London supported them. The action of the city, on the 20th of November, 1645, in supporting the petition of the London ministers complaining of

---

[1] *Letters*, ii., 307-8.
[2] Baillie, ii., 317-18, 14th October, 1645.
[3] C. J., iv., 324.
[4] Baillie, ii., 326, 25th November, 1645.

defects in the directions of the Parliament of 19th CHAP. II. August, and in the ordinance of 20th October, will 1645. be detailed in its own connection (*infra*, under Juris-diction). Certain portions of this petition, how-ever, concerned the mere machinery or framework of presbytery. The powers given to the tryers of the elections of elders were not explicit. The Chapel of the Rolls, the two Serjeants' Inns, and the four Inns of Court, although made a classis, were not included in the London province. There was as yet no ordinance plainly authorising and commanding the election of elders.[1]

From 28th November the Grand Committee of Some defects in the ordi- the House sat in consideration of the petition, nance of 19th turning its attention firstly to the powers of the August, 1645, remedied. tryers.[2] On the 5th of December it resolved that the Chapel of the Rolls, the Serjeants' Inns, and Inns of Court should be divided into two classes and form a province of themselves.[3] The Grand Committee was still engaged in the consideration of the remaining portions of this petition concern-ing scandal when, on the 16th of January, 1645-46, the Common Council of London presented its second petition to Parliament,[4] pressing for the settling of Church government and decrying a toleration. In this petition the Common Council inform the Houses that in the city elections of the preceding December, 1645, most of the city wards had petitioned their respective aldermen to move the Council for an address to Parliament for the

---

[1] L. J., vii., 714, 20th November, 1645.
[2] Whittaker, 490.
[3] *Ibid.*, 492 ; C. J., iv., 365.   [4] C. J., iv., 408.

speedy settling of Church government within the city. In proof of this the Council appended to their petition the representation of the ward of Farringdon Within at their wardmote.

To his account of this petition Baillie adds some significant words :—[1]

> There are but few of the city ministers about the first and secret wheeles of the businesse. I make it a part of my task to give them [the city ministers] weekly my best advyce and incouragement, and, blessed be God, with such successe hitherto that it is worth my stay here.

The usual intermediary between Baillie and the city ministers seems to have been Francis Roberts, minister of St. Augustine's, and Baillie's *Letters* contain frequent indications of his direct intervention and instigation.[2]

On the 12th of February, 1645-46, the Assembly adopted from its own committee a petition to the House pressing for the establishment of the classical presbyteries, with a view to carrying out the ordinance for ordination, "and that where there cannot at present be any presbyteries settled, the next presbytery adjoining may have power to ordain for those that want ".[3] The petition was presented to the Lords on the following day, and to the Commons on the 16th of February.[4] It was as a result of this representation that the Commons, on the 18th of February, passed its three resolutions authorising and commanding a choice of elders to

---

[1] *Letters*, ii., 336-37.

[2] See a particular instance in *Letters*, ii., 333, and *infra*, p. 292, under Presbyterian Discipline.

[3] Mitchell, 186.   [4] L. J., viii., 166 ; C. J., iv., 443.

be made forthwith through England and Wales,[1]
votes which were agreed to punctually by the
Lords three days later.[2] It is evident from Whit- The clergy
taker's report of this transaction that these three still dissatis-
fied with the
resolutions were not at first intended to stand Parliament's
ordinance.
alone.[3] They formed part of the draft ordinance
which was reported on the 18th of February
from the sub-committee to the Grand Committee
for Religion, the remainder of the ordinance dealing
with the provision for the election of Commissioners
of Appeals (*q.v.*, *infra*, pp. 285-288). The determination to separate the resolutions from the
remainder of the ordinance, and to issue them
separately, can only be explained by a supposition
that the House believed that the clergy waited
only for a direct and categorical ordinance, enabling
and commanding them to set up the Presbyterian
system, and that immediately on its passing they
would proceed to act upon it. The clerical spirit,
however, was as yet not sufficiently broken to
accept such a conclusion without a struggle.
Nothing was done upon the resolutions pending
the passing of the ordinance for scandal, and when
that ordinance, with its scheme of clerical commissioners, finally passed, on the 14th March, the
ministers folded their arms.

It mars us to set up anything (says Baillie).[4] Oft we
have been on the brink to sett up our Government, but Sattan
to this day has hindered us. The ministers and elders are not

[1] C. J., iv., 446.
[2] 20th February, 1645-46, L. J., viii. 178. Husband's *Ordinances*,
(folio) p. 809.
[3] Whittaker, 510.
[4] *Letters*, ii., 357, 6th March, 1645-46 ; ii., 360, 17th March.

willing to sett up and begin any action till they may have a law for some power to purpose; all former ordinances have been so intolerablie defective that they could not be accepted.

The ordinance of 14th March, 1645-46 (the *ordinance for Scandal*, see *infra*, p. 288), reproduces textually in its first three clauses the above-quoted three resolutions of 20th February.

1. Be it ordained that there be forthwith a choice made of elders throughout the kingdom of England and dominion of Wales in their respective parish churches and chapels.

2. Notice of the election to be given by the ministers in the public assembly the next Lord's day but one before.

3. Electors to be members of the congregation who have taken the National Covenant, being over age, and not servants.

It then proceeds to provide for the trial by the Tryers of exceptions against the elders nominated, for the exemption of the Houses of the King or of Peers of the Realm from the ordinance, for the inclusion of the Savoy in the eleventh classis of London, and for the establishment of the Inns of Courts, Serjeants' Inns, and Chapel of the Rolls as two classes separate from the London province. It finally provides that the meetings of the classes should be held monthly or oftener if need be, the classes being constituted of two elders or more, not exceeding four, and one minister from each congregational eldership. The remainder of the ordinance was concerned with the question of jurisdiction over scandals (see *infra*, pp. 288 *seq.*).[1]

For nearly three months the ordinance remained unacted upon, until the House had made some

[1] C. J., iv., 463.

slight concession on the question of jurisdiction,
and had consented, by way of accommodation, to
replace the courts of Commissioners of Appeals in *The London*
each county by a single Parliamentary Committee *clergy yield to the Parlia-*
of Appeal. The final ordinance for this accommo- *ment's delimitation*
dation passed the Upper House on the 5th of *of the Pres-*
June. With this concession the clerical spirit had *byterian sys-tem, June,*
perforce to rest content : and grudgingly and with *1646.*
an ill-grace it at last gave way and consented to
co-operate in setting up the Presbyterian system
thus elaborated and delimited by the Parliament.
Four days later the Commons issued an order
requiring the ministers in the parishes of the
Province of London, and the Classes of the Inns of
Court, forthwith to put in execution the ordinance
concerning Church government. The members of
the House for London and Westminster were likewise thereby ordered to send copies of the ordinance
to the several parishes, "and to take care that the
government may be speedily settled and put in
execution ".[1]

> For the matter of our Church (writes Baillie), with
> much adoe we gott the Provinciall Commissioners laid aside
> and soe resolve to act. The ministers of the Assemblie did
> meet with those of London and agreed upon a declaration for
> acting ; so the next week they purpose to set up. I pray God
> be with them.[2]

At last the Presbyterian machinery, which had
been so long in forging, was to be set in work.

---

[1] C. J., iv., 569, 9th June, 1646.
[2] *Letters*, ii., 377, 26th June, 1646.

§ III.—*Presbyterian Discipline or the Spiritual Jurisdiction of the Eldership.*

The origin of the idea of Consistorial discipline in the Reformed Churches.

In the Reformed Churches, those, *i.e.*, of Switzerland, France, the Netherlands and Scotland, the codified system of internal spiritual government came to be known by the name *Discipline*. At first glance it might seem that this discipline occupied for those churches the place which the Canon Law occupied for the Church of Rome, and the inference might be drawn therefrom that the one institution derived from the other. Neither opinion is more than half true, if so much. The word itself does indeed occur in the *Decretum* of Gratian, and the phrase " ecclesiastical discipline " was evidently in use among the Canon jurists,[1] but only as applied to the actual administrative rule of the bishop over his diocese. He is to rule his clergy by love rather than by blows.

Discipline in the Roman Canon Law

But of the specialised consistorial discipline of the Reformed Church the Canon Law of the Church of Rome knew nothing. In the first place the Canon Law was a more or less complete body of jurisdiction, dealing with persons and things, grandly organised, standing side by side with and in a sense competing with the Civil Law of the various European nationalities. In the second place, of any special regulation for the safeguarding of the Sacrament the Roman Church was careless. They who partook of the Sacrament

---

[1] *Decretum*, part i., Distinctio xlv., chap. 9. For the phrase *ecclesiastica disciplina*, see Lyndwood, p. 352, referring to the Sext. 1, tit. vi., and Clementines 1, tit. iii., cap. iv.

unworthily, partook of it to their own damnation. No grace came to them thereby. Such unworthy partaking did not defile the Sacrament, it only increased the perdition of the partaker. And there the Roman Church left the matter.[1] Theoretically, communion was as much the duty of all in the Christian Commonwealth, good and bad alike, as the partaking of the Passover had been the duty of the whole Jewish community, good and bad alike.

The sentence of excommunication in the Canon Law stood simply for any equivalent form of outlawry in the Common Law, and its application was as wide and as diverse. Whoever broke the peace of the king or kingdom, or delayed justice, whoever as an advocate offered malicious exceptions in matrimonial causes, was to be excommunicated, and so on *ad infinitum*.

On the other hand, the consistorial discipline of the Reformed Churches had none of this civil and multifarious character. It was special, purely spiritual in its import, and restricted as to its intention to the safeguarding of the Sacrament and to a censorship of morals.

How did these Churches come by this idea of discipline? The answer springs readily to the lips—from the genius of Calvin. But there is both truth and untruth in such an answer. The question requires much more painstaking investigation than it has yet received. Very briefly the course of the development of this institution may be summed up thus: (1) Everywhere the Reforma-

Discipline in the Reformed Churches.

---

[1] *Decretum*, iii., Dist., ii., chaps. 24, 25, 65-68.

tion had a *moral* purpose, and all the reformed states with varying degrees of certainty and clearness seized upon the idea of excommunication as an engine against immorality. (2) This engine was appropriated to itself by the state or civil power, which everywhere unhesitatingly assumed the undivided heritage of the Papal power and of the Canon Law. (3) It was Calvin who vindicated or usurped this machine of excommunication as the possession of the Church. He led the revolt of the Reformation Church against the Reformation State.

The juridical reorganisation of the Reformed Church.   The sweeping away of the ecclesiastical and juridical organisation of the Catholic Church left a gap. Everywhere the temporal power stepped into the gap, and the old structure was replaced by an ecclesiastical and juridical organisation at the bidding, and under the auspices of, that temporal or civil power. It was so, for instance, in the In Saxony. home of the Reformation. In Saxony the old ecclesiastical jurisdiction of the Catholic bishops was transferred to the Consistories which became patterns for the rest of Protestant Germany. These consistories or courts owed their origin entirely to the civil power, and throughout the sixteenth century they were completely dependent upon it. In 1537 the Standing Committee of the Estates at Torgau proposed to the elector the erection of four Consistories. The proposition was submitted by the elector to a committee of four theologians, Justus Jonas, Cruciger, Bugenhagen and Melancthon, and two jurists. In their report thereupon this committee sanctioned the idea of

the erection of four Consistories for the electoral
dominions, with competence over all cases which
had previously appertained to the ecclesiastical
jurisdiction under the Catholic regime, and with
power to inflict excommunication, corporal punishment or monetary fines. The jurisdiction of the
courts was to be directed especially to : (1) false
doctrine (with appeal to the Elector and the
Elector's court) ; (2) immorality and usury ; (3)
violence to parents and to spiritual persons ; (4)
blasphemy ; (5) neglect or disturbance of divine
service ; (6) witchcraft.[1]

The mere history of the erection of these Consistories in accordance with this report lies outside
our subject. It may be noted, however, that the
committee of divines and jurists had proposed a
single judge for the consistories, but that the
form actually adopted was that of a college or
commission—in close imitation of the temporal
or political administration. The first Consistory,
which was erected at Wittenberg, comprised four
assessors, two jurists and two theologians. The
others were erected at different later times, and
with occasionally slightly varying constitutions.

In the Saxony churches, therefore, the Consistories, together with the Superintendent who
exercised the function of visitation, represented
the juridical and administrative reorganisation of
the Church.

In the case of the Swiss churches there was In Switzerland.

[1] Dr. George Müller, " Verfassung und Verwaltungsgeschichte der
Sächsichen Landeskirche," vol. ix. of the *Beiträge zur Sächsichen
Kirchengeschichte*, Leipzig, 1894.

every reason why that reorganisation should take a different form. The Swiss Republics were small —simply towns or unions of towns—so small that a large and elaborate territorial organisation was not necessary, and so small again that the town Council, in each case having to deal with a small area and with citizens directly and daily under its own eye, felt no difficulty in the assumption of a mixed authority—spiritual as well as temporal. At Zurich in 1521 the council published an edict enjoining preachers to preach only according to the Word of God. The town council of Berne and Bâle did the same two and three years later (1523, 1524), as did also the Council of 300 at Geneva in June, 1532, *i.e.*, before the arrival of Farel in the town, before the adoption of the Reformation, and before the rejection of the authority of the Bishop of Geneva—showing the universal assumption by these states of authority over the organisation of the Church.

Complete assumption of ecclesiastical powers by the Civil State.

But more than this, in Switzerland as elsewhere, the Reformation was intimately connected with a determined censorship of morals. One of the first results of the adoption of the new faith or law was the appointment of a Consistory, or some form of consistorial authority, to watch over the public morals. It was so at Berne in 1528, *i.e.*, thirteen years before a Consistory was adopted at Geneva. Bâle declared for the Reformation in 1529, and in the following year the council declared that those should be excluded from the Sacrament of the Lord's Supper who were designated by the councils of the parishes as impenitent sinners.

The exercise of this power, directly over the organisation and doctrine of the Church, and indirectly (through the appointment of the Consistory and the supervision of its proceedings) over the moral life of the people, was purely and solely an attribute of the civil state. Not only was it assumed as such by the town council without any trace of hesitation, it was not even disputed by the theologians. Œcolampadius was alone among them—*i.e.*, in the days before the advent of Calvin —in desiring to initiate the exercise of excommunication as a theological function. Zwingli did not wish to hear speak of it, opining that faithful magistrates constituted a sufficient protection for the Church. More explicitly still Bullinger declared [1] "excommunication does not enter into the attributes of the Church. It is a function of the Christian state"—meaning the civil state.

In a more detailed and interesting way still the same is demonstrable of Geneva. For 400 or 500 years before the Reformation, Geneva had been an estate of Holy Church; its prince was the Bishop of Geneva, formerly as unchecked in his authority in the town as any German Prince bishop. One of the bishops created a precedent; he granted the little town a charter of liberties, and henceforth Geneva was a little Republic, with its tiny town council [of 50 (subsequently the council of 60)] supplemented by a larger council [of 300], and a popular assembly occasionally summoned—all working under the shadow, the

Particularly in Geneva.

---

[1] Letter to Leo Juda in 1532. Roget, *L'Etat et l'Eglise à Genève*, p. 19. Hottinger, *Geschichte Zurich*, i., 3.

temporal as well as the ecclesiastical rule, of a bishop imposed on them by the Pope. So long as the bishops were patriotic there was harmony, but from the time when they lent themselves to the designs of the neighbouring house of Savoy against the town, the hour of revolution and therein also of Reformation had sounded for Geneva.

From the moment of the declaration of the Reformation in Geneva—and in a less degree for the few years antecedent, during which the authority of the bishop had been gradually set aside—the magistracy of Geneva (the syndics and the councils) had put itself purely and simply into the bishop's vacant place. The civil power of the State was substituted for that of the ecclesiastical overlord. The Council organised the great religious dispute in June, 1535, and constituted itself the sole judge thereof. It interdicted the Mass and disposed of the goods of the Church. It imposed penalties on libertinage and made the attendance on Divine service obligatory under a penalty. In January, 1537, it approved the Confession of Faith drawn up by Farel and Calvin; it decided upon the method of the celebration of the Lord's Supper and baptism; it assumed to itself the right of pronouncing in matrimonial causes after having consulted the divines; it prohibited the celebration of feasts or holy days. Practically, one may say, that before the arrival of Calvin in Geneva the main outlines of the ecclesiastical reorganisation had been laid down, and that by the civil power—the *Petit Conseil* had stepped into the place of the bishop and had assumed his jurisdiction.

From the point of view, therefore, of the historical progress of the Swiss Reformation, Calvin is not the inventor of the idea of discipline. His law-giving and formulating influence belong to a second and later phase of that history—the phase and period in which the right to and exercise of that discipline was in dispute between the civil and the religious power.

In another direction also, *viz.*, literary, the credit of origination and formulation is still less his. Fifteen years before the publication of the first edition of Calvin's *Christianæ religionis Institutio*, Melancthon had attempted in his *Loci Communes rerum theologicarum seu hypotyposes theologicæ* a formulation of the theological position of the Protestant movement. Melancthon's work had grown out of his lectures on the Epistle to the Romans [1] in the summer and winter of 1520. In its first tiny form the work is more philosophical than either theological or juridical, but it distinctly anticipated some of the features of Calvin's later work. In the twenty-second paragraph, *de participatione mensæ Domini*, he stumbled upon that very verse in the eighteenth chapter of Matthew which was to become the grand basis of the Presbyterian system. "The keys," he says, "belong to all, not to one. But expediency demanded some

---

[1] For the history of this work see the introduction to Plitt and Kolde's edition of it; Krafft's *Briefe und Dokumente aus der Zeit der Reformation;* Melancthon's letter to Hess (*Corp. Reformat.*, i., 158; xi., 49); and Schwarz, *Melancthon's Entwurf zu den Hypotyposen*, in "Theolog. Studien und Kritiken," p. 75, 1855.

CHAP. II. form of deputation or procuration which should place the ecclesiastical administration in the hands of skilled persons."

Four years after the appearance of Melancthon's *Loci*, Zwingli published at Zurich his *Commentarius de Vera et Falsa Religione*, 1525, and some years later, but still before the date of the first edition of Calvin's *Institutes*, William Farel had issued his *short and summary declaration*.[1] In method and matter both these works resemble Melancthon's and anticipate Calvin's. In a preliminary way, and with much of disorder and illogicality of arrangement, they are attempts at an *Institutio*—a book of principles of the reformed religion, partly theological, partly philosophical, partly juridical.

That Calvin knew of these works can hardly be doubted. How far he was influenced by them is a question.

Advance in Calvin's theocratic position between 1536 and 1559.

The first edition of Calvin's *Institutio* was published at Bâle in 1536. Three editions followed at Strassburg, 1539, 1543, 1545, and three others at Geneva, 1550, 1553 and 1554. The last Latin edition which was not subject to further alteration was that of 1559 at Geneva, which formed the basis of the French translation of 1560, Geneva.

Now, the noticeable feature of this work is that in its earliest seven editions it contains neither

[1] *Summaire briefve declaration daucuns lieux fort necessaires a ung chascun Chrestien pour mettre sa confiance en Dieu et ayder son prochain. Item ung traicte de Purgatoire nouvellement adjouste sur la fin.* Printed at Serrières, near Neufchâtel, some time before 1535.

draft of Church discipline, after the consistorial pattern, nor draft of Church organisation, after the pattern of primitive times. It is only in the 1559 edition that Calvin expounds both, and thereby became the law-giver of presbytery.

What is it that bridges over the gulf between those editions—between the literary standpoint of Calvin in 1536 and in 1559? Simply the events of his life in Geneva—his continual struggle with the civil power of the little State. When Calvin first arrived in Geneva, in the latter half of 1536, he was preoccupied with only one thing—the excesses of the Church of Rome and her representatives. Accordingly in that part of the sixth or last chapter of the 1536 *Institutio*, in which he treats *de Potestate ecclesiastica*, he hardly raises the fringe of the question of the internal organisation of the Church. It does not enter his thoughts. He is concerned only with a precise vindication of the rights of the civil magistrate. Exactly similar was the attitude of Melancthon in his *Loci* fifteen years before. "Concerning ecclesiastical rulers," says Melancthon in the twenty-fourth *locus de magistratibus*, "thus we think—firstly, bishops are ministers or servants. They are not a power (*potestas*) or a magistracy, therefore they have not the right of making laws."

The steps by which Calvin passed from such a position to that of the law-giver of a theocracy in conflict with the civil power could only be adequately explained at great length. The ordinarily accepted account of the struggle between him and the civil power in Geneva is very wide of the truth.

Explicable by Calvin's experience in Geneva, 1536-1559.

From 1538 to 1541 Calvin was in exile from the town. He returned on the 10th of September of the latter year, and three days later presented himself before the Council with a demand for measures to be taken for the ordering of the Church. The Council appointed a commission, and the propositions of this body were definitely accepted in November by the Council of 300 and the General Assembly. Thereupon the Consistory was immediately installed, and from December, 1541, proceeded to act.

Nature of the Consistory established in Geneva, 1541.

The only purpose of the Consistory was the regulation of manners. Its only weapon was admonition. It had no jurisdiction over doctrine —that was not so much reserved to the council as considered to be inherent in it of simple right and course. The majority of the members of the Consistory were laymen. Calvin was only a member, he never presided. The Consistory had neither right nor power to exclude from the Sacrament. Its only function was to admonish, and thereupon report to the Council, and the magistracy would thereupon proceed to judge and punish. This the Council of Geneva laid down in most categorical terms in March, 1543. A month before, the magistracy of Berne had, with equal decisiveness, refused the right of excommunication to the ministers of Lausanne.

The Consistory claims the function of excommunication.

It was upon this ground that the contest developed itself between Calvin and the Genevan State. The reformer was determined to vindicate for the Church the complete right of administration of the sacraments. The contest lasted twelve years, and was in the end decided in Calvin's favour only by a, for him, fortunate accident. In the first place, the ministers demanded, in March, 1547, that the delinquents who had been tried by the Council on the presentation of the Consistory should be sent back to the Consistory. The Council compromised by allowing it in the case of the impenitent, "but as for the repentant, they shall be let depart in peace".[1]

In September of the following year, 1548, the Council laid down emphatically that the Consistory had only the power of admonition and not of excommunication, and thereupon ordered that a certain Guichard Roux should be admitted to the Sacrament. It made a similar order as late as January, 1552. It was not until September of the following year, 1553, that the ministers at last openly revolted, and the struggle came to a head. They refused the Sacrament to Berthelier, although he had the regular authorisation of the Council for his admission. Berthelier appealed to the Council. That body, after hearing Calvin, declared again that Berthelier should be admitted to communicate. Calvin declared that he would rather die than submit. On its side the Council was as definite and obstinate. It expressly reiterated its right to order the administration of the Sacrament to whomever it pleased. It added a further resolution, some days later, to the effect that persons punished or reprimanded by itself were dispensed with from being again brought before the Consistory, and that when a resolution had been taken

---

[1] Roget, *L'Eglise et l'Etat à Genève*, p. 41.

in the Council for the admission of anybody to the Lord's Supper, it ought to be put in force *instanter* without any further resort to the Consistory.

As one man the Consistory and the ministers revolted against the Council. The larger Council of 300 were assembled. It ranged itself on the side of the smaller Council. To avoid an open rupture the latter body thereupon consented to submit the question to the Swiss Churches. That opinion was obtained, but naturally threw no light on the question, and the quarrel dragged its length through 1554. It was only decided in the following year, 1555, in Calvin's favour by the influence of the new burgesses—the French refugees who were thronging in crowds to Geneva, and whose admission to the rights of burgesses was only settled in May of that year, after an almost revolutionary strife.

The claim conceded by the State, and Consistorial Discipline thereby established, 1555.

From 1555 the Consistory remained in uncontested possession of the right of administering or refusing the Sacrament. It had carried the mere point of excommunication.

There remained the further question of the penal sanction for this new jurisdiction. A year later, in June, 1556, the Consistory proposed that such members as wilfully separated from the Church should be chased from the city. The Council again resisted, and it was only in June, 1557, that it consented to a more mitigated penalty —persons debarred from the Sacrament and remaining impenitent for a year were to be exiled from the city for a twelvemonth. Practically further than this Calvin did not in his lifetime go.

We are thus carried to within little more than a year of the date of the final Latin edition of the *Institutio*, in the fourth book of which Calvin laid down the bases at once of Presbytery (see chapter iii., *Of the Ministers of the Church*) and of Discipline (chapter xi., *Of the Jurisdiction of the Church*, and chapter xii., *Of the Discipline of the Church*).

The mantle of Calvin's Presbytery and Discipline fell first upon the Reformed Churches of France. In May, 1559—the very year of the last Latin edition of the *Institutio*—the first national Synod of the Reformed Churches of France met at Paris. Three ministers went from Geneva to it, and Calvin's correspondence at the time shows the painful interest he took in it.[1]

The Synod adopted a Confession of Faith and a form or scheme of Discipline, which has been preserved. This Discipline provided for the representation of the separate churches in the " colloques or synodes by a delegated minister or elder for each, and for a consistory or senate in each church, composed of ministers, elders and deacons, for the judgment of scandals and other like things ".[2]

All the subsequent national Synods concerned themselves with the redaction of this Discipline, but practically the principles of a Presbyterian system and of a disciplinary code were outlined so clearly in this first Synod that very little or no

---

[1] *Histoire ecclésiastique des églises réformées au royaume de France*, Baum and Cunitz's edition, i., 201, 215; Aymon, *Actes ecclésiastiques*, etc., i. 98 ; Quick, *Synodicon*, i., pp. xvi., and 3.

[2] See Ch. L. Frossard, *Etude sur la discipline ecclésiastique des églises réformées de France*, in " Bulletin de la Société de l'histoire du Protestantisme Francais," 1886.

CHAP. II.

And in the Netherlands, 1568.

And in Scotland, 1560.

development of principle is needed to carry us to the standpoint of the French Churches in the middle of the seventeenth century, when the question of presbytery came to agitate the English State. In the Low Countries the French refugees carried with them this twofold inheritance of presbytery and discipline. As early as 1560 the Walloon Churches met in synod at Tournay. In 1563 their first regular synod was held at Oudenarde. The first convention or synod of which record has survived, was held at Wezel in November, 1568.[1] It treated of Church organisation, presbyters, and discipline. The succeeding synod at Emden, October, 1571, subscribed the confession of faith of the French Churches, elected representatives to attend the next French synod, and sketched a distribution of the Netherland and Rhine Churches into eight classical organisations.

Besides the republication of their Discipline, in the most heated times of the Church disputes of the Civil War period, these Netherland Churches were constantly in touch during the years 1643-47 with the Presbyterian party in the Assembly of Divines, as appears both from the Assembly's "minutes" and, more explicitly, from Baillie's *Letters*.

To turn to Scotland. Knox returned to Scotland in June, 1559, after having been for some

[1] F. L. Rutgers, *Acta van de Nederlandsche Synoden der Zestiende eeuw.*, Utrecht, 1889. B. van Meer, *De Synode te Emden.* See also *Règlemens du Synode des églises Wallonnes des provinces unies des Pays-Bas*, 1705. *Règlemens généraux et particuliers a l'usage des églises wallonnes du royaume des Pays-Bas*, 1847.

time at Geneva Calvin's intimate friend. He resided in St. Andrews from November, 1559, to April, 1560. It was doubtless due to his influence that the canons of the church of St. Andrews declared for the Reformation, and established the Consistory or Kirk Session there as early as July, 1559—one month after his return. From the 25th of July, 1559, the Kirk Session of this particular church was formally constituted of ministers and elders. Its records are preserved.[1] Knox's individual influence, therefore, had effected an entry for the Discipline before it had even been brought before the reforming parliament. It was not until 1560 that the Convention adopted the Confession of Faith, and not until January, 1561, that the *First Book of Discipline*, which had been composed by Knox and five other reformers, was ratified by the Secret Council.[2]

The seventh head of this first *Discipline* treats of ecclesiastical discipline, which consists in the reproving of faults which the civil sword neglects or is unable to punish. "Blasphemy, adultery, murder, perjury, pertain to the civil sword, being worthy of death. But drunkenness, excess, fornication, oppression of the poor, deceit, wantonness, pertain to the Church of God, to punish in accordance to the Word." The *Discipline* then proceeds to lay down the manner, firstly of admonition, and then of excommunication, for private and public offenders.

Marginal notes:

CHAP. II.

The *First Book of Discipline*.

---

[1] Scottish History Society, vols. iv., vii.
[2] It is printed in its draft form and with the marginal notes of the Lords of Secret Session upon it in Knox's *Works*, ii., 185.

As to presbytery, the essentials of it are contained in the eighth head of the *Discipline*, " of the election of elders and deacons," in the provision for the yearly election of elders in each church, and for the exercise of their jurisdiction as a Consistory.

Further than this the first *Discipline* did not go in the matter of the organisation of pure presbytery. What it did for the higher ranges of the organisation was to propose the appointment of ten or twelve superintendents, successors in some sort to the bishops, with power to plant churches and visit them, and to set order and to appoint ministers. The Consistory of the superintendents' church might have developed into a classical presbytery, but in reality such a development was never in question. Only five superintendents were ever actually nominated, and the institution served merely as a lever for the designs of King James against unalloyed presbytery.

The first step towards the organisation of classical presbyteries and provincial synods—the higher ranges of the Presbyterian system—was taken by the Assembly of 1576, which ordered the restoration of the Exercises formerly appointed by the first *Discipline* to meet at particular centres or towns. Five years later the General Assembly at Glasgow, April, 1581, ordered the erection of presbyteries at Edinburgh and twelve other places to serve as examples for the rest.

The *Second Book of Discipline*. Concurrently with this development—or slightly before, *viz.*, in July, 1580—the *Second Book of Discipline* received the sanction of the Church. In the seventh chapter this *Discipline* treats of elderships, assemblies and discipline, specifying four kinds of assemblies, particular, provincial, national, and œcumenical, *i.e.*, the classical presbytery is not yet either expressed or existent.

Apart from this change, however, the difference between the *First* and *Second Book of Discipline* is rather one of spirit—of Melville's spirit as contrasted with Knox's, of the hierarchical as opposed to the democratic; the rights of the eldership were strengthened as against those of the congregation, and the assertion was explicitly made that it was the duty of the magistrate to enforce the decisions of the ecclesiastical courts by civil penalties. For the discipline itself, it was claimed to be enjoined by Scripture, and to be in accordance with the Primitive Church and of perpetual authority— implying a claim of *jus divinum* for the discipline itself, if not for the presbytery.

I am here concerned only with the origin and nature, or ground plan, of the Scottish Presbytery. With its chequered history up to the National Covenant of 1637 I have nothing to do.

The Reformation in England had not so immediate and drastic an effect on the spiritual courts as it had in Upper and Lower Germany. The renunciation of the Papal supremacy led to the ascription of juridical authority to the king. For appeals to the Pope were substituted appeals to the King in Chancery, *i.e.*, to the Court of Delegates, constituted the supreme tribunal of appeal in ecclesiastical causes by 25 Henry VIII., c. 19.

The English Reformation and its juridical reconstruction of the ecclesiastical organisation.

As for the Canon Law itself, the provision for the revision of it was not acted upon in the reign of Henry VIII. Under Edward VI. three several commissions were issued for it, under the Act 3 & 4 Edward VI., c. 11, and the work was actually accomplished, mainly by Cranmer and Peter Martyr. The *Reformatio Legum Ecclesiasticarum*, in which their labours were embodied, was not confirmed by either Edward VI. or Elizabeth, and therefore never became law. As, therefore, by the last section of the Act of 25 Henry VIII., c. 19, the provision was made that until the revision of the Canon Law was complete all the existing canons and constitutions, not repugnant to the law or the royal prerogative, should still stand and be executed, the only inference can be that on the failure of the project of revision the old Canon Law remained in force. In actual practice, however, the Canon Law was discredited in three ways :—

1. By direct inroads made upon it by Statute Law.
2. By the cessation of the study of the Canon Law.
3. By the wholesale opprobrium cast upon it under the new order of things—alike by legislator and by civil and common lawyer.

Henceforth the knowledge and practice of the Canon Law tended to become a mere appendage to that of the Civil Law.

The Canon Law, therefore, applicable in the English ecclesiastical courts from the Reformation to the Revolution of 1640, must be regarded as diminished in its authority and changed in its content. The annulling of the Papal authority must have greatly restricted the *matter* of the

Canon Law which was applicable to the Church of England; and, on the other hand, there was now to be added to the body of this law (*a*) the king's ecclesiastical laws; (*b*) such canons or bodies of canons as might be passed in Convocation and receive the royal authorisation. Up to the period of the Civil War this latter source had added to ecclesiastical law the canons of 1597, 1604 and 1640. The two former received the royal assent and were regarded as binding on the clergy, but not on the laity, as not having been sanctioned by Parliament. The latter, the canons of 1640, were regarded as binding neither on clergy nor laity.

Equally with the Canon Law itself the ecclesi-astical courts remained after the Reformation, and with far less of change either in structure or procedure. In the manner of citations certain alterations were made by 23 Henry VIII., c. 9, whilst by the later Act of 37 Henry VIII., c. 17, laymen were made eligible for the office of judges in the ecclesiastical courts.

The spiritual courts in England, 1538-1640.

Whilst, however, the actual constitution of the ancient courts were not materially changed, their working must be regarded as in great measure paralysed by—

1. The uncertainty as to the Canon Law itself whilst under revision.

2. Such Acts as gave to the civil courts concurrent action in ecclesiastical matter, *e.g.*, the Act of 1 Edward VI., c. 1, against irreverent speaking of the Sacrament, and the two Acts of Uniformity, 2 & 3 Edward VI., c. 1, and 5 & 6 Edward VI., c. 1.

3. By the interference of the supreme judicial power of

the king through commissions of visitation and jurisdiction, which must be regarded as for the time being superseding the jurisdiction of the Ordinaries.

4. By the obligation under which some of the bishops placed themselves of taking out commissions for the exercise of their ordinary jurisdiction.

The High Commission Court, 1559-1640.

To this structure of ecclesiastical courts the reign of Elizabeth made one very material addition. The Court of High Commission was created in 1559, under the power of the statute 1 Elizabeth, c. 1, with authority to inquire into offences against the Acts of Supremacy and Uniformity, and into cases of heresy, seditious books, offences in church or offences against Divine service or ministers, abstention from church, or any other offences which could be dealt with by any spiritual or ecclesiastical power. With many and important changes in the terms of the written commission, the court lasted up to the outbreak of the Revolution.

This double organisation of High Commission and Episcopal or Archideaconal Courts sufficed the English Church from the Reformation to 1641 for purposes at once of discipline and of judgment of doctrine. For instance, Bartholomew Legatt and Edward Wightman, who were burned in 1612 for heresy, were tried, the one by the Consistory Court of the Bishop of London, the other by the Bishop of Coventry and Lichfield.[1] Again, in 1622, the Chancellor of Norwich excommunicated a female for refusing to wear a veil when she was churched.[2]

For the action and jurisdiction of the High

---

[1] Howell, *State Trials*, ii., 727.   [2] Palmer's *Reports*, 297.

Commission itself during this period there is much fuller illustration available. The extent of its activity, however, being concurrent with that of the Consistory Courts, can only be regarded as having superseded, so far, that of the latter, so that according to Hacket [1] the Consistory Courts of the suffragans in the Province of Canterbury, became in a manner despicable in the reign of Charles I.

Upon this structure the Long Parliament threw The Long itself with a fury bred at once of the professional Parliament attacks the hatred of the common lawyer for the Civil and spiritual courts and Canon Law, and of the national revolt against the destroys the existing Laudian Church system. juridical organisation

The Act of 16 Charles I., c. 11 abolished the of the Church. High Commission Court and (by section 4) deprived the ordinary ecclesiastical courts of all penal jurisdiction from and after 1st August, 1641. It was followed in the same year by the Act 16 Charles I., c. 27, which disenabled all persons in holy orders to exercise any temporal jurisdiction or authority. Finally the abolition of Episcopacy itself swept away the courts themselves at a blow. Together the three Acts abolished all ecclesiastical jurisdiction in England, and all the then existing mechanism for the regulation of the clergy and ecclesiastical causes.

There was, indeed, probably no other department of the legislative and executive action of the Long Parliament which was so instantaneously revolutionary in character as this in dealing with the ecclesiastical courts and judicature. On this

[1] *Scrinia reserata*, p. 97.

CHAP. II. head the lay and the Common Law element were at
one, and the combination was irresistible. From
the first moment of its assembly the Parliament
commenced to interfere with the Consistory Courts,
the High Commission and Convocation, reviewing
ecclesiastical sentences, and inquiring into the
abuses of the spiritual courts.

Individual instances of review by the Parliament of ecclesiastical sentences.

The cases of review of ecclesiastical sentence
included ministers persecuted for not reading the
book of sports,[1] prosecutions in the Consistory
Courts for tythes,[2] wrongful suspensions from
divinity lectures in Oxford by the vice-chancellor
of the university,[3] imprisonment of laymen for
thirteen years in the Bishops' Prison for refusing
the oath *ex officio,* wrongful deprivation or institution to vicarages,[4] sentences on laymen for hearing
sermons out of their parish churches,[5] excommunication and arrests of churchwardens for refusing
to rail in the communion table,[6] illegal proceedings
in the obtaining of injunctions to stop trials of
right at Common Law,[7] wrongful suspensions and
sequestrations of clergymen by ordinaries[8] or
bishops, etc.

It would be almost impossible to enumerate the
individual cases of injustice and illegality committed
by the inferior ecclesiastical courts, which throng
the pages of the *Journals* of both Houses, in the
years 1640-43, irrespective altogether of the more
notorious cases of injustice by the High Commission,
e.g., Bastwick, Dr. Smart of Durham, and so on.

[1] C. J., ii., 39.   [2] *Ibid.,* ii., 56.   [3] *Ibid.,* ii., 57.
[4] L. J., iv., 152, 155, 181, 273, 410.   [5] *Ibid.,* 156.
[6] *Ibid.*   [7] *Ibid.,* 183.   [8] C. J., ii., 192, 227.

In these individual cases the method of either House (for the petitions were promoted indifferently in the Lords or the Commons) was summary and severe. By the mere order of the House pending proceedings were instantly stopped, judgments were reversed, and wrongfully deprived clergymen were restored,[1] and reparation ordered by money fine or restoration to benefice—a procedure which, from a legal point of view, can only be styled revolutionary.

Against the ecclesiastical courts themselves, however, the Parliament determined to proceed constitutionally. On the 1st of December, 1640, long before it had made up its mind as to any reform of Church polity, a bill was introduced into the Commons *for the reformation of divers abuses in ecclesiastical courts.*[2] The measure, however, did not get beyond its second reading. A few weeks later a special committee was empowered to examine into all matters concerning the ecclesiastical courts and officers in the diocese of Lincoln, where abuses had been particularly rife.[3]

The proceedings against the ecclesiastical courts, 1640-4.

To prevent this subject of the ecclesiastical courts being dropped out of sight in the onrush of multifarious legislation, the Commons, on the 11th of January, 1640-41, again ordered the Grand Committee to be empowered to consider "the ecclesiastical courts and the government of the Church as it is now exercised".[4] There is no

---

[1] L. J., iv., 181 ; *ibid.*, vi., 16.

[2] C. J., ii., 40. Read a first time, 1st December, 1640. Read a second time, 27th April, 1641, and committed (C. J., ii., 128). The committee ordered to sit 5th May, 1641 (*ibid.*, ii., 134).

[3] *Ibid.*, ii., 56, 22nd December, 1640.   [4] *Ibid.*, ii., 66.

trace, however, of any further direct or special legislation on the subject. The fate of the ecclesiastical courts was necessarily involved in that of the Episcopal system itself, so that the discussion of the juridical system became virtually an appendage to the debates on Episcopacy which have been already detailed.

One special feature of the question, *viz.*, the infliction of fines and corporal punishments by spiritual courts, was particularly and especially condemned in the Act (*infra*) for the abolition of the High Commission, but otherwise the fate of the courts was left to depend and did depend upon that of the various Bishops' Bills already detailed.

Until the prescription of the Episcopal system, therefore, the spiritual courts nominally remained at work. As late as October, 1642, the Commons sanctioned this by contemplating a declaration for these courts to " proceed upon those statutes that are in force concerning tythes ".[1] The abolition of Episcopacy, however, (see *supra*, p. 121) swept the whole system away as will be seen.

Proceedings against the High Commission Court, 1640-1.

Two days after the first introduction of the Bill for the Reformation of the Ecclesiastical Courts, the Commons appointed a committee to consider of the jurisdiction of the High Commission Courts of Canterbury and York, and the abuses committed in those courts or by any judges or officers of them.[2] It would appear from an order of three months later, however, requesting the committee to resume, that its sittings had been interrupted.[3]

---

[1] C. J., ii., 811, 17th October, 1642.
[2] *Ibid.*, 44, 3rd December, 1640.   [3] *Ibid.*, 95, 2nd March, 1640-41.

The result of this order was seen in the introduction, on the 25th of March, 1641, of a Bill " for the repeal of a branch of a statute made, 1 Elizabeth, concerning commissioners for causes ecclesiastical ".[1] This Act, which received the royal assent in the following July, not only abolished the High Commission Court, but prohibited any archbishop, bishop or ecclesiastical court whatever from inflicting any fine, penalty or corporal punishment, or to administer an oath *ex officio*.

Higher than the Ecclesiastical Commission stood Convocation itself. Without the slightest hesitation the Parliament assumed the same attitude and authority over it that it did towards every other item of the Church system. No direct attack upon Convocation as such was ever made, and when it fell, it fell only as an adjunct or part of the Episcopal system generally. But both Lords and Commons were at one in scrutinising and attempting to define for the future the exercise

Attitude of the Long Parliament towards Convocation.

---

[1] Read a first time 25th March, 1641 (C. J., ii., 112) ; a second time, and committed (*ibid.*, ii., 115, 3rd April, 1641). Reported with amendments, and ordered to be engrossed, 29th May (*ibid.*, ii., 161). Read a third time and passed on the 8th of June, and carried up to the Lords on the following day (*ibid.*, ii., 171). Read a first time in the Lords 11th June (L. J., iv., 272), a second time on the 17th of June, and committed to the whole House (*ibid.*, 278). Before reading it a third time the Lords moved for a conference with the Commons on amendments suggested by the judges (*ibid.*, 289 ; C. J., ii., 191, 25th June). The Commons considered these amendments on the 29th or 30th of June (C. J., ii., 192, 194). On the 1st of July the Lords reconsidered these amendments and read the bill the third time, and sent it down (L. J., iv., 196). The Commons accepted the amendments on the 3rd of July, and the royal assent was given to it on the 5th of July (*ibid.*, 299 ; C. J., ii., 197). The statute is printed among the " Statutes of the Realm," v., as 16 Charles I., c. 11.

of its function. The condemnation of the canons of 1640 has been already referred to as one of the earliest acts of the Parliaments. The mere judgment of the canons themselves implied a judgment of Convocation. But the Commons were not satisfied to leave it to mere implication. The resolutions of the 15th of December, 1640, laid down a ruling—it can hardly be styled more for it was merely declaratory—which, from the point of view of ecclesiastical law, was at the time open to grave question. But it laid it down emphatically for all that.

Resolved upon the question *nullo contradicente* that the clergy of England convented in any Convocation or Synod or otherwise have no power to make any constitution, canons or acts whatsoever in matter of doctrine, discipline or otherwise to bind the clergy or the laity of this land without common consent of Parliament.[1]

The accompanying resolution condemned the particular canons of 1640 as a corollary. This claim of the Commons to a legislative consent to canons was reiterated in another resolution a few months later.

Resolved upon the question that this House doth declare that such persons as shall be admitted into holy orders or hereafter instituted or inducted into any living ought to be so admitted, instituted and inducted without any other oath or subscription to be required of them but such as are enjoined by the statutes of the realm, and being instituted or inducted, ought not to execute any power by virtue of any canon not warranted by Act of Parliament.[2]

Behind the ecclesiastical organisation stood the

[1] C. J., ii., 51.   [2] *Ibid.*, 152.

body of the clergy themselves. In every way in which the clergy were liable to jurisdiction the Parliament instantly assumed such jurisdiction to itself with revolutionary violence. In individual cases, without waiting for legislation on the point, clergymen were put out of Commissions of Peace [1] by the Lords, whilst the Commons went the length of requesting the Lord Keeper of the Great Seal and the Chancellor of the Duchy to leave out all clergymen from the Commissions of Peace on the renewal of the commissions at the assizes.[2]

Concurrently with this highly characteristic proceeding the Commons were legislating by bill against the secular employments of the clergy, and also discussing them in the abstract in a third connection, *viz.*, in the debates on the Ministers' Remonstrance (*vide supra*, pp. 29, 47-53). The interference with the political status of

Margin note: Chap. II. Attitude of the Long Parliament towards the juridical and political status of the body of the clergy.

[1] L. J., iv., 136.

[2] C. J., ii.; 79, 5th February, 1640-41. This matter was subsequently the subject of a conference between the two Houses (C. J., ii., 94, 1st March, 1640-41). This conference resulted in the introduction of a bill " disabling any clergyman to exercise any temporal or lay employment or commission as justices of the peace in England and Wales ". Read a first time 2nd March, 1640-41 (C. J., ii., 95), and a second time on the 8th of March. On the occasion of the second reading Hollis moved to add to the bill the taking away of bishop's votes in the Lords. The Commons' committee, however, which was then sitting on the Ministers' Petition, had made up its mind to effect this latter object by a separate bill. D'Ewes, speaking with a knowledge of what had taken place at the Ministers' committee, opposed Hollis' motion : " It would be well if we could have it granted after long debate in this House, and it would deserve a bill alone " (D'Ewes, i., 294). Owing to the progress of this later bill, the first Bishops Bill, the clergy Disabilities Bill was considered to be superseded, and was dropped 21st April, 1641 (C. J., ii., 125). The legislative history of the first and second Bishops Bill will be found *supra*, pp. 60-5 and 118.

Revolution-
ary seizure by
the Long
Parliament of
ecclesiastical
jurisdiction
in every
branch.

clergymen, which the Commons thus deliberately made even without awaiting the outcome of its own legislation, by no means sums up the total of its revolutionary seizure of power and jurisdiction. On the slightest provocation, whether of petition from parishioners or of rumour of disaffected words spoken, either House ordered clergymen to be sent for as delinquents by its own serjeant-at-arms. Without hesitation they were committed to prison, questioned for their life, morals, or title, their livings were sequestered, and other men presented by mere command of Parliament, and the institution of the new nominees forcibly insisted upon. When Laud or his officials proved recalcitrant to such orders their jurisdiction was sequestered. The whole of this phase of the action of the Long Parliament will be detailed later in connection with the general question of patronage (see *infra*, ii., 218). It is here noticed only in reference to the wider subject of clerical jurisdiction generally, and of its abrupt revolutionary assumption by the Long Parliament. Not content, indeed, with dealing with the general body of the clergy, hitherto amenable in such matters only to their own spiritual courts, the two Houses went behind them, and assumed to itself such jurisdiction over the body of the laity generally as had hitherto pertained confessedly to the spiritual courts. Either House called to its bar laymen for disturbances in churches (see *supra*, p. 106), for holding conventicles, or for absenting themselves from their parish churches,[1]

---

[1] L. J., iv., 133.

or for preaching when not ordained.[1] Further, Parliament interfered in the Universities, ordering the subscription demanded of the scholars in accordance with the Thirty-sixth Article of the canons of 1603 not to be pressed on any, as being against the law and liberty of the subject.[2] On the same ground the enforcement of academical garments was prohibited.[3]

To complete the circle of the assumption by the Long Parliament of jurisdiction in ecclesiastical matters there remained only the point of doctrine. The course of its dealings with the Assembly throughout the years 1644-46 will show with what peremptory decision the Parliament assumed to itself this right also as a matter of course. Whilst paying every respect to the expert opinion of divines, its attitude was the same from the first. In May, 1641, the Commons ordered the Stationers' Company to suppress a book called *The Saints' Belief*, and directed the author, John Turner, to be sent for as a delinquent "for his boldness in causing a new belief to be printed without authority, sitting the Parliament".[4]

The Parliament assumes authority over doctrine.

Similarly, a few months later, complaint was made to the Lords of the preaching of dangerous and seditious doctrine in St. Margaret's Church, Westminster, by the oversight or neglect of Williams, who, as Dean of Westminster, was ordinary of the parish. The House thereupon ordered him to take more care thereof, and that all preachers there should be allowed by him

[1] C. J., ii., 168. [2] *Ibid.*, 70, 117, 922; L. J., v., 559.
[3] *Ibid.*, 969. [4] *Ibid.*, 148, 18th May, 1641.

before they preached.[1] More distinctive reference will be made to this in another connection. It is indicated here simply as an exemplification of the unscrupulous and revolutionary seizure by the Parliament of every part of the domain of ecclesiastical jurisdiction which had hitherto in whole or part belonged peculiarly to the spiritual courts.

Gap left in the Church system by this action of the Long Parliament.

But in truth the violence of this action overshot the mark. The abolition of all distinctly ecclesiastical jurisdiction in the country left a gap. The House of Commons could not step into that gap without demeaning itself to the level of a (factious) court of law, and bewildered though it was with its multiplicity of affairs, it had no intention of turning so astray. There can be little doubt that even if the Long Parliament had reformed the Church on the basis of a Primitive Episcopacy, it would have been driven sooner or later to face the question of evolving some method form or structure of ecclesiastical regime or discipline, which would have raised the old point of ecclesiastical courts and ecclesiastical jurisdiction.

Presbyterian Discipline adopted to fill this gap.

As it was, the course of the Revolution ended in the adoption of a Presbyterian system, and to the ordinary non-legal mind the inevitable accompaniment of presbytery, i.e., Presbyterian discipline, may have seemed at first sight as elegible a system as any other to fill the gap. It is only by such a consideration that we can at all account for the amount of support which the proposal of the Presbyterian form of discipline did actually come

[1] L. J., iv., 299, 5th July, 1641.

to receive within the bosom of the Long Parlia- CHAP. II.
ment itself. On the other hand, the opposition of
the common lawyer to any such proposal was a
foregone certainty from the first. The Erastianism But essen-
of the Long Parliament sprang from the common tially modified by the
lawyers, nurtured on the traditional enmity of the Erastianism
of the Long
Common to the Civil and Canon Law, before it Parliament.
became a lay or national movement in any sense.
The whole history of the transactions of the years
1645-46, between the Parliament and the Assembly
on the matter of discipline, turns on the deep-seated
antagonism thus revealed.

On the 12th of October, 1643, the Parliament
ordered the Assembly to confer upon such a
Discipline and Government of the Church as might
be most agreeable to the Word of God, and most
apt to preserve the peace of the Church at home
and nearer agreement to the Church of Scotland
and other Reformed Churches abroad ; to be settled
in place of the present Church government by
archbishops, etc., etc.[1]

The large question of the jurisdiction of Church The Assembly
officers—of the internal government of the Church of Divines
commences
—had been referred to the second of the three the debate of
ecclesiastical
Assembly committees. On the 8th of January, jurisdiction
and disci-
1643-44, a report from this committee was pre- pline, January, 1644.
sented concerning the work of pastors and teachers.
" Pastors and teachers have power to inquire and
judge who are fit to be admitted to the sacraments
or kept from them ; as also who are to be excommunicated or absolved from that censure." [2]   The

---

[1] Husband's *Ordinances* (folio), p. 362, and *supra*, pp. 153-4.
[2] Lightfoot, 105-6.

proposition met with the decided opposition, not only of Independents, but also of the Erastians under Selden, and in the end it was recommitted to the second committee to take the whole business of excommunication and censures into consideration.

On the 19th of the same month this committee reported that " there is a power of censuring and absolving from censures in the Church,"[1] and proposed as the plan of its deliberations to inquire (1) what the Church is that is to exercise censures ; (2) what kind of censures these are ; (3) by whom and in what manner they are to be exercised. Incidentally the Assembly touched on a portion of these questions in the heated debate on presbytery during the following February.[2] But this portion of the Assembly's debate is to be held strictly to belong to the theoretical debate of presbytery.[3]

From the second committee Dr. Staunton reported six propositions on the 5th of February, 1643-44,[4] and a further series of eight propositions on the 5th of March.[5] In their entirety these propositions are as follow :—

Doctrinal propositions concerning Government and Discipline, Feb.-March, 1644.

1. There is one general visible Church in the New Testament.

2. The ministry and ordinances are given for the perfecting of the Church.

3. Particular visible churches and members of the general Church are by the institution of Christ.

4. Particular churches in the primitive times were made up of visible saints and believers.

---

[1] Lightfoot, 115.   [2] *Ibid.*, 138-60.   [3] See *supra*, p.
[4] Gillespie's *Notes*, p. 10.   [5] Lightfoot, 192-94.

5. In great cities there either were or might be more such Chap. II. saints and believers than could meet together in one place to 1644. partake of all the ordinances.

6. So many of these saints as dwelt together in one city were but one Church as touching Church censures, whether they were one congregation or not.

7. When believers multiply, so that they cannot meet in one place, it is lawful and expedient that they divide into distinct and fixed congregations.

8. We find no other way of dividing than by the bounds of their dwellings.

9. Single congregations ought to have such officers, ordinances, and administrations as God had instituted for edification.

10. There is a measure of liberty and privilege belonging to single congregations, as of exception against their officers.

11. When congregations are divided and fixed they need all mutual helps one from another.

12. No single congregation may ordinarily take to itself all and sole power in elections, ordinations and censures, or in forensical determining controversies of faith, cases of conscience, and things indifferent.

13. All the elders of a city in the apostles' time did join in one to order and govern the congregations thereof, as in other things so for censures.

14. The elders of several congregations in our times have like power and authority as they—as much need of association among smaller congregations in villages as amongst them in cities, and they may reap as much profit by it, and *ergo* ought they to be joined also to make up ample presbyteries upon the same ground and to the same end that city congregations are united.

No systematic debate appears to have taken place on these doctrinal propositions. The second proposition was discussed and voted on Thursday, 28th March; the third on 2nd April;[1] the fourth on Friday, 26th April; the sixth was debated on

[1] Lightfoot, 235-37.

29th April and two following days, and for the moment waived.[1] The seventh and eighth propositions were voted on the 1st of May, the ninth on Monday, 3rd May, with some alteration.[2] The twelfth proposition held in debate from Tuesday to Friday, 7th to 10th May, and was finally voted *in terminis* by 27 to 19, having been "managed with the most heat and confusion of anything that had happened among us".[3]

Division of opinion concerning the jurisdiction of the congregational eldership, May, 1644.

On the 15th May, Dr. Staunton reported from the second committee a series of reasons in proof of this twelfth proposition, and hereupon the hot debate again waged for two days.[4] The points scrupled by the Independents are succinctly and repeatedly stated by Baillie in his *Letters*. But on this head the division of opinion was not merely between Independent and Presbyterian.

For our Assemblie matters we are daylie perplexed; not only we make no progresse, and are farr from the sight of any appearance of ane end, but also matters oft are in hazard of miscarriage. The Independents so farr as we can yet see are peremptor to make a schisme, and their partie is very strong and growing, especiallie in the armies. The leading men in the Assemblie are much at this time divided about the questions in hand of the power of congregations and synods. Some of them would give nothing to congregations denying peremptorilie all examples, precept, or reason for a congregational eldership. Others and many more are wilfull to give to congregationall eldership all and intire power of ordination and excommuni-

---

[1] Lightfoot, 256.

[2] "In every congregation there ought to be one at the least to labour in the word and doctrine and to rule. It is also requisite that there be others to assist him in ruling, and some to take care for the poor, the number of each of which is to be proportioned according to the condition of the congregation" (Lightfoot, 262).

[3] *Ibid.*   [4] 15th and 16th May, *ibid.*, 266-67.

cation and all. Had not God sent Mr. Henderson, Mr. Rutherfoord, and Mr. Gillespie among them, I see not that ever they could have agreed to any settled government.[1]

Besides the above propositions there were at the same time two other competing series before the Assembly. The Committee for Accommodation, which had been appointed on 8th March, 1643-44, at the close of the fierce debates of the preceding February on presbytery,[2] reported on the 14th of March the following propositions, accepted by the Independents as the basis of agreement :—[3]

1. That there be a presbytery or meeting of many neighbouring congregations' elders to consult upon such things as concern these congregations in matters ecclesiastical: and such presbyteries are the ordinance of Christ, having His power and authority.

2. Such presbyteries have power in cases that are to come before them to declare and determine doctrinally what is agreeable to God's Word; and this judgment of theirs is to be received with reverence and obligation as Christ's ordinance.

3. They have power to require the elders of those congregations to give an account of anything scandalous in doctrine or practice.

On the conclusion of this report there was some debate as to the policy of continuing this Committee for Accommodation, as it was feared by some from the tone of its report that it would anticipate the work of the Assembly by taking into consideration the matter of Church censures. It was, however, finally voted that the committee should stand, and should have power to deliberate upon and bring

[1] Baillie, ii., 177, 9th May, 1644.
[2] See *supra*, p. 171.   [3] Lightfoot, 214.

in anything that might tend to accommodation between the Independents and Presbyterians.

Accordingly, on the 21st of March,[1] Marshall reported from it an addition to proposition one above and two additional propositions, numbers four and five, as follow :—

1. . . . At these meetings let them pray and preach, handle practical cases, or resolve hard questions.

4. The churches and elderships being offended, let them examine, admonish, and in case of obstinacy declare them either disturbers of the peace or subverters of the faith or otherwise, as the nature and degree of the offence shall require.

5. In case that the particular church or eldership shall refuse to reform that scandalous doctrine or practice, then that meeting of elders which is assembled from several churches and congregations shall acquaint their several congregations respectively, and withdraw from them and deny Church communion and fellowship with them.

Hereupon there arose, as on the occasion of the previous report, a debate as to the desirability of continuing the Committee for Accommodation. And, as before, in the end it was again decided to let the committee stand. The only account of the meetings of this committee are contained in Baillie's letter of 2nd April, 1644.[2]

We have mett some three or four times alreadie, and have agreed on five or six propositions, hoping by God's Grace to agree in more. They [the Independents] yield that a presbytrie, even as we take it, is ane ordinance of God which hath power and authoritie from Christ to call the ministers and elders or any in their bounds before them to account for any offence in life or doctrine, to try and examine the cause, to

---

[1] Lightfoot, 229.   [2] *Letters*, ii., 147.

admonish and rebuke, and if they be obstinate to declare them as ethnicks and publicans, and give them over to the punishment of the magistrates; also doctrinally to declare the mind of God in all questions of religion with such authoritie as obliedges to receave their just sentences; that they will be members of such fixed presbytres, keep the meeting, preach as it comes to their turne, joyne in the discipline after doctrine. Thus far we have gone on without prejudice to the proceedings of the Assemblie.

When the committee was in the act of going on to the rest of the propositions concerning this matter of jurisdiction, the Assembly was suddenly turned aside to the more pressing question of ordination,[1] and as far as these propositions concerning Church Discipline are concerned, this is the last that was heard of them, though the Committee for Accommodation itself will be found emerging later.

It is very indicative of the want of order in the Assembly's proceedings that, on the same day, 21st March, 1644, on which the above report was made from the Committee for Accommodation, a parallel report on the same subject of Church government was made from another quarter. Mr. Coleman reported from the first committee concerning presbytery the acts of presbytery, viz. :—

1. Ordination.
2. Censures and release.
3. Resolving of doubtfull and difficult cases.
4. Ordering things concerning the worship of God.[2]

On the report no proceedings or debates were taken in consequence of the obtrusion of the question of ordination,[3] which held far into April,

---

[1] See infra, pp. 323-4.   [2] Lightfoot, 229-30.
[3] See under Ordination, infra, pp. 323 seq.

1644, and subsequently of that of presbytery.[1] But when, in the third week of April, the Assembly had finished the consideration of ordination and shelved for a moment its resolutions concerning presbytery, the larger question of jurisdiction as a part of Church government again came to the front.

The work of the Assembly's Committee for the Summary of Government, April-, 1644.

On the 25th of April a committee was, upon Mr. Seaman's motion, chosen to hasten and draw up a summary of the whole Church government.[2]

Five days later the House of Commons resolved that "Mr. Salway should from this House desire the Assembly of Divines to proceed to the expediting and settling this question of the government of the Church."[3] Under the influence of this demand for speed, the Assembly's committee for the summary of Church government reported, on the 14th of May, the following draft propositions for debate :—

The jurisdiction of the congregational eldership.

(a) Concerning the officers of particular congregations they have power—

(1) Authoritatively to call before them scandalous or suspected persons.

(2) To admonish or rebuke authoritatively.

(3) To keep from the Sacrament authoritatively.

(4) To excommunicate.[4]

As preparatory to these propositions the committee had debated and concluded that "the government of the Church belongs either to congregations or presbyteries or synods," and had

---

[1] See under Presbytery, *supra*, pp. 172 *seq.*, from 10th April.

[2] Lightfoot, 254.   [3] C. J., iii., 473, 30th April, 1644.

[4] Lightfoot, 262-63.

thereupon drawn up the above propositions as concerning the first item in this system of Church government.

Writing on the day preceding this debate, Baillie again throws much side-light on the engineering of the Assembly's proceedings :—

> On Friday [12th May],[1] after a week's debaite, we carried albeit hardlie that no single congregation had the power of ordination. To-morrow we begin to debaite if they have any right of excommunication. We gave in long agoe a paper to the Great [the Treaty] Committee wherein we asserted a congregationall eldership for governing the private affaires of the congregation, from the 18th of Matthew. Mr. D. Calderwood, in his letter to us, has censured us grievouslie for so doing; shewing us that our books of Discipline admitts of no Presbytrie or Eldership but one; that we put ourselfe in hazard to be forced to give excommunication and so entire government to congregations, which is a great stepp to Independencie. Mr. Henderson acknowledges this, and we are in a pecke of troubles with it.[2]

After some debate the committee's reported preamble and first proposition were in substance passed on the same day,[3] and as far as related to the third proposition, the following general proposition was voted on the 21st of May, after two days' debate :[4] "Authoritative suspension from the Lord's table of a person not yet cast out of the Church is agreeable to the Scripture". The Scriptural proofs of this proposition held the Assembly for two more days.[5]

<small>Power of suspension carried, May, 1644.</small>

The debates on the Directory interrupted any further immediate pursuit of the subject of excom-

<small>The subject of excommunication postponed.</small>

---

[1] Lightfoot, 262.   [2] Baillie, ii., 182.   [3] Lightfoot, 264-65.
[4] *Ibid.*, 268-73.   [5] 22nd to 23rd May, *ibid.*, 273-77.

munication, and when incidentally the Committee for the Directory found itself obliged to touch upon the question of the celebration of the communion and the exclusion of the scandalous and ignorant, it simply submitted a report of two clauses for that purpose, drawn in an alternative and non-controversial form.[1]   The report was read in the Assembly without debate.[2]   The actual debate of the two propositions four days later was itself perfunctory.[3]   The question of excommunication and suspension was too burning a one to be decided on such a side-issue as the wording of an order in the Directory.

> Since our Friday fast (writes Baillie on the 31st of May) we have made good speed in the Assemblie. Our Church Sessions, to which Independents gave all and their opposite nothing at all, we have gotten settled with unanimity in the Scots fashion. Our great debate of the power of excommunication we have laid aside {and taken in the directory}.[4]

For the whole of June, July, and till the middle of August, the Assembly was engaged almost exclusively on the Directory.   On the 20th of August Mr. Palmer reported from the Grand Committee

---

[1] (1) The communion or supper to be celebrated frequently, etc. (2) None to be admitted but such as being baptised are found, upon careful examination by the ministers before the officers, to have a competent measure of knowledge of the grounds of religion and ability to examine themselves, and who profess their willingness and promise to submit themselves to all the ordinances of Christ.   *Or thus*, who give just grounds in the judgment of charity to conceive that there is faith and regeneration wrought in them.   The ignorant, scandalous, etc., not to be admitted, nor strangers unless they be well known.

[2] 6th June, Lightfoot, 279-80.   [3] 10th June, *ibid.*, 282.

[4] *Letters*, ii., 186-87.

[the Treaty Committee] certain suggestions for the conduct of the further debates of the Assembly. Items three to·five of this agenda paper, already noticed,[1] ran as follows :—

3. The committee for the summary [of Church government][2] [to] hasten their report about Church government.
4. The Assembly to return to the government.
5. Then to handle excommunication.

As usual, Baillie here again throws light on the workings behind the scenes :—

So soon as my Lord Warriston came up we resolved on the occasion of his instructings and the letters of our General Assemblie both to ourselves [the Scotch Commissioners] and this Assemblie [at Westminster], which he brought to quicken them a little who had great need of spurs. My Lord Warriston very particularlie declared in the Assemblie the passionate desires both of our parliament, assemblie, armies, and whole people of the performance of the covenanted uniformity; and withall we called for a meeting of the Grand Committee of Lords, Commons, Assemblie, and us, to whom we gave a paper penned notablie well by Mr. Henderson, bearing the great evills of so long a delay of settling religion, and our earnest desyres that some wayes might be found out for expedition. This paper my Lord Say took to deliver to the House of Lords, Mr. Solicitor also for the House of Commons, and a third copy was given to Mr. Marshall to be presented to the Assemblie . . . also we have the Grand Committee to meet on Monday to find out wayes of expedition ; and we have gotten it to be the work of the Assemblie itselfe to doe no other thing till they have found out wayes of accelerating; so by God's help we expect a farr quicker progress than hitherto.[3]

It was, however, not until the 4th of September that the Assembly found itself at liberty to act upon the suggestions of the Grand Committee.

[1] *Supra*, p. 176.   [2] Lightfoot, 305.
[3] Baillie, *Letters*, ii., 220-21, 18th August, 1644.

On that day, having finished the Directory and ordination, it took up the question of government. After much preliminary debate as to the order of discussion, whether to treat first of government or excommunication, it was decided to fall first on government, the question being finally proposed in the form already particularised.[1] The account of the debate of this proposition has been already given.[2] Having at last voted the existence of the several Church Assemblies, outlined in the plan of government, the divines, on the 4th of October, approached the question of the jurisdiction to be assigned to them. The debate was grounded upon a report that day made by Dr. Temple from the third committee[3] to the following effect :—

1. The Assemblies mentioned have power to convent and call before them any person within their bounds.

2. To hear and determine such causes and differences as come orderly before them.

3. They have also some power of or to dispense censure.[4]

The first clause was voted the same day, after being narrowed down by the addition of words restricting the reference to ecclesiastical business. The second clause was voted on the 7th, and the third on the following day.[5]

Having settled the question of the seat of jurisdiction, the Assembly next approached that of the nature of the jurisdiction itself, and on the 14th of October sat down to debate of excommunication *an sit et quid sit*,[6] on the proposition

---

[1] *Supra*, p. 177, Lightfoot, 308, 4th September.   [2] *Supra, ibid.*
[3] Lightfoot incorrectly says the first committee, 314.
[4] Lightfoot, 314 ; Gillespie, 86-87.   [5] Gillespie, 88.   [6] *Ibid.*, 91.

"there is such a Church censure as excommunication; to wit, the shutting out of a person from the communion or fellowship of the faithful ".[1]

The *an sit* was voted affirmatively, after three days' debate, 16th to 18th October.[2] On the question of the *ubi sit* (in whom the power of excommunication resided—the second committee having voted it to be in the presbytery) the Assembly, again a prey to itself, turned aside from excommunication to suspension, and voted this latter to be the prerogative of the officers of a particular congregation.[3]

The question as to the seat of Disciplinary power.

From this latter date until late in December the Assembly was occupied with its two "*humble advices*" containing its draft of Church government [organisation], and with the dispute over the "*Reasons*" of the Dissenting Brethren.[4] On the 23rd of December, 1644, in reply to the demand of the House of Commons for the despatch of the remaining parts of Church government, the Assembly explained to the House, through the mouth of Dr.

---

[1] On the following day, 15th October, an unusual incident occurred in the Assembly and took up the whole of its session. The Grand or Treaty Committee sent to desire an account of what the Assembly had done in the item of excommunication in the programme proposed from them on the 20th of August previous. In reply, the scribe of the Assembly drew up a report from his books, showing that the Scotch Commissioners had pressed that the Assembly might first fall upon the several sorts of Assemblies and their subordination, and that the Assembly had now entered upon the report of the second [? third] committee [concerning excommunication]. Hereupon a dispute arose as to the authority of the Assembly to make any report at all to other than the two Houses (Gillespie, 92).

[2] Gillespie, 93-95 ; Lightfoot, 317-21.

[3] Gillespie, 96 ; Lightfoot, 320-21, 24th to 25th October.

[4] See *supra*, pp. 181, 183.

Burgess, that all the material parts of Church government [so far, *i.e.*, as related to the form or organisation of it] had been already sent into the Parliament.[1]

> There remains only the point of Excommunication. They have found that there is that point of Excommunication, but the *ubi* is a theological dispute which they have not yet agreed upon, but have thought upon some general rules in the meantime, the which they doubt not will be generally agreed unto.[2]

This hopeful view was shared by the Scotch Commissioners.

> If the Directorie were once out of our hands (writes Baillie, on the 26th of December), as a few days will put them, then we will fall on our great question of Excommunication, the Catechise, and Confession. There is here matter to hold us long enough, if the wrangling humour which long predomined in many here did continue; but thanks to God that is much abated and all inclines towards a conclusion.[3]

On the 20th of December, 1644, the Assembly, having at last practically finished the Directory and the draft of Church Government, and completed its answer to the Dissenting Brethren, passed a resolution for the drafting of a directory for the practical part of discipline and government.[4] With a view to the impending discussion of what Baillie calls this great question of excommunication, Henderson, on behalf of the Scotch Commissioners, had drawn up a draft directory for Church censures and excommunication in which, whilst eschewing speculative questions, he had kept to the practice of the Scotch Church. The Scotch-

The Scotchmen draft a directory for excommunication.

---

[1] See *supra*, p. 182. [2] C. J., iii., 733, Monday, 23rd December, 1644.
[3] *Letters*, ii., 248.   [4] Mitchell, p. 22.

men were in hopes[1] that it would please all parties, even the Independents. The leading Presbyterians of the Assembly to whom the draft had been submitted had expressed satisfaction with it,[2] and if the Independents still proved unaccommodating, the Scotchmen yet hoped that at least the debates of such speculative questions might be either eschewed or shortened.[3]

There can be no doubt that this directory emanating from the Scotch Commissioners had been compiled before the 26th of December, 1644. It may possibly have been drawn up in consequence of the Assembly's vote of 20th December. But the alternative probability is much greater than it had been drafted prior to that vote, and had been kept in readiness to be offered to the Assembly when the right moment and occasion had been engineered.[4]

On the 27th of December, a week after the order for the draft of a directory of excommunication, the Assembly appointed a committee of five Presbyterians to take into consideration the report concerning excommunication.[5] As we are here reduced to the single and meagre testimony of the Assembly's "minutes," it is not clear what report is intended, but it is most likely that the reference was to Dr. Temple's belated report of 4th October, 1644, on excommunication.[6] If so,

---

[1] Baillie, ii., 248, 250.   [2] Baillie, *ibid.*; Gillespie, 97.
[3] Baillie, ii., 248.
[4] In January Baillie and Gillespie left London to be present at the meeting of the General Assembly at Edinburgh, and till his return on 9th April we miss the invaluable assistance of his letters.
[5] Mitchell, 23-24.   [6] See *supra*, p. 248.

CHAP. II.

1644.

Their draft
introduced
into the
Assembly,
Dec., 1644.

it would indicate that the Assembly was intending to proceed on its own initiative. It could therefore hardly have been pleased when three days later the Scotchmen, through Mr. Marshall, offered to it their ready drafted directory of excommunication.[1] That the Assembly consented to consider it at all from such a source is proof at once of its own abjectness and of the powerful influence of the Scotchmen at the moment. As it was, the Independents, through Nye, opposed the bringing of it in, but the Assembly called to have it read. "It was drawn up by Mr. Henderson," says Gillespie[2] with ludicrous candour, "and given to Mr. Marshall, who, first by himself then with divers others, thought upon it and made some alteration."

In order to save appearances, Dr. Temple moved that it might be referred to a committee, so that it could be brought into the Assembly under the formality of a report. But even this was waived, and the Assembly voted to consider of the directory as presented.[3] Accordingly from the following day the Assembly sat down to the systematic debate of this Scotch directory for excommunication.[4]

The discussion raised by the Independents turned upon the nature of the sins which should be taken cognisance of by the eldership for the purpose of Church censures, and on the 1st of January the Assembly made a memorandum that something should be considered of to set out such

---

[1] 30th December, Mitchell, 24 ; Gillespie, 97.   [2] Gillespie, 97.
[3] *Ibid.,* Mitchell, 24.
[4] Lightfoot, 344 ; Gillespie, 97-98 ; Mitchell, 24-25, 31st December.

sins.[1] But when, on the 7th of January, the divines reached the crucial question of the *ubi*, the repository of the power of excommunication whether in the congregation, the congregational eldership or the classical eldership, the Independents objected against the method of adopting a directory drafted by the Scotch Commissioners, and to which the Assembly had been originally no party at all.[2] The Scotchmen had naturally placed the power of excommunication in the classis, and the Independents as determinedly maintained it as pertaining to the congregation. After a heated debate, in which Marshall felt himself obliged to explain his own proceedings in his transaction with the Scotchmen, the paragraph was referred to a Committee for Accommodation.[3]

On the 14th of January the remainder of the directory was committed to the same committee.[4] It was reported on the 16th by Mr. Marshall, and again on the 21st after a recommitment. On the following day, 22nd January, Mr. Marshall further reported the sins worthy of excommunication.[5] This first draft of a catalogue of excommunicable sins came from the above-named Committee for Accommodation, but in the following session the Scotch Commissioners offered a paper of their own on the subject,[6] as representing the ultimate concessions they were able to make by way of accommodation on the point of doctrinal error of opinion as an excommunicable sin. " If you give way to that paper," said Henderson, referring evidently to the

CHAP. II.
1644-5.

Breach with the Independents on the question of the seat of jurisdiction.

A Committee for Accommodation— its work.

The first catalogue of sins.

---

[1] Mitchell, 27.   [2] *Ibid.*,30.   [3] *Ibid.*, 32-33,
[4] *Ibid.*, 37.   [5] *Ibid.*, 41.   [6] 23rd January, 1644-45, *ibid.*, 41-42.

first draft of sins from the Accommodation Committee, " I see not how any error can be suppressed." [1]

Form after form was proposed of a clause to conciliate the Independents on this their idol of a permissible liberty of opinion in things not subversive of Church order, until on the 30th of January, a fresh committee was appointed for the consideration of the point. [2] Pending its report, the Assembly on the following day continued its consideration of the catalogue of sins as in the paper from its own Committee of Accommodation, when after a heated debate in which the Independents renounced the whole accommodation to which in the said committee they had been a party, the entire directory for excommunication was ordered to be drawn up by the committee formerly appointed for the wording of the votes of the Assembly. [3]

The directory for excommunication forcibly passed and sent up, Feb., 1645.
It was accordingly in the following session [4] reported, read, adopted and ordered to be sent up under the incentive of a message from both the Lords and Commons for the hastening of the remainder of Church government in view of the Treaty of Uxbridge. [5] The five Independents as before formally entered their dissent, handing in a paper of their reasons.

For four sessions [6] the Assembly was engaged hotly upon these " *Dissenters' reasons* " and its own answer thereto.

---

[1] Mitchell, 42.   [2] *Ibid.*, 44.   [3] *Ibid.*, 45.
[4] 3rd February, *ibid.*, 46.   [5] L. J., vii., 169 ; C. J., iv., 40.
[6] 4th to 7th February, *ibid.*, 46-48.

On the latter day a committee was appointed to draft clauses relating to appeals and the remainder of the directory. These clauses were brought in on the 10th of February,[1] and instantly considered. Through seven sessions, 10th to 18th February, The question the Assembly hotly debated this moot point of appeals temporarily appeals, the Independents striving with all their postponed. force of argument against the admission of regular appeal from the congregation or the congregational eldership.[2] The conclusion of the debate does not appear in the Assembly's "minutes," but it would seem that on the 18th of February the question was diverted from appeals as such to the precedent question of the jurisdiction and subordination of synods.

The Assembly apparently appointed a committee to report on this latter subject, and from the following day, 19th February, when that committee reported, the debate ran upon the article of synods and their powers, especially of their excommunicating.[3]

The proposition affirming the power of synods to excommunicate would appear to have been passed on the 17th of March.[4] Thereupon the divines descending the scale of the Church Assemblies fell upon the jurisdiction of the classis. On the 18th of March, Dr. Temple reported from the sub-committee propositions concerning the powers of classes. Part of the report was accepted and part recommitted,[5] and then the Assembly at

---

[1] C. J., iv., 48.   [2] Mitchell, 49-62.
[3] Ibid., 62-70.   [4] Ibid., 69.
[5] 18th and 19th March, ibid., 70.

CHAP. II.

1644-5.

The Independents'
propositions
concerning
the power of
congregations, March,
1645.

last reached the consideration of the right, power and practice of particular congregations.[1]

With a view to meeting, or at any rate focussing in one expression, the views of the Independents, they were requested by the Assembly to bring in their opinions on this subject.[2] Accordingly six days later Mr. Nye presented the Independents' propositions concerning particular congregations.[3] For a moment the Assembly appears to have been staggered by the breadth of these propositions which strayed back over ground that had been already made the subject of accommodation. Eventually the Dissenting Brethren were desired rather to bring in a platform of Government concerning particular congregations.[4]

That such a proposal was merely a ruse to get rid of the Independents for a while, or to catch them on the horns of a dilemma, is frankly avowed by Baillie,[5] and was doubtless perfectly well known to the Independents themselves.[6]

Without waiting a moment for this " platform " from the Dissenting Brethren, the Assembly proceeded in its debate, and from the following session (28th March), discussed the matter of the power of congregational churches on a report by Mr. Reynolds.[7]

The conclusion of the debate does not appear in the Assembly's very imperfect record. But that

[1] 19th March, Mitchell. [2] 21st March, *ibid.*
[3] 27th March, *ibid.*, 72. [4] *Ibid.*, 73, 27th March.
[5] *Letters*, ii., 266, 271.
[6] See *a copy of a Remonstrance lately delivered in to the Assembly*, 1645. Hanbury *Historical Memorials*, iii., pp. 1-6.
[7] Mitchell, 74.

the question was carried, in a sense, adverse to the Independents is evident from Baillie's words : " The Assemblie hath now, I may say, ended the whole body of the Church government, and that according to the doctrine and practice of the Church of Scotland in everything materiall ".[1]

In the meantime, so much of its conclusions, and of the directory of excommunication, as the Assembly had passed by the 3rd of February preceding, had now reached the Parliament. On the 4th of February, 1644-45, the Assembly through Dr. Burgess presented them to both Houses in the shape of two papers :— *The question of the power of the congregational eldership debated in the Commons, Feb., 1645.*

1. The Humble Advice of the Assembly of Divines now by ordinance of Parliament sitting at Westminster concerning excommunication.

2. The Humble Advice of the said Assembly concerning a directory for admonition, excommunication and absolution.[2]

On Monday, the 10th of February, the Commons, taking up these two papers, referred it to a committee of the whole House to consider " what power the officers of a particular congregation shall have over the members of the said congregation concerning their knowledge and spiritual estate, and likewise to consider of the propositions in the paper presented from the Assembly of Divines touching this matter, and further to consider what other power is fit to be given to the officers of a particular congregation ".[3]

[1] *Letters*, ii., 266, 25th April, 1645.
[2] C. J., iv., 41 ; L. J., vii., 176.
[3] C. J., iv., 45 ; Whittaker's *Diary*. Brit. Mus. *addit. MSS.* 31116, p. 382. Whittaker was throughout chairman of this Grand Committee, and his *Diary* enables one to fill in gaps in the *Commons*

The failure of the Treaty of Uxbridge, for which this draft of a directory for suspension had been pressed forcibly through the Assembly, deprived them of their momentary relevancy.

In addition, the individual consideration of these papers of advice was further for the time being interrupted by the presentation of the more immediately practical question of the erection of the Church system which had at last been accepted in its main outline by both Assembly and Parliament. Consequently the first form in which the Parliament at last definitely approached the question of excommunication was in connection with, or as a logical appendix, to the *"ordinance for the election of elders."*

On the 6th of March, 1644-45, the divines presented to both Houses a paper touching the settling of a preaching ministry, and touching the keeping of ignorant and scandalous persons from the Sacrament.[1] Both Houses sat down instantly to the consideration of it, the Lords appointing a committee to draw it up in the form of an ordinance. This latter was reported on the 10th of March, and the Lords instantly adopted and ordered it to be sent down to the Commons. In the Lower House it was read on the same day as *" an ordinance* [2] *for*

Journals, as the latter only note the committee's work when reports were made and do not note the sub-committee at all.

But it is a disappointingly meagre *Diary, e.g.,* his entry for the day, 10th February, is simply as follows: " Proceeded in the propositions concerning Church government, and in the afternoon the House was resolved into Grand Committee, myself in the chair. We proceeded touching the power of suspension from the Lord's Supper by the congregationall elderships ".

[1] C. J., iv., 70 ; L. J., vii., 265.   [2] L. J., vii., 267 ; C. J., iv., 74.

the election and establishing of elders in every con-
gregation". It was read a first and second time on
the same day, 10th March, and committed to a
committee of the whole House with a special recommendation to take into consideration in the
first place the clause contained in it concerning the
keeping from the Sacrament of the Lord's Supper
ignorant and scandalous persons.[1] Not content
with having originated the ordinance, the Lords
sent down a somewhat impatient message three
days later putting the Commons in mind of it, and
desiring its speedy expediting.[2]

On the 21st, the Commons sat upon it in full
committee ; and, after debate, resolved to refer it to
the Assembly to express the particulars of that
ignorance and scandal for which they considered
persons ought to be suspended from the Sacrament.[3] The message was taken to the Assembly
the same day by Sir Robert Harley,[4] and a Committee of Divines was immediately appointed to
draw up a report. On the 24th of March the committee brought in the required particulars to the
Assembly, and on the following day they were
forwarded to the House.[5]

Particulars
of ignorance
and of scan-
dalous ex-
communi-
cable sins
demanded by
the Parlia-
ment.

The House thereupon went into committee.
But, before the committee would begin to debate
upon the Assembly's answer, it passed two votes

[1] C. J., iv., 74. On the same day the ministers of London, assembled
at Zion College, presented to the Lords a petition for the adoption of
some course by Parliament for keeping back ignorant and scandalous
persons from the Sacrament (L. J., vii., 268).

[2] C. J., iv., 77, 13th March, 1644-45.

[3] *Ibid.*, 85, 21st March ; Whittaker's *Diary*, 399.

[4] Mitchell, 71.

[5] *Ibid. ;* C. J., iv., 89, 25th March, 1645.

That there be some persons so grossly ignorant and so notoriously scandalous that they shall not be admitted to the Sacrament of the Lord's Supper.[1]

Two days later the Commons resolved, after a whole sitting's debate in the Grand Committee

" That a person not having a competent measure of understanding concerning God the Father, Son and Holy Ghost shall not be admitted to the Sacrament."

Concurrently, however, with this, it again re ferred itself to the Assembly for a statement of the particulars of such competent measure of understanding concerning God the Father, etc.[2]

The divines debated this message the next day, 28th March, and on the 29th their reply was presented to the House.[3] Some of these particulars the Commons proceeded to adopt on the 1st of April, but it again referred itself to the Assembly to set down in particular what they conceive to be such a " competent measure of understanding concerning the state of man by the creation, and by his fall, the redemption," etc., etc.[4] As before, the Assembly instantly took the message into consideration (2nd April), but it was not until 4th April that its committee reported, and not until 10th April that the report was forwarded to the Commons.[5]

Hereupon, on the 17th of April, Whittaker reported from the Grand Committee of the House its votes concerning the point of the ignorant and

[1] C. J., iv., 89, 25th March, 1645.   Whittaker's *Diary*, 401.

[2] C. J., iv., 90, 26th-27th March, 1645 ; Whittaker's *Diary*, 401-2.

[3] C. J., iv., 92 ; Mitchell, 74.   [4] C. J., iv., 95.

[5] Mitchell, 75-76 ; C. J., iv., 105.

scandalous, and they were immediately adopted by Chap. II.
1645. formal resolution of the House.   In brief, this series of votes excluded from the Sacrament (1) adulterers, etc., drunkards, swearers, blasphemers; (2) such as have not a competent measure of understanding concerning the state of man by creation, etc., the redemption of Jesus Christ, etc., the way and means to apply Christ, etc., the nature and necessity of faith, etc., repentance, etc., the nature and use of the Sacraments, etc., the condition of man after this life, etc.   In each case the particulars of the "competent knowledge" were set out in explicit words in the resolution.

In conclusion, the House adopted a resolution that the examination and judgment of such persons as should not be admitted for the above-specified scandals or ignorances was to be in the power of the eldership of every congregation.   A committee was then appointed to draft an ordinance in accordance with the terms of these resolutions.   The composition of this committee is significant.[1]

Having settled the matter of the jurisdiction of the eldership, the Commons turned to the manner of it.   On the 17th of April it had resolved that this jurisdiction rested in the hands of the congregational eldership.   This was, however, by no means intended as a final pronouncement on the point.   The question was debated again in full committee of the House on the 21st and 24th of

Debate as to
the manner
of this
disciplinary
jurisdiction.

[1] C. J., iv., 114, 17th April.   Rouse, Sir John Cooke, Sir Wm. Masham, Selden, Sa Browne, Serj. Wilde, Salloway, Tate, Rigby, Nicholas, Sir Benj. Rudyard, Mr. Holland, Mr. Lisle, Sir Ro. Harley, Sir Henry Mildmaye, Mr. Younge.

April, and 1st and 3rd May. On the latter day the House adopted the following composite resolutions on report from Committee :—

1. Power shall be given to the eldership of every congregation to examine any person complained of for such matter of scandal as is passed by vote of this House, and upon confession of the party before the eldership to suspend him from the Sacrament, *pro tempore*.

2. The eldership of every congregation to suspend from the Sacrament any person lawfully convicted of any matter of scandal passed by vote of this House.

3. The cognisance of capital offences shall rest with the civil magistrate, who upon committal shall certify the eldership of the congregation who shall thereupon have power to suspend the accused.[1]

In the succeeding session (Monday, 5th May), the Commons added to the above resolutions a fourth :—

4. Matters of scandal, not capital, voted by this House, shall be examined by the eldership of every congregation, who upon just proof made thereof shall have power to suspend the accused.[2]

On the following day, 6th May, these votes were sent up to the Lords for their concurrence.[3] Without waiting for the expression of their concurrence, however (which was given by the Lords on the 9th of May),[4] the House continued its consideration of the method of the exercise for jurisdiction by the eldership. It adopted[5] two resolutions from its committee empowering congregational elderships to judge upon the testimony

[1] C. J., iv., 131 ; Whittaker's *Diary*, 411-12, 414-15.
[2] C. J., iv., 132.   [3] *Ibid.*, 133, 6th May.   [4] L. J., vii., 360.
[5] 8th May, C. J., iv., 134 ; Whittaker's *Diary*, 416.

of two witnesses, and to administer an oath, but
upon a division the motion to send these resolutions also to the Lords was lost by 49-39. The
meaning of this division was made more clear five
days later, when upon report from the Grand
Committee, the Commons adopted the following
additional resolutions :—

1. Satisfaction shall be given to the eldership of every
congregation by sufficient manifestation of the offender's repentance or the party's innocency appearing, before the suspended,
as above, shall be readmitted to the Sacrament.

2. If any person suspended from the Sacrament of the The Com-
Lord's Supper shall find himself grieved with the proceeding mons' plan of
appeals from
before the eldership of any congregation, he shall have liberty the elder-
to appeal to the Classical Assembly, from thence to the Pro- ships' jurisdiction, May,
vincial, from thence to the National, and from thence to the 1645.
Parliament.[1]

Writing on the 25th of April, 1645, Baillie
throws light on what had been going on in the
Commons' Committee.

The Parliament have passed many of our votes of Government purposing quickly to erect the ecclesiastick courts of [kirk]
Sessions, Presbyteries and Synods and thereafter to pass so
much of our government as they think necessare. We will
have much to doe with them to make sundrie of our votes
pass, for most of their lawyers are strong Erastians, and would
have all the Church government depend absolutelie on the
Parliament : For this end they have past a vote in the House
of Commons for appeals from [kirk] Sessions to Presbyteries,
from these to Synods, from these to Nationall Assemblies, and
from these to the Parliament. We mind to be silent in this
least we marr the erection of the ecclesiastick courts, but when
we find it seasonable we mind to make much adoe before it goe
so. We are hopefull to make them declare they meane no

[1] 13th May, C. J., iv., 140 ; Whittaker's *Diary*, 418.

other thing by their appealls from the Nationall Assemblie to a Parliament than a complaint of an injurious proceeding which we did never deny.[1]

In his despondency at the triumph of this Erastianism in the Parliament, Baillie attributed it to the weakness of the Scotch army and to its delay in marching South.

These things have made us [the Scotch in London] look almost contemptible, and this contempt hath occasioned jealousie and provocations which may (if not provided for) prove dangerous.[2]

That Baillie's advice to show no immediate resentment at the blow to a pure presbytery, which the last vote of the Commons implied, was followed is evidenced by the fact that until the following month the Assembly made no reference whatever to the question of scandal and excommunication. Its time during these weeks was to all appearance given wholly to the preparation of its various advices for, and negotiations with, the sub-committee of the Commons then actively engaged in the settlement of the classical and provincial system.[3] On the The Assembly returns to the subject of excommunication, June, 1645. 4th of June, however, the Presbyterian spirit of the Assembly again broke loose, and yielding to temptation the divines adopted an addition concerning scandals to the particular paper of advice to the sub-committee, which it was at the moment considering.[4] The sub-committee apparently received the paper the same day, and immediately thereupon requested the Assembly to consider of a catalogue of sins, with the intention of having

[1] *Letters*, ii., 267.   [2] *Ibid.*
[3] See *supra*, pp. 188 *seq.*   [4] Mitchell, 100.

them added as particulars to the former vote of CHAP. II.
the House. That a fierce faction fight was pro-1645.
ceeding in the sub-committee is quite apparent,
although all details are hidden from us. But it is
further plain, as will be seen, that the sub-committee, which included the indefatigable Presbyterian member, Rouse, was strongly inclined to
propitiate the clerical spirit.

Immediately on receiving the sub-committee's A second
enumeration
request for this fresh or additional enumeration of of scandals.
sins, the Assembly set to work to draft it,[1] 5th to
13th June. Not content, however, with preparing The Assembly
the catalogue, it proceeded to appoint a committee desires an
unlimited
"to draw something to be added by way of desire jurisdiction
over the
that there may be some general proposition to eldership,
but tempo-
leave it to presbytery to proceed in other cases or rarily shelves
the demand.
scandals [not enumerated] of the like nature as in
those [enumerated], and some reasons for such
a clause,"[2] adding a request to the Scotch Commissioners to assist in the preparation. This
addition was completed on the 13th of June, and
at once taken to the sub-committee of the Commons.[3] The latter body, however, would appear
to have demurred to the responsibility of receiving
such a paper as out of its power (being not strictly
relevant to the only matter which it had in hand on
reference from the House, *viz.*, Church government and its erection). The Assembly was therefore confronted with the necessity of leaving out
the catalogue or of presenting it direct to Parliament itself, as advice concerning the Sacrament.
The latter course was adopted, 16th June. A

[1] Mitchell, 100-104.   [2] *Ibid.*, 103.   [3] *Ibid.*, 104.

committee was appointed to draft it, and on the following day it was presented to the House by Mr. Marshall.[1] It would appear, however, that at the last moment, for prudential reasons, the important additional clause in which the Assembly desired a practically unlimited jurisdiction was withdrawn and only the simple request for a fresh catalogue of sins was given in. No immediate notice of this paper was, however, possible. Through the remainder of this month, and the most of July, both House and Assembly were busily occupied with the discussion of the completed draft of Church government and the proposals for the instant erection of presbytery. Accordingly, it was not until late in July that the Commons could return to the consideration of the Assembly's desires concerning excommunication.

The Commons consider the Assembly's demands, July, 1645.
On the 25th of that month, the day on which the Commons practically agreed to the directions for the elections of elderships, it ordered "the last paper from the Assembly of Divines concerning scandal" to be referred to the consideration of the Grand Committee for Religion.[2]

On the same day the Assembly appointed a committee to draw up a petition and a narrative to be presented to both Houses for the hasting of the business of the sacraments.[3] This paper was reported, debated and adopted at the following session on Monday, 28th July, and on the 31st ordered to be sent up to both Houses in the name of the Assembly.[4] On the 1st of August it was,

[1] Mitchell, 104; C. J., iv., 176, 17th June, 1645.
[2] C. J., iv., 218.   [3] Mitchell, 116.   [4] Ibid., 117.

accordingly presented as the Assembly's "*humble* petition in pursuance of their humble advice formerly delivered into the House concerning persons not to be admitted to the Sacrament*".

At the time of the presentation of this fresh paper from the Assembly, the Commons was actually engaged on the consideration of the preceding paper of 17th June. Several votes had aleady passed in Grand Committee adopting other notorious and scandalous sins, as requested by the divines in that paper. Accordingly, when the deputation from the Assembly came with their new request for additions to be made to the catalogue of scandals, the House, possibly with some surprise, informed them that the matter had been in consideration all day, and that many of their desires were already granted.[1]

This new petition of the Assembly, however, desired something more than an addition to the catalogue of sins. It contained that clause concerning a general remainder jurisdiction which had formerly been proposed for insertion in the paper of 17th June, 1645, but which may very possibly have been prudentially kept out of that earlier petition.[2] The present "humble petition" desired in brief that all [not a selected and strictly defined list] of scandalous persons should be kept from the sacraments, "for if any scandalous sins deserve abstention, then likewise all other scandalous sins do lie under the same demerit, and by parity of reason should undergo the like censure".

CHAP. II.
1645.

The Assembly's "Humble petition," August, 1645.

The demand for an unlimited jurisdiction formally made.

---

[1] Whittaker's *Diary*, 446, 1st August; C. J., iv., 226 ; L. J., vii., 522; Mitchell, 118.   [2] See *supra*, p. 266.

Five days later Mr. Vines made a motion in the Assembly " to move the Houses for the preserving of the sacraments pure, because the ordinance is drawing [in either the Grand Committee or the sub-committee of the Commons] up only for seven sins ".

The Assembly thereupon appointed a committee to consider what was fit further to be done by them to discharge their duties and consciences in this important matter.[1] It may be significant that Calamy and Dr. Temple moved for leave to be absent for some days from the Assembly, and that Dr. Lightfoot entered his dissent. But the Assembly was resolute, and, after nominating the committee, desired the Scotch Commissioners to assist at it. On the following day, 7th August, the committee reported a petition which was instantly read, debated and voted to be sent up.[2] Accordingly, on the 8th of August, this third petition was presented to both Houses. In presenting it, White, the Assessor of the Assembly, informed the Commons " that there is not a matter of higher concernment for the glory of God and peace of this Church than the matter of this petition, nor was anything ever presented to the House with more zeal and tenderness of conscience ".[3]

Anticipating the conclusions of the Parliamentary Committee—of whose debates it could not be supposed cognisant—the divines appealed to the Solemn League and Covenant, pleaded that the power of excluding from the Sacrament could

[1] Mitchell, p. 118-19, 6th August.   [2] *Ibid.*, 119.
[3] C. J., iv., 234 ; L. J., vii., 532 ; Mitchell, 120.

not be arbitrary seeing it was limited by the Chap. II.
1645. exactest law, the word of God, nor could be styled inconsistent with the liberties of the subject, seeing the Sacrament was not a matter of civil liberty or right, and pointed to the example of other Christian states which had given to the eldership full exercise of the power of censures. They even concluded with a threat : " Should things be so ordered (which God forbid) that any wicked and scandalous person might without control thrust himself upon this Sacrament, we do evidently foresee that not only we but many of our godly brethren must be put upon this hard choice, either to forsake our stations in the ministry, which would be to us one of the greatest afflictions, or else to partake in other men's sins ". For the moment both Houses returned a civil answer. The Commons promised to take it into further consideration.[1]

It is to this period that belongs Baillie's undated letter, ii., 306, in which he gives so vivid an account of the agitation which the question produced.

The most part of the House of Commons, especiallie the *Agitation* lawyers, whereof there are many and divers of them very able *caused by the question.* men are either half or whole Erastians, believing no Church government to be of divine right but all to be a humane institution depending on the will of the magistrates. About this matter

Whittaker's *Diary*, 448, 8th August. The House in Grand Committee, myself in the chair. Proceeded to consider how the ministers of the Assembly might be satisfied in their desire of having some other scandalous sins expressed. A sub-committee was appointed to consider thereof to call unto them some of the divines to advise and debate with them concerning it.

Speaker in the chair. Divers ministers of the Assembly came concerning suspension, alleging divine right with a threat of resignation.

we have had at diverse tymes much bickering with them : now it is come to a shock.   Ever since the directorie came out we have been pressing for a power to hold all ignorant and scandalous persons from the table : with much adoe this was granted ; but soe as we behooved to sett down the poynts of knowledge the want whereof should make one ignorant, upon this we agreed. But for the scandalous, where we had long essayed, we could not make such ane enumeration, but alwayse we found more of the lyke nature which could not be expressed ; therefore we required to have power to exclude all scandalous as well as some.   The generall they would not grant as including ane arbitrarie and illimited power.   Our advyce was that they would goe on to sett up their Presbyteries and Synods with so much power as they could gett, and after they were once settled then they might strive to obtain their full due power.   But the synod [the Assembly of Divines] was in ane other mind ; and after diverse fair papers at last they framed a most zealous, clear and peremptor one wherein they held out plainlie the Church's divine right to keep off from the Sacrament all who were scandalous, and if they cannot obtaine the free exercise of that power which Christ hath given them, they will lay downe their charges and rather choyse all afflictions than to sinne by prophaning the Holy table.   The House is highly inflamed with this petition, and seems resolute to refuse it. The Assemblie is also peremptor to have it granted.   For upon this point they say depends their standing, all the godly being resolved to separate from them if there be not a power and care to keep the prophane from the Sacraments.   If the Lord assist us not in this difficultie it may be the cause of great confusion among us.   The House has appointed a conference with us to-morrow afternoon, and we purpose to require a Grand Committee thereafter that we may press our interest of uniformity : we are hopefull by God's help to obtaine our poynt if this jarr delay it not.[1]

On the return of the divines to the Assembly, Mr. Rouse informed them that a sub-committee of the House had been appointed, and that it desired

[1] *Letters*, ii., 307.

the advice of such members of the Assembly as it might appoint.[1]

On the following Monday, 11th August, accordingly the Assembly proceeded to nominate a committee of twenty-four, to whom they desired the Scotch Commissioners might be added, "to advise and debate with the sub-committee of the House of Commons concerning a course to be settled touching suspension from the Sacrament of the Lord's Supper".[2]

Having elected the committee the divines proceeded to pass resolutions strictly limiting the sphere of its action.

Ordered.—This committee is not to present any list of scandalous sins till they have further order from the Assembly, nor in the debate and advice to recede from the sense of the Assembly declared in their votes and petitions till the Assembly is acquainted therewith.

Ordered.—Not to conclude anything *de novo* till the Assembly be acquainted with it.

Ordered.—The committee are to apply themselves especially to these two particulars in their advice and debate : (1) the *jus divinum* of a power in church officers to keep scandalous persons from the Sacrament ; (2) the impossibility by any enumeration of sins to make a catalogue so sufficient as to preserve the Sacraments pure.

Ordered.—This committee is to prepare a character of scandalous sins, and to report it to the Assembly with all convenient speed.[3]

Instructions from the Assembly to its own sub-committee.

On the following day a request was communicated to the Assembly from the sub-committee of the Commons "that the divines be desired to advise what notorious and scandalous sins, besides

Its transactions with the Commons' sub-committee.

[1] Mitchell, 120.   [2] *Ibid.*, 121.
[3] *Ibid.*, 121, 11th August, 1645.

those that are already voted by the Houses, and how such persons as are guilty of them shall be suspended from the Sacrament of the Lord's Supper, and touching a course to be settled for suspension from the said Sacrament ".[1]   Upon debate of this message the Assembly resolved to draw up an enumeration of some particular sins to be added by way of instance.   The preparation of this reply agitated the divines through their two succeeding sessions, 13th and 14th August.[2]

A third
enumeration
of scandals
prepared.

On the 18th of August Palmer reported to the Assembly rules about suspension from the Sacrament, which were thereupon debated and ordered to be presented to the sub-committee, together with clauses relating to the examples and instances of the discipline of other [foreign] churches, reported on the same day by Dr. Burgess.   From the Parliamentary sub-committee these papers were passed on to the House.

On the 20th of August, when the House was in Grand Committee, Mr. Tate reported from the sub-committee " a list of notorious sins which had been presented to them [the sub-committee] to be added to the other sins formerly voted in the House, and also a relation of the form used in many Protestant churches beyond sea in suspension, and of the form used in primitive times, and of the opinion of the Greek fathers and other divines, but the resolving of other notorious and scandalous sins to be added as aforesaid was deferred till another sitting ".[3]

[1] Mitchell, 121-22.   [2] Ibid., 122-23 ; Baillie, ii., 309.
[3] Whittaker's Diary, 453.

Meanwhile the city clergy — Presbyterian by CHAP. II.
this time almost to a man—had taken up the   1645.
cause of the Assembly.   The city
On the 25th of August the divines of London clergy join in
presented a petition to the Commons[1] on this the fray.
subject of the safeguarding of the Sacrament, and
praying for fulness of power without unnecessary
restraint to be left in the hands of the presbyteries.

Under the combined influence of Scotch Commissioners and city divines, the Grand Committee temporarily gave way on this momentous
issue, and on the 26th of August voted that the
words *and other notorious scandalous sins* should
be added to the offences formerly voted.

Which vote I reported to the House, but the House had
a long debate about it and could not that day resolve it but
deferred it till next sitting.[2]

Again, on the 29th, the House debated this The Com-
report of Whittaker's from the Grand Committee, mons tem-
but could come to no resolution.[3]   porarily
                                               falter in their
                                               opposition
In the Assemblie (writes Baillie[4]) we are goeing on to the
languidlie with the Confession of Faith and Catechisme. The demand.
mindes of the Divines are much enfeebled by the House, their
delay to grant the petition, a power to seclude from the table all
scandalous persons as well as some.

Again, on the 3rd of September, the House

[1] C. J., iv., 253 ; L. J., vii., 558.
[2] Whittaker, 455. This is, as far as I know, the single but quite
sufficient authority for the statement in the text, and the entry
constitutes Whittaker's one great contribution to the history of the
subject. The Journals of the House of Commons and all the ordinary
authorities are absolutely silent about this unexpected (but happily
averted) surrender of its position by the Parliament.
[3] *Ibid.*, 455-56.   [4] *Letters*, ii., 315.

proceeded to take into consideration the report. The recommendations consisted of two :—

1. The addition of the words " and other notorious scandalous sins " to be added to the offences justifying exclusion from the Sacrament.

2. A new proposition empowering elderships when first constituted to admit persons to the Sacrament only after trial and examination.

But Whittaker in his *Diary* only refers to the former of these as presenting the great difficulty. "After the long debate, the variety of opinion was such that they thought fit to recommit it to the consideration of the Grand Committee."[1]

Three days later, 7th and 8th September, the Grand Committee proceeded in the renewed discussion of the above clause, "and after long debate, resolved that some cautions should be considered of to limit the cognisacion of the presbytery, that it should not extend to causes of such and such nature ".[2]

But compromise by the adoption of cautions.

In addition to taking this action, which was undoubtedly meant by way of compromise, the Grand Committee further discussed, through its sessions of the 10th, 12th and 19th, other scandalous offences, presented from the sub-committee, to be added to the list.[3] But, returning on the 23rd September to the more vital question of the safeguards to be erected against the presbytery itself, it resolved that a "Standing Committee of Lords and Commons should be nominated to consider of such other causes of suspension as should be pre-

---

[1] Whittaker's *Diary*, 458.
[2] *Ibid.*, 459.   [3] *Ibid.*, 461, 462, 464.

sented to them from the eldership, and by that committee to be presented to Parliament, and Par- liament not sitting, that committee to be judges of it ".[1] Three days before this, on the 20th of September, the House of Commons had been made acquainted with a paper which was being busily canvassed in the city for subscriptions touching this matter of Church government, then under debate in the House. They promptly voted it scandalous to their proceedings, and appointed a committee to prepare a declaration concerning the matter of the paper, and to find out the authors of it.[2] Without suffering itself, however, to be turned aside by such an incident, on the 26th of September the Grand Committee reported several votes concerning such other particular sins for which persons guilty should be suspended from the Sacrament. In brief these votes were as follows :—[3]

The Presbytery may exclude from the Sacrament worshippers and makers of images, etc., persons confessing themselves not to be in charity, senders or carriers of challenges, any using dancing, gaming, masking, etc., etc., on the Lord's Day, or resorting to plays, or selling or travelling on that day, any repairing to witches, wizards or fortune-tellers, any who assaults his parents, magistrates or elders, any person legally attainted of barratry, forgery, extortion, perjury or bribery.

Two cautions the committee had itself recommended :—

1. That the presbytery should not have cognisance of any matter concerning payments, contract, demand, conveyance or title.

2. No use should be made at a trial of any confession or proof made before the eldership.

---

[1] Whittaker's *Diary*, 465-66.
[2] *Ibid.*, iv., 282. [3] C. J., iv., 288-90.

To these the Commons proceeded to add a more drastic safeguarding clause, adopting the suggestion bodily from the Grand Committee, "that there be a Standing Committee of both Houses of Parliament to consider of causes of suspension from the Sacrament not contained in the ordinance which is to be framed for that purpose, unto which committee any eldership shall present such causes to the end that the Parliament if need require may hear and determine the same".

The Commons concluded by ordering the subcommittee of the Grand Committee for Religion to prepare an ordinance to be brought in to comprehend all the votes passed in the House concerning Church government.

These votes of the 26th of September were sent up to the Lords and agreed to by them on the 29th.[1] Two days later the Scotch Commissioners presented to the Lords a paper pressing this matter for the safeguarding of the Sacrament.[2] But, without regarding the Scotchmen, the Commons proceeded with their ordinance.[3]

[1] L. J., vii., 609, 620.

[2] *Ibid.*, 620 (paper dated 30th September, presented 1st October).

[3] The discussion on the Scotch paper took place in the Commons on the 6th October. *See* Sir Robert Honeywood's letter to Sir H. Vane, senior (S.P.D., Car. I., DXI., no. 9, Oct. 7, 1645). "The chief thing of the moment which has lately been agitated was the debate yesterday in the House of Commons upon a paper some days since delivered in by the Scots containing a reproach to the parliament for the payment of their army, their not settling the Presbyterian Government, in which business they used some sharp language and the very words of a petition projected to have been delivered from the city to the House for settling of said Government, which petition the House upon precognizance had voted to be false and scandalous . . . to all which there was an inclination in the House to answer with neglect

On the 3rd of October the Grand Committee CHAP. II.
1645. with Whittaker in the chair "all forenoon and afternoon debated concerning the power to be given to the presbytery for suspension, and an ordinance was brought in from the sub-committee containing the votes formerly passed in the House concerning the subject [of suspension]".[1]

Drawn up as it was, the whole ordinance was a heavy blow to the Presbyterian clergy. "The Assembly is much discouraged," writes Baillie. "They find their advyce altogether slighted; a kind of [nominall] Presbyterie sett up ; sects daily spreading over all the land."[2] In their extremity the Assembly resolved upon a fast for the further carrying on of their advice to the Parliament that God might guide the House in a due way.[3]

Disappointment of the clergy with the Parliament's proposals.

On the 8th of October, on a report from the Grand Committee for Religion, which had at last, Whittaker thought, made a vote tending to the conclusion of the business, the House proceeded to adopt an additional series of votes.

Persons keeping stews, etc., or marrying Papists, or consenting to their children marrying Papists, were made liable to suspension from the Sacrament, and with regard to the further extension of the catalogue of excommunicable sins an additional

enough, but I am told that my brother [in law] Vane Jun[r] showed great judgment in turning all into a fair way by proposing . . . and for the Presbyterian government it was ordered to be set up, but not with that latitude of power which the Assembly of Divines desired, which the sense of the House could not admit ".

The resolutions in the *Commons Journals*, iv., 298, do not notice the Church question at all.

[1] Whittaker's *Diary*, 470. [2] *Letters*, ii., 320.
[3] Mitchell, 134-47, 6th October.

regulation was made that such sins not enumerated in the above votes might be certified from the congregational eldership to the classis, and from the classis to the above-specified committee of the House of Commons, " to the end that Parliament, if need require, may hear and determine the same ".[1]

On the same day the draft of an ordinance for putting in execution these several votes concerning the keeping of scandalous and ignorant persons from the Sacrament was reported, read a first and second time and committed.[2]

On the 10th of October, the amendments to the ordinance were reported and debated, and upon a division it was resolved by 43-40 to add the decisive words " and not otherwise until it be otherwise declared by both Houses of Parliament " [voted to be added to the clauses concerning the eldership's jurisdiction].[3]

Whittaker[4] puts the matter more plainly, " The ordinance was brought into the House from the committee to which it was committed, and with a negative clause that there should be no other causes of suspension but those, except such as should be allowed by both Houses of Parliament," 10th October.

On the 15th of October, 1645, the ordinance was read a third time in the Commons,[5] a proviso

<hr />

[1] C. J., iv., 300 ; Whittaker's *Diary*, 471.   [2] C. J., *ibid.*
[3] C. J., iv., 303.   [4] *Diary*, 471.
[5] C. J., iv., 308.   Cp. S.P.D., Car. I., DXI., no. 14.   Sir H. Vane, junior, to Sir H. Vane, senior, Oct. 14, 1645.   " For church government the ordinance is to be read the third time to-morrow when the great dispute will be whether the clause of restraining the Presbytery from suspending from the sacrament [for unenumerated scandals] will

added, and the whole adopted and ordered to be
sent up to the Lords.

The proviso is not specified, but it appears to be contained in the following resolution of the same day :—

Resolved that it be referred to the members of this House that are of the committee on the ordinance for establishing rules and directions for suspending ignorant and scandalous persons from the Sacrament of the Lord's Supper, to consider how it may be held forth to all the world, how other notorious and scandalous sinners not named in the said ordinance may be kept from the Sacrament of the Lord's Supper.[1]

The ordinance was read in the Lords for the first time on the 16th of October, and a second time on the 18th. On the 20th it was read a third time, after some delay over the question of hearing the Divines of the Assembly before passing the ordinance. This proposal was negatived, and the ordinance was adopted and ordered to be forthwith printed and published.[2]

The ordinance of the Lords and Commons assembled in Parliament together with rules and directions concerning suspension from the Sacrament of the Lord's Supper in cases of ignorance and scandal is accordingly dated 20th October, 1645.[3]

The first Parliamentary ordinance for scandal, 20th October, 1645.

On the 22nd, finding that the ordinance had been incorrectly printed, Parliament called it in, and ordered it to be suppressed, and referred it to the care of the Committee for Plundered Ministers to see to the proper printing thereof.[4]

be agitated, though the House upon the second reading and engrossing resolved it in the affirmative."

[1] C. J., iv., 309. [2] L. J., vii., 649, 652. [3] *Ibid.*, 649.
[4] The two texts can be compared in L. J., vii., 649, and C. J., iv., 309.

As a matter of course, the divines, and the clerical spirit generally, were not contented with the ordinance, and did not for a moment intend to accept it as a final form or as satisfactory.

There can be no doubt that the Parliament consented to recur to the subject primarily under the impulse of the poignantly expressed discontent of the clerical mind at the insufficiency of the ordinance which had just passed. Only three days after its first and incorrect printing, Marshall moved in the Assembly for some consideration of the ordinance. " It is so short in some things that according to my present light we shall not be able to proceed in our ministry with a good conscience." [1] He moved for a petition, and a committee was in the end appointed to draw some such petition for further relief or help from Parliament in the matter of the Sacrament. The form of it was reported the same day and agreed to, with the dissent of Goodwin and others.[2] As the Assembly's Committee could not find an opportunity on the following day, the 24th of October, for the presentation of their paper to the Commons, it was kept in hand till the succeeding Monday, the 27th, when some addition was presented to it. On the following Thursday, 30th October, this latter was still in debate. It is therefore clear that this paper being unpresented could not be the ostensible cause of the order which the Commons made on the 27th of October,[3] when it resolved to send a message to the Assembly to desire the divines to present to the House "such other notorious and

The Parliament reopens the matter and asks for an additional catalogue of scandals 27th Oct., 1645.

[1] Mitchell, 157.   [2] *Ibid.*, 158.   [3] C. J., iv., 324.

scandalous sins in particular for which they desired
that persons guilty thereof may be suspended from
the Sacrament of the Lord's Supper ". This message was brought into the Assembly on the 30th
of October, at the very moment that the divines
were debating concerning their petition to the
House on that identical subject.[1] The Assembly
at once named a committee to consider the message, desiring the Scotch Commissioners to be
present.[2] It was not until the 7th of November
that the additional enumeration of scandals was
reported from this committee of the Assembly, and
it was only delivered to the House on the 12th.[3]
Meanwhile the Commons had been proceeding as
before on their own initiative. On the 31st it sat
in Grand Committee with Whittaker in the chair,
and "proceeded in consideration of a directory for
admonition and suspension and excommunication,
which was heretofore[4] sent into us by the Assembly : and only entered [began] it ".[5]

At the same time the House, with a view to
vindicating itself from the reflections which the
attitude of the clerical mind towards its ordinance
implied, had prepared a declaration touching its
proceedings in the matter of Church government.[6]
At last, on the 12th of November, 1645, the
Assembly presented to the House its *humble advice*

---

[1] Mitchell, 160.   [2] *Ibid.*   [3] *Ibid.*, 161-62.
[4] 4th February, 1644-45, see *supra*, p. 257. From February to
November the directory had lain practically unconsidered and neglected by the Commons.
[5] Whittaker's *Diary*, 479 ; C. J., iv., 327.
[6] 28th October, C. J., iv., 326. For the time being, however, this
was laid aside on the 8th of November (*ibid.*, 336).

CHAP. II.
1645.

The additional catalogue presented 12th November, 1645.

Impolitic and unconstitutional interference of the London clergy, 19th November, 1645.

and request touching some more particulars to be added to the catalogue of scandalous offenders, according to the order of this House of 27th October, 1645. As usual the paper was read and referred to the Grand Committee for Religion.[1]

Two days later, 14th November, this committee met with Whittaker in the chair, "and having voted two of the additional sins, and finding a difficulty in the third concerning the having of images of any person of the Trinity in a man's house, the committee referred it to be further considered of by the sub-committee, calling to them some of the Assembly of Divines to advise with them thereupon ".[2]

The succeeding meeting of the Grand Committee, on the 19th of November, was interrupted by the presentation, through the aldermen of the city, of the petition of the ministers of London complaining of divers passages in the recent ordinance, instancing defects in the enumeration of scandals and elsewhere, and desiring the establishment of presbytery forthwith and greater power to be put in the hands of the tryers in regard to the election of elders. The House was highly incensed, both at the implied censure of its own proceedings and at the method of the presentation of the petition, and after a long debate it returned a very sharp answer.[3]

[1] C. J., iv., 339.   Whittaker's *Diary*, 484-85.

[3] Whittaker's *Diary*, 486 ; C. J., iv., 348 ; L. J., vii., 346. After the House had voted to return this answer requesting the divines to forbear in future to misrepresent and forejudge the proceedings of the House, the ministers themselves came and presented the same petition to the House (Whittaker, 486). It was presented to the Lords on

Leaving for future censure the offence thus Chap. II.
given by the ministers, the Grand Committee con- 1645.
tinued, on the 21st of November, its consideration of
the Assembly's paper concerning suspension, "and
after long debate a sub-committee was appointed
to consider of some questions to be moved to the
Assembly concerning that matter, and to present
them to the Grand Committee".[1]

A week later the Grand Committee sat in consideration of certain questions brought in by the
sub-committee to be offered to the Assembly concerning Church government, with the object of
removing the obstructions that hindered the putting
in execution the directions concerning the electing
of elders, and the ordinance concerning scandal.
It resolved to refer it to the same sub-committee
to consider what power is fit to be granted to
tryers of elders, and to present a draft of an Act
for the purpose.[2]

On the 2nd of January, 1645-46, the Grand
Committee again sat on these matters, and considered of both the above points complained of by
the divines, "and of some good way to settle

the following day, and met with a similar reception (L. J., vii., 714).
The Commons referred it to the Committee for Examinations to
inquire concerning the origin of the petition, and the method of its
presentation to the Common Council (C. J., iv., 348, 19th November,
1645). On the 14th of March, 1645-46, a report was made concerning
the breach of privilege by the Common Council of London in their
petition concerning Church government (Whittaker, 518). Five days
later the Common Council presented their excuses, desiring that the
petition might be obliterated from the Journals (ibid., 520; C. J.,
iv., 479).

[1] Whittaker's Diary, 487.
[2] Ibid., 490; C. J., iv., 357, 28th November.

them". Both questions were referred to a sub-committee, "and Wednesday, seven night, was fixed for a fast to prepare us for settling of this great work of Church government".[1]

Notwithstanding the severe rebuke which the London ministers had received at the hands of the Parliament, they did not rest till they had inveigled the city into an outspoken championship of their cause. On the 15th of January, 1645-46, the aldermen and common council presented a petition to the Parliament for the settling of Church government.[2]

> We have gotten it (says Baillie [3]) thanks to God, to this point that the mayor, aldermen and common councill and most of the considerable men are grieved for the increase of sects and heresies and want of Government. They have yesterday had a publick fast for it, and renewed solemnly their Covenant by oath and subscription; and this day have given in a strong petition for settling of Church government and suppressing of all sects without any toleration. No doubt if they be constant they will obtain all their desires, for all know the Parliament here cannot subsist without London: so whatsomever they desyre in earnest and constantlie it must be granted. Wherefore albeit they gave them a baffling answer to their former petition a moneth agoe, yet considering the addresse of this in all its progresse, they have thanked them for it and promised a good answer speedilie. The Independents and all sects are wakened much upon it, and all will sturre, which way we doe not know yet.

Acting under the incentive of this petition, the Grand Committee on the following day, 16th January, at the order of the House, returned to

[1] Whittaker's *Diary*, 502.
[2] C. J., iv., 407 ; L. J., viii., 104.
[3] Baillie, *Letters*, ii., 337.

the question of the suspension of the scandalous CHAP. II.
"and in whom that power should be placed, 1645-6.
and how other scandalous offences, besides those The Com-
already enumerated should be judged ".[1]   On the mons adopt an alternative
21st, on Whittaker's report from this committee, scheme for the trial of
the House passed a series of resolutions extending unenu-
the list of excommunicable offences, and making merated scandals,
provision for the trial, by the tryers, of exceptions 21st January, 1646.
against elders elected.   For the vexed question of
the trial of unenumerated offences, the resolutions
were as follows :—

7. There shall be Commissioners appointed in every pro- Provincial or
vince who shall have power to judge of any scandalous un- County Commissioners of
enumerated offence presented unto them for which the guilty Appeal pro-
may be suspended. posed.

8. Upon the certificate of the judgment of said Commissioners to the eldership that such an offence presented to them
is scandalous, the said eldership may proceed to suspend.

12. Upon certificate made of such a scandalous offence not
enumerated, the above Commissioners shall make certificate of
the case, with their opinions thereof, to both Houses of Parliament with all speed.

13. Upon such a certificate the House shall proceed to a
final determination of the case.[2]

Part of these votes were considered of and
passed in the Lords on the 16th of February.[3]
The part concerning the commissioners was in
debate on the 16th, when on a division the votes
were equal.[4]

It was speedily apparent, however, that such
an arrangement as the proposed commissioners

---

[1] Whittaker's *Diary*, 508 ; C. J., iv., 408.

[2] C. J., iv., 412-13 ; 21st January, 1645-46.

[3] L. J., viii., 168, 174.   [4] *Ibid.*, 187.

CHAP. II.
1645-6.

The proposal proves even more objectionable to the clergy.

gave the intensest dissatisfaction to the clergy. That presbytery should be under the control of a committee of Parliament was bad enough, but it was quite intolerable that for a central, and therefore manageable Parliamentary Committee, should be substituted a series of decentralised local lay bodies, wholly unmanageable by the clergy, and very probably at heart antagonistic to them.

It concerns you (says Baillie,[1] writing to Roberts, the minister of St. Augustine's, London), to be advysed without delay what is needful to be done. I think the Lords will make some alterations if they were dealt with. I wish by all means that unhappie Court of Commissioners in every shyre may be exploded. If it must be so, let the new cases of scandals come to the Parliament by the letters of the eldership, or any other way, but not by a standing Court of Commissioners. You had need to be at your witts' end quicklie. . . .

The Parliament will have a Court of Civil Commissioners erected in every shyre on pretence to make report to the Houses in every new case of scandall, but reallie to keep down the power of the Presbyteries for ever, and hold up the head of sectaries. It's our present work to gett that crushed, and I hope we have done some good in this.[2]

It may be a mere coincidence that on the 29th of January, in the Assembly, Mr. Dury made report from the second committee, concerning Church officers and censures.[3] But it is certainly significant of the agitation, as well as uncertainty of the mind of the House of Commons, that a few days later, in response to a communication made from the Committee for Accommodation,[4] a pro-

The Commons waver for a moment.

---

[1] Baillie, ii., 346.
[2] *Ibid.*, 348. Baillie to Dickson.
[3] Mitchell, 183.　　　　[4] *Infra*, ii., 48-50.

posal was made to give the Grand Committee power to find out some expedient for settling the business concerning keeping the scandalous from the Sacrament, "notwithstanding any former order or resolution passed in this House".[1] The motion to put this proposal was negatived. Instead of it the House ordered the Grand Committee to receive Mr. Bacon's report concerning the digesting into an ordinance the votes passed in both Houses concerning the matter of Church government.[2]

Accordingly, on the 18th February, the subcommittee reported to the Grand Committee the draft ordinance for the election of elders throughout the kingdom, and of commissioners in every province to receive complaint concerning such persons as should be suspended from the Sacrament.[3] On Whittaker's report to the House, however, that body only voted the portions relating to the election of elders.[4] These portions were passed by the Lords two days later,[5] and on the 26th ordered to be printed and published.[6]

The Commons, meanwhile, were proceeding steadily with their ordinance for Church government, of which the above votes were a part only. The whole ordinance was reported from the Grand Committee on the 27th of February. The last article concerning provision for appeals by elders was referred back to the sub-committee. The

[1] C. J., iv., 428, 4th February.
[2] 10th and 11th February; C. J., iv., 436.
[3] Whittaker's *Diary*, 510.
[4] C. J., iv., 446, 18th February, 1645-46.
[5] L. J., viii., 177.
[6] *Ibid.*, 187. See *supra*, pp. 202-3.

remainder of the ordinance was voted, read a first and second time, and recommitted to the Grand Committee.[1] The recommitted portions of the ordinance were reported on the 3rd of March, and on the 5th of March the whole ordinance was read a third time, and after the offering and debate of several provisos, was passed and ordered to be sent up to the Lords.[2] On the following day the title of the ordinance was presented and voted, and on the 7th Holles, accompanied by the whole House, carried it up. " The soul of all laws," said Holles, in his speech at the bar of the Lords, " is execution, which this ordinance doth to those votes and ordinances formerly passed the Houses. This is the dawning of a glorious day which our ancestors hoped to have seen but could not.[3] On the 13th of March the Lords voted the crucial item No. 14, which provided for commissioners of appeals, ten Lords entering their protest against it.[4] On the following day the ordinance passed the Upper House, with some slight amendments, promptly accepted by the Commons, and was forth-

The second Parliamentary ordinance for scandal, 14th March, 1646.

with ordered to be printed[5] as *an ordinance for keeping of scandalous persons from the Sacrament of the Lord's Supper, the enabling of congregations for the choice of elders, and supplying of defects in former ordinances, and directions of Parliament concerning Church government.*[6]

Such portions of this ordinance as related to

[1] Whittaker's *Diary*, 512 ; C. J., iv., 455.

[2] *Ibid.*, 513-16 ; *Ibid.*, 460, 463.

[3] L. J., viii., 202.   [4] *Ibid.*, 208.

[5] C. J., iv., 475 ; L. J., viii., 209 ; Whittaker's *Diary*, 518.

[6] 14th March, 1645-46.

the large and vital question of jurisdiction were as Chap. II.
follow :—

iv., v., vi. The tryers of elders shall have power to try Its provisions
exceptions concerning the elections of said elders, to examine concerning
the qualifications of elders, to remove the disqualified. jurisdiction.

xiii. All renouncers of the true Protestant religion professed in the Church of England, all who maintain such errors
as are subversive of the Articles of that religion, all makers of
images or pictures of the Trinity, all in whom malice appears
and they refuse to be reconciled, may be upon just proof suspended from the Sacrament.

xiv. In every Province persons shall be chosen by the
Houses of Parliament that shall be Commissioners to judge of
scandalous offences, not enumerated in any ordinance of Parliament, to them presented : and the eldership of that congregation, where the said offence was committed, shall upon
examination and proof of such scandalous offence (in like
manner as is done in the [case of] offences enumerated) shall
certify the same to the said Commissioners, together with the
proofs. And before the said certificate the party accused shall
have liberty to make such defence as he shall think fit before
the said eldership, and also before the Commissioners, before
any certificate shall be made to the Parliament. And if the
said Commissioners, after examination of all parties, shall determine the offence so presented and proved to be scandalous,
and the same shall certify to the congregation, the eldership
thereof may suspend such person from the Sacrament of the
Lord's Supper, in like manner as in cases enumerated in any
ordinance of Parliament.

xv. (Qualifications of such Commissioners).

xvi. In case of offences committed on the day of the Sacrament the minister may temporarily suspend the accused,
certifying the offence to the Commissioners within eight days,
who shall proceed thereupon and certify the Parliament with
all speed, and thereupon the Parliament shall proceed to a
final determination.

xvii. Said Commissioners shall assemble in a convenient
place in each Province.

Chap. II.

1646,
March.

xviii. The Congregational Eldership, the Classis and the Province, shall have power by warrant under their hands, in all cases whereof they have cognisance by any ordinance of Parliament to convent before them all persons against whom complaints shall be made, and the witnesses in the case. Upon complaint to the next Justice of Peace, the party refusing obedience to such warrant shall be brought before him, and in case of obstinate persisting shall be committed by the said Justice of Peace till he submit to the order.

xix. Persons suspended in one congregation not to be received to Communion in another without a certificate from said congregation.

xx. Ministers and elders may be suspended similarly as above.

xxi. In all cases of appeal the Classical, Provincial or National Assembly shall have power to proceed thereupon by examination of witnesses in like manner as the Congregational Eldership is enabled.

xxii. On manifestation of repentance the suspended person may be readmitted.

Disappointment of the clergy and Scotch

Baillie was well-nigh in despair over the Ordinance—as well he might be.[1]

The Sectarian party is very malicious and powerfull. They have carried the House of Commons and are lyke also to carry the House of Lords to spoile much our Church government. They have past an ordinance, not only for appeale from the Generall Assemblie to the Parliament, for two ruleing elders, for one minister in every church meeting, for no censure except in such particular offences as they have enumerat; but also, which vexes us most, and against which we have been labouring this moneth bygone, a Court of Civill Commissioners in every county, to whom the congregationall elderships must bring all cases not enumerat, to be reported by them, with their judgment, to the Parliament or their committee. This is a trick of the Independents invention of purpose to enervat and disgrace all our [Church] government, in which they have

[1] *Letters*, ii., 357, 6th March, 1646.

been assisted by the lawyers and the Erastian partie. This Chap. II.
troubles us all exceedingly, the whole Assemblie and ministrie 1646,
over the kingdom. The body of the citie is much grieved with March.
it, but how to help it we cannot well tell.

In a letter of approximately the same date, Baillie reveals to us the state of mind in the city (as seen through the Scotch spectacles) on the point of these County Commissioners of Appeal.

The order of the House of Commons for Commissioners in and of the
every shyre, though it be not as yet reported to the House of city.
Lords, is far advanced. The burgesses of Southwarke and some
others of the nearest have named their Commissioners. The
burgesses of London before they would name theirs were
pleased to signify to my Lord Mayor their purpose ; whereupon
yesternight a Common Councell was called, which appointed
a committee, the same that drew the petition [*ut supra*,
pp. 282-3] to consider of that business, and if they found it
convenient, without more adoe to advyse with their burgesses
upon the persons to be nominate. This day they mett : they
were like, unanimouslie, to finde that Court of Commissioners
contrarie to the Covenant and to be disavowed, but Alderman Foulkes did change them, and did perswade that what
had passed the vote of the House should not be called by
them contrare to the Covenant: yet the business is put off
till Monday. If your burgesses [of London] have allowance,
yea, were it but a connivance from the citie to name these
commissioners, they will be received in the whole kingdome.
It were needful to take this business to serious consideracion.[1]

Baillie's state of mind, as representing that of the Presbyterians generally, is indicated by the feverish frequency of his letters at this moment. Writing on what must have been the same or following day he assures his correspondent, Francis Roberts, minister of St. Augustine's, that the com-

[1] *Letters*, ii., 358.

mittee of the Common Council disliked the idea of these Commissioners the more they thought upon them, "and so doe other Common Councell men. I have good ground to conceave that it will be quite disclaimed". In a third letter, following immediately after, he even proposed a scheme to the same Roberts for attempting to obstruct the passing of the ordinance in the Lords.

Yesterday Mr. Rouse and Mr. Tate came to confer with us.[1] From them we learned that the new Ordinance whereby the most of your [the London minister's] grievances are remeeded is sent up to the Lords, that it is in [the Earl of] Manchester's hand to be reported speedilie; that if he will carry it soe as the Lords scrape out all that concerns the Commissioners for shyres and put in their rowme the Classical Presbyteries to be reporters to the Parliament of all the not enumerat cases of scandalls, they are confident to carry in their House [*i.e.,* the Commons] according to the Lords' amendment. Consider therefore if it were not expedient for you to speak with Mr. Ashe, that with all possible speed he might go to [the Earl of] Manchester and obtaine of him leave to peruse with you and Mr. Clerk that Ordinance. I am very hopeful that his Lordship will doe his uttermost endeavour to make the House of Lords assent not only to the mentioned amendment bot to others which you may find necessar to move on the sight of the Ordinance. If Mr. Ashe find it more expedient for you to go with him lest my Lord scruple to give the writings out of his House, you will doe well in my mind to goe. Allen's business and the citie's zeale has much altered in a few dayes the temper of the House [of Commons]. Our friends there lift up their head, the sectaries are lower; strick the iron while it is hott.[2]

[1] Rouse, as a Parliamentary member of the Assembly of Divines, acted consistently as the go-between between the House and the Presbyterians of the Assembly. Tate had been chairman of the sub-committee of the Commons for the drafting of the ordinance in question, and was a perfervid Presbyterian (Whittaker's *Diary, passim*).

[2] Baillie, *Letters,* ii., 358-9 Baillie to Mr. Ramsay.

When, however, in spite of the protest in the Chap. II.
Lords, the measure passed in the form in which it
had left the Commons, the blow to the Presbyterian The clergy revolt, March, 1646.
party was too heavy to be borne in patience.
Baillie openly indicates the intended resistance to
it.

The Erastian and Independent party joyning together in
the Houses to keep off the [Presbyterian] Government so long
as they were able, and when it was extorted to make it as
lame and corrupt as they were able : yet at last, yesterday an
ordinance came forth to supply the defects of all the former
that soe without further delay we might goe to worke. We
laboured so much as we were able before it came out to have it
so free of exceptions as might be : but notwithstanding of all
we could doe it is by the malignity of the fore-mentioned
brethren in evill so filled with grievances that yet it cannot be
put in practice. We for our part mind to give in a remonstrance against it, the Assemblie will doe the like ; the city
ministers will give the third ; but that which by God's help
may prove most effectual is the zeale of the city itselfe. Before
the ordinance came out they petitioned against some materialls
of it. This both the Houses voted to be a breach of their
privilege to offer a petition against anything that is in debate
before them till once it be concluded and come abroad. This
vote the city takes very well : its likelie to go high betwixt
them.[1]

On the 20th of March the Assembly, acting
under the instigation of Marshall, on whose con- The Assembly's petition against the Ordinance, 20th March, 1646.
science some things in the ordinance lay very
heavy, appointed a committee to prepare a petition
to the Parliament.[2] It was drawn up the same
day and presented to both Houses on the 23rd of
March.[3]

[1] *Letters*, ii., 360-1, 17th March, 1645-6.
[2] Mitchell, 208.
[3] C. J., iv., 485 ; L. J., viii., 227, 232 ; Whittaker's *Diary*, 521.

The petition complained of defects in the enumeration of scandalous sins, very many such ordinarily committed in all places and formerly presented by the Assembly being still omitted, and it characterised the Courts of Commissioners as so contrary to that way of government which Christ hath appointed in the Church that they dared not practice according to that provision. They therefore prayed to be enabled to keep back all scandalous from the Sacrament, a power belonging to them by Divine right. The petition was practically a threat of open disobedience on the part of the Presbyterian clergy, and the House was naturally highly incensed and determined to express its displeasure, finding it no less a breach of privilege than the previous petition from the Common Council of the city.[1]

The Parliament's resentment of the petition.

[1] On the 27th of March, the House appointed the Grand Committee to consider of the petition and the manner of its presentation, with power to hear the divines, put questions to them, and receive their answers in writing (Whittaker, 523 ; C. J., iv., 492). The Grand Committee debated this question of the breach of privilege on the 1st of April (Whittaker, 524), and again on the 8th, " a debate that took up the whole day from morning till night without any intermission, and divers questions were propounded but no vote passed " (*ibid.*, 527).

On the 11th of April, it was voted a breach of privilege (*ibid.*, 528 ; C. J., iv., 506), and on the 16th the House appointed a committee to state the particulars of the breach of privilege, and to present to the divines certain questions reported from the sub-committee of the Grand Committee concerning the power of ruling elders and divine right (Whittaker, 529 ; C. J., iv., 511).

On the following day the House adopted, and ordered to be printed, a declaration for taking off the misrepresentations put upon the Parliament, especially with regard to this article of religion (C. J., iv,, 513).

On the 18th of April, the Committee of the House reported the narrative of fact concerning the breach of privilege and the questions to be proposed to the divines (Whittaker, 529 ; C. J., iv., 514).   On the

Furthermore, as it proved, the hopes of the Chap. II. Presbyterians that the city clergy and the city itself would .support the Assembly in their temerous action was doomed to disappointment. The city shamefully succumbed, and by a few words were made as dumb as fish, whilst the remonstrance put in by the Scotch Commissioners against the ordinance received no answer, and though the ministers of London subscribed a petition a good deal higher than either the Assembly's or the Scotchmen's remonstrance, there is no record of its presentation.[1]

1646, April.

The city falters in its support of the clergy.

> The city ministers (writes Baillie) are to give in one [petition] much higher, not so much upon hope of success as resolution to deliver their conscience. The citizens say they will give in ane other for the same end, but we doe not believe them ; their fainting has given our cause one of the greatest wounds yet it has gotten.[2]

What, therefore, finally induced the House to reconsider the whole question of the Commissioners of Appeal does not appear on the surface. Possibly it was the presence of the king as a prisoner in the Scottish camp, and the sense of growing danger from the Independents. Whatever the cause, on the 18th of May, 1646, the Commons had a long debate concerning a further enumeration of scandals.[3]

The Commons nevertheless re-open the subject, May, 1646,

21st the narrative was adopted in the House and eight of the questions (*ibid.*, 517). The remainder was adopted on the following day, and are entered in the *Journals* (C. J., iv., 519, 22nd April, 1646). The vote and questions were communicated to the divines on the 30th of April (Mitchell, 225). For the continuation of this subject, see under *Jus Divinum*, *infra*, pp. 305 *seq.*

[1] *Letters*, ii., 366-7.

[2] *Ibid.*, 356, 23rd April, 1647.   [3] C. J., iv., 549.

The *Journals* only record the appointment of a committee *ad hoc* with power to advise with the Assembly therein, but Whittaker adds in his *Diary* the words : " And that there should be also some consideration had of the lay Commissioners established in the last ordinance ".[1]

On receipt of the order the Assembly promptly appointed a committee to attend on the Committee of the House of Commons for the purpose of advice.[2]

Three days later, 21st May, the House resolved after a long debate by 110-99, " that leave be given at this time to take into consideration that part of Church government which concerns the Commissioners ".[3]

The substance of the adjourned debate on the following day is not stated in the *Journals*. But in Whittaker's *Diary* it is stated very succinctly, " very long debate whether they should consider of laying aside the lay Commissioners and find out some expedient to supply that which was to be performed by them, whether by prohibitions or some other way ; but resolved upon nothing but that to-morrow they would hear what could be said for or against them ".[4]

On the following day a member, Sam Browne, offered an expedient for taking away lay Commissioners in every Province, and putting in their place a Standing Committee of Parliament to sit at Westminster—a proposal which practically carried the House back to the first position which it had

[1] Whittaker's *Diary*, 538.   [2] Mitchell, 233.
[3] C. J., iv., 552 ; Whittaker's *Diary*, 539.
[4] Whittaker's *Diary*, 540, 22nd May, 1646.

assumed on this important question.[1] The sub- CHAP. II.
stance of the proposal was adopted and ordered to 1646,
June.
be drawn up into an ordinance, after a long debate
which lasted till 4 P.M., the committee being in-
structed to alter it on certain points which were
controverted.

Under the stimulus of a strong Presbyterian
petition[2] from the city, the House, on the 2nd of
June, read the ordinance a first and second time
and committed it with the proviso that it was to
be in force for only three years.[3] On the following
day it was reported, adopted and ordered to be
sent up to the Lords.[4]

On the 5th the Upper House agreed to the The final
ordinance unanimously,[5] and four days later the ordinance for
scandal, 9th
ministers of the Province of London were ordered June, 1646.
to put the Church government into execution.[6]

In this final form the ordinance contained no
further enumeration of scandalous offences, although
the Committee of the Assembly had distinctly
offered an addition.[7] It merely appointed a Committee of Lords and Commons as judges of unenumerated offences in place of the previous bodies of
Commissioners in the respective Provinces and
Counties, and prescribed the method of its pro-

[1] 23rd May, C. J., iv., 553 ; Whittaker's *Diary*, 540.

[2] 26th May, 1646, C. J., iv., 555 ; L. J., viii., 334.

[3] Whittaker's *Diary*, 543 ; C. J., iv., 561.

[4] 3rd May, Whittaker's *Diary*, 543-44 ; C. J., iv., 562.

[5] L. J., viii., 358.

[6] C. J., iv., 569, 9th June.

[7] On the 20th of May the Assembly resolved that the drinking of
healths be added to the enumeration as a scandalous offence (Mitchell,
233-35). On the following day they added also " neglect of family
prayer " and refusal to instruct families in religion.

cedure, *viz.*, elderships to certify offences and proofs direct to said committee, complaints of irregular procedure in the eldership to lie before the next three Justices of Peace who are likewise to certify said committee.[1]

With this ordinance the Presbyterian clergy had, perforce, to be content. Although with qualifications and safeguards the wooden sword of excommunication had been at last in reality put into their hands. It only remained for them to get their system erected and to wield the weapon.

§ IV.—*The Jus Divinum of Presbytery.*

Almost from the opening days of the Westminster Assembly the question of the Divine right of Church institutions and government had been in agitation. It was not so much that the conceit of Divine right had laid hold on the clerical mind from the outset of the struggle. It was simply Origin of the that in the orderly course of its constructive dclaim of the Divine Right bates the Assembly was thrown back at every of Presbytery. point on to the precedent question—what was the corresponding or original form or office in the Primitive Church,—what had Christ himself instituted? Was, for example, the doctor or teacher an ordinary and perpetual officer in the Church *ex instituto Christi*, and therefore of perpetual endurance, or was he merely temporary without any institution of full office for the time to come? Similarly for the question of the office of the ruling lay elder. In the debates of December, 1643, the

---

[1] C. J., iv., 562.

laymen of the Assembly wished the matter to be
argued from the point of view of expediency. The
divines persisted in arguing it only from analogy
with the institutions of the Jewish 'and early
Christian Church.[1]

There needed only such an environment as that
of the events of the years 1643-46 to produce from
such a root a full-grown doctrine of Presbyterian
jus divinum. At the very outset of the debates on
Church government, the Scotch Commissioners and
the Independents (at one for once) had desired
that the debate should be so ordered as to treat,
firstly, the question whether a platform of Church
government at all is laid down in the Scriptures,
before proceeding to the logically subsequent question, *viz.,* what, if so, that platform was. In the
end, however, the Assembly, overruling for once
both its friends the Scotch Commissioners and its
enemies the Independents, proceeded in the reverse
order. It concluded a sovereign power of government in Christ, the Head and King of the Church,
and that the Apostles had received the keys from
His hands immediately, and did exercise them in
all Churches of the world and upon all occasions.
Only after establishing so much did the Assembly
proceed to inquire whether there was any such
government now in the Church, unanimously resolving it in the affirmative. The result was equivalent to a declaration that the government of the
Church which Christ had instituted was in the
Church to-day, *i.e.,* that it was of Christ's institution for all time, and therefore of Divine origin and

[1] Lightfoot, xiii., 54, 74, 77, 82-83.

right. The subsequent course of the Assembly's debates on this head has been already described.[1]

The point to notice is not the minor one of the difference between Presbyterian and Independent as to the proper order of the debate, but the greater one of the agreement between them on the abstract question of the *jus divinum*. They were at one in the conviction that the form of Church government had been instituted by Christ, that it was of Divine origin and right. They differed only in their opinion as to what that form actually was which Christ had instituted.

Of course such a result was not achieved merely in the Westminster Assembly, and in the year 1644. It had been the heritage of presbytery from the days of Calvin; it was implied in the very beginnings of Independency, and had been proclaimed in explicit terms by Henry Jacob. But it was only by and through its formulation in the Westminster Assembly that the doctrine of a *jus divinum* of Church government appears as an official phenomenon in Commonwealth Church History, and as such came into conflict with the lay sense of the nation as concentrated and represented in the Parliament.

Instinctive opposition of the Parliament to the claim from the very outset. From the first the Commons were quick-sightedly jealous on the point. D'Ewes has preserved an entry in his MS. *Diary* pointedly demonstrating this for a period as early as March, 1643-44. The Assembly had sent a letter to the Churches in Zealand, and received a reply. On the 13th of March both letters were read in the Commons, and

---

[1] See *supra*, pp. 155 *seq.*

the Assembly's letter was ordered to be printed. So much alone the *Commons Journals*[1] record. But D'Ewes continues :—

It was moved also to the House by the Speaker to know if they would have the other letter [the reply of the Zealand Churches] printed, but Mr. Selden spake earnestlie against it, shewing that in that letter they challenged an ecclesiastical or Church government to be *jure divino*, with which the civil magistrate had nothing to do, and this he saied was contrarie to the ancient law of England and the use heere received, and therefore advised that we should forbeare to print that letter, which after some debate was thought to be the best way.[2]

In the matter of ordination, too, as will be seen, the Erastian action of the Houses, both Lords and Commons,[3] had been equally decisive.

This decided attitude of the Parliament at such an early date is all the more remarkable as indicative of its permanent disposition ; for explicitly, and in so many words, the Assembly had not yet formulated a claim to the *jus divinum*—not from any want of desire, but from what can only be described as policy. So much appears conclusively from Marshall's speech on the 27th of March, 1645, on the occasion of the introduction by Nye of the Independents' propositions concerning the power of congregations.

Some of these propositions (he said) concern Church government general and some particular congregations. . . . The first run upon this, a *jus divinum* of the platform and of the particular officers. . . . Concerning this by a vote in the Assembly you did lay aside the disputing of that point whether

[1] C. J., iii., 426.
[2] D'Ewes' *Diary*, Harl. MS. 166, fo. 40.
[3] See *infra*, pp. 325-32.

CHAP. II.

a perfect platform of government [is prescribed in the Scriptures] . . . and for the *jus divinum* you have been careful to go this way not to seek for a Divine institution. It's contrary to the whole way you have gone, and to the intent and purpose of the Parliament.[1]

The Assembly commits itself to a claim of *jus divinum*, June, 1645.

It was not until the question of jurisdiction came to be disputed between the Assembly and the Parliament that the divines committed themselves purposely and definitely to a claim of *jus divinum*. In response to the desire of the subcommittee of the House of Commons, which had requested the divines to prepare an additional catalogue of scandalous excommunicable sins, the Assembly had, in June, 1645, appointed a committee to draw the addition. Not content with the mere specifying of certain further scandals, they also drafted, as has been seen, a general clause to include all "like" sins unenumerated,[2] and as a corollary to this they debated "about adding another reason to show and hold out the *jus divinum. We claim our power of Jesus Christ.*"[3]

Accordingly, the Assembly's petition of 1st August, 1645, contains both the claim and the assertion thus meditated.

Albeit there may be amongst learned and pious men difference of judgment touching the particular kind and form of ecclesiastical polity, and some particular points and officers thereunto belonging : yet in this one point there is a general consent that as Christ hath ordained a government and governors in His Church and according to His will to order the same, so one special and principal branch of that government is to exclude

[1] Mitchell, 72.

[2] *Ibid.*, 101, 103, 5th and 12th June, 1645.

[3] *Ibid.*, 103, 13th June.

from ecclesiastical communion such as shall publicly scandalise
and offend the Church . . . nor do we find that there hath
been any great doubt or question made thereof in the Church,
until Erastus, a physician, who by his profession may be supposed to have had better skill in curing of the diseases of the
natural than the scandals of the ecclesiastical body, did move
the controversy.

Eleven days later, as the controversy between
the Assembly and the sub-committee of the House
of Commons developed, the divines appointed their
own committee to negotiate, ordering it not to
recede from the already declared sense of the
Assembly's votes, but in their negotiations to
apply themselves to two particulars, of which the
first was " the *jus divinum* of a power in Church
officers to keep scandalous persons from the Sacrament ".[1]

The course of the succeeding strife or dispute, Incidentally
as has been already seen, held through the suc- the Assembly debates the
ceeding ten months. But before that strife had *jus divinum* under the
reached the point of the *jus divinum*, the Assembly Confession of Faith, March,
had been drawn a second time, and in another 1646.
connection, into a formulation of its views and
claim in regard to it. The debate of the 25th
Article of the Confession of Faith (" of the Church ")
had involved the question of the institution by
Christ of Church government in the hands of
Church officers as distinct from the government of
the civil magistrate. The debate hereupon held
the Assembly from the 6th to the 17th of March,
1645-46,[2] and the defence, which would seem to
have fallen entirely on Coleman, took the purely

[1] Mitchell, 121, 11th August, 1645.
[2] *Ibid.*, 193-206.

Erastian line of argument that the Church of the New Testament held out no such distinction between civil and ecclesiastic government. Selden's name is not mentioned in the debate, and Lightfoot spoke little and only eclectically. The discussion, synchronising as it did with the publication of the Ordinance for Church government of March, 1645-46, had the effect of compelling the Assembly, on the 19th of that month, to appoint a fresh committee " to prepare something for the Assembly to assert the *jus divinum* of Church censures, and in whose hands *jure divino* they are ".[1] And in the petition which was drawn up on the following day against the Parliament's ordinance the divines reiterated their claim " as an attribute of that way of government which Christ hath appointed in His Church to keep back from the Sacrament . . . of which we must, as formerly in our petition we have done, say it expressly belongeth to them by Divine right and by the will and appointment of Jesus Christ "[2]

Beyond the wording of this petition it is not certain whether the last named Committee of the Assembly for the *jus divinum* ever made a report on its reference or not. On the 26th of March it was ordered to make a report on the following Tuesday, but the parallel matter which occupied the Assembly from that latter date through several sessions seems to have originated in a report of two articles of the Confession of Faith (*viz.*, Articles 26 and 30 " of the Church " and " of Church censurers "[3]). It is

[1] Mitchell, 207.
[2] *Ibid.*, 209-10 ; L. J., viii., 232.   [3] *Ibid.*, 212-15.

therefore probable that the action of the House of
Commons anticipated the work of the Assembly's
Committee.

The Assembly's petition of the 19th of March The As-
had been presented on the 23rd.[1] On the 27th the sembly's
petition of
Commons appointed a committee to consider of 19th March,
1646, leads to
the manner of presenting it, and on 11th April the Parlia-
ment's
voted it a breach of privilege. They further drew Queries con-
cerning the
up a declaration for taking off the misrepresenta- *jus divinum.*
tion put upon the Parliament, in which they declared their inability to consent to the "granting of
an arbitrary and unlimited power and jurisdiction
to near 10,000 judicatories to be erected within
this kingdom, and this demanded in such a way as
is not consistent with the fundamental laws and
government of the kingdom, and whereof we have
received no satisfaction in point of conscience or
prudence ".[2]

At the time of the appointment of the committee
of 27th March, the Commons had further empowered it to propound to the divines what questions they should think fit, and to receive their
answers thereunto in writing.

This committee, which is subsequently described
as the sub-committee of the Grand Committee for
Religion (doubtless the sub-committee which had
throughout been in close touch and negotiation
with the Assembly on this matter of discipline), had
prepared at some time previous to the 16th of April,
1646, a series of questions to be propounded to the
divines. On the latter date these questions were

[1] C. J., iv., 485 ; L. J., viii., 232.
[2] C. J., iv., 513, 17th April, 1646.

read in the House, and were practically handed over to the discretion of a new Committee for the Breach of Privilege to revise as they saw fit.[1]

Two days later Sir Arthur Haselrig reported the narrative of the matter of fact concerning the breach of privilege together with the draft questions.[2] The narrative was adopted by the House on the 21st April and the questions on the 22nd.[3] The latter were as follows :—

The Queries concerning the *jus divinum*, 22nd April, 1646.

Whereas it is resolved by the House of Commons that all persons guilty of notorious and scandalous offences shall be suspended from the Sacrament of the Lord's Supper, the said House desires to be satisfied by the Assembly of Divines in these questions following :—

1. Whether the parochial and congregational elderships appointed by ordinance of Parliament or any other congregational or presbyterial eldership are *jure divino* and by the will and appointment of Jesus Christ, and whether any particular Church government be *jure divino* and what that government is ?

2. Whether all the members of the said elderships as members thereof, or which of them, are *jure divino* and by the will and appointment of Jesus Christ ?

3. Whether the superior assemblies or elderships, *viz.*, the classical, provincial and national, whether all or any of them

---

[1] C. J., iv., 511, 16th April, 1646.

Resolved—That the questions to be propounded to the divines, considered by a sub-committee of the Grand Committee for Religion, and read in the Grand Committee, shall be now read in the House.

Resolved—That further power shall be given to the committee (for the breach of privilege) to prepare questions to be propounded to the divines upon the matter of Divine right for them to return their answer in writing. They are likewise to consider of the former questions considered of by the Grand Committee, and what alterations and additions are fit to be made to those questions, and what other things are fit to be propounded.

[2] *Ibid.*, 514, 18th April.

[3] *Ibid.*, 517-18.

and which of them are *jure divino* and by the will and appointment of Jesus Christ?

4. Whether appeals from congregational elderships to the classical, provincial and national assemblies or to any of them, and to which of them, are *jure divino* and by the will and appointment of Jesus Christ, and are their powers upon such appeals *jure divino*, and by the will and appointment of Jesus Christ?

5. Whether œcumenical assemblies are *jure divino* and whether there be appeals from any of the former assemblies to the said œcumenical *jure divino* and by the will and appointment of Jesus Christ?

6. Whether by the Word of God the power of judging and declaring what are such notorious and scandalous offences for which persons guilty thereof are to be kept from the Sacrament of the Lord's Supper, and of conventing before them, trying and actual suspending from the Sacrament of the Lord's Supper such offenders accordingly, is either in the congregational eldership or presbytery or in any other eldership, congregation or persons, and whether such powers are in them only or in any of them and in which of them *jure divino* and by the will and appointment of Jesus Christ?

7. Whether there be any certain and particular rules expressed in the word of God to direct the elderships or presbyteries, congregations or persons or any of them in the exercise and execution of the powers aforesaid, and what are those rules?

8. Is there anything contained in the word of God that the supreme magistracy in a Christian State may not judge and determine what are the aforesaid notorious and scandalous offences and the manner of suspension for the same and in what particulars concerning the premises is the said supreme magistracy by the word of God excluded?

9. Whether the provision of Commissioners to judge of scandals not enumerated (as they are authorised by the ordinance of Parliament) be contrary to that way of government which Christ hath appointed in the Church and wherein are they so contrary?

In answer to those particulars the House of Commons desire of the Assembly of Divines their proofs from Scripture to be set down, the several texts of Scripture in the express words of the same, and it is *ordered* that every particular minister of the Assembly of Divines that is or shall be present at the debate of any of these questions do upon every resolution which shall be presented to this House concerning the same subscribe his respective name either with the affirmative or negative as he gives his vote; and that those that do dissent from the major part shall set down their positive opinions with the express text of Scripture upon which their opinions are grounded.[1]

The questions, together with the narrative of the breach of privilege, were delivered to the Assembly on the 30th of April, 1646, by a committee of the Commons, several of whom made most notable speeches of which we can still discern the main outline from the Assembly's disjointed minutes :—

The Commoners'
speeches on
the delivery
of the Queries
to the Assembly, 30th
April, 1646.

We trust (said Sir Jo. Evelyn) that no division is now to arise between us. If there shall, you will give occasion to all the world to say that as you were willing to serve the Parliament a while, so you were willing to have them serve you for ever after. . . . Do not think that the Parliament is unwilling to submit their yoke to Jesus Christ; His yoke is easy. If it be a galling, vexing yoke it is not His and we [will not bear it].

Fiennes continued in the same strain :—

The Parliament doth not pretend to an infallibilty of judgment, and the Parliament suppose this Assembly will not do so neither. If, therefore, the question be but of a human judgment subject to error, preserved only by means common, they must and do claim privilege that they have the supreme judgment in making laws. . . . Something in the matter . . . that all power in all causes should be derived from them [the Parliament]. You derive it in part from Jesus Christ to the presbyteries. For that concerning the Divine right though the Houses have not been so positive yet till that be made clear unto them. . . .

[1] C. J., iv., 519, 22nd April, 1646.

Fiennes was followed by Browne, a member who,
as has been seen, was subsequently responsible for
the expedient which was accepted by the Presbyterians as a compromise on the point of the lay
Commissioners :—

The Commons (he said) have declared that by the fundamental laws the Parliament is the supreme judicature . . .
spiritual and ecclesiastical . . . there was never any writ but
[the king's] for matters concerning the Church . . . in the
first of Elizabeth . . . if the Parliament of England had not
settled it then good, . . . this power of judicature they may
delegate to what person they please. . . . But the great question is whether of Divine right it's fit that those that are to
declare it so should find it to be so. Nothing come to them
yet hath satisfied them [on this]. . . . Heretofore both Lords
and Commons have been very serious in considering of anything offered to be *jure divino*. . . . Many thing offered to the
Parliament *jure divino* that the Parliament hath been very
careful to weigh and consider . . . and is it not cause they
should ? . . . If it be of God it must not alter. . . . It is much
pressed for the point of the Covenant. We all agree that the
word of God is the rule and must be the rule, but say there be
no positive rule in the word are we by the Covenant bound to
follow the practice of Reformed Churches in case it be against
the fundamental law of the kingdom ? You must interpret the
Covenant so as that all parts may stand. We are bound to
maintain the liberties of Parliament and kingdom. If I do any
act against this I am a breaker of the Covenant. If I should
encourage any by petition. . . . For this of Commissioners,
this unheard of word, it hath been in the English Church ever
since the Conquest to judge of ecclesiastical things. Thirty-
seven of Henry VIII. the judges did resolve that the king
might grant a commission in ecclesiastical causes to determine
spiritual causes. . . . It is the doctrine of the Pope to take
from princes the power that God committed to them, to judge
of the maladministration. . . . For this exorbitant power we
have smarted for it and you have smarted with it.

More incisive still, and even minatory, was Sir Benjamin Rudyard :—

The matter you are now about, the *jus divinum*, is of a formidable and tremendous nature. It will be expected you should answer by clear, practical and express Scriptures, not by far-fetched arguments which are commonly told before you come to the matter. . . . I have heard much spoken of "the pattern in the Mount," so express. . . . I could never find in the New Testament [such a pattern]. The first rule is " Let all things be done decently and in order " to edification. Decency and order are variable, and therefore cannot be *jure divino*. Discipline is but the hedge. I desire you would make your answer in plain terms. I have heard it often very well said the present Assembly are learned and pious men, but a Parliament is to make laws for all sorts of men. . . . We are pressed as to our Covenant. I believe we have done nothing against the word of God. Neither do all the Churches agree throughout. . . . The civil magistrate is a Church officer in every Christian Commonwealth. . . .[1]

The Queries debated in the Assembly but never answered.

After the speeches and the reading of the Queries, the staggered Assembly adjourned. It appointed a day of humiliation in reference to "this great business," and sent letters to all the member divines to attend on the debate, which opened on the following Monday, 4th May. After a preliminary discussion, the Queries were referred to the usual three committees, *viz.*, the nature of *jus divinum* in reference to Church government in general to the first committee ; the nature of Church government, and wherein it doth consist, to the second ; and to the third, whether the Church government be in the hands of Church officers only.[2] Ten days later the Dissenting

Brethren, at their own request, were made a separate committee for the questions.[1]

Once for all it may be premised that the Assembly never reached the conclusion of its agitation of the Queries, and that they remained unanswered by it to the day of its dwindled and discredited close. How far such a result was due to accident or to design can hardly be decided. Intermittently for more than two months, 15th May to 6th July, they were busily and determinedly debated.[2] On the 1st of July a "most comprehensive" answer to the first query was reported from the first committee, although it was admitted in the report that some of the members of the committee had strongly opposed it. In the consideration of this report the Assembly resolved on the 6th of July, *nemine contradicente*, "that Jesus Christ, as Head and King of the Church, hath Himself appointed a Church government distinct from the civil". Following this on the next day, elaborate regulations were made concerning the method of attesting the answers by the subscriptions of the divines.[3] Even so little progress would indicate a determination on the part of the Assembly to proceed with the work, but that there were cross currents is evident.

The work of the Assemblie these bygone weeks (says Baillie[4] on the 14th July), has been to answer some very captious questions of the Parliament about the clear Scriptural warrant for all the punctilios of the government. It was thought

---

[1] Mitchell, 231, 468, 14th May, 1646.
[2] *Ibid.*, 231-50, 469.   [3] *Ibid.*, 250-51.
[4] *Letters*, ii., 378 ; 14th July, 1646.

it would be impossible for us to answer, and that in our answers there should be no unanimitie; yet by God's grace we shall deceave them who were waiting for our halting. The committee has prepared very solide and satisfactory answers already almost to all the questions, wherein there is like to be ane unanimitie absolute even with the Independents. But because of the Assemblie's way and the Independents' miserable unamendable designe to keep all things from any conclusion, its like we shall not be able to perfyte our answers for some tyme; therefore I have put some of my good friends, leading men in the House of Commons, to move the Assemblie to lay aside our questions for a time, and labour . . . the perfecting of the Confession of Faith and the Catechism.

Before Baillie's motion took effect, the Assembly had resolved [1] several clauses of its answer to the first query, and the divines were still engaged upon it when the message was brought from the House requesting them to hasten the perfecting of the Confession and Catechism.[2]

In his letter Baillie takes all the credit of this diversion to himself.

The Queries laid aside, July, 1646.

In the Assemblie we were like to have stucken many moneths on the "*questions*," and the Independents were in a way to gett all their differences debated over againe. I dealt so with Mr. Rouse and Mr. Tate that they brought in an order from the House to lay aside the "*questions*" till the Confession and Catechise were ended. Many took it for a trick of the Independents and Erastians for our hurt, but I knew it was nothing less.[3]

Although Baillie's assertion is to be taken with a certain amount of reserve (as is evident from the fact that on the 7th of December in the same year, 1646, the House sent to desire of the Assembly to

[1] Mitchell, 251-53, 255-57.
[2] *Ibid.*, 258, 22nd July.   [3] *Letters*, ii., 388.

speedily send in their answer to the queries),[1] yet

the result achieved was practically that which he asserts. For nearly two years, from July, 1646, to May, 1648,[2] the further consideration of the Queries was interrupted in the Assembly by the debates on the Confession and the Catechism. When, on the 9th of May of the latter year, the divines resumed the discussion of their answer to the Queries, they commenced with the still unanswered first Query. The work proceeded dilatorily, and apparently without reference to the progress previously made, although Baillie distinctly asserts that the committee of 1646 had prepared for report full answers to all the Queries. In June, 1648, *e.g.*, it was resolved to divide the Assembly into several committees to draw up their several answers to the Queries.[3] Five days later the divines returned to the subject in a lackadaisical way,[4] but from this date onwards to its close, no further reference occurs in their debates to the Queries. The Assembly melted away into oblivion, with its claim of the *jus divinum* still upon its head dishonoured and unsubstantiated.

With the outside and merely literary phase of the contest which waged between these clerics and the lay Erastians I am not so much concerned, save to indicate the general tenour of the argument.

The work which the Assembly as a body never accomplished was undertaken by the London clergy with a greater sense of freedom and irresponsibility towards the Parliament.

The *jus divinum regiminis ecclesiastici, or the*

The controversy taken up by the London clergy, Dec., 1646.

---

[1] C. J., v., 2.   [2] Mitchell, 516-19.
[3] *Ibid.*, 523.   [4] *Ibid.*, 525, 21st June, 1648.

Divine right of Church government asserted and evidenced by the Holy Scriptures . . . by sundry ministers of Christ within the city of London, was published on the 2nd of December, 1646.

It is entirely on the lines laid down through three years of bitter and wearisome warfare in the Assembly. It asserts that there is a Church government *jure divino* now under the New Testament declared in the Scriptures, shows what that government is, and concludes that neither the supreme civil magistrate as such, nor consequently any commissioners or committees nominated under, or by them, are or can be, the proper subject or wielder of the formal power of Church government.

In Baillie's opinion the answer was complete.

We have no more adoe in the Assemblie, neither know we any more work the Assemblie has in hand, but ane answer to the nine queries of the House of Commons about the *jus divinum* of diverse parts of the government. The ministers of London's late *jus divinum of Presbytery* does this abundantly, also a committee of the Assemblie has a full answer to all those queries ready. The authors repents much of that motion. Their aime was to have confounded and divided the Assemblie by their insnaring questions, but finding the Assemblie's unanimitie in them, the Independents' principles forceing them to join with the rest in asserting the Divine right of these points of government, whereupon the Parliament does most sticke, the movers of these questions wishes they had been silent.

It is possible that the answer which Baillie here asserts to have been fully drawn by the Assembly's Committee is represented in a controversial way by an anonymous *answer*, which was published late in 1646, as *an answer to those questions propounded*

by the Parliament to the Assembly of Divines touch-
ing the jus divinum *in matter of Church government.*
Wherein is clearly proved from Scripture that the
Presbyterial government is jure divino *of Divine in-*
stitution and according to the will and appointment
of Jesus Christ.[1]

The answer is comprehensive. All the nine Revolution in political theory implied in the attitude of the Presbyterian clergy of 1646 on this subject of the *jus divinum*.
Queries are gone through, though the bulk of the
reply is naturally devoted to the first. In discussing the crucial point, " whether any Church government be *jure divino*," the anonymous author raises
the large question of constitutional theory, and it
is for his explicit pronouncement upon it, and for
the method of his argument, that he is to be taken
as a complete representative of the revolution in
matter of political theory which had overtaken the
members of the English Church. As a separate
national Church it had been borne under the
shadow of the royal supremacy, and had been
subject at every point to the interference of the
civil or regal power. Even when it had been most
Calvinistic in doctrine, it had still been most territorial in constitution. But when, from being
merely Calvinistic in doctrine, it came to adopt a
Calvinistic Presbyterianism in matter of Church
government, it was obliged to fling away the political traditions of a century, and to reconstruct its
constitutional theory anew. Of such reconstruction of political theory this particular tract is most
aptly illustrative.

I shall answer this [first question] (he says) by dividing
the officers in the Church and bounding them in their place

---

[1] Bodlein Library (B., 20, 16, Linc.).

and station where Christ hath set them, and to prove that the one hath a Divine right of government from Christ in the State and not in the Church; and the other hath a Divine right of government in the Church but not in the State. I prove it thus: Christ hath two kingdoms, the one temporal the other spiritual (p. 10). . . . If kings and magistrates should rule in the Church as emperors rule the State, this were to dethrone Christ . . . to confound the spiritual kingdom of Christ with the kingdoms of men (p. 12). . . . The supreme magistracy is to judge and determine of sins by the positive laws of the land, and punish the offenders according to those laws in the temporal kingdom of Christ, but he may not judge and determine of them in the Church (p. 20). . . . Christ alone is to give both offices and officers and also their names, but Christ never gave any such for His Church as commissioners, neither must Parliaments create any names, or offices, or officers, as their creatures to be set up and appointed their work in the Church; it is a great affront to Christ, the Head of the Church, to do it . . . the authority of the Parliament will not bear them out when Christ will disclaim them as usurpers whom He never placed in the Church.[1]

Nothing could be more precise than such statements, and at the same time nothing could be more antagonistic at once to the whole traditions of English constitutional and ecclesiastical history, to the earliest principles of the Reformation, and to the prevailing trend of political thought and theory in the middle of the seventeenth century. The earliest Reformation had never proclaimed such a separation of the civil from the ecclesiastical government. It was the fatal and malignant heritage of the genius and life of Calvin, and how adversely it has affected the later history of European progress can hardly yet be estimated.

It matters little, from the point of view of this

[1] Mitchell, 525, 21st June, 1648.

narrative, that such a claim or theory was wrecked Chap. II.
by the success of the army ; the important point is
that it should ever have been advanced, and that
the English clergy even in part should ever have
given themselves over to it. The answer which it
received was as complete as it was representative.[1]

From the point of view of political theory, however, the most significant and complete reply is
contained in the *Leviathan.* Hobbes deduced the Hobbes'
rights of sovereign power and the duty of subjects reply.
thereto from the principles of nature only. Mon-
archical, aristocratical or democratical, all these
sorts of power are sovereign and coercive. Christ
left no coercive power, but only a power to pro-
claim the kingdom of Christ, and to persuade men
thereunto (chap. xlii.). If a man, therefore, should
ask a pastor his authority for the execution of his
office, he can make no other just answer but that
he doth it by the authority of the Commonwealth,
given him by the king or Assembly that repre-
senteth it. All pastors, except the supreme, execute their charges in the right ; that is, by the
authority of the civil sovereign that is *jure civili.*
But the king and every other sovereign executeth
his office of supreme pastor by immediate authority
from God ; that is to say, in God's right or *jure
divino.*

In intention Hobbes' lance, so far as it was
poised in controversy at all, was poised against

---

[1] See *The difference about Church government ended by taking
away the distinction of government into ecclesiastical and civil, and
proving the government of the civil magistrate only [alone] sufficient
in a Christian kingdom,* J. M., London, 30th May, 1646. See also
Saltmarsh's *Divine Right of Presbyterie,* 7th April, 1646.

Bellarmino and the temporal power of the Papacy, but the same shaft* that slew the Pope slew Presbytery.

§ V.—*Ordination.*

Logically, the Assembly, after having concluded on the 1st of January, 1643-44, the constructive portions of its debates on Church officers should have followed this work up by the consideration of the jurisdiction of those officers as exercised in the Church Assemblies, parochial sessions, classical presbyteries and provincial synods. That this course was not punctually pursued is to be attributed partly to the want of system in the Assembly's debates and partly also to the intrigue which Baillie details in his account of the debate of 29th December, 1643.[1] If, as may be gathered from Baillie's narrative, this intrigue was checked on the 29th of December, the check was not for long, for on Tuesday the 2nd of January, 1643-44, the Assembly deliberately resumed the consideration of the report made, the 5th of December preceding, by the second committee on the character of Apostles, their power to ordain in all Churches, to order all the service and worship, and to determine controversies of faith.[2]

Baillie, glossing over what must have been a severe tactical defeat of the Scotch Commissioners, merely says that the Assembly having reached certain conclusions concerning Church officers, before going on, "thought meet to consider some things further in the officers both extraordinar and

---

[1] *Supra*, pp. 164-5.   [2] Lightfoot, xiii., 98-99.

ordinar, some mor characters of the apostles, their
power to ordain " . . . etc.
Putting aside, however, the want of system in
the Assembly's debates, and the further question of
the war of parties, Presbyterian *versus* Independ-
ant among the divines themselves, there was a
pressing practical reason for the instant considera- Pressing
tion of this question of ordination, *viz.*, the actual need for some
need of the kingdom for some supply of new system of
ministers and some mechanism for presentation
and ordination. " There were divers motions and
reasons made and given to hasten that business
[of ordination] because of the great necessity of it
in the kingdom." [1]

The proposition as to the apostles' power to
ordain was passed on the first day's debate.[2] Their
power to appoint evangelists to ordain was voted
on the 4th.[3] Unlike the above two propositions,
which were hotly contested, their power to order
all the service and worship, and to determine
controversies of faith, passed on the 8th without
debate or difference, a fact which Lightfoot notes
as hitherto unexampled in the Assembly's history.[4]

After this preliminary or postliminary survey
which, according to Baillie, had ended in agreement after commencing in hot dispute from the
jealousy that the point had been raised " for pre- The As-
judice and far ends," [5] the Assembly settled down to the subject
to the more orderly discussion of the work of of ordination.

---

[1] Lightfoot, xiii., 102.
[2] *Ibid.*, 100, 2nd January, 1643-44.
[3] *Ibid.*, 103.   [4] *Ibid.*, 105.
[5] *Letters*, ii., 128-29.

ordination on a report thereon made by Dr. Temple from the third committee.[1]

The first contest on this report arose out of the third clause in it—who are to ordain? In the New Testament Apostles, Evangelists and preaching presbyters did ordain. "Because Apostles and Evangelists are officers extraordinary and not to continue in the Church, and since in Scripture we find ordination in no other hands, we humbly conceive that the preaching presbyters are only to ordain."[2]

The preamble or declaratory portions of this proposition were passed by the 16th of January,[3] and on the following day, Wednesday, 17th January, 1643-44, the Assembly approached the substantive part of it—"preaching presbyters are only to ordain," an alternative statement being offered in the following words: "Ordination is only in the hands of those who by office are to attend the preaching of the word and administration of the Sacrament".[4]

"When it was ready to go to the question whether this should be debated, there was a motion made by Mr. Calamy, and backed by Mr. Gillespie, that we might not fall as yet upon it. And so it was moved also by others. And this held us in debate whether we should fall upon this or no till twelve o'clock; and then upon a motion of Mr. Seaman's, there was a committee of Independents chosen that should state the question concerning ordination, and so we adjourned."[5]

[1] Lightfoot, xiii., 107, Tuesday, 9th January, 1643-44.
[2] Ibid., 107-9.   [3] Ibid., 113.
[4] Ibid., 114.   [5] Ibid.

Through the mouth of Mr. Nye this Independents' Committee reported two days later[1] in two
propositions (1) that as far as the participation of
the elders in that work is concerned, ordination Position of
the Indepen-
is simply the solemnisation of the officers' outward dents.
call; (2) there is no proof that in the act of ordination there is a derivation from the elders as such
of such power as gives formal being to an officer.[2]

On this report the Assembly spent very little
debate. The paper was laid aside, and the divines
almost instantly fell back upon the statement of the
question as drawn up on the preceding Wednesday,
viz., that ordination is only in the hands of
preaching elders.[3] Hardly had they reached this
determination, and commenced the debate, when
they received an order from the House of Lords
requiring them to dispatch the matter of ordination.
A committee was accordingly chosen to that end.
With commendable despatch the committee reported at the following meeting,[4] and in view of
the pressing need of the moment, and of the The abstract
question post-
practical nature of the report, the Assembly for poned before
the moment laid aside its wrangle as to the seat of the need for
some interim
the power of ordination.[5] ordination
machinery.

[1] Friday, 19th January, 1643-44; Lightfoot, 115.

[2] The proceedings of the Independents' Committee, and of the
Assembly, thereupon were the subject of bitter controversy in print
in 1645. See the Independents' *"copy of a remonstrance,"* B.M., E.
$\frac{300}{4}$, and the Assembly's *"answer"* thereto. The latter details the proceedings had on the matter of ordination at this particular juncture
by both Independents and the Assembly, *see* Hanbury, iii., pp. 1-31.

[3] Lightfoot, xiii., p. 116.

[4] Monday, 22nd January, *ibid.*, 116-17.

[5] In their *" copy of a remonstrance"* the Independents charge the
Assembly with having adopted the course it did at the above juncture

The report was as follows :—

1. In extraordinary cases, and until a settled order can be had, extraordinary means may be employed.

2. It is lawful, and according to the word, that certain ministers of the city be desired to ordain ministers in the vicinity *jure fraternitatis.*

The first of these propositions was passed on the following day,[1] 23rd January, after a hot protracted debate. The second was discussed on the 25th,[2] and later days. The reason of the bitter opposition of the Independents to this proposition lay in their fear that the operation of selecting some of the London ministers to carry on the work of ordination would " come too near a presbytery," that such ordination being a matter of jurisdiction those that performed it might also excommunicate, and that to settle so much at such a stage would be to prejudge the whole larger question of presbytery itself.[3] After holding through six days' obstinate debate (26th January to 2nd February), this question of the London ministers performing ordination was temporarily laid aside on the urgent motion of Lord Saye, and, spite the bitter opposition of the Independents, the precedent question of presbytery itself—the union of many churches under one presbytery—was ordered to be discussed in a proposition from a committee thereto appointed.[4] From this date until the 18th of March,

merely as a ruse to snatch a decisive vote for presbytery on a side issue.

[1] Lightfoot, 117-18.
[2] *Ibid.,* 120-21.   [3] *Ibid.,* 126, 129-30.
[4] Thursday, 1st February, *ibid.,* 131.

the large abstract question of presbytery was hotly
contested in the Assembly,[1] and it was only on its
conclusion, and on the decisive routing of the Independents, that the Assembly could resume the
subject of ordination, to which it was, in addition,
importuned by both the Earl of Warwick and the
Earl of Manchester, from the need of a supply of
divines for the navy and the Eastern Association.[2]
In consequence of the urgent request of the latter,
the Assembly at last, on Friday 15th March,[3] voted
to fall upon ordination, and the work was begun
on the following Monday, on a report from the
third committee. After two days' debate the
Assembly resolved, as preparatory to the whole
subject, that such as were to be ordained ministers
should be designed to some particular church or
other ministerial charge.[4] On the following day it
voted that no man should be ordained minister to a
particular congregation if that congregation could
show any just cause of exception against him.[5]
The formalities of ordination by the hands of
preaching presbyters were then successively agreed
upon by votes of 22nd and 25th March.[6] The
whole scattered series of votes thus passed concerning the doctrinal part of ordination were then
referred to a committee to be drawn up in proper
form. From this committee Dr. Burgess reported
on the 3rd April a series of twelve[7] propositions

---

[1] See *supra*, pp. 165-8.

[2] Lightfoot, xiii., 207, 217.   [3] *Ibid.*, 218.

[4] 20th March, *ibid.*, 228 ; Gillespie, 43-6.

[5] Lightfoot, 233 ; Gillespie, 45.

[6] Lightfoot, 233-5 ; Gillespie, 45-6.

[7] See them in Lightfoot, 237-8 ; and see Gillespie, p. 47.

on the doctrinal part of ordination, as representing the substance of the previous votes. The propositions were under acrimonious debate for most of that day, and were still unfinished when the Earl of Warwick intervened with an order from the House of Lords requesting the Assembly, now that it had concluded the doctrinal part of ordination, to fall upon a directory for the managing of it,[1] "that so both the navy and many congregations which want ministers may be timely furnished".[2]

In the afternoon of the same day, accordingly, the Assembly appointed a committee of eight to consider of some such Directory of Ordination, requesting at the same time the presence and assistance of the Scotch Commissioners in the work, and meanwhile the propositions concerning the doctrinal part of ordination were laid by till the completion of the said directory.[3]

On the 18th of April, Dr. Temple reported from this committee the Directory for Ordination so far as drafted, i.e., minus the preface and the questions to be proposed to candidates. It was thereupon passed on the same day, and ordered to be drawn up, so as to be sent to the two Houses.[4]

The Directory for Ordination and the twelve doctrinal propositions on ordination sent up to the Parliament, 20th April, 1644. On the following day, the preface and the ordination questions were reported from the committee and adopted, and thereupon the Assembly resolved to send up to the two Houses the completed directory together with the twelve propositions concerning the doctrinal portion of ordination.[5]

[1] Lightfoot, xiii., 239, Wednesday, 3rd April.
[2] L. J., vi., 498.   [3] Lightfoot, 240, 250.
[4] Ibid., 250-51; Gillespie, 53-4.
[5] Lightfoot, 252-53, and see supra, pp. 172-4.

This was accordingly done on the 20th of April,
1644, by Dr. Burgess and a committee on behalf
of the whole Assembly.[1]

At scattered intervals the House turned to the
matter in Grand Committee,[2] but practically the
effectual debate upon it did not begin till the 6th of
June, 1644, " when the committee first considered
whether to begin with the doctrinal part of the
divines report or with the practical portion of it
which was a directory for an extraordinary way of
putting it into a speedy practice for the present.
The Grand Committee resolved that a sub-committee should be appointed to consider both of the
positive rule in the doctrinal part, and of an extraordinary way to put it into practice *pro tempore*." [3]

On the 26th of June, the Commons ordered the
Grand Committee, and this sub-committee for the
matter of ordination, to make use of the advice
of the Divines of Assembly as they should find
occasion.[4] The meaning of such an order is
graphically explained by Baillie in his letter of
28th June, a letter which throws a strong light on
the Erastian proceedings of the sub-committee
from the time of its appointment three weeks
before.

[1] C. J., iii., 466 ; L. J., vi., 524. The subsequent debates in the
Assembly from 29th April, and more particularly from 8th May to
14th May, on the power of a congregation or of the preaching presbyters respectively to perform the work of ordination, is to be regarded
as pertaining to the theoretical debate of Presbytery, *ut supra*, pp.
172-5, 243. Gillespie, 55-64.

[2] 30th April, 2nd May, 24th May, 6th June, C. J., iii., 476, 506 ;
Whittaker's *Diary*, 267.

[3] Whittaker's *Diary*, 285.

[4] C. J., iii., 542 ; Lightfoot, 290.

After great labour we give in as our first fruits a paper for ordination of ministers to both the Houses. Oft had they called for it before it came. When it had lyen in their hands neglected for many weeks, at last it was committed to a few of the Commons to make a report to their House about it. We heard surmises that this committee had altered much of our paper; but I finding by Mr. Rous, the chief of that committee, that the alterations were both more and greater than we suspected, and that the committee had closed their report, and were ready to make it to the House without any further meeting, I persuaded him it would be convenient before the report was made and either House engaged in anything which was against the mind of the Assemblie and of our nation [Scotland] to confer privately with some of us anent these alterations. Upon this he obtained an order of the House for that committee to call for any of the Assemblie they pleased. This he brought to the Assemblie, and called out Marshall and me to tell us his purpose. We gave him our best advyce. On his motion the Assemblie named Marshall, Vines, Burgess, Tuckney, and the Scribes to wait on; and withall requested us [the Scotch Commissioners] to be with them. Great strife and clamour was made to have Mr. Goodwin joined, but he was refused by a vote. Marshall came not. At meeting we found they had past by all the whole doctrinall part of ordination and all our Scriptural grounds for it; that they had chosen only the extraordinarie way of ordination, and in that very part had scraped out whatever might displease the Independents or patrons, or Selden and others, who will have no discipline at all in any Church *jure divino*, but settled only upon the free will and pleasure of the Parliament. Mr. Henderson and the rest reasoned against the dangerousness and disgrace of this their way so clearlie that sundry of the gentlemen repented of their alterations; yet the most took all to advysement. We in private resolved we would by all means stick to our paper; else this being the first if we yielded to these most prejudicial alterations, which the Independents and civilians underhand had wrought, the Assemblie's reputation was clean overthrowne and Erastus' way would triumph. What will be the end of this debate God knows. If the Assemblie could stand to their deed, we hope to have the Parliament reasonable, for they will

be loth to loose the Assemblie and us for the pleasure of any
other party. But we fear the fainting of many of our House:
this holds our mind in suspense, only we are glad we have
taken the matter before it came to the House.[1]

In a subsequent letter of 12th July, Baillie
returns to this transaction with the Commons.

In our last debate with the Committee of Commons for our
paper of ordination we were in the midest over head and ears
of that greatest of our questions, the power of the Parliament in
ecclesiastick affairs. Its like this question shall be hotter here
than anywhere else: but we mind to hold off for yet its very
unseasonable. As yet we are come to no issue what to do with
that paper.[2]

Baillie's hopes of a favourable intervention of
providence in behalf of Scotch Commissioners
and presbytery were, however, disappointed. The
Battle of Marston Moor was fought on the 2nd of
July, and prevailing rumour attributed the victory
to Cromwell rather than to Leslie and the spirits
of the Independents were correspondingly raised.

Our Independents continews and increases in their obsti-
nacie (writes Baillie on the 23rd of July). Much is added to
their pride and hopes by their service at the battell of Yorke
albeit much of their valour is grounded on very false lies pre-
judiciall to God, the author, and to us the true instruments of
that day's honor. The politick part in the Parliament is the
stronger, who are resolute to conclude nothing in the matters
of religion that may grieve the Sectaries whom they count
necessitie for the moment.[3]

On the 19th of July, according to the *Commons* The Com-
Journals,[4] the first portion of the report of the Grand mittee's
Committee was adopted. According to Whittaker's report, July-
August, 1644.

---

[1] *Letters*, ii., 198-99. [2] *Ibid.*, 205.
[3] *Ibid.*, ii., 211. [4] C. J., iii., 565.

Diary [1] the Grand Committee reported through its chairman, Sir Thos. Widdrington, the first article for a temporary provision of ordination till the fundamental rules could be resolved upon. This article provided that ministers to be ordained should take the Covenant, be twenty-four years of age, and have a testimonial of learning, degrees, etc. "This was reported to the House, but not then resolved." [2]

Five days later the Grand Committee was ordered to meet every Tuesday and Thursday upon the matter. [3] It accordingly met hereon on the 2nd of August [4] when it proceeded with the directions for ordination as they were brought in from the sub-committee and from the Assembly of Divines, "and resolved to have twenty-three ministers about the city of London for the present until the form of Church government might be settled by the Assembly". [5]

The debates of the Grand Committee were continued on the 11th and 12th of August, and on Wednesday, the 14th of August, Sir Thos. Widdrington reported from it the rules for ordination and the votes and opinions of the committee upon the whole matter. [6] The House thereupon proceeded to adopt the report by resolution, and in conclusion ordered Mr. Rouse to deliver a copy of the whole business to the Assembly.

The draft ordinance, as it left the hands of the Commons, contained not so much a directory for ordination as a plan or scheme, or rough and ready

---

[1] p. 301.   [2] *Ibid.*   [3] C. J., iii., 568, 24th July.
[4] *Ibid.*, 576.   [5] Whittaker's *Diary*, 305.
[6] C. J., iii, 589; Whittaker's *Diary*, 308.

outline of a machinery for the practical work of ordination for the moment. It contained no reference whatever to the twelve doctrinal propositions on ordination. It merely appointed twenty-three presbyters, unnamed, of the city of London, or any one of them to examine, approve and ordain according to rules therein expressed.

In this form it took the divines by surprise. When Rouse presented it from the Commons to the Assembly on the 15th of August, Vines asked if the form was meant only for London, or for the rest of the kingdom. Rouse replied: " It is only for London for the present, but in time will be thought a pattern for the rest of the kingdom ". The House further resolved, on the 17th of August, in reply to a scruple from the Assembly, that the rules were to be only *pro tempore*.[1]

Attitude of
the Assembly
towards the
Commons'
draft Ordi-
nance.

To encourage the Assembly to reject the Commons' paper, the Scotch Commissioners disavowed it in their prayers, and set down their reasons in writing against it.[2] The Assembly thereupon (16th August) applied for leave to debate the Commons alterations as a whole before proceeding to nominate the divines, and, on leave, proceeded to the discussion.[3]

Neglecting the bellicose incitations of the Scotchmen, the divines proceeded to merely express their desires for changing most of the alterations.[4] Accordingly, on the 29th August, Dr. Burgess presented to the Commons " *the humble*

[1] C. J., iii., 593.   [2] Baillie, 221.
[3] Lightfoot, xiii., 305-7 ; C. J., iii., 592 ; Baillie, 223.
[4] Lightfoot, xiii., 305-7.

advice and request of the Assembly of Divines touching ordination pro tempore ".[1]   The Commons proceeded to accept most of the merely verbal alterations, but the clauses which the Assembly had appended to the advice met with a different fate.   In the 16th clause the divines wished to extend the mechanism for ordination, so as to include other places than London.   They therefore proposed that a " proportionable number of presbyters, according to the extent of each county, should be appointed in the several counties which were at the time quiet and undisturbed, for the ordaining of ministers for those counties ".   To this the House agreed with the addition of the words " to be approved by the Houses" after the word presbyter.

The Commons ignore the material part of the Assembly's objections.

The succeeding proposition " that the present directory for ordination *pro tempore* be no prejudice to the humble advice of the Assembly touching the doctrine or directory of ordination of ministers in the ordinary way formerly sent up to the honourable Houses of Parliament " was laid aside without anything being done thereupon.

Mr. Rouse and Mr. Tate were appointed to acquaint the Assembly with the action of the House.   On the 4th of September following, Dr. Burgess read to his fellow divines the return which the Assembly's Committee had drawn on the two points raised by the Commons.   The divines again desired (1) that ordination might be expressed to be " by the ordinance of Christ," (2) and " that it might be inserted that ministers were set over us as

[1] C. J., iii., 610.

rulers,"[1] both desires being reassertions of points intentionally omitted by the Commons.

The return was read in the Commons the same day, but the debate on it put off till the following Saturday.

On the 7th and 9th following, it was considered in Grand Committee.[2]

> Wee proceeded to a further debate touching the first point wherein the divines had made an alteration, which was the inserting these words " by the ordinance of Christ," which words because it was very strongly alleadged by many in the House that by the inserting of them the divines would bring in an acknowledgment of the House that the ordination of ministers by imposicon of hands is *jure divino* which was not conceived fit to be yeelded unto, noe such thing having been heretofore resolved upon either in the Church of England or in any other Reform'd Church, it was determined that theis words should not be inserted in that place but it was resolved upon the question thus farre that that ordinacon, that is a setting apart of some person or persons for the exercise or function of the ministrye in the Church of Christ, is of Christ's institucon. But for imposition of hands it was debated, but not at this tyme resolv'd."[3]

On the 13th of September the second amendment desired by the divines touching declaring preaching presbyters to be set over their charge in the Lord, was accepted and resolved by the House.[4] On that day, therefore, the whole ordinance (with the exception of another clause tendered from the Assembly[5] and passed on the 15th to 16th of September, providing that ordination should be by the

---

[1] Lightfoot, 308 ; Whittaker's *Diary*, 315-16. Gillespie, 65, attributes the action of the Commons to the influence of Selden.

[2] C. J., iii., 617, 620, 622.

[3] Whittaker's *Diary*, 317, 8th and 9th September.

[4] *Ibid.*, 319. [5] *Ibid.*, 320.

hands of the preaching presbytery) was passed, with blanks left for the names of the twenty-three divines for which latter it was again sent to the Assembly.[1] The names, ten of the Assembly and thirteen of the city divines, were chosen by a committee of the Assembly and presented on the 18th of September,[2] when they were inserted and the ordinance carried up to the Lords by Mr. Rouse.[3] It was read for the first time in the Lords on the 21st of September and a second time on the 23rd, being committed to a committee of the whole House.[4] On the 30th the Lords agreed to it with some alterations and a proviso.[5] The alterations consisted of the omission of the words that ministers were "set over us by the Lord"; the proviso was to the effect that the ordinance should remain in force for only twelve months. On a division, and after a long debate, the Commons voted to agree with the Lords on the omission of the abovesaid words.[6] The proviso was at the same time accepted, and on the following day, 2nd October, the ordinance was ordered to be printed.[7]

The ordi-
nance for
ordination
pro tempore
passed 2nd
Oct., 1644.

The care of printing it was referred to the Assembly, and when that body saw the ordinance in its final shape, they noticed the Lords' omission of the clause " to rule over them in the Lord ". Some debate was had concerning the reinstating of the clause, but the matter was allowed to drop and

---

[1] C. J., iii., 625.

[2] Lightfoot, 312 ; C. J., iii., 620-21.

[3] L. J., vi., 709 ; Whittaker's *Diary*, 321.

[4] L. J., vi., 712.   [5] *Ibid.*, vii., 3.

[6] Whittaker's *Diary*, 326 ; C. J., iii., 647, 1st October.

[7] C. J., iii., 648.

some merely trivial alterations of phrase were proposed by the Assembly to the Commons, Thursday, 3rd October, 1644. They were at once assented to by both Houses.[1]

In the course of the following month, on the 25th of November, 1644, the two Houses ordered a committee of twenty-one divines of the county of Lancaster to have power, according to the ordinance of 2nd October, for the ordaining of ministers *pro tempore*, within the county of Lancaster. Persons preaching or exercising any ministerial office, not ordained or thereto allowed by seven of the said ministers, were to be reported to both Houses of Parliament to be dealt with as they should think fit.[2]

Five months later, on the occasion of reports of the preaching of unordained and unqualified laymen in the army, the two Houses made an order against the preaching of any person not being an expectant on trial, or not ordained either in the English or some other Reformed Church.[3]

With the exception of these two measures, the subject of ordination was neglected by both the Assembly and the Parliament for the greater part of the succeeding year. With the prospect, however, of the establishment of presbyteries, the larger question of a settled method of ordination, to take the place of the temporary scheme adopted by the House, of necessity came to the front.

The subject of ordination recurs, 1645, September.

---

[1] Lightfoot, 314; Gillespie, 86; C. J., iii., 652; L. J., vii., 11. The ordinance is printed in its final form in the journals of the House of Lords, vii., 13-6.

[2] C. J., iii., 705.

[3] 25th April, 1645; C. J., iv., 122; L. J., vii., 337.

On the 26th of September, 1645, in connection with the votes concerning the enumeration of ex-communicable scandals, the House resolved that the ministers in the Province of London should ordain ministers within their several classes according to the Directory for Ordination already passed. It was ordered to be referred to a sub-committee of the Grand Committee how the resolution might most conveniently be put in execution. On the 22nd of October the Grand Committee of the House, acting doubtless on a report from the sub-committee, resolved that at the next sitting of the House an ordinance should be brought in to enable the presbyteries generally to ordain ministers. The task was committed to Tate and Rouse.[1] When, however, two days later the House adopted the ordinance as presented, they added a clause limiting its duration to twelve months.[2] The ordinance was read a first time in the Lords on the following day,[3] a second time on the 3rd of November,[4] and finally passed on the 8th of November.[5]

The second Ordinance for Ordination, 8th Nov., 1645.

This second Ordinance for Ordination provided that the several and respective classical presbyteries, within their respective bounds, should examine, approve and ordain presbyteries according to rules detailed, *viz.*, the expectant to bring certificates of having taken the Solemn League and Covenant, of his studies and degrees; to be examined touching the Grace of God in him and his call to the ministry, his knowledge and power to

---

[1] C. J., iv.. 317, 22nd October, 1645; Whittaker's *Diary*, 476-77.
[2] C. J., iv., 319, 24th October.   [3] L. J., vii., 659.
[4] *Ibid.*, 675.   [5] *Ibid.*, 682-83.

defend the orthodox doctrine ; to preach before the
classis, and then before his intended flock three
days ; his instrument, or *si quis*, then to be sent
to the congregation from the classis, and affixed on
the church door for any exceptions to be put in
against him ; the expectant then to be ordained in
the church to which he should minister with a solemn
fast and prayer, etc. Variations were allowed for
chaplains appointed to the army, navy or colleges.
The ordinance ended with the above provisos for
its endurance for twelve months only.

As yet, however, the ordinance was merely on
paper and ineffectual—pending the erection of the
presbyteries. The practical need for ordination
drove the Assembly again and again to agitate the
question of the erection of the classes. In January,
1646, there was a cry for ministers in Cumberland
and Westmoreland—no isolated case. The committee of the Assembly had had candidates for
vacant places before it, " only they are not in
orders. They do not scruple orders, but would
accept it if any to ordain them. The committee
would not send them down [to the country] without orders, but desire to take this hint to send a
message to the House of Commons that they
would set up a way of ordination." [1] Three days
later the Assembly appointed a committee of its
own body to consider of an expedient for present
way of ordination to be presented to both Houses
of Parliament. [2]

On the 12th of February, the Assembly decided

[1] Mitchell, 180, 20th January, 1645-46.
[2] *Ibid.*, 182.

after debate, to petition the House for the erection
of presbyteries in order that some machinery of
ordination might be set in work in the counties
in accordance with the late ordinance. The
Assembly's petition was presented on the 16th
February, 1645-46,[1] but practically the matter was
forced into abeyance until the settlement of the
question of classical jurisdiction enabled the erection of the Presbyterian system to be taken seriously in hand. On the eve of that event, the House
of Lords, on the 18th of May, 1646, appointed a
committee to consider of drawing up an ordinance
for ordinations to be indefinite.[2]

The object of the proposed measure was doubtless to place the exercise of ordination in the hands
of the classes about to be erected. There is no
trace of the measure having progressed any further
in the Lords. But towards the end of July, after
the classes had been actually established in London,
the Commons took up the matter independently,
though in an identical spirit. Harington and
Rouse were ordered to bring in an ordinance.[3] On

Final ordi-
nance for
ordination,
27th August,
1646.
its presentation, on the 27th of August, it was
rushed through the three readings without being
committed, and was passed the same day in the
Lords [4] as " *The Manner of Ordination of Ministers
in Classical Presbyteries, together with Rules for
examination*". This third ordinance contained a
proviso limiting its duration to three years only.

---

[1] C. J., iv., 443 ; L. J., viii., 166.
[2] L. J., viii., 320.
[3] C. J., iv., 630, 31st July, 1646.
[4] *Ibid.*, 653 ; L. J., viii., 474 ; Scobell, i., 99.

The comprehensive ordinance of 29th August, 1648,[1] for Church government, which incorporated the above ordinance of August, 1646, had no such clause limiting its duration.

§ VI.—*The Directory for Worship.*

In the order of the House of Commons of 18th September, 1643, which was finally passed as an ordinance of both Houses on the 12th of October, 1643, the Parliament had empowered the Assembly to debate and propound concerning a Directory of Worship, or Liturgy, hereafter to be used in the Church.[2]

The subsequent order of 17th October, by which the Parliament instituted the joint committee of Lords, Commons and Divines to treat with the Scotch Commissioners of the General Assembly, had given to this committee also power to treat concerning a Directory of Worship.[3]

As might easily be supposed, the Scotchmen were much more eager than the general body of the Assembly to approach such a subject. It was part of the design, which Baillie so naively confesses, to postpone a rupture with the Independents by turning the reforming zeal of the latter against the Book of Common Prayer.

It was my advice (he writes),[4] which Mr. Hendersone presentlie applauded, and gave me thanks for it, to eschew a publick rupture with the Independents till we were more able for them. As yet a Presbytrie to this people [Englishmen generally or Independents] is conceaved to be a strange

---

[1] Scobell, i., 165.   [2] *Supra*, pp. 153-4.
[3] C. J., iii., 278.   [4] *Letters*, ii., 117.

CHAP. II.
1643-4.

The Scotch-
men make
common
cause with
the Inde-
pendents
against the
Book of Com-
mon Prayer,
Dec., 1643.

monster. It was our good therefore to go on hand in hand so far as we did agree against the common enemie; hopeing that in our differences, when we behoove to come to them, God would give us light; in the meantime we could assay to agree upon the Directorie of Worship, wherein we expect no small help from these men [the Independents] to abolish the great idol of England, the Service Book, and to erect in all parts of worship a full conformitie to Scotland in all things worthie to be spoken of.

Haveing proposed these motions in the ears of some of the chieffe [Presbyterians] of the Assemblie and Parliament (but [except] in a tacit way all had been spoyled), they were well taken, and this day, as we resolved, were proponed by Mr. Solicitour, seconded by Sir Harie Vane, my Lord Say, and my Lord Wharton at our committee [the Joint Treaty Committee of Lords, Commons, Divines and Scotch Commissioners], and assented to by all, that a sub-committee of five, without exclusion of anie of the committee, shall meet with us of Scotland for preparing a Directorie of Worship to be communicate to the Great Committee [the Treaty Committee as above], and by them to the Assemblie. The men also, were, as we had forethought, Mr. Marshall, chairman of the committee, Mr. Palmer, Mr. Goodwin, Mr. Young, Mr. Herle, any two whereof with two of us make a quorum. For this good beginning we are very glad.

This particular letter of Baillie's is undated, but there is internal reason to assign 15th December, 1643, as the date of the transaction it records.

For the proceedings of this sub-committee of five, to which we have specific reference down to as late as 10th June, 1644, we are reduced to the authority of Gillespie's two pages of notes (pp. 101-102) and of Baillie's letters, with the further disadvantage that, besides being occasionally undated, some of his letters are really of the nature of *résumés* written upon different days and covering rather wide chronological spaces.

In the succeeding letter to the above-quoted, he thus describes the first work of the sub-committee :—

We had,[1] as I wryte, obtained a sub-committee of five to joyn with us for preparing to the Great Committee some materialls for a Directorie. At our first meeting for the first hour we made prettie progress to see what should be the work of ane ordinare Sabbath separate from fasts, communions, baptismes, marriage. Here came the first question about Readers. The Assemblie has past a vote before we came that it is a part of the Pastor's office to read the Scriptures ; what help he may have herein by these [Readers] who are not Pastors is not yet agitat. Always these of best note about London are now in use in the desk to pray and read on the Sunday morning four chapters and expone some of them, and cause sing two psalms and then to goe to the pulpit to preach. We are not against the minister's reading and exponing when he does not preach ; but if all this work be laid on the minister before he preach, we fear it put preaching in a more narrow and discreditable roume than we would wish. My overture was to pass over that block in the beginning and all other matter of great debaite till we have gone over these things wherein we did agree. This was followed. So beginning with the Pastor in the pulpit and leaving till afterward how families should be prepared in private for the work of the Sabbath, and what should be their exercise before the Pastor came to the pulpit, our first question was about the preface before praying. As for the minister's bowing in the pulpit we did misken it; for, besides the Independents' vehemencie against it, there is no such custom here used by any ; so we thought it not seasonable to move it in the verie entrie, bot mynds in due tyme to doe the best for it we may. A long debate we had about the conveniencie of prefaceing, yet at last we agreed on the expedencie of it. We were next settling on the manner of the prayer, if it were good to have two prayers, as we use, before sermon or bot one as they use, if in that first prayer it were meet to take in the King, Church and Sick, as they doe or leave these to the last prayer

Proceedings of the sub-committee for the Directory, Jan.-April, 1644.

[1] *Letters*, ii., 122-23.

as we. While we are sweetlie debaiting on these things, in came Mr. Goodwin, who incontinent assayed to turn all upside downe, to reason against all directories and our verie first grounds, also that all prefaceing was unlawfull, that according to 1 Tim. ii. 1 it was necessare to begin with prayer and that in the first prayer we behooved to pray for the King. . . . That day God opened my mouth somewhat to my own contentment to Goodwin's new motions; I thought I gott good new extemporall answers. However, he troubled us so that after long debates we could conclude nothing. For the help of this evill we thought it best to speak with him in private, so we invited him to dinner and spent an afternoon with him verie sweetlie. It were a thousand pities of that man; he is of manie excellent parts; I hope God will not permitt him to goe on to lead a faction for renting of the kirk. We and he seemed to agree prettie well on the most things of the Directorie. Always how all will be I cannot yet say, but with the next you will hear more; for we now resolve to use all meanes to be at same poynt.

In a later letter of 18th February, 1643-44, Baillie [1] briefly relates the proceedings of the succeeding meeting presumably in the first or second week of January.

> Likewise we pressed the sub-committee to go on in the Directorie. At that meeting Mr. Goodwin brought Mr. Nye with him; which we thought an impudent intrusion, but miskent it. After that all we had done had been ranversed we had so contrived it that it was laid, by all, upon us [the Scotch members

---

[1] Baillie, ii., 131. In the same letter he writes: "We had so contrived it with my Lord Wharton that the Lords that day did petition the Assemblie they might have one of the divines to attend their house for a week, as it came about, to pray to God with them. Some dayes thereafter the Lower House petitioned for the same. Both their designes was gladlie granted, for by this means the relicks of the Service Book which till then were every day used in both Houses are at last banished (*ibid.*, 130). See Lightfoot, xiii., pp. 103, 111, under dates 4th January and 11th January for these requests from the two Houses.

of the sub-committee, or the Scotch Commissioners in a body?] to present at the next meeting the matter of all the prayers of the Sabbath Day. This with much labour we drew up and gave in at the third meeting; whereupon as yet they are considering. By this ye may perceive that though our progress be small, yet our endeavours are the uttermost of our strength.

Again, later, speaking apparently of the second or third week of February, Baillie refers [1] to the work of the sub-committee as follows :—

In committee for the Directorie, we gave in the matter of publick prayer. It was well taken by all the committee, and I hope shall pass. It was laid on [us the Scotch members of the sub-committee, or the Scotch Commissioners generally] to draw up a directorie for both Sacraments; on Mr. Marshall for preaching; on Mr. Palmer for catechising; on Mr. Young for reading of Scriptures and singing of psalms; on Mr. Goodwin and Mr. Herle for fasting and thanksgiving. Had not the debate [in the Assembly] upon the main point of differing (the Presbyterie) withdrawne all our mind, before this these tasks had been ended. However, we expect by God's grace shortlie to end these. What is behind in the Directorie will all be committed the next time to the forenamed hands; and if it had past these, we apprehend no great difficultie in its passing both the Great Committee and the Assemblie and Parliament.

The sub-committee's distribution of the work of preparing the Directory.

At this point Gillespie's notes of the sub-committee's debates open with an account of the discussion on the 4th of March on the manner of receiving at the Communion.

It is to this hotly disputed subject that Baillie

---

[1] Baillie, ii., 140. The passage occurs in a letter dated 18th February, 1643-44. The latter part of the letter was added at a later date, which Baillie himself by a clerical error puts down as 3rd January. The editor of these letters alters it to 3rd February—a quite impossible emendation as it occurs after Baillie has been describing debates in the Assembly which took place as late as 16th February.

refers. In a letter of the 2nd of April,[1] he refers to the proceedings of the sub-committee on some occasion prior to that date :—

As for our Directorie, the matter of prayer which we gave in is agreed to in the committee. Mr. Marshall's part anent preaching, and Mr. Palmer's about catechising, though the one be the best preacher and the other the best catechist in England, yet we no wayes like it; so their papers are past in our hands to frame them according to our mind. One paper anent the Sacraments we gave in. We agreed so farr as we went except in a table. Here all of them opposeth us, and we them. They will not, and saith the people will, never yield to alter their practise. They are content of sitting albeit not as of a ryte institute; but to come out of their pews to a table they deny the necessitie of it. We affirme it necessare and will stand to it. The Independents' way of celebration seems to be very irreverent. They have the Communion every Sabbath without any preparation before or thanksgiving after; little examination of people, their very prayers and doctrine before the Sacrament uses not to be directed to the use of the Sacrament. They have, after the blessing, a short discourse and two short graces over the elements, which are distributed and participate in silence without exhortation, reading or singing, and all is ended with a psalme without prayer. Mr. Nye told us his private judgment that in preaching he thinks the minister should be covered and the people discovered, but in the Sacrament the minister should be discovered as a servant and the guests all covered.

The Assembly appoints its own Committee for the Directory, 3rd April.

Up to this point the matter of the Directory had rested entirely with the sub-committee of the Treaty Committee. On the 3rd of April, however, the House of Lords at last took notice of the matter, and in the order of that day, in which they requested the Assembly to draw up a directory for the practice of ordination, they also desired

[1] *Letters*, ii., 148-49.

"that the Assembly may be hastened to agree upon directions for worship, and especially for the administration of sacraments".[1] This order was reported to the Assembly by the Earl of Warwick on the same day. The Assembly considered the order on the afternoon of the same day, and passed a resolution that the [12] Divines of the Assembly formerly appointed as its members of or contribution to the Grand Treaty Committee of Lords, Commoners, Scotchmen and divines, should be a committee as from the Assembly for the work of the Directory. At the same time the desire was expressed that the sub-committee of five of the Grand Treaty Committee which had hitherto busied itself with the provisional drafting of the Directory should hasten that work.[2] A week later the Scotch Commissioners offered " something for the Directory of Worship," desiring the Assembly to take it in hand,[3] with a view to making a good report to the General Assembly in Scotland, which was to meet in the following month.

It was not, however, until Tuesday, the 21st of May that the Assembly took notice of the matter. On that day Mr. Rutherford moved for the speeding of the Directory for Worship. The motion was backed by Mr. Marshall, and an order thereupon made to bring in some report on the following Friday.[4] On the day appointed, Friday, 24th May, the chairman from the Assembly's committee for the Directory reported largely concerning the Lord's

CHAP. II.

1644,
April-May.

The Directory for Worship in the Assembly, May-Nov., 1644.

---

[1] L. J., vi., 498.

[2] Minutes of the Westminster Assembly, i., 419 b ; Dr. Williams' Library ; Lightfoot, p. 239.

Lightfoot, 242, 10th April.   [4] Ibid., 268.

Day, and prayer and preaching. These portions held the Assembly all the succeeding week, when the portions concerning the Sabbath and the directory for prayer were passed.[1]

Writing on the 31st of the same month, Baillie for once expresses content with the speed of the Assembly's progress :—

> Our great debate of the power of excommunication we have laid aside and taken in at last the directory. Already we have past the draught of all the prayers, reading of Scripture, and singing of psalms on the Sabbath Day *nemine contradicente*. We trust in one or two sessions to get through also our draught of preaching. If we continue this race we will amend our former infamous slowness. Always I can say little till once we pass the directorie of the Lord's Supper in the committee [which] we found there very sticking ; the Independents and all love so well sundry of their English guyses which we must have away. However, we are in better hope of a happie speed than before.[2]

The Directory for Preaching.

The Directory for Prayer.

The Directory for the Sacrament.

The Directory for Preaching was under debate when Lightfoot returned to Westminster on the 4th of June, and held through 5th June to 15th.[3] The Directory for Prayer was passed in a single sitting on the 14th June.[4] The Directory for the Sacrament, however, was a much more difficult matter. On the preceding 6th of June, Mr. Marshall had made a report from the committee for the Directory of two prefatory propositions in substance as follows :—

1. The Communion to be celebrated frequently.

2. Unbaptised, ignorant, scandalous, or strangers not to be admitted.[5]

---

[1] Lightfoot, 277. [2] *Letters*, ii., 187.

[3] Lightfoot, 277-85.

[4] *Ibid.*, 284-85 ; Gillespie, 102. [5] Lightfoot, 279.

These propositions were under discussion on Monday, 10th June,[1] but laid aside apparently for the moment in favour of the more practical parts of the Directory for the Sacrament, which were under discussion from the 18th June.[2] The point of sitting at the Table, and of coming in successive companies to partake, was only resolved on the 5th of July after an exceedingly bitter struggle between the Scotchmen and the Independents,[3] and was almost immediately undone by a committee appointed for accommodation.

We are proceeding in our Assemblie (writes Baillie in an undated public letter[4]). This day before noone we gott sundrie propositions of our directory for the Sacrament of the Lord's Supper past. But in the afternoone we could not move one inch. The unhappie Independents would mangle that Sacrament. No catechising nor preparation before ; no thanksgiving after ; no Sacramental doctrine or chapters on the day of celebration ; no coming up to any table, but a carrying of the element to all in their seats athort the Church ; yet all this with God's help we have carryed over their bellies to our practise. But exhortations at tables yet we stick at. They would have no words spoken at all. Nye would be at covering the head at the receaving. We must dispute every inch of our ground.[5]

Again, on the 28th of June, Baillie writes :—[6]

This day we were vexed also in the Assemblie ; we thought we had passed with consent sitting at the Table ; but behold Mr. Nye, Goodwin, and Bridge cast all in the howes denying to us the necessity of any table, but pressing the communicating of all in their seats without coming up to a table.

---

[1] Lightfoot, xiii., 282.   [2] *Ibid.*, 285.
[3] *Ibid.*, 286-93.
[4] ? 8th June or end of June, 1644 ? ; see Lightfoot, xiii., 289.
[5] *Letters*, ii., 195.   [6] *Ibid.*, ii., 199.

Messrs. Henderson, Rutherford, and Gillespie all three disputed exceeding well for it with arguments unanswerable, yet not one of the English did joine with us, only Mr. Assessour Burgess, who then was in the chair, beginning to speak somewhat for us but a little too vehementlie, was so mett with by the Independents that a shamefull and long clamour ended their debaite. This has grieved us that we feare the end of our worke, allwayes we expect it shall be better.

The day after the appointment of the Committee for Accommodation on this fantastically disputed point that body reported, proposing to omit from the Directory all the passages concerning coming in companies to the table, retaining only "the communicants orderly sitting about the table ".[1]

The Scotchmen accepted the compromise with very bad grace, desiring that they might impart so much to their General Assembly, promising withal, perhaps in irony, to do it with all reverence and respect to the Assembly of Divines.

Directory for Baptism.

On the following day the Assembly commenced the Directory for Baptism, Thursday, 11th July.[2]

On the 12th of July, Baillie writes :—

In our Assemblie we goe on as we may. The Independents and others keeped us long three weeks upon one point alone, the communicating at a table. By this we came to debate the diverse coming up of companies successively to a table ; the consecrating of the bread and wine severallie ; the giving of the bread to all the congregation, and then the wine to all, and so twice coming up to the table, first for the bread and then for the wine : the mutuall distribution, the table exhortations and a world of such questions, which to the most of them were new and strange things. After we were overtoyled with debate, we were forced to leave all these things and take us to generall

---

[1] Lightfoot, 296, 10th July.   [2] *Ibid.*, 296.

expressions, which by a benigne exposition would infer our Church practices, which the most promised to follow so much the more as we did not necessitate them by the Assemblie's express determinations. We have ended the matter of the Lord's Supper, and these last three dayes have been upon Baptisme. We have carryed with much greater ease than we expected the publicness of Baptisme. The abuse was great over all this land. In the greatest parish in London scarce one child in a year was brought to the Church for Baptisme. Also we have carried the parent's presenting of his child, and not their midwives, as was their universall custome.[1]

Several days' debate were spent on the question of dipping *versus* sprinkling, and the matter was only in fine evaded by omitting reference to dipping, and resolving that sprinkling was not only lawful but sufficient and expedient.[2]

On the 8th August, the Directory for Baptism was completed and passed,[3] and in the next meeting Friday, 9th August, Mr. Marshall reported for debate a Directory for Thanksgiving, which was passed a week later.[4]

On the 20th of August, in accordance with the recommendations reported by Mr. Palmer from the Grand Treaty Committee, the Assembly chose a committee of three to draw up the Directory in whole into a model form.[5]

"The most of the directorie is past" (writes Baillie on the 28th of August), "and the rest is given to hands to prepare the models for the Assemblie."[6]

In the second week of October, the Assembly

---

[1] *Letters*, ii., 204.   [2] Lightfoot, 301, 8th August.
[3] *Ibid.*   [4] Friday, 16th August, *ibid.*, 305.
[5] *Ibid.*, 305.   [6] *Letters*, ii., 224.

spent two days on additions to the Directory for Baptism.[1] A fortnight later, the Commons requested the Assembly to speed the Directory for Worship and to send it in.[2] The message was delivered on the following day, and in reply to it the Assembly resolved that the Directory should be brought in [*i.e.*, from the Assembly's Committee to the Assembly itself] on the ensuing Monday or Tuesday, 28th or 29th October.[3]

Writing on the 1st of November, Baillie sums up the progress achieved in these words :—

> The preface of our directorie casting out at doores the Liturgie and all the ceremonies *in cumulo* is this day past. It cost us diverse dayes debate, and these sharp enough with our best friends.[4]

The Preface.
The concluding clauses of the preface were under debate on the 7th and 8th November.[5] On the 11th, and following day, the whole Directory was read through with the purpose of a general review.[6]

---

[1] 9th to 10th October, Lightfoot, 314; Gillespie, 88-91.

[2] C. J., iii., 675, 24th October.

[3] Lightfoot, 321; Gillespie, 96.

[4] *Letters*, ii., 240.

[5] Lightfoot, 322, 324.

[6] *Ibid.*, 325-27. One alteration made in this review is noticeable. The Scotch Commissioners expressed their dislike of the wording of the paragraph which related to sitting at the table at the Sacrament. Their engagements or instructions from Scotland were to take the clause only in the sense of sitting to the table. "And therefore they either desired a recommittment of this passage or that their sense might be expressed in the margin—which cost a long and large debate: at last it was concluded thus to have it in the text 'about the table or at it as in the Church of Scotland' and so they retain their custom and we of England are left at liberty, and so it was the sense of the Assembly that we might at liberty either cause the communicants to sit at the table or at some distance about it" (Lightfoot, 326).

With the exception of the wording of the pre- CHAP. II.
face, the whole Directory was finished on the latter
day (12th November, 1644) and voted to be sent
up to the Parliament.

1644,
November.

Pending the transcribing of the whole form, the
Assembly, on the 19th November, turned to the debate of the preface as reported by Dr. Burgess, and
passed it in the next meeting after some heated
opposition from the Independents on the ground of
the reference to the Solemn League and Covenant.[1]
A committee was thereupon appointed to carry
up the Directory and preface to the Parliament.
Accordingly, on the following day Dr. Burgess
presented to both Houses " *the humble advice of*
the Assembly of Divines sitting by ordinance of
Parliament at Westminster, concerning a Directory
for the public Worship of God in the three kingdoms ".[2]

The Di-
rectory for
Worship
transmitted
from the
Assembly to
the Parlia-
ment, 21st
November,
1644.

For once Baillie was jubilant :—

> That which comforts us most is the Directorie.   All that we
> have done in it is this day sent up with a full unanimity of all :
> many a wearisome debate has it cost us, but we hope the sweet
> fruit will over-balance the very great toyle we had on it.   The
> last passage was sensibly guided by God.   After with huge deal
> of adoe we had past the parts that concerned prayers, reading
> of scripture, preaching, both the Sacraments, ordination and
> santification of the Sabbath, there was many references to the
> preface ; and in this piece we expected most difficulty ; one
> party purposing by the preface to turn the Directorie to a
> straight Liturgie, the other to make it so loose and free that it
> should serve for little use ; but God helped us to get both these
> rocks eschewed.   Always here yesterday when we were at the
> very end of it the Independents brought us so doubtful a dis-
> putation that we were in very great fear all should be cast in

[1] Lightfoot, 334 ; Mitchell, 4, 5.

[2] C. J., iii., 701 ; L. J., vii., 71, Thursday, 21st November.

CHAP. II.
1644,
November.

the howes and that their opposition to the whole Directorie should be as great as to the Government; yet God in His mercy guided it so that yesterday we gott them and all others so satisfied that *nemine contradicente* it was ordered altogidder to be transmitted to the Houses, and Goodwin to be one of the carryers, which this day was done to all our great joy and hope that this will be a good ground of agreeance betwixt us and them eider soon or syne. What remains of the Directory anent marrying and burial will soon be despatched.[1]

Supplementary portions of the Directory.

The elaboration of the supplementary portions of the Directory are detailed in the footnote.[2]

[1] *Letters*, ii., 242, 21st November, 1644.

[2] The *Directory for Observation of the Sabbath* was reported from the second committee on Tuesday, 12th November, 1644, and debated on the two following days, and again on the 19th and 20th November (Lightfoot, 325, 327-30, 334; Mitchell, 3, 6). It was finished on the latter day, and ordered to be sent in on the 21st to the Parliament along with the Directory for Worship *ut supra.*

The *Directory for Marriage* was reported from the second committee on the 21st of November, and debated (Lightfoot, 335; Mitchell, 7) on that and the following 22nd, 25th, 28th (Mitchell, 11), 29th (Lightfoot, 337; Baillie, ii., 244), Monday, 2nd December (Lightfoot, 338), and was passed on the latter date on an urgent message from the House for the finishing of these concluding parts of the Directory in view of the laying by of the Common Prayer Book, which could not be done till the whole was completed. On the following day, 3rd December, it was transcribed, read and concluded upon to be transmitted to Parliament (*ibid.*, 339).

The *Directory for Burial* was reported on the 3rd December, 1644 (Lightfoot, 338; Mitchell, 13), and debated on the 4th and 6th (*ibid.*, 539, and 14-15), and concluded on the 9th, after a great controversy about funeral sermons, which the Scots objected to, but which the English wished to retain (*ibid.*, 340, and 16; Baillie, ii., 245). In its final form, it was read on the 13th of December, passed and ordered to be sent up (Lightfoot, 342-43).

The *Directory for Thanksgiving for the Churching of Women* was reported and ordered to be waived on the 13th of December (Mitchell, 20; Lightfoot, 343).

The *Directory for Visitation of the Sick* was reported, debated and voted on the 11th of December (Lightfoot, 342; Mitchell, 19).

Writing on the 26th of December, 1644, Baillie sums up the progress made upon the Directory in terse jubilant words :—

We daily now make good progresse in the Assemblie. We have sent up our Directorie for Marriage and Thanksgiving ; we have also gotten through Buriall. We have some little thing to say of Fasting and Visiting of the Sick ; and so our long looked for Directory will be closed : its exceedinglie lyked by all who sees it. Every piece of it passes the House as fast as we send it.[1]

On the 16th it was read, voted and ordered to be sent to the Parliament (Mitchell, 20).

The *Directory concerning Fasting Days* was reported on the 13th of December, but being exceeding long and full of controversial matter was recommitted (Lightfoot, 343 ; Mitchell, 20). It was again reported on the 16th (Mitchell, *ibid.*), and debated on the 19th (*ibid.*, 21 ; Lightfoot, 344), 20th (Mitchell, 22), and 27th, when it was passed and ordered to be sent up (*ibid.*, 23).

The *Directory for Psalms.* Reading of Scripture and the Psalms had been referred by the sub-committee to Mr. Young, see *supra,* p. 341. On the 22nd and 23rd of May, 1644, his draft of a directory for this branch was debated in the sub-committee (Gillespie, p. 101-2). The Directory was ordered on the 12th of December to be prepared by the Assembly's committee (Mitchell, 19). It was reported on the following day (*ibid.*, 20 ; Lightfoot, 343), and debated on the 19th of December (*ibid.*, 21, and 343). The Directory was finished and passed in the absence of the Scotch Commissioners, and on their entering the Assembly they expressed dislike at the permission accorded of reading the psalms line by line. It was accordingly referred to them to draw up something on the point, and to present it to the Assembly (*ibid.*, 21, and 344). On the 27th the final report was made, and the Directory adopted and ordered to be sent up (*ibid.*, 23).

The *Directory for Holy Days and Holy Places* was reported to the Assembly on Monday, 25th November, 1644, and read (Mitchell, 11). It was debated on the 10th December (*ibid.*, 17 ; Lightfoot, 341), on the 11th (*ibid.*, 342), and 19th and 27th (Mitchell, 23), when an appendix to it was reported and debated.

The *Directory for Public Thanksgiving* was reported on the 6th of December (Lightfoot, 339 ; Mitchell, 16).

[1] *Letters,* ii., 247.

CHAP. II.

1644,
November.

The Directory
debated in
the Parliament, November, 1644,
to January,
1645.

The House of Commons was indeed, for once, acting promptly.

On the 22nd of November, 1644, and following days, the day after the Assembly's "*humble advice concerning a directory for the public worship of God in the three kingdoms*" had been presented, the Commons sat down at eight o'clock in the morning peremptorily to consider it. Clause by clause it was read, and each particular title and paragraph voted and passed upon the question. Alterations were made—slight, but significant. In the clause of the chapter relating to the Sacrament of the Lord's Supper, which concerned the sitting at or about the table, the words "as in the Church of Scotland" were voted to be omitted by 57 to 34.[1]

On the 23rd [2] of November, the substance of the Directory for Worship was passed, with the exception of the clause relating to the admission to the Sacrament, a clause which the House referred to a committee. On the following Saturday, 30th November, this committee reported advising the omission of the clause as it stood in the "*humble advice*," and proposing in the place of it the words "the ignorant and the scandalous are not fit to receive the Sacrament of the Lord's Supper". These words were accordingly adopted and ordered to be inserted.[3] On the same day the Ordinance for taking away the Book of Common Prayer, and for establishing and putting in execution the Directory, was introduced into the House, read a first and

[1] C. J., iii., 702, 705.
[2] Whittaker's *Diary*, 351, says the 26th of November.
[3] C. J., iii., 709.

second time, and committed.[1] The amendments to
the Ordinance were reported and adopted on the
12th of December.[2]

On the 28th of December, the completed
Directory, together with the Ordinance establishing
it, was passed and ordered to be engrossed. On
the 1st of January, it was taken up to the Lords by
Mr. Rouse.[3] Although the Lords had received the
various portions of the Directory concurrently with
the Commons, they do not appear to have done
more than ceremonially read them, waiting apparently for the initiative of the Lower House.
They, however, proceeded immediately to the consideration of the Ordinance and the Directory on
receipt of them from the Commons, and passed them
with some amendments on the 3rd of January.[4]
On the following day these amendments were the
subject of a conference between the two Houses,
and were finally agreed upon.

The Ordinance itself, which is prefixed to the
Directory, is incorrectly dated 3rd January, 1644-45.

The Ordin-
ance for the
Directory
passed, 1644-
45, 4th Jan.

[1] C. J., iii., 709.

[2] *Ibid.*, iii., 722. The subsidiary portions of the Directory were
adopted successively as they were sent up from the Assembly.

The *Directory for Marriage* was brought into the House on
the 4th of December, and was adopted on the 6th (C. J., iii., 713,
715). The report concerning Burial was brought up on the 13th of
December (L. J., vii., 97). Visitation of the Sick presented 16th and
17th December (C. J., iii., 724 ; L. J., vii., 103), and adopted on the
26th and 28th of December, with alterations (C. J., iv., 2 and 3).
The remaining portions concerning Public Fasts, Thanksgiving and
Singing of Psalms, were brought to the House on the 27th of December.
The appendix touching Days and Places for Public Worship was sent
into the House on 1st January 1644-45, and adopted the same day
(C. J., iv., 6 ; Whittaker's *Diary*, 366).

[3] C. J., iv., 3, 6 ; L. J., vii., 119.   [4] L. J., vii., 125 ; C. J., iv., 9.

The Directory accepted in Scotland.

On the 27th of February, 1644-45, the Scotch Commissioners from the General Assembly informed the House of Lords, through the Treaty Committee presumably, that the Directory for Public Worship had passed the Assembly and Parliament of Scotland unanimously, and without alteration. On their desire that it might be referred to the Assembly of Divines to make a title to the work, and that it might be printed, the Lords passed an order to that effect.[1]

In the report, however, which was given to the House of Commons by Mr. Tate, on the 5th of March, 1644-45, certain alterations in the Directory for Public Worship were brought in as being desired by the General Assembly of Scotland. They were passed in both Houses on the same day.[2] On the following day the title to the Directory was reported from the Assembly and adopted[3] as "*a Directory for the Public Worship of God throughout the three kingdoms of England, Scotland and Ireland, together with an Ordinance of Parliament for the taking away of the Book of Common Prayer, and for establishing and observing of this present Directory throughout the kingdom of England and dominion of Wales*".

The first Ordinance for the Directory, 5th March, 1645.

The speed with which the Directory had been pushed in its final stages, through both Assembly and Parliament, was due entirely to the wish to present it as an enacted and completed whole to the king in the Treaty of Uxbridge.

[1] L. J., vii., 255.
[2] C. J., iv., 70; L. J., vii., 264, where the alterations are detailed.
[3] C. J., *ibid.*; L. J., *ibid.*, 265.

The failure of the negotiations practically left the Directory as a dead thing in the hands of the Commons, for as yet no steps had been taken to enforce it, or to disperse it through the country.

On the 17th of April, 1645, however, the Commons resolved that an ordinance should be forthwith brought in for the dispersing of the Directory for Worship into all the parish churches and chapels in England, Wales and Berwick, for the putting of it into present execution and for abolishing the Book of Common Prayer together with some penalties to be imposed on all who should make use of the Book of Common Prayer or neglect the Directory, or should write, preach or publish any book written in contempt or depravation thereof.[1] The matter was referred to a sub-committee; and, under the influence of the Scotch Commissioners,[2] a measure was drafted which in its first state was of a rigour satisfactory even to Baillie.

> For preachers or wryters or publishers against it, were they dukes and peers, their third fault is the loss of all their goods and perpetuall imprisonment.

In this form it was reported to the House on the 27th of June, 1645, read a first and second time and committed.[3] The committee's amendments were debated on the 25th of July, 1645,[4] and on the 6th of August the ordinance passed and was sent up to the Lords.[5] On the 12th of August it was read twice in the Upper House, and committed to a committee of the whole House.[6] Eleven

[1] C. J., iv., 113.   [2] Baillie, *Letters*, ii., 271.
[3] C. J., iv., 187.   [4] *Ibid.*, 218.
[5] *Ibid.*, 232.   [6] L. J., vii., 532.

Chap. II.

1645,
August.

The second
Ordinance for
the Directory,
23rd August,
1645.

days later, the Lords agreed to the Ordinance with certain amendments, which were instantly assented to by the Commons. It was then ordered to be forthwith printed and published [1] as "*an ordinance of the Lords and Commons assembled in Parliament for the more effectual putting in execution the Directory for Public Worship*".

The defect of the previous Ordinance had consisted in its not prescribing a penalty for the use of the Book of Common Prayer, or for neglecting to use the Directory, "by means whereof there has been as yet little fruit of the said Ordinance". The new Ordinance, accordingly, required the Parliamentary committees of the various counties to distribute copies of the Directory to each parish and chapelry, to be delivered by the constables or other officers to the respective ministers of the same, to be openly read in the churches the Sunday after receipt of the book. Persons reading the Common Prayer-book thereafter were to pay £5 for a first offence, £10 for a second, and for a third to suffer a year's imprisonment without bail.

Ministers neglecting to use the Directory were to pay 40s. for every neglect; persons depraving the same, either by speech or writing, to suffer a fine of not less than £5, and not more than £50. Charges to be preferred before the next or General Sessions, or at the next General Quarter Sessions, and the trial to be according to the law of the land.

Within a month of the publication of the ordinance all copies of the Common Prayer-book

---

[1] C. J., iv., 251; L. J., vii., 547, 551, 23rd August, 1645.

remaining in parish churches or chapels were to

be carried by the churchwardens or constables to the respective County Committees to be disposed of as the Parliament shall direct.

Stringent as the Ordinance was in this its final form, it fell far short of the savage rigour of the first draft of it, on which Baillie had gloated with such Presbyterian glee.

§ VII.—*The Confession of Faith.*

The Confession of Faith and the Catechisms were regarded by Baillie and his contemporaries as the final work of the Assembly.[1]   By later Presbyterians it has been regarded as not only its final but also its greatest production.   As, however, throughout the course of construction, both of Confession and of Catechism, there was no essential difference of opinion either on matters of doctrine, or still less on any constitutional question at all, the record of its passage through the Assembly is a merely annalistic and uninteresting one.   We no longer meet with any of those revelations of party strife or state policy which mark the path of the construction of, *e.g.*, the Ordinance for Scandal or Ordination.

On the 17th of April, 1645, the House commenced the adoption of its series of votes specifying the degrees of ignorance and scandal which should justify exclusion from the Sacrament.   The defini- tion of ignorance led of necessity to the need of a formulation of a Confession of Faith, and the

Need of a Confession of Faith for the purposes of a sacramental test.

---

[1] Baillie, *Letters*, ii., 300.

House by direct resolution thereupon desired the Assembly, with all convenient speed, to resolve upon some such Confession of Faith of the Church of England, and present it to the House.[1] It is probably this order to which the minutes of the Assembly refer, under date 18th April, when a committee was appointed.[2]

The Assembly's work on the Confession, April, 1645, to June, 1646.
On 21st April, 1645, the divines ordered the committee for the Confession of Faith to meet on the following Wednesday.[3] The committee would appear to have subdivided, for on the 9th of May following, two days after a request from the House to hasten the Confession,[4] the Assembly ordered that the best way to expedite it should be debated on the following Monday, 12th May, and that the two committees for the Confession should be put into one.[5] On the day appointed, accordingly, after debate, the Assembly appointed a committee of seven, with the assistance of the Scotch Commissioners, to draw the first draft of the Confession.[6]

It was not until the 4th of July that the matter again came before them. On that day the sub-committee was ordered to report on the following Monday, 7th July, so much of the Confession as they had in their hands concerning God and the Scriptures.[7] As ordered, the report was made so

---

[1] C. J., iv., 113. Nine months before receiving this order, the Assembly had, in a preliminary way, approached the task of drawing up a Confession, appointing a committee for it under the chairmanship of Dr. Temple. Lightfoot, xiii., 305, 308, 20th August and 4th September, 1644.

[2] Mitchell, 83.   [3] Ibid., 83.
[4] C. J., iv., 133.   [5] Mitchell, 90.
[6] Ibid., 91, 12th May, 1645.   [7] Ibid., 109.

far as concerned the Scriptures, and after debate

thereupon it was resolved that Reynolds, Herle and Newcomen should take care of the wording of the Confession as voted in the Assembly from time to time, reporting thereupon as occasion arose after consultation with the Scotch Commissioners.[1]

On the 11th of July it was ordered, doubtless for greater despatch, to divide the body of the Confession among the three committees of the Assembly.[2] The report of the proposed heads was made on the 16th of July,[3] and adopted as follows :—

The first committee to prepare the heads God and the Holy Trinity, God's decrees, predestination, election, etc., the works of creation and providence, man's fall.

The second committee : Sin and the punishment thereof, free-will, the covenant of grace, Christ our Mediator.

The third committee : Effectual vocation, justification, adoption, sanctification.

To this enumeration was added on the 18th of November, 1645, a further distribution of heads as follows :—[4]

To *the first committee :* Perseverance, Christian liberty, the Church, the Communion of Saints.

To *the second committee :* Officers and censures of the Church, councils or synods, sacraments, Baptism and the Lord's Supper.

To *the third committee :* The law, religion, worship.

Similarly, on the 23rd of February, 1645-46, a third distribution of heads took place as follows :—[5]

To *the first committee :* Christian Sabbath, the civil magistrate, marriage and divorce.

---

[1] Mitchell, 110, 8th July, 1645.   [2] *Ibid.,* 112.
[3] *Ibid.,* 113.   [4] *Ibid.,* 164.   [5] *Ibid.,* 190.

To *the second committee :* Certainty of salvation, lies and equivocation, the state of the soul after death.

To *the third committee :* The resurrection, the last judgment, life eternal.

On the 8th of December, 1645, Tuckney, Reynolds, Newcomen and Whitaker were appointed a committee to review the Confession of Faith as it was finished in the Assembly.[1]

After the interruption of these debates, caused by the question of the *jus divinum,* the Assembly returned to its Confession on the 17th June, 1646, when Mr. Arrowsmith was added to the committee for perfecting it.[2]

Further, to this committee was given power, on the 19th of June, 1646, "as they see things imperfect" in the Confession to complete them, and make report to the Assembly.[3]

After, therefore, a year's interrupted and changing discussion, the committee for perfecting the Confession began the reporting of it piecemeal on the 17th of June, 1646. From that date to the 30th June the Assembly passed the bulk of the articles of the Confession *seriatim.*

The remaining portions were resumed into consideration from the 22nd of July, 1646, on receipt of an order from the two Houses[4] requesting them earnestly to expedite the Confession, an order which was itself due to the letter from the Assembly of the Kirk in Scotland of the 18th of June, read in the Lords on the 9th of July.[5]

[1] Mitchell, 168.   [2] *Ibid.,* 244-45.
[3] *Ibid.,* 245.   [4] *Ibid.,* 258.
[5] L. J., viii., 425 ; C. J., iv., 621.

Still later, on the 16th of September, 1646, the Commons made an order calling for such parts of the Confession as were perfected.[1] The order was read in the Assembly on the 18th of September, 1646, and a proposition was thereupon made to consider the Confession, what errors were not obviated in it, or in any of the confessions of the Church of England or Scotland, and to that end to have a review of the Articles of the Church.

The motion was not carried, evidently from a desire of not prolonging the debates which had already endured intermittently for eighteen months. At the following session, accordingly, 21st September, 1646, Dr Burgess reported the Confession transcribed so far as perfected.[2]

The title was reported and adopted, 25th September, 1646, and on that day it was resolved to send up the first nineteen chapters to the Commons under the title, "*to the Honourable the House of Commons assembled in Parliament, the humble advice of the Assembly of Divines, now by authority of Parliament sitting at Westminster, concerning part of a Confession of Faith*".[3] The House graciously received it at the hands of Dr. Burgess, and appointed the reading of it for the following Friday.[4]

The Commons read this first part of the confession perfunctorily on the 6th of October, 1646,[5] and three days later it was debated in Grand Committee. According to Whittaker's *Diary*,[6] the

CHAP. II.

1646,
Sept.-Oct.

Part of the
Confession
sent up to the
Parliament,
25th Sept.,
1646.

[1] C. J., iv., 670. [2] Mitchell, 286.
[3] *Ibid.*, 290; C. J., iv., 677.
[4] For some reason the same paper was not presented to the Lords till 1st October (L. J., viii., 505).
[5] C. J., iv., 685. [6] p. 569.

debate in the committee was whether to proceed
with the paper or not. In the end it was decided
to print it for the use of the House, and to request
the divines to supply the Scriptural proofs for the
margin, and to hasten the remainder of it.

The Assembly evidently found the task of affix-
ing Scripture proofs a heavy one, for they asked
for time.[1] The Commons, therefore, sanctioned
the printing of the part of the Confession without
the Scriptural proofs on the margin for the time
being.

The Lords
proceed upon
it.
Meanwhile the Lords had sat down methodi-
cally from the 29th of October, 1646, to the consideration of the same paper, voting chapter by
chapter.[2] By the 4th of November they had completed their votes upon it, and sent it down to the
Commons, with a warm recommendation for the
concurrence of the Lower House, " it being necessary that the Protestant churches abroad, as well
as the people of this kingdom at home, may have
knowledge how that the Parliament did never intend to innovate matters of faith ".[3] In the meantime the Commons did nothing whatever in the
matter.

More than two months later the Lords, evidently
impatient at the carelessness of the Commons in
the matter, proceeded with the second instalment
of the Confession, voted systematically all the remaining chapters (20-33), and sent down this portion also with a tart reminder of the incongruity of
having a fast by the appointment of both Houses

[1] Whittaker's *Diary*, 569; Mitchell, 295; C. J., iv., 692.
[2] L. J., viii., 549.　　　　[3] *Ibid.*, viii., 558.

for heresies and schisms while still the Confession
of Faith was unpublished.[1]

CHAP. II.
1646,
December.
The re-
mainder of
the Confes-
sion sent up
to the Parlia-
ment, 4th
Dec., 1646.

On the 26th of November, 1646, the Confession
of Faith was finished in the Assembly, and after
giving formal thanks to the committee for perfecting it, the divines ordered the whole of it, including
the nineteen chapters already sent in, to be transcribed, read and sent into the Parliament.[2] A
delay was, however, made over a preface,[3] and over
alterations which were put in successively on 17th
November[4] and 2nd December,[5] in chapters 19,
21, 22, 29, 31. Finally, on the 4th of December,
the whole, as transcribed by Dr. Burgess, was reported and ordered to be presented to both Houses
by all the divines of the Assembly.[6]

The Commons received the complete Confession
on the same day, and three days later ordered it
to be printed for the members' use without the
marginal scriptural proofs, the latter being still expected from the divines.[7] As usual Baillie, with
his wealth of innuendo, throws a partial light on
the situation of faction in the House :—

Our Assemblie for over twenty days posted hard, bot since
hes gotten into its old pace. The first halfe and more of the
Confession we sent up to the House : the end of these [in the
House] who called for it was the shuffling out the ordinance
against errors [Heresies] ; yet our friends [the Presbyterians in
the House] hes carried to goe on with that ; but others hes
carried the putting of Scriptures to the margin of the Confession, which may prove a very long business if not dexterously
managed.[8]

[1] 16th February, 1646-47 ; L. J., ix., 17, 18.
[2] Mitchell, 303.   [3] Ibid., 304.
[4] Ibid., 304.   [5] Ibid., 307.   [6] Ibid., 309.
[7] C. J., iv., 739 ; v., 2.   [8] Letters, ii., 403.

At a later date Baillie again complains of these tactics :—

The third point [of Uniformity], the Confession of Faith, I brought it with me, now in print as it was offered to the House by the Assembly without considerable dissent of any. It's much cryed up by all, even many of our greatest opposites, as the best Confession yet extant; it's expected the Houses shall pass it as they did the Directorie without much debate. Howbeit the retarding party has put the Assemblie to add Scriptures to it which they omitted only to eschew the offence of the House, whose practice hitherto hes been to enact nothing of religion on Divine right or scripturall grounds but upon their owne authoritie alone. This innovation of our opposites may well cost the Assemblie some time, who cannot do the most easie things with any expedition; but it will be for the advantage and strength of the work.[1]

Scriptural
proofs added.

It was not till the 5th of April, 1647, that the Assembly completed these scriptural proofs and reached the stage of reviewing the Confession as a whole in committee.[2] This review occupied the divines during the early part of April, and on the 26th a committee was appointed to carry the completed Confession with the scriptural proofs to the Houses.[3] The Parliament received it on the 29th of April, but it was not until the 19th of May that the Commons commenced the methodical debate of the whole. Beginning with the 1st chapter, it voted it paragraph by paragraph, with the exception of paragraph 8, " of the Holy Scriptures," which was respited for conference with the divines thereupon.[4]

The completed Confession in the Commons, May, 1647.

The debate of the doctrinal parts of the Con-

---

[1] *Letters*, iii., 2.   [2] Mitchell, 345.
[3] *Ibid.*, 354.
[4] C. J., v., 177, 189, 19th and 28th May, 1647.

fession, Articles, i.-v., xx-xxix., xxxii-xxxiii., was
not finished in the Commons until the 17th of
March, 1647-48.[1]

On the latter day, the title was by resolution of
the House altered from the form, "*A Confession of
Faith*" to the form "*Articles of Christian religion
approved and passed by both Houses of Parliament
after advice had with the Assembly of Divines by
authority of Parliament sitting at Westminster*".[2]

A fortnight later, the Commons handed these
portions with their corrections to the Lords at a
conference, with the desire that it might be published for the benefit of the kingdom, as the parts
concerning discipline, which were still under consideration, might require time.[3] Early in May the
Lords agreed to the corrections made by the
Commons,[4] except in the article concerning marriage.

The last alterations by the Lords were accepted
by the Commons on the 20th of June, 1648, and
the "Articles" ordered to be printed.[5] ·

Further than this the Long Parliament never
got in its review of the celebrated Confession.[6]

It is not part of our purpose to tell the story

[1] Debated 4th February, 1647-8, C. J., v., 455-6 ; 11th February,
ibid., 461-2 ; 3rd March, *ibid.*, 478 ; and 10th March, *ibid.*, 489-92.

[2] *Ibid.*, v., 502, 17th March, 1647-48.

[3] L. J., ix., 167, 3rd April, 1648 ; Rushworth, vii., p. 1035.

[4] L. J., x., 239, 2nd May, 1648; 301, 3rd June, 1648.

[5] C. J., v., 608.

[6] See *Ibid.*, vi., 270, for the appointment of a committee to take
into consideration the articles of Christian Religion, and to consider
what is further fit to be done with them. See note *infra*, p. 376. The
mere details of the genesis of the Confession in the Assembly and
of its partial passage through the Commons are given in the note
infra, pp. 367-372.

CHAP. II.
1652-60.

of the reception of the Confession in Scotland.[1] Its practical lack of authorisation at the hands of the English Parliament renders it of little further interest to our national history.

Subsequent attempts at the formulation of a Confession of Faith, 1652, 1654, 1657 and 1660.

In the subsequent years of the Commonwealth three half-hearted attempts were made to revive such a Confession, without counting the abortive essay of the Independent divines in 1652 at a definition of fundamentals of belief, see *infra*, ii., pp. 81-4.

On the 11th of September, 1654, Cromwell's first Parliament resolved upon the calling of a fresh Assembly of Divines to be consulted with concerning matters of religion.[2] For the purposes of consulting with this body, a committee of the House was nominated, and by this committee twenty "*Articles of Faith*," with their scriptural proofs, were reported to the House on the 12th of December, 1654. The House received them with thankfulness, and requested the divines to perfect what they had further prepared.[3] The first instalment thus offered was ordered to be printed. Nothing further however was heard of the articles.[4] But in the debates on the "*Address and Remonstrance*," in February, 1656-57, Cromwell's second Parliament returned to the project of establishing some Confession[5] by its resolution that "a Confession of Faith, to be agreed by His Highness and the Parliament, according to the rule and warrant of the Scripture, be held forth and recommended to the people of these nations".

[1] See Mitchell, *Minutes of the Westminster Assembly*, 418.
[2] C. J., vii., 367.   [3] *Ibid.*, 399, 12th December, 1654.
[4] See *infra*, ii., pp. 86-90.   [5] C. J., vii., 506-7.

In February, 1659-60, the reassembled Rump CHAP. II. returned to the old, and as yet, unauthorised Confession of the Westminster Assembly. A committee was appointed ·to consider of it,[1] and two days later the Confession was agreed to by the House, except chapters 30 and 31, concerning Church censures [2] and synods. The ordinance for the Confession in accordance passed on the 5th of March.[3] Needless to say that the enactment was perfectly futile and unregarded.[4]

[1] 29th February, 1659-60, C. J., vii., 855.

[2] Whitelock, iv., 401, 2nd March.

[3] C. J., vii., 862.

[4] *The genesis of the Confession of Faith in the Assembly, and its treatment in the House of Commons.* In order to avoid a dull repetition of dates and references, the detailed account of the progress of the Confession of Faith in the Assembly and Parliament is here given in a note :—

Title referred to the committee for perfecting, 3rd September, 1646 (Mitchell, 273). Scriptural proofs concluded, 5th April, 1646-47 (*ibid.*, 345). Title altered by resolution of the House of Commons, 17th March, 1647-48 (C. J., v., 502).

Article I. *Scripture* (subsequently *of the Holy Scriptures*).—Debated in the Assembly, 7th, 11th, 14th, 16th, 17th and 18th, July, 1645 (Mitchell, 110, 111, 113, 114, 115). Passed and ordered, 18th June, 1646 (*ibid.*, 245). Scriptural proofs debated, 7th to 15th January, 1646-47 (*ibid.*, 319-22). Debated in the Commons on the 19th and 28th May, 1647 (C. J., v., 177, 189). The respited eighth clause again debated and accepted, 17th March, 1647-48 (*ibid.*, v., 502).

Article II. *Of God and the Holy Trinity* (at first proposed separately *of God*, 23rd July, 1645, Mitchell, 115, and *of Trinity, ibid.*, same date). The two titles combined, 18th June, 1646 (*ibid.*, 245). Scriptural proofs debated, 8th and 18th January, 1646-47 (*ibid.* 319, 322). Debated in the Commons, 28th May, 1647 (C. J., v., 189).

Article III. *Of God's Eternal Decree* (proposed as *God's Decrees*, 29th August, 1645, Mitchell, 126. Altered to *God's Eternal Decree*, 18th to 19th June, 1646, *ibid.*, 245-46).—Debated, 29th August ; 2nd, 3rd, 9th and 11th September (*ibid.*, 127, 129, 130). Scriptural proofs added, 13th, 19th, 20th and 21st January, 1646-47 (*ibid.*, 321-23). Debated in the Commons, 28th May, 1647 (C. J., vi., 189).

CHAP. II. § VIII.—*The Larger and Smaller Catechisms.*

The first reference in the records of the Westminster Assembly to the preparation of a Catechism

Subsidiary to this Article were the following, at first proposed in the Assembly as separate heads :—

Reprobation.—Debated, 3rd, 6th, 7th and 11th November, 1645 (Mitchell, 160-62).

Redemption of the Elect only by Christ.--Debated, 22nd to 24th October (*ibid.*, 152-60).

Predestination.—Debated, 3rd, 17th, 20th and 21st October (*ibid.*, 134, 150-52).

Article IV. *Of Creation.*—Debated, 17th to 20th November, 1645 (*ibid.*, 164-65), ordered, 19th June, 1646 (*ibid.*, 246). Scriptural proofs added, 15th, 21st and 28th January, 1646-47 (*ibid.*, 322-24). Debated in the Commons, 2nd October, 1647 (C. J., v., 323).

Article V. *Of Providence.*—Debated, 27th and 28th November ; 2nd and 4th December, 1645 (Mitchell, 166-67), ordered, 19th June, 1646 (*ibid.*, 246). Scriptural proofs debated, 28th and 29th January, 1646-47 (*ibid.*, 324). Debated in the Commons, 2nd October, 1647 (C. J., v., 323).

Article VI. *Of the Fall of Man, of Sin, and the Punishment thereof.* —Debated, 17th and 21st November, 1645 ; 22nd and 25th June, 1646 (Mitchell, 164-65, 246). Scriptural proofs debated, 2nd February, 1646-47 (*ibid.*, 325) ; not accepted by the Commons.

Article VII. *Of God's Covenant with Man* (title proposed as *of Covenants*, 9th October, 1645 (*ibid.*, 147)); altered as above, 25th June, 1646, *ibid.*, 246). Debated in the Assembly, 9th, 10th and 17th October ; 6th, 14th and 17th November ; 23rd December, 1645 ; 25th June, 1646 (*ibid.*, 147-48, 150, 161, 163-64, 172, 246). Scriptural proofs debated, 3rd and 5th February, 1646-47 (*ibid.*, 325-26).

Article VIII. *Of Christ the Mediator.*—Debated in the Assembly, 29th August ; 2nd to 4th, 8th, 9th, 11th, 12th and 15th September ; 14th November, 1645 ; 25th June, 1646 (*ibid.*, 126-31, 163). Scriptural proofs debated, 8th February, 7th April, 1647 (*ibid.*, 326, 346-47).

Article IX. *Of Free-will.*—Debated in the Assembly, 15th and 17th December, 1645 ; 29th to 30th June, 1646 (*ibid.*, 170, 247-48). Scriptural proofs debated, 2nd and 9th February, 1646-47 (*ibid.*, 325, 327).

Article X. *Of Effectual Calling.*—Debated in the Assembly, 9th, 17th, 25th and 29th September ; 6th November, 1645 ; 30th June, 1646 (*ibid.*, 129, 132-33, 161, 248). Scriptural proofs debated, 3rd and 9th February, 1646-47 (*ibid.*, 325, 327).

Article XI. *Of Justification.*—Debated in the Assembly, 2nd, 3rd,

occurs on the 2nd of December, 1644, when a Chap. II.
committee was appointed for summing one up.[1]   1644,
                                                  December.

8th to 11th, 16th December, 1645; 23rd July, 1646 (*ibid.*, 166-70, 259).
Scriptural proofs debated, 4th, 10th, 11th February, 1646-47 (*ibid.*, Question as
326, 328).   to the his-
                                                                       torical origin
    Article XII. *Of Adoption.*—Debated in the Assembly, 20th Nov- of the Cate-
ember, 1645; 23rd July, 1646 (*ibid.*, 165, 259). Scriptural proofs de- chism.
bated, 5th and 11th February, 1646-47 (*ibid.*, 326, 328).

    Article XIII. *Of Sanctification.*—Debated in the Assembly,
20th and 24th November, 1645; 16th and 23rd September, 1646 (*ibid.*,
165-66, 284, 288-89). Scriptural proofs debated, 5th and 12th February,
1646-47 (*ibid.*, 326, 329).

    Article XIV. *Of Saving Faith.*—Debated in the Assembly, 20th
August to 1st September; 9th September, 1646 (*ibid.*, 271, 276-77).
Scriptural proofs debated, 5th and 12th February, 1646-47 (*ibid.*,
326-29).

    Article XV. *Of Repentance unto Life* (proposed as *Of Repentance
and Good Works*, 19th August, 1646, *ibid.*, 270; title altered as
above, 10th September, 1646, *ibid.*, 278).—Debated in Assembly, 19th
August; 10th, 17th, 18th and 21st September, 1646 (*ibid.*, 270, 278,
284, 286). Scriptural proofs debated, 12th February, 1646-47 (*ibid.*, 329).

    Article XVI. *Of Good Works* (see under title of Article XV.).—
Debated in the Assembly, 19th August and 9th September, 1646
(*ibid.*, 270, 277-78). Scriptural proofs debated, 15th February,
1646-47 (*ibid.*, 329).

    Article XVII. *Of the Perseverance of the Saints* (title proposed as
Of Perseverance, 19th December, 1645, *ibid.*, 171).—Debated in the
Assembly, 16th, 26th December, 1645; 14th September, 1646 (*ibid.*,
171, 173, 281). Scriptural proofs debated, 17th February, 1646-47
(*ibid.*, 330).

    Article XVIII. *Of Assurance of Grace and Salvation* (title pro-
posed as *Of Certainty of Grace and Salvation*, 24th July, 1646, *ibid.*,
259; altered to *Of Certainty of Salvation*, 14th September, 1646, *ibid.*,
281-82).—Debated in the Assembly, 24th and 30th July; 14th September, 1646 (*ibid.*, 259-60, 281-82). Scriptural proofs debated, 17th
and 18th February, 1646-47; 7th April, 1647 (*ibid.*, 330-31, 347).

    Article XIX. *Of the Law of God* (title proposed as *The Law,
Ceremonial and Judicial*, 29th January, *ibid.*, 182).—Debated in

[1] Lightfoot, 327, 338. Dr. Mitchell in his *Catechism of the Second
Reformation* refers to the Committee for the Directory (December,
1643, Baillie, ii., 118, 140) as if engaged in the preparation of a catechism. It was only engaged on the Directory for Worship (including
a *directory* of catechising), not on a catechism.

According to Lightfoot, this committee was a new creation. According to the minutes of the Assembly, it was formed by adding Marshall,

the Assembly, 1st, 7th, 9th, 12th, 13th and 29th January; 2nd and 9th February, 1645-46; 20th August, 1646, to 3rd September; 15th and 17th September, (*ibid.*, 173, 177-78, 182-83, 185, 271-74, 282, 284. Scriptural proofs debated, 19th and 22nd February, 1646-47 (*ibid.*, 331-32).

Article XX. *Of Christian Liberty and Liberty of Conscience* (title proposed as *of Christian Liberty*, 29th January, 1645-46, and *Of Liberty of Conscience*, proposed as a separate Article at first, 10th March, 1645, *ibid.*, 182, 205. The two heads or titles united, 26th March, 1646). —Debated, 29th January, 1645-46 ; 9th to 12th and 16th February ; 10th, 26th, 27th, and 30th to 31st March, 1646 ; 23rd to 25th September ; 1st, 7th to 9th, 13th to 14th, 16th, 21st and 30th October (*ibid.*, 182, 185-87, 196, 205, 211, 213-15, 289-90, 292-98. Scriptural proofs debated in Assembly, 25th to 26th February, 1646-47 ; 4th, 11th and 12th April (*ibid.*, 332-35, 337). Debated in the Commons on the 4th February, 1647-48, when paragraph 4 was respited till the consideration of Article XXX. (C. J., v., 455).

Article XXI. *Of Religious Worship and the Sabbath Day* (title originally proposed as *Religion and Worship*, and altered to *Of Religious Worship*, 5th March, 1645-46. *The Sabbath* proposed as a separate head, 9th March, *ibid.*, 192, 195. The two heads united as above, 12th October, 1646, *ibid.*, 295.) Debated in the Assembly, 1645-46; 5th, 9th, 10th and 20th March ; 26th March, 1646 ; 6th April ; 12th October ; 30th October ; 20th and 23rd November, 1646 (*ibid.*, 192, 195, 205, 209-10, 215-16, 295, 298, 302, 303). Scriptural proofs debated, 2nd February, 1646-47 (*ibid.*, 331). Debated in the Commons, 4th February, 1647-48 (C. J., v., 455).

Article XXII. *Of Lawful Oaths and Vows* (title proposed as *Of Lawful Oath*, 8th January, 1645-46. Altered as above, 12th October.) —Debated in the Assembly, 8th, 13th, 15th, 16th, 19th, 20th and 21st January, 1645-46 ; 12th October, 1646 ; 3rd, 6th and 23rd November, 1646 (Mitchell, 177-81, 295, 298-99, 303). Scriptural proofs debated, 18th February, 1646-47 (*ibid.*, 331). Debated in the Commons as above (Article XXI.).

Article XXIII. *Of the Civil Magistrate* (title proposed as *Of the Magistrate*, 26th March, 1646, *ibid.*, 210).—Debated in the Assembly, 26th March ; 24th and 27th April ; 12th to 15th October ; 9th November ; 4th December, 1646 (*ibid.*, 210, 223-24, 295-96, 299, 308). Scriptural proofs debated, 3rd March, 1646-47 (*ibid.*, 335). Debated in the Commons, *ut supra*, under Article XXI., significant alterations

Tuckney and Newcomen to Mr. Palmer for the
purpose of hastening the Catechism.[1] The fact

made in paragraph 4, and the remainder respited till the consideration of Article XXX.

Article XXIV. *Of Marriage and Divorce* (presented as separate heads of marriage, 17th June, 1646, *ibid.*, 244 ; *Of Divorce*, 10th August, 1646, *ibid.*, 266 ; the two heads united, 12th October, 1646, *ibid.*, 295).
—Debated in the Assembly, 17th June ; 23rd July ; 3rd, 4th and 10th August ; 10th and 11th September ; 12th October ; 9th, 10th and 11th November, 1646 (*ibid.*, 244, 259, 262-64, 266, 279-80, 295, 299-300).
Scriptural proofs debated, 3rd March, 1646-47. Debated in the Commons, 4th and 11th February, and 3rd March, 1647-48 (C. J., v., 455, 461, 478, and alterations made).

Article XXV. *Of the Church.*—Debated in the Assembly, 16th, 23rd, 26th and 27th February, 1645-46 ; 2nd, 5th, 6th and 18th March, 1646 ; 3rd, 7th to 10th, 13th to 17th, 20th to 22nd April, 1646 ; 13th and 17th November (*ibid.*, 188, 190-203, 206-207, 215-221, 301-302).
Scriptural proofs debated, 3rd March, 1646-47 (*ibid.*, 335). Debated in the Commons, 10th March, 1647-48 (C. J., v., 489).

Article XXVI. *Of the Communion of Saints.*—Debated in the Assembly, 17th February ; 3rd to 5th March, 1645-46 ; 13th, 17th, 19th and 20th November, 1646 (*ibid.*, 188, 192, 301-2). Scriptural proofs debated, 3rd March, 1646-47 (*ibid.*, 335). Debated in the Commons, 10th March, 1647-48 (C. J., v., 489).

Article XXVII. *Of the Sacraments* (title proposed as *Of the Sacraments in general*, 2nd December 1645, *ibid.*, 167).—Debated in the Assembly, 2nd, 5th, 11th, 12th, 15th, 16th and 24th December, 1645 ; 10th November, 1646 (*ibid.*, 169-70, 172, 299). Debated in the Commons, *ut supra*, under Article XXVI.

Article XXVIII. *Of Baptism.*—Debated in the Assembly, 29th December, 1645 ; 1st, 2nd, 5th, 6th, 8th, 9th, 16th, 21st and 26th January, 1645-46 ; 11th September, 1646 ; and 10th November (*ibid.*, 173, 175-79, 181-82, 280, 299). Debated in the Commons, *ut supra*, under Article XXVI.

Article XXIX. *Of the Lord's Supper.*—Debated in the Assembly, 1st and 26th December, 1645 ; 11th to 13th, and 16th November, 1646 (*ibid.*, 166, 173, 300-302). Scriptural proofs debated, 5th March, 1646-47 (*ibid.*, 336). Debated in the Commons, *ut supra*, under Article XXVI.

Article XXX. *Of Church Censures* (title proposed as *Of Church Officers and Censures*), 29th January, 1645-46 (*ibid.*, 182).—Debated in the Assembly, 29th January, 1645-46 ; 23rd April ; 13th, 23rd and

[1] Mitchell, 13.

would seem to be that the joint committee for the Directory [1] had assigned the drafting of a directory for catechising (not the preparation of a catechism) to Palmer. That divine's draft of it, however, did not please the Scotch, and his papers were handed over to them to frame according to their mind. [2] When Baillie later refers to the " catechise " as almost ready in April, 1644, [3] and as drawn up in November, it is uncertain whether he is referring to the " directory for catechising " or to a catechism of their own which the Scotch Commissioners had drawn, as they had previously drawn a directory of worship—on chance, *i.e.*, without authority from

26th November, 1646 (*ibid.*, 182, 222, 301, 303). Scriptural proofs debated, 5th March, 1646-47 ; 2nd April, 1647 (*ibid.*, 336, 345).

Article XXXI. *Of Synods and Councils.*—Debated in the Assembly, 4th to 7th, 10th to 11th, 13th to 14th, 19th to 20th August ; 13th and 26th November, 1646 (*ibid.*, 264-71, 301, 303). Scriptural proofs debated, 5th March, 1646 47 ; 2nd April, 1647 (*ibid.*, 336, 345).

Article XXXII. *Of the State of Men after Death and of the Resurrection of the Dead.* Debated in the Assembly under two separate heads. (1) *Of the State of the Soul after Death*, 24th and 31st July, 1646 ; altered to *Of the State of Man after Death*, 26th November, 1646 (*ibid.*, 259, 261-62, 303). (2) *Of Resurrection.*—Debated, 4th August and 4th September, 1646 (*ibid.*, 264, 275). Scriptural proofs of the united heads debated, 5th March, 1646-47 ; 2nd April, 1647 (*ibid.*, 336, 345). Debated in the Commons, *ut supra*, under Article XXVI.

Article XXXIII. *Of the Last Judgment* (title proposed as *Of the Last Judgment and Life Eternal*, 4th September, 1646, Mitchell, 275). —Debated in the Assembly, 20th August to 1st and 4th September ; 26th November, 1646. Scriptural proofs debated, 3rd March, 1646-47 ; 2nd April, 1647 (*ibid.*, 336, 345). Debated in the Commons, *ut supra*, under Article XXVI.

Besides the above Thirty-three Articles, the Assembly, on the 2nd of January, 1645-46, debated of *Dedication to God* (Mitchell, 175). If not represented by Article XII. it must have been omitted in the final draft of the confession.

[1] See *supra*, p. 341.
[2] Baillie, ii., 118, 140, 148.   [3] *Ibid.*, 172, 242.

either Assembly or Parliament, and simply to be
held in readiness to be produced in the Assembly
whenever the project of a catechism should come
to be broached there. Baillie says as much as this
in his public letter of 26th December, 1644.

We [the Scot Comm^rs (?) or the Grand Treaty Committee]
have near also agreed in private on a draft of catechise, whereupon when it comes in publick we expect little debate.[1]

On the 7th of February, 1644-45, Reynolds and
Delmé were added to the Assembly's Committee for
the Catechism.[2] From this committee a report was
made on the 13th of May, 1645,[3] concerning the
method or principles of catechising. On the 1st
of August following, Palmer made report of the
Catechism, and a spasmodic debate of it commenced.[4] Although, however, on the 20th of that
month, the Assembly appointed Palmer, Staunton
and Young to draw up the whole draft of the catechism with all convenient speed, nothing further
was heard of it for nearly a year, in consequence
of the interposition of the debates on the Confession of Faith. In July, 1646, the House sent
impatiently for the Confession and Catechism, and
on the 14th of September the Assembly resumed
the systematic debate of it.[5] From that date to
January, 1646-47, with a considerable break devoted to the Confession, the Assembly considered
the Catechism.[6] On the 14th of that month, how-

---

[1] *Letters*, ii., 248.

[2] Mitchell, 48. For other additions, see *ibid.*, 258-59, 400, 477.

[3] *Ibid.*, 91-94; C. J., iv., 133.

[4] Mitchell, 118; Baillie, ii., 306.

[5] C. J., iv., 622.   [6] Mitchell, 281-321.

CHAP. II.

1647,
April-Nov.

The Assembly decides to prepare Two Catechisms.

The Larger Catechism, April-Oct., 1647.

The Shorter Catechism, August-Nov., 1647.

ever, a resolution was taken that the Committee for the Catechism should prepare a draft of two catechisms, a larger and a smaller, the smaller one having special bearing on the Confession of Faith.[1]

Without discarding all their previous work, both committee and Assembly from this point practically recommenced their labours on this subject. The report of the Larger Catechism began on the 14th of April, 1647,[2] and with certain slight breaks the debate of it continued in the Assembly up to October, 1647.[3] On the 22nd of the latter month, it was delivered to both Houses, and graciously received.[4] The Shorter Catechism had, meanwhile (5th August, 1647), been committed to the Prolocutor of the Assembly, with Palmer, Temple, Lightfoot, Gunn and Delmé as assistants.[5] At a later date, 19th October, 1647, a different committee is referred to as ordered to prepare it, but probably only in the sense of reviewing the preparation of the previous committee, for the purpose of reporting in the Assembly.[6] From the 21st of October the Lesser Catechism was in debate until the 22nd of November,[7] when it was finished. Three days later it was presented to both Houses.[8] On the occasion of its delivery the Commons requested the divines to affix scriptural proofs to both the Larger and Lesser Catechism, and on this work the Assembly was engaged, as its last task, till near the time of its dwindled and discredited close. The discussion of these scriptural proofs occupied the divines from

---

[1] Mitchell, 321, 474. [2] Ibid., 349.
[3] Ibid., 349-485. [4] L. J., ix., 488; C. J., v., 340.
[5] Mitchell, 408. [6] Ibid., 485. [7] Ibid., 485-92.
[8] C. J., v., 368; L. J., ix., 543, 25th November, 1647.

30th November, 1647, to the 12th of April, 1648.[1]
Two days later they were delivered to both Houses.[2]
It was not till the 12th of June, 1648, that the
Commons condescended to review the Larger Catechism.[3] With two slight corrections, the House
finished the consideration of it on the 24th of July,
when it was passed and sent to the Lords with a
desire for its publication.[4] On the same day the
Shorter Catechism was proceeded with, passed
and ordered to be sent up.

On the 18th and 25th of August the Lords committed the Larger Catechism for reconsideration,
but passed the Shorter Catechism, and sent it down
to the Commons,[5] with the title (reported from the
divines) " *The grounds and principles of religion
contained in a Shorter Catechism according to the
advice of the Assembly of Divines sitting at Westminster to be used throughout the kingdom of
England and dominion of Wales*".

The Commons agreed to the Lords' order for the
Shorter Catechism on the 22nd of September, 1648.[6]

The Larger Catechism was never passed by the
Lords. Later in the Commonwealth period Cromwell's second Parliament returned to the subject of
catechising, and drafted a bill enjoining that duty
on ministers and others. In connection with this
bill which passed the House, but was refused
by the Protector,[7] the Shorter Catechism of the

---

[1] Mitchell, 493-511.

[2] C. J., v., 530 ; L. J., x., 204.　　　[3] C. J., v. 633.

[4] *Ibid.*, v., 645.　　　[5] L. J., x., 443, 452, 455.

[6] C. J., vi., 27. The order for the printing of the Shorter Catechism in L. J., x., 511.

[7] Burton's *Diary*, ii., 203-5.

Assembly was revised and presented to the Commons to be made part of the bill and to be publicly taught.[1]

This is practically the last reference in English constitutional history to the work of the Westminster Assembly. It is not a little curious that those portions of its accomplished work which have remained through later times the most distinct and memorable accomplishment of the Assembly—*i.e.*, the Confession of Faith and the Larger Catechism —should have never received the assent of the Parliament which had called the Assembly into being, and at whose behest it had prepared those works.[2]

[1] C. J., vii., 482, 13th February, 1656-57.

[2] The account of the reception of the Confession and Catechism by the General Assembly of the Church of Scotland is detailed in a note to Mitchell's edition of *The Minutes of the Westminster Assembly*, pp. 418-24, 514-15. In the *Narrative of the Proceedings of the Parliament of England in the Work of Reformation*, which was printed on the 8th of August, 1648, and which is reprinted in *Parliamentary History*, xvii., 373-81, the Long Parliament claimed as follows in its list of accomplished works :—

" They have approved and passed *The Confession of Faith or Articles of Christian Religion* as it came from the Assembly of Divines with some small alterations, only some small part is yet under consideration, the rest being printed and published by authority of Parliament.

" They have passed a *Greater and Lesser Catechism* that came from the Assembly of Divines."

It must be clearly understood, however, that this declaration emanated from the Commons alone and speaks, in these items certainly, only of the legislative work of the Lower House which, when alone, did not of course give constitutional enactment. The very preamble of this "*narrative*" commences with the words " we the Commons assembled in the Parliament of England ".

In the final negotiation with Charles, the Commons sent up a message on the 1st of November, 1648 (L. J., x., 572), requesting the Lords' concurrence in an order instructing the Commissioners then treating with Charles in the Isle of Wight, to desire his consent concerning

§ IX.—*The Metrical Version of the Psalms.*

The last and least important of the constructive works undertaken by the Assembly concerned the Psalter. In this matter, however, it pursued no independent plan of its own, but had to remain—and was apparently well pleased to remain—content with perusing, revising and sanctioning an existing version. The fact may of course be partly due to the terms of the reference from the Parliament—behind which the Assembly dared not ordinarily go.

On Monday, 20th November, 1643, the Commons made an order desiring the advice of the Assembly "whether it may not be useful and profitable to the Church that the Psalms set forth by Mr. Rouse be permitted to be publicly sung, the same being read before singing, until the books be more generally dispersed ".[1]

Rouse's version commended to the Assembly.

the Catechism. The Lords agreed to it on the same day. It is not clear what reference is meant in this entry, but presumably it related to the *Shorter Catechism.*

The corresponding order in the Commons on the same day (C. J., vi., 67) mentions "the catechisms," doubtless implying both. The difference is probably intentional—the Commons having passed both, and the Lords not.

[1] C. J., iii., 315. For an account of Rouse's version, see the appendix to Laing's edition of Baillie's *Letters,* iii., 532. It was first published in April, 1643, the imprimatur of the Committee of the Commons for printing being dated on the 17th of that month. The revised version of it was published in 1646 with an imprimatur of the Commons' Committee of date 4th November, 1645. The competing contemporary versions of Sir William Mure of Rowallane and of Zachary Boyd do not appear to have been ever brought officially before the notice of our Westminster Assembly, although Baillie repeatedly referred to Rowallen's, as he called it (*Letters,* ii., 101, 121, 332).

Writing apparently before the receipt of this order from the Commons, Baillie refers to Rouse's version in somewhat disparaging terms.[1]

> Ane old most honest member of the House of Commons, Mr. Rous, hes helped the old Psalter, in the most places faultie. His friends are verie pressing in the Assemblie that the book may be examined and helped by the author in what places it shall be found meet, and then be commended to the Parliament, that they may injoin the publick use of it. One of their considerations is the great private advantage which would by this book come to their friend. But manie do oppose the motion, the most because the work is not so well done as they think it might. Mr. Nye did speak much against a tie to any Psalter, and something against the singing of paraphrases as of preaching of homilies. We, underhand, will mightly oppose it [*i.e.*, this anti-Psalter attitude of the Independents] for the Psalter is a great part of our uniformitie, which we cannot let pass till our Church be well advised with [regarding] it. I wish I had Rowallen's Psalter here. For I like it much better than anie yet I have seen.

The Assembly at work on it, 1643, Nov.-December.

The very limited and precise order of the Commons was communicated to the Assembly on the 22nd of November, 1643, by Sir Benjamin Rudyard,[2] and was immediately referred to the usual three committees, each committee being assigned fifty Psalms. To judge by the example of the particular committee of which Lightfoot was a member, these committees further delegated the work, for on the 11th of December, 1643, that body distributed the part of Rouse's Psalms which had been assigned to it, to six of its members, Walker, Burroughs, Caryl, Hall, Whittaker and Lightfoot.[3]

On the 22nd of the same month it was pro

[1] *Letters*, ii., 121.

[2] Lightfoot, 60.   [3] *Ibid.*, 79.

posed in the Assembly that a select committee of Hebrew scholars should be chosen to confer with Rouse on his work.[1] The proposal, however, does not appear to have been acted upon, and in the subsequent onrush of hotly debated business the whole subject of the metrical version sank out of the Assembly's sight for almost two years.[2]

The first trace of a return to the subject in the Assembly occurs on the 12th of September, 1645, when Mr. Wilson reported as follows :—

> This Assembly doth humbly advise and desire that those Psalms set forth by Mr. Rouse, with such alterations as are made by the Committee of the Assembly appointed to review it, may be publicly sung in Churches as being useful and profitable to the Church.[3]

Upon this report the Assembly voted to read over the said Psalms in its own Grand Committee without the allowance of any debate. " Those that desired to be satisfied in anything, they are to consider of it together with the committee that have already examined." At this point the orderly evolution of the work was interrupted by a merely personal incident. One William Barton, M.A., having composed in English metre two books of David's Psalms, first published in 1644, presented his book to the House of Lords with a petition. The Lords thereupon referred it to the Assembly to be read over, judged and reported upon by

Barton's version commended to the Assembly, 1645, Oct.

[1] Lightfoot, 90.

[2] The reference in Baillie's *Letters*, ii., 140, 259, to the subject of the reading of the Scriptures and singing of Psalms relates entirely to the Directory for Psalms and of the several portions of the Directory for Worship, for which see *supra*, pp. 341, 351.

[3] Mitchell, 131.

them, "that such further direction may be given touching the same as shall be meet".[1]

In response to this message, the Assembly referred the fresh partial version to its Committee for the Psalms, that body being strengthened by the addition of six members [2] in the succeeding month.

On the 14th of November, 1645, the Assembly came to the following conclusion :—

The Assembly's revision and allowance of Rouse's version, 1645, 14th Nov.

Ordered that whereas the Honble House of Commons hath by an order bearing date the 20th of November, 1643, recommended the Psalms set out by Mr. Rous to the consideration of the Assembly of Divines ; the Assembly hath caused them to be carefully perused and as they are now altered and amended do approve of them and humbly conceive that it may be useful and profitable to the Church that they be permitted to be publicly sung.[8]

The vote was at once forwarded to the Commons. At the same time a more comprehensive answer was despatched to the Lords, in which, after detailing that the Assembly had with much care perused Rouse's version and concurred [*sic* for conferred] with him thereupon to amend and perfect his copy, they expressed a preference for his said version over that of Mr. Barton.[4]

Immediately on the receipt of the Assembly's report, the House of Commons resolved "that the Book of Psalms set forth by Mr. Rouse and perused by the Assembly of Divines be forthwith printed, and that it be referred to Mr. Rouse to take care

---

[1] L. J., vii., 627, 7th October, 1645. For another competing contemporary version of the Psalms by Mr. Roberts see Lightfoot, 266.

[2] Mitchell, 147, 9th October, 1645.   [3] *Ibid.*, 163.

[4] L. J., vii., 703, 705, 14th November, 1645.

for the printing thereof, and that none do presume to print it but such as shall be authorised by him ".[1]

This order of the Commons is not to be regarded as more than a formal allowance of the Psalter. It did not as yet enjoin its public use. One reason for delaying the latter decisive step doubtless lay in the fact that the Scotch Commissioners in the Assembly had throughout insisted that the Psalter should first be submitted to the judgment of the Scotch Church. Periodically, as the work progressed in the Assembly, it had been despatched to Scotland by the said Commissioners— the last batch of fifty psalms of Rouse's version being sent off about the middle of June, 1645.[2]

The Commons order it to be printed, but do not enjoin its use —pending the Scotch revision, 1645, 14th November.

As late as the 25th of November of the same year (*i.e.*, after the Assembly had practically adopted the version by resolution), Baillie informed his countrymen that it was " not to be perused [presumably in the House of Commons] till they be sent to you and your animadversions returned hither, which we wish were so soon as might be ".[3]

It is not, however, quite clear when the corrections and suggestions of the Scotch Church were actually received in London. On the 14th of July, 1646, Baillie states " that the corrections of the Scotch had been friendlily received and almost all of them followed [*i.e.*, adopted]. Its like the Assembly and Parliament here will ere long authorise the use of that oft corrected Psalter." [4]

[1] C. J., iv., 342, 14th November, 1645.

[2] Baillie, *Letters*, ii., 279, 293.

[3] *Ibid.*, ii., 326. For other references to the first Scotch revision of the Psalter see *ibid.*, 280, 286, 293, 321, 326, 329-31, 379, 401.

[4] *Ibid.*, ii., 379.

CHAP. II.

1646,

The Commons enjoin the Psalter, 1646, 15th April.

The difficulty with regard to this letter (presuming the date of it correct) is that the House of Commons had already two months before returned to the subject and definitely authorised the version. On the 15th of April, 1646, the Commons ordered that Rouse's Psalms, as perused by the Assembly, should be forthwith printed, "and that the said Psalms and none other shall after the first day of January next be sung in all Churches and Chapels within the Kingdom of England, Dominion of Wales and town of Berwick-upon-Tweed ".[1] This order and the Psalter were then sent up to the Lords, who three days later read the book twice and committed it to a committee of their own.[2] It was not until the 23rd September, 1646, that the Lords' amendments to the Commons' order were passed and voted to be sent down, and it does not appear that these amendments were accepted by the Commons.[3] The delay in the formal concurrence by the Lords in the Commons' order would appear to be attributable to the opposition of the Independents, who disliked the injunction of any uniformity in the matter of singing.

In October, 1646, Baillie distinctly attributes the delay to this faction as he styles it :—

Our long labours on the Psalmes when readie to be put in practice are like by a faction to be altogether stifled ; they will have a liberty to take what Psalter they will.[4]

There was, however, in the case of the Lords an additional and more personal motive. They do not appear to have been satisfied with the Assembly's answer on the 14th of November, 1645,

[1] C. J., v., 509, 511. [2] L. J., viii., 277, 16th April, 1646.
[3] L. J., viii., 500, [4] *Letters*, 504 ii., 401.

with regard to Barton's version. Upon that answer Barton had promoted a second petition to the Lords, who thereupon requested the Assembly to state why his Psalms might not be sung in churches as well as other translations by such as were willing to use them.[1] The Assembly appointed a committee to satisfy the Lords,[2] and this committee's reply was reported and voted on on the 22nd of April, and forwarded to the Lords on the 25th.[3]

The reply steadily deprecated the employment of more than one version. A further play of motive too is revealed in Baillie's letter of 26th January, 1647 :—

> The Commons past their order long agoe; but the Lords joyned not, being solicited by divers of the Assemblie, and of the ministers of London, who loves better the more poetical paraphrase of their colleague Mr. Barton. The too great accuracie of some in the Assemblie, sticking too hard to the originall text, made the last edition more concise and obscure than the former. With this the Commission of our Church wes not so weell pleased; but we have gotten all these obscurities helped; so I think it shall pass. Our good friend Mr. Zacharie Boyd hes putt himself to a great deale of paines and charges to make a Psalter, but I ever warned him his hopes were groundless to get it receaved in our Churches; yet the flatteries of his unadvysed neighbours makes him insist in his fruitless designe.[4]

The result was that the House of Lords was swept away before it had agreed with the Commons on the subject of the latter's order of injunction.[5] On the 4th of April, 1648, on Barton's petition, the Lords gave leave for the publication of "*an exact emendation of the whole*

---

[1] L. J., viii., 236, 26th March, 1646.

[2] Mitchell, 216, 9th April, 1646.   [3] *Ibid.*, 221 ; L. J., viii., 283-84.

[4] Baillie, *Letters*, iii., 3.   [5] See L. J., ix., 280.

CHAP. II.

1648-54.

book of Psalms begun by Francis Rouse, Esq., and perfected with sundry hymnes thereunto annexed by William Barton, M.A." [1]

Barton's version allowed, 1654.

Three years later, on the 27th of September, 1650, Barton petitioned the Commons with regard to this his version. In reply the Commons appointed six divines "to peruse and consider of the translation of the Psalms set out by Mr. Rouse, and since reviewed by the said William Barton, and if they shall approve of the same then to license the printing thereof".[2] Ultimately Barton's version received the imprimatur of the Protector and his Council, January, 1653-54, and it is noticeable that the 1654 edition differs materially from those of 1644, 1645 and 1646. The mere licensing his version for the press was, however, and of course, quite a different matter from the public enjoining of it for purposes of worship.

The final result, therefore (speaking of the period 1640-60), was (1) that Rouse's version, though revised by the Westminster Assembly and by the Scotch Church, and accepted by the Commons, was never accepted by the Lords, and therefore never legally enjoined. (2) That no other version either was enjoined.

Very strangely the fate of the English (unaccepted) version was more kindly in Scotland. As adopted by the Assembly it was subject to much critical handling by the Scottish Kirk during the years 1647-49, but was finally adopted by the General Assembly in November, 1649, and ratified by the Committee of Estates in January, 1654.[3]

[1] L. J., x., 178.   [2] C. J., vi., 474.   [3] See Baillie, *Letters*, iii., 60, 97, 540-52.

END OF VOL. I.